THE PARADOX OF POWER

THE PARADOX OF POWER

Statebuilding in America, 1754–1920

Ballard C. Campbell

University Press of Kansas

Published by the University Press of Kansas (Lawrence, Kansas 66045), which was organized by the Kansas Board of Regents and is operated and funded by Emporia State University, Fort Hays State University, Kansas State University, Pittsburg State University, the University of Kansas, and Wichita State University

Library of Congress Cataloging-in-Publication Data

Names: Campbell, Ballard C., 1940– author.
Title: The paradox of power : statebuilding in America, 1754–1920 / Ballard C. Campbell.
Description: Lawrence, Kansas : University Press of Kansas, 2021. | Includes bibliographical references and index.
Identifiers: LCCN 2021003517
ISBN 9780700632558 (cloth)
ISBN 9780700632565 (paperback)
ISBN 9780700632572 (ebook)
Subjects: LCSH: Federal government—United States. | United States—Politics and government. | United States history.
Classification: LCC JK311 .C36 2021 | DDC 973—dc23
LC record available at https://lccn.loc.gov/2021003517.

British Library Cataloguing-in-Publication Data is available.

Printed in the United States of America

10 9 8 7 6 5 4 3 2 1

The paper used in this publication is acid free and meets the minimum requirements of the American National Standard for Permanence of Paper for Printed Library Materials Z39.48-1992.

CONTENTS

FIGURES AND TABLES

FIGURES

TABLES

PREFACE

America's political history is a fascinating paradox. The United States was born with the admonition that government posed a threat to liberty. This apprehension became the foundation of the nation's civic ideology and was embedded in its constitutional structure. Yet the history of public life in the United States records the emergence of an enormously powerful national state during the nineteenth century. By 1920 the United States was arguably the most powerful country in the world. This book traces that evolution and offers an explanation of how it occurred.

I am not the first person to see a contradiction between theory and practice in American civic life. Many eminent observers have noted this discrepancy. Yet the dynamics that account for the accretion of political power over the nation's history warrant further analysis and clarification. This explanatory deficiency is partially due to the belief that there was no state in America until the twentieth century. The nation's republican ideology, which pivoted around the notions of liberty and democracy, and the federal system, which fragmented power across governments and space, made it appear that the United States was "stateless," at least in the European sense of the term. This book argues that the state in America is rooted in its colonial experience and evolved over subsequent decades. The first task of this book is to synthesize evidence for this contention by reviewing governance at all levels of the American polity—local, state, and national—between 1754 and 1920. I do not claim that my summary represents a comprehensive inventory of public activity, for the archive of American governmental actions is immense and largely unorganized. But I hope my synthesis offers a valid representation of the historical reality.

The second task of this book is to explain the dynamics that propelled the expansion of the American state. Answering "why" depends heavily on tracing "how" the development occurred, an assignment that argues the utility of a historical perspective. The roots of the American state were situated in its British colonial history and the Revolution, which established the base from which civic action evolved over the next century and a half. The narratives used in this book are intended to capture the situational character of a sequence of critical events that lined this historical path, one filled with crises of war, economic depression, and political confrontation. Narrative story lines cannot, however, fully illuminate the dynamics of political change. Concepts that delineate broad, sometimes amorphous megainfluences are required to tease out more subtle causal dynamics. *The Paradox of Power* poses five critical causal elements: war, geography, economic development, identity (including citizenship and nationalism), and political capacity. This last factor embraces law and constitutionalism, administration, and political parties. The structure of the book emphasizes the role of these orienting concepts.

The third task of this book is related to the direction of historical writing about American government. There are several parts to this story. Historians seldom used the concept of the nation-state in their writing until political scientists in the 1980s and afterward addressed the topic, a period when civic history had begun to lose much of its former attraction for historians. Designating the state as the point of orientation can help rekindle interest in the nation's civic past and fill in gaps in our understanding of it. Another part of the task facing scholars of American governance is to envision the polity in its entirety, which means integrating municipal, town, county, and state governments into the portrait of governmental history. Beginning in the 1890s, writing about America's political past focused increasingly on the federal government, but an exclusive focus on national history does an injustice to civic life in the United States. Major dimensions of American governance, now and in the past, are undertaken locally. This fact poses formidable challenges to researchers, given the massive number of governmental entities in the United States. There is, however, an immense literature of original documents and secondary works available to facilitate this task. My synthesis of governance during two centuries necessarily rests primarily on the work of other scholars. Mining these studies and original sources can be—and probably should be—an interdisciplinary enterprise, as no one discipline has a monopoly on method and theory.

Several talented historians read portions of the manuscript and offered valuable suggestions: my thanks to Philip R. VanderMeer, Michael Les Benedict, James Leamon, Alan Lessoff, and William B. Murphy. I also benefited greatly from the comments by two anonymous readers for the University Press of Kansas and my editor David Congdon. Collectively, their advice has substantially improved the book. So too has Linda Lotz's editing of my prose, affirming the axiom that a good editor is an author's best friend. I also want to express my appreciation to the authors of the books and articles that informed my understanding of American governance and statebuilding. The scholarly works cited in the pages that follow, as well as numerous uncited works, are a testimony to why an extended historical portrait is a community effort.

I

The Dynamics of American Statebuilding

Within the span of two lifetimes, thirteen British colonies in North America evolved into an enormously wealthy and powerful national state. "America," as the world called this new society, evoked myriad images: a people that passionately embraced liberty and cherished individual rights and equality, an abundance of natural riches, widespread economic opportunity, political democracy, and, eventually, massive military might. Less celebrated but central to America's history were the genocidal war on Native Americans, repeated use of coercive force against residents and foreign foes, support of slavery, persistent racism, gender inequality, and business monopolies. These blemishes have contributed to an American political history that is both distinctive and paradoxical.

On the eve of the American Revolution, 3 million persons, mainly free British subjects and their slaves, were concentrated on the coastal plain of the Atlantic from Maine to Georgia. In 1920 the United States was home to 106 million people, making its population the fourth largest in the world. By the early twentieth century Americans lived on lands that stretched 3,000 miles across North America from the Atlantic to the Pacific and from the Great Lakes to the Gulf of Mexico. This geography made the United States the fourth largest country on earth, and in terms of fertile soil, the second largest. Even before World War I, which confirmed the United States' membership in the club of world powers, the size of its economy exceeded that of all others, and its workers' wages were among the highest anywhere.

By the mid-nineteenth century the United States was already the world's largest democracy. Its citizens possessed broad legal protections that were the envy of the world, despite racial, ethnic, and gender inequalities. In the early twentieth century the United States had the world's largest system of free education, probably the highest percentage of homeownership, and more motor vehicles than any other nation. Millions of immigrants abandoned familiar surroundings to share in the opportunities that America offered. In addition to the reproduction of American institutions across the continent, the United States inserted its influence in the Caribbean and across much of the Pacific basin at the dawn of the twentieth century. This development resulted in the fusion of diverse dynamics that turned a group of "little republics" into a powerful national state between the 1760s and 1920. What propelled this political transformation?

THE AMERICAN PARADOX

The evolution of the American state began with European outposts in North America. The largest were colonies of Great Britain, which had built a strong central state and possessed a formidable military. Most residents of Britain's American colonies were proud to be members of the British Empire. But resentment of Britain's effort to force colonial loyalty to a "tyrannical" king led to revolution and independence. America was thus born denouncing monarchy and central state authority (Parliament and the king's ministers), enshrining the axiom that government, especially the central regime, was an ever-present threat to liberty. This conviction became the central theme of the new republic's ideology and was seared into its civic DNA. Political leaders and cultural tradition perpetuated this antistatist outlook, which was engraved into the country's constitutions. Given that the United States possessed the most pronounced antistatist ideology in the modern world, how did it become the world's most powerful state?

This question disputes the contention that there was no "state" in America before the twentieth century. Recent reassessments have challenged this traditional view, but a composite portrait of the process is needed.[1] The history of the long nineteenth century (1763–1920) shows that America always acted like a state. The antecedents of American statebuilding began in the colonial period, when local governments assumed a broad range of authorities. Local officials had the authority to use deadly force to defend the homeland. They sent individuals to the gallows for theft, rape, and unwed pregnancy. Homegrown lawmakers levied taxes to support militias and sometimes drafted men to fill their ranks. Colonial and later state militias defended Europeans from Native Americans and drove the latter from their lands. These actions represent the application of powers that lie at the core of statehood.

After independence, a triumvirate of governments—local, state, and national—shepherded the country into existence as a national state. The federal (i.e., national) government remained small in its early decades, yet its officials were hardly impotent. Despite the well-known constraints on their authority, federal officials played a significant role in American statebuilding. The national government has always asserted its right as a sovereign to enforce its laws in all territories claimed by the United States.

American history thus presents a paradox. The country's defining ideology preached restraints on civic authority, but the actual uses of governmental power repeatedly contradicted this stricture. There is no simple explanation for this disjuncture. American history, however, suggests that most decisions to use governmental power have been situational in nature. That is, practical actions were taken in response to particular circumstances that were usually seen as problematic. These situations assumed various forms, ranging from crises, such as an attack on the United States, to conflicts that evolved over decades, such as slavery and dislocations traceable to industrialization. Time and again, specific circumstances arose that either triggered a public demand for remedial action or served as a rationale for actions taken by power holders. Time and again, pragmatic responses to problems trumped America's cautionary ideology.

Attitudes were not uniform across society or among lawmakers. Ideology is not an undifferentiated catechism; variations in belief exist among individuals and groups. These differences and the material conditions associated with them spawned conflicting interests (e.g., North and South, capitalist and worker, Republican and Democrat) that opened pathways for policymaking within the maze of ideological and constitutional constraints.[2] Nonetheless, politicians are skilled at justifying their actions in terms of their consistency with the nation's civic heritage.

A second reason for the paradoxical relationship between theory and action in American politics is the existence of many "states" in the United States. Most Americans live in several jurisdictions—namely, in the United States (under the federal government), in a state (or states) of residence, and in a particular city or town. These overlapping structures of government and their respective legal authorities have always been present in America. During most of the long nineteenth century the national government remained weaker than its European counterparts, while matrices of state and local governments performed most civic tasks and took on more responsibilities as time advanced.

Skeptics may reply that the subnational governments were not really components of a state, that they did not constitute a central regime. It is true that the American scheme of governance fragmented civic authority and distributed it broadly. But this fact does not negate the existence of state powers. Individual state and local governments exercised authority over specified territories with clearly marked boundaries. They possessed the power to tax (i.e., to take property from residents) and to use coercive force such as capital punishment, deployment of militias, and enforcement of social regulations. Federal and state courts consistently recognized the constitutional legitimacy of these powers. By any reasonable criteria, civic entities that could tax, use deadly force, and regulate social relations within a specified territorial arena held powers that lay at the heart of a state.

The federal system has obscured much of this history. James Bryce, a perceptive British observer of American government, emphasized this impaired ability to track political activity in the United States. The union, he wrote at the end of the nineteenth century, is "more than an aggregate of States and the States are more than parts of the Union." The United States, he continued, "is a Commonwealth of commonwealths." Hence, Americans have "two loyalties, two patriotisms." Understanding American civic life, Bryce opined, required recognition of this "double organization."[3] That is, one must study both levels of government—the federal and the subnational tiers.

Another reason that the pragmatic tradition in American governance has been underappreciated has to do with the incremental growth of governmental power. Deference to antistatist ideas surfaced repeatedly, as political conditions waxed and waned. Yet, over the course of the long nineteenth century, the scope and scale of state power expanded. During this evolution, government at all three levels took on more tasks, developed greater administrative capacity, and acquired more revenue to fund these activities. Gauging the growth of the American state requires the reconstruction of these trends.

THE NATURE OF A STATE

States have a long history, originating in antiquity, and sometimes took the form of empires. Most scholars agree that "modern" states emerged in western Europe after 1500. These new regimes had three fundamental elements. First, they were territorially bounded, with defined borders and a central government that possessed the authority to rule (the capacity to make law) in the areas for which it claimed jurisdiction. In our own time these territorial realms are plotted conspicuously on maps. Second, states were independent in the sense that they were self-governing; in the language of international law, they had sovereignty. Within their own territory, political leaders were autonomous decisionmakers, owing allegiance only to their state and to its monarch, its constituents, or both. The king's ministers and the nation's president negotiated with the leaders of other countries within the system of states, with powerful nations possessing hegemonic influence over lesser countries. Third, states had the authority to take property from inhabitants, usually in the form of taxes, and they possessed a legal monopoly on the use of lethal force, which could be utilized to enforce their rules. Coercive and fiscal functions are customarily assigned to specialized personnel, such as military forces, police, and revenue officers. These two legal entitlements—to use coercive force and to extract wealth from residents—differentiate states from other entities. Territorial jurisdiction, the sovereign authority to govern, and the capacity to take life and property make states extraordinarily powerful entities.[4]

As modern states matured they acquired additional attributes—notably, bureaucracy, whereby administrative units were devised and officers were appointed to superintend particular civic tasks. Administrative personnel assumed defined roles within hierarchical organizations whose purpose was defined by law, and they established relationships with groups outside of government. Over time, administrative organizations became institutionalized; rules and routines for overseeing policy objectives become fixed, and bureaucracies assumed semiautonomous status. In the popular mind, bureaucracy is often equated with government.

Scholars have noted two additional characteristics that became integral to states by the late nineteenth century. The first was nationalism, which denotes a sense of common identity among the inhabitants of a country and a sociopsychological allegiance to the state it represents. These sentimental attachments form the emotional fabric of a nation, which rests on a widespread sense of belonging to a cultural community by virtue of ethnic background, language, religion, and history. The synchronization of a nation with its formal civic apparatus results in a nation-state.[5] Because nationalism helps empower a state's capacity, elites attempt to cultivate popular attachment to the regime.

The other feature of states that became increasingly visible during the nineteenth century was the recognition of citizenship and rights. With the transition from kingly domains and colonies to nation-states, most notably in western Europe and North America, the inhabitants of a territory were transformed from the subjects of a ruler to citizens with rights and entitlements. Members of democratic states expect to vote for their leaders and to have their civil liberties protected. In return for these benefits, they recognize that they owe taxes to the regime and may be required to serve in the nation's armed forces. Modern states, therefore, have formed complex relationships with residents regarding their rights and obligations.

THE DYNAMICS OF STATE FORMATION

The origin of the modern European state is entwined with the region's history. Scholars debate the causes of its development, but there is agreement about the most prominent factors. All agree that the rise of the modern state was a historical process in which institutions and rulers reacted to and interacted with conditions that evolved over time. Only a close examination of specific episodes can reconstruct these sequences, but several general patterns can be summarized. The feudal arrangement that had dominated medieval Europe eroded after 1500 in the face of social, economic, and political pressures such as the Protestant Reformation, which challenged the political influence of Latin Christianity. Cities grew in wealth and size with the rise of commerce, spurring the formation of modern capitalism and the creation of economic interest groups such as merchants and bankers. The Renaissance and the Enlightenment offered new ideas about social and natural phenomena and posed alternatives to older orthodoxies.

Against this background statebuilding took shape within the more specific dynamics of change, none more critical than war. And no single military development was more instrumental in undermining the medieval political order than the invention of gunpowder and its use in cannon. This new technology, as well as personal firearms and oceangoing sailing vessels capable of mounting cannon, revolutionized military tactics and strategy. Cannon rendered castles and knights—the foundation of medieval warfare—obsolete. In place of small militias at the command of nobles and hired mercenaries, state leaders created military forces that relied on full-time paid armies and navies that trained regularly, were barracked separately from citizens, and were provisioned with modern arms. Maintaining this new coercive system was expensive, so regimes were forced to seek increased revenue, which they obtained by imposing new taxes and improving tax collection mechanisms. This demand stimulated the expansion of centralized political controls, principally by improving administrative capacities. The story of statebuilding between 1500 and 1800 evolved in large measure from the interactions among the creation of professional militaries, the adoption of revenue policies to support them, and the establishment of effective bureaucracies to coordinate the modernized military-fiscal complex. As Peter the Great, tsar of Russia (1682–1725), characterized this interaction: "money is the artery of war." And as Philip Bobbitt observed, the state is a "war-making institution."[6]

Charles Tilly, a historical sociologist, offered an important caveat to this process: civic leaders seldom pursue a specific model for building a state; rather, they respond to situations as they arise in the course of managing their immediate civic concerns.[7] Rulers periodically confront crises, such as insurrection at home or military threats from rival states. Economic or epidemiological crises may prompt remedial action in the face of adverse circumstances. The system of states not only engendered competition among countries but also diffused new technologies and practices. No large state shunned the acquisition of cannon, for example. Economic and political changes after 1500 generated a host of interest groups that sought favors from state leaders, who recognized the importance of cultivating the support of wealthy inhabitants. Various inducements coaxed rulers to expand their states territorially. An estimated 300 political communities existed in Europe in 1500; that number had dwindled to 30 by the late twentieth century.[8] While this brief summary of statebuilding in Europe only skims the surface of a complex history, it suggests factors with a bearing on the governance of America.

DIMENSIONS OF AMERICAN STATEBUILDING

Although modern states exhibit some similarities, each has its own history and cultural makeup. These distinctions were especially important for statebuilding in the United States during the long nineteenth century. To orient this analysis, I have selected five major contextual influences that can be thought of as "causes," in the sense that they identify conditions that affected historical development: geography, war and military power, economic development, identity, and political capacity. While there is no airtight historical model that explains American statebuilding, the identification of major causal influences establishes references on which to base conjecture and explanation.[9]

Geography

Modern states are territorially defined. Their boundaries demark an area over which a governing regime claims sole jurisdiction. Territory, of course, encompasses the physiographic, socioeconomic, and political attributes of its space. The spatial reach of the United States grew rapidly and extensively in its first seventy years, spanning North America from east to west. This huge continental mass endowed the American state with a diverse topography ranging from coastal plains to broad grasslands to towering mountains, many deep-water harbors, an array of lengthy navigable waterways, and a rich storehouse of natural resources. As settlers built towns and cities, they developed these natural resources and established pathways of commerce, giving rise to regional cultures. By the last decades of the long nineteenth century the reach of American society not only stretched across the continent but also extended outward, notably into the Caribbean and the Pacific.

Geography may not be destiny, but it clearly plays a role in shaping human societies. America's geographic endowment had a major impact on the country's economic growth, its diplomatic outlook, and its cultural orientation. Traversing numerous climatic zones and physiographic regions, the American landmass contained topography suitable for a wide variety of agricultural and extractive activities. Seacoasts and coastal harbors, networks of rivers, and numerous lakes served as major transportation arteries. The thousands of miles of seacoast from Maine to the Gulf of Mexico and along the Alaskan shore and the Pacific coast from the Strait of Juan de Fuca to

San Diego Bay supported fishing industries and safe harbors for maritime commerce. A long list of mineral and natural resources made American real estate especially valuable and valued.

The nation's continental expanse and geographic separation from Europe and Asia had a marked impact on its foreign and domestic policies during the nineteenth century. The ocean separating the United States from the powerful states of Europe influenced American attitudes toward national security, especially after 1815. Within North America, the availability of cultivable land at comparatively low cost offered millions of families home and hope, a condition compatible with the spread of republican political institutions. Geography was connected to the regional cultural differences that culminated in the Civil War.[10]

Geographic perspectives on history can illuminate the diffusion and shifts in political, cultural, and economic patterns. As historical geographer D. W. Meinig notes, "Geography and history are bound together by the very nature of things."[11] The geographic perspective in this book embraces the environment, including climate and weather. Meteorological disruptions in the form of droughts, severe winters, or prolonged periods of abnormal temperatures or wet conditions have impacted economic activity, such as depressing agricultural production. Economic calamities, particularly in the era before industrialization, commonly generated significant social stresses that contributed to poverty, migration, delayed family formation, and increased levels of sickness and mortality. Like other determinants of economic activity, meteorological influences varied in form and impact over the immense territory of the United States.[12]

Maps are powerful instruments for visualizing spatial and relational properties of human activity. They also constitute historical evidence. As part of the retained archive of geographic knowledge, maps from the past shed light on how contemporaries viewed their environment and how they imaged their geographic future. The study of historical maps, the subject of historical cartography, illuminates dimensions of statebuilding.

Modern states arose in tandem with the development of cartography, whereby statebuilders sought measured descriptions of territory. This new form of knowledge helped rulers assert authority over specific units of space. Maps are thus legal documents that delineate the spatial terrain of a national state, as well as subunits within it. The very shape of national entities can convey powerful ideas about the nature of a state. In our own time, most of us are aware that international borders are fenced at places and that passage between countries is subject to official control and documentation of individuals' identities. The history of this modern reality is linked to the territorial specificity of modern states.

Mapmakers began depicting the national boundaries of states in the sixteenth century. By the eighteenth century cartographers institutionalized this practice, often coloring each national territory and its colonial holdings with a distinct hue to delineate its territory (including noncontiguous colonies) from that of other national entities. This cartographic convention gave the impression that the regime possessed full control over its lands and implied a homogeneous culture within them. Reality contradicted these assumptions, of course, yet older maps were not politically neutral; they were tools of statecraft, or, in the language of cartographic scholars, "socially" constructed. The close connection between the rise of national states and the creation of atlases contributed to the development of national pride, whereby residents increasingly formed emotional bonds with their states. Maps, in short, were tools of statebuilding.[13]

War and Military Power

The connection between war and statebuilding is filled with irony. Fear of centralized power and the expenditures required for military action kept the regular army and navy of the United States small during the nineteenth century. Thomas Paine, the English exile who urged American independence, agreed with these reservations, writing in 1787 that war released "a train of unforeseen circumstances" yet was certain to increase taxes and debt. Fear of unchecked militarism led the framers of the Constitution to give Congress the power to declare war. Despite this ideological apprehension, the United States engaged in six major wars between the American Revolution and World War I. If one counts the continuous clashes between Euro-Americans and Native Americans as a discrete military episode, campaigns against Indians constitute a seventh war. In addition, national and state militaries were marshaled on many occasions to quell domestic rebellions, riots, and strikes. American forces were deployed in the Mediterranean against state-based pirates in the early nineteenth century and in Mexico in the early twentieth century. The rise of municipal and state police added another layer of organized force that evolved in the United States.[14]

One of the great paradoxes of American history is the juxtaposition between its small-military tradition and its repeated use of coercive force. No generation of Americans failed to witness a military campaign during the long nineteenth century. And although the US Army remained tiny for most of its early history, it ballooned to become the world's largest during the Civil War. Two million Americans were sent to France during World War I. These engagements played a prominent role in American statebuilding. As Theda Skocpol aptly observed, "wars punctuate the biographies of nations."[15]

The American military took on a variety of tasks besides combat. Before the Civil War the army loaned engineers to private transportation ventures and explored, mapped, and surveyed much of the western United States. The navy surveyed coastal waters, providing valuable information to a country with a maritime tradition. The army's command structure and logistical organization provided a model for corporate and governmental bureaucracy. Many scholars have noted that American wars stimulated surges of nationalism that generated popular support for the country's political leaders, at least for a time.[16]

Military engagements had important economic effects. Expenditures for military procurement stimulated business and employment, especially during the Civil War and World War I. The larger the scale of the engagement, the higher its cost, which meant that major wars left the nation with a much larger debt. Paying down these loans was one reason, along with the provision of veterans' benefits, that peacetime public spending was higher after war than prior to it. Major wars, in short, caused dislocations in the economy, governmental finance, and social life.[17]

Economic Development

To say that a country's economy has a critical bearing on its society and government is to state the obvious. Economics concerns how people organize production for their survival, create wealth, and consume the fruits of their labors. History offers considerable guidance on these issues. A symbiotic relationship occurred in Europe between the rise of capitalism and the emergence of modern states, which taxed private wealth largely to fund militaries. Political leaders realized that expanding economies enhanced the potential to raise public revenue. The development of capitalism in the seventeenth and eighteenth centuries contributed to the formation of economic interest groups such as merchants, bankers, and landlords, which became increasingly important to political leaders. Because they understood the state's dependence on the private economy, governmental actors promoted and protected commercial classes. In the United States the emergence of laissez-faire economics, the doctrine that government should not interfere with private enterprise, nurtured these relationships. Despite this ideological veil, American government was not a neutral player in the economy.[18]

Economic growth was propelled by numerous factors. America's bountiful natural resources have already been referenced. A growing population, fueled in part by massive immigration that brought ideas as well as labor, enlarged the workforce (supply) and added consumers (demand). Americans emphasized education, which spread literacy and broadened the skills of workers. Receptivity to technological innovation had a transformative influence on commerce and business, as demonstrated by the arrival of steam power and steel. Government had a hand in these developments, including approving new forms of business organization (corporations in particular) and legal protections for trade and commerce. Although explaining how these factors interacted is difficult, it is clear that the American economy became the largest and wealthiest in the world over the long nineteenth century.

This development, however, did not proceed at an even pace. Rather, it assumed an undulating pattern in which recurring expansions were punctuated by sharp and sometimes prolonged slumps, occasionally called panics, that usually preceded depressions. The most severe downturns caused widespread bankruptcies and business failures, loss of real estate due to mortgage foreclosure and tax delinquency, high unemployment, and elevated social distress. Nine major economic depressions occurred between the 1780s and 1920.[19]

Economic downturns warrant attention because they have had significant repercussions for society and government. Major depressions brought hardship and uncertainty to workers, families, and businesses, which pressured policymakers to take remedial action. The effects of these demands took several forms, such as triggering electoral realignments that altered political coalitions and inducing workers and entrepreneurs to formulate new coping strategies. Whatever vectors these shock waves followed, memory of the calamity could linger for years. Failure to defuse the anger and fear generated by economic reversals could undermine the groups in power. Depressions constituted critical moments in history when unexpected crises unleashed powerful dynamics for political change.[20]

Together, wars and depressions are two potent forces that have repeatedly impacted public life in the United States. Only two decades during the long nineteenth century—the 1790s and the 1880s—failed to record at least one *major* war or depression, and even these fortunate decades experienced minor recessions and military actions. Both types of shock to the polity figured prominently in American statebuilding.[21]

Identity

How individuals perceive their place in society—what I call identity—plays a central role in statebuilding. It combines several components. A key relationship between residents and the state is embodied in nationalism, or a sense of peoplehood whereby individuals share cultural bonds and consider themselves members of a wider community. As nationalism evolves, inhabitants of a country become aware of ties to nonfamily members in society, usually through linkages created by history and tradition, ethnicity, religion, and language. The fusion of cultural identification with a society's civic and ideological foundations gives birth to a nation-state.[22]

The concept of nationalism may appear to be homogeneous, but it can have multiple expressions. As geographer D. W. Meinig and others have reminded us, American identity was embedded in numerous geographic and sociopolitical contexts. From the first European settlement, American society has possessed regional distinctions in which "differences in ethnic content, social character, religious expression, and political culture" were geographically diffused. Regional cultures, Meinig argues, "were fundamental to the shaping of America." The contest between national sentiments and regional loyalties (and antinational attitudes) rendered American nationalism a paradox, particularly before the Civil War.[23]

The transformation of North American colonies into the American nation-state paralleled the transition in the status of individuals from subjects to citizens. The American Revolution marks the moment when most free male residents of the North American colonies renounced their allegiance to King George III of England and became citizens of the United States. Their new status confirmed and conveyed various rights and obligations. The classic enumeration of rights in the United States is the Bill of Rights in the Constitution. The individual American states also wrote their own bills of rights, some of them earlier and much longer than the national version. American citizens thus live under a dual legal framework that, in theory, protects their rights from governmental deprivation. Voting in elections for public officials is perhaps the most recognized right of citizenship. With citizenship came the obligation for males to serve in the military (when drafted or by volunteering) and for property holders to pay taxes.

Citizenship has a contested history in the United States. A perennial issue was how to integrate immigrants into the community and prepare them for citizenship. Complicating this transition were habitual complaints that newcomers had not conformed to the cultural norms of their adopted society. The barriers to full citizenship have been high even for some native-born Americans, namely, African Americans, Native Americans, Latinos, and women. Gender has long influenced the American polity, especially with regard to political participation and policy advocacy.[24]

Political Capacity

The final orienting referent concerns civic entities' ability to govern. This dimension concerns the political process, especially the selection of officeholders, the making of policy, and administration. These processes are conditioned by a regime's underlying authority, such as its ideological mantra, and its institutional expressions. Formal, written constitutions became the holy grail of civic life in the United States. These documents allocated powers and responsibilities to public officials, created institutional structures (e.g., legislatures and courts), and set forth procedures for their operation (e.g., specifying a four-year term for the president). They also set limits on the power of officeholders. The evolution of constitutional law through amendments, court rulings, and political practices, as well as the adoption of statutes and patterns of administrative practices, all have a bearing on political capacity.

Political power lies outside the structure of government as well as within it. Ideology, which permeates various corners of the polity both inside and outside the halls of government, reflects how people view the role of the state and sets informal boundaries on permissible and impermissible actions. Beyond some general homilies, the largest segment of the population probably gave little thought to the theoretical foundations of the government. Actual governance derived primarily from practical concerns. Demands filtered into the political arena through the requests of lobbyists and interest groups; from prominent figures in society, such as newspaper editors and religious leaders; and via elections, which acted as conduits of information from constituencies. Elections that realigned party coalitions had significant effects on policy.[25]

Reconstructing this history is complicated by the nation's federal system, which divided governing prerogatives between the states and the central government. The shape of this legal-constitutional bifurcation changed through political practice and court interpretations after 1788, yet throughout the long nineteenth century, a broad consensus persisted that state and local governments should handle most day-to-day governance. Yet no *comprehensive* history of subnational (state and local) governance exists for the nineteenth century. Despite this handicap, tracking American statebuilding is incomplete unless *all* governing units (national, state, local, and special) are included in the analysis.[26]

PART I

Colonial Times through the Civil War and Reconstruction

2

Rise of the Little Republics

Had Google Earth scanned North America in 1750, it would have displayed a scattering of settlements along the Atlantic coast. South of the continent's northern tundra, in an area then controlled by the British Hudson's Bay Company, it would have revealed small communities situated along the St. Lawrence River, inhabited by people of French ancestry. Heading southeast into the Gulf of St. Lawrence, the Google satellite would have spotted British and Acadian residents clustered along the shores of Newfoundland, Prince Edward Island, and Nova Scotia. Swinging southward, larger British settlements would have come into view, beginning with the Massachusetts colony, which included present-day Maine, and continuing 1,200 miles south to Savannah, Georgia. Most of these residents, mainly of European birth or descent, lived within a hundred miles of the sea, with the densest communities located near bays, such as Chesapeake Bay, and navigable rivers—the Kennebec, Connecticut, and Delaware in the North and the Potomac, James, and Savannah in the South. Barely visible would be scattered pockets of settlers west of the Appalachian Mountains.

These aerial images would have detected a handful of denser settlements, all of which were port cities, including Boston, New York, and Charlestown, South Carolina. Philadelphia, the largest, had an estimated 34,000 residents in 1776. Baltimore, the sixth largest, was home to fewer than 6,000 souls. Google's view of Boston would have shown one- and two-story structures on a small spit of land jutting into Boston Harbor. New Yorkers congregated on the lower reaches of Manhattan Island. The density of these eighteenth-century cities contrasted with the rural panorama of farms and villages scattered along the coastal plains. Most residents from Maine to Georgia were of British background. A small scattering of people resided beyond the Appalachian Mountains in the Ohio and Mississippi River valleys in lands claimed by France. Hundreds of miles to the west, across the grassland plains, rose the towering Rocky Mountains, although few European colonists knew of their existence in 1750. Euro-Americans were aware that the Pacific Ocean established the western border of North America. Hope still circulated that a water route across the continent existed. To the south of Georgia lay New Spain, with settlements around Santa Fe, New Mexico; in southern Texas; along the northern shore of the Gulf of

Figure 2.1. Map of North America, circa 1750. This was probably based on Bowen's 1747 map. *Source:* Library of Congress, Washington, DC, control number 73694927.

Mexico, including New Orleans; and at St. Augustine and other Florida locations. Spanish colonies also reached southward into Central America, Cuba, and Puerto Rico. Spain, Great Britain, France, and the Netherlands all had claims in the West Indies archipelago. Russia had a toehold in North America on the Alaskan coast.

Google Earth also would have spotted indigenous peoples. These Amerindians were divided into hundreds of tribes, spoke innumerable languages, and were spread over the entire continent, although few continued to live where Europeans were numerous. As Google's eye in the sky panned the forest canopy stretching from the Mississippi to the eastern coastline, the largely treeless Great Plains, the Rocky Mountains, and the Pacific coast, it would have noted swarms of wild animals, including bison, which ranged as far east as New York. It would have surveyed an immense land area with varied topographies and physical properties that played a pivotal role in shaping the American state.[1]

THE BRITISH EMPIRE AND NORTH AMERICA

Euro-American colonists of the 1750s did not have access to the internet, of course, but some of them owned maps and atlases. These works conspicuously displayed the territories of the powerful European states that had staked claims in the Americas. Britain had been particularly successful in acquiring international holdings and collecting them into an "empire," a term in use during the eighteenth century. Besides its colonies in North America and the Caribbean, which included the islands of Barbados and Jamaica, Britain had established footholds in Central and South America, supported the ventures of the private East India Company in India, colonized Ireland, and fused Wales, Scotland, and England to form Great Britain. The impetus behind this imperial expansion was multifaceted and included a competitive rivalry with other states, a desire to enlarge Britain's commercial radius, and the availability of its Royal Navy, a potent instrument of state power. By the seventeenth century the major European states had developed heavily armed oceangoing vessels, which afforded them military control over weaker regimes. Britain became the world's naval superpower in the mid-eighteenth century, possessing 141 "ships of the line," the battleships of their day.[2]

British immigrants in North America took pride in Great Britain's naval prowess, which protected trade and commerce in the Atlantic region and guarded against advances from France and Spain, both ruled by Catholic monarchs. American colonists of English descent, virtually all of them Protestant, considered themselves loyal British subjects. Most took considerable pride in their British heritage, which entitled them to the customary rights of British subjects and protection by the king's professional army and the Royal Navy.

Maintaining these forces was costly. The key to their funding was Britain's capacity to raise money, first by establishing reliable revenue streams and second by borrowing when political-military crises increased the need for funds. Foreign and domestic trade played a prominent role in financing this system, with customs and excise taxes accounting for more than 70 percent of British tax revenue in the 1750s. One-fifth of the nation's exports came from its thirteen North American colonies. Steady income meant good credit, so when additional funds were needed, such as during wartime emergencies, the ministry could turn to the Bank of England, founded in 1694, for loans. Britain's naval might was based in large measure on a workable tax system and its creditworthiness.[3]

Settlements in Virginia and Massachusetts, founded in the early seventeenth century, were Britain's first North American possessions south of Nova Scotia. They eventually increased to thirteen colonies between Maine and Georgia. Their governors were appointed by British officials in the eight "royal" colonies and by proprietors in Maryland, Delaware, and Pennsylvania; governors were elected in the "charter" colonies of Rhode Island and Connecticut. In all the colonies, with the exception of Massachusetts, governors appointed a council that functioned as a body of advisers and as the highest court in some cases. Governors had the power to veto legislation adopted by colonial assemblies, whose members were elected in all thirteen colonies. A Board of Trade in England had the authority to disallow laws passed in the colonies, a power it used sparingly. Most day-to-day civic business was undertaken by local governments, principally by towns in New England and the middle colonies and by counties in colonies south of Pennsylvania.

British officials saw their North American colonies primarily as economic adjuncts for the benefit of the home islands. The seventeenth century had given rise to mercantilism, a system that sought to enhance the nation's economy through command controls. Britain's primary interest in North America was to encourage the export of grains, forest products (including naval stores), and cattle, which it did by offering colonial producers access to British markets.[4] The commercial monopolies granted to the British East India Company grew out of this approach. Beginning in 1651 Parliament enacted the Navigation Acts, which formulated mercantilist regulations for the empire's colonies: exports were restricted to ships that had been built in Britain or America and had British crews; most imports into the colonies had to pass through Britain, as did most colonial exports; and manufactured products that competed with British businesses were prohibited. In the mid-eighteenth century Parliament tried to ban the colonial issue of paper money in an attempt to dampen inflation, which harmed British creditors.[5]

Though seemingly stringent on its face, British commercial policy was lax in practice. Administrative enforcement of commercial regulations was porous, and evasion of customs duties was widespread, especially in New England, which specialized in merchant shipping. Americans realized that Great Britain was a favored market for American products, which enjoyed protection by the Royal Navy while in transit. Few residents in British North America contested Parliament's authority to regulate the Atlantic trade.

THE AMERICAN COLONIES

North Americans accepted the British commercial system because it added to their prosperity. Numerous factors contributed to the growing colonial economy, with the availability of productive land the first in importance. America's colonial economy was based primarily on cultivated commodities such as wheat, tobacco, rice, cattle, and horses and the harvest of native products such as timber, beavers, and fish. Numerous Atlantic harbors aided marine activity, especially the shipment of products to other colonies, the West Indies, and Europe. Lacking was a sufficient workforce, which lured streams of migrants to North America. Newcomers played a major role in an economy that benefited from population growth.[6] The thirteen colonies that became the United States grew from 250,000 non-native people in 1700 to ten times that number in 1775.

Land was the pivotal attraction. Preindustrial civilizations were resource-based, extractive communities where survival and advancement depended on planting and husbandry, harvesting natural products, and mining. Roughly 90 percent of the population in mid-eighteenth-century North America was sustained by agriculture or by harvesting nature's bounty. Merchants, artisans, military personnel, and a few professionals, such as lawyers, were found mainly in the continent's few cities and constituted a small fraction of the workforce. For most, the clearest path to economic security in the New World lay in landownership; they worked the land by their own sweat or that of slaves and tenants, or they held it for speculation.[7]

George Washington filled all these roles. As a Virginia planter (an agriculturalist with a large farm operation), he oversaw five working farms consisting of 5,000 acres on his Mount Vernon estate, initially acquired by inheritance and marriage. Washington also gained control of tens of thousands of additional acres in his native Virginia and throughout Pennsylvania, New York, and the Ohio River basin, obtained through grants for military service from Virginia governors and private purchases. He took considerable pains to protect these investments by evicting squatters and enhanced their value by supporting transportation ventures that made his frontier properties more accessible. Washington is an oversize example of a colonial planter-speculator; his vast landholdings and several hundred slaves made him one of the richest men in Virginia. Most colonists were modest farmers whose activities centered around a household economy; this was especially true in New England, where livelihoods depended on consuming the fruits of one's labors and selling or bartering small surpluses in a personalized economy in which hard currency was scarce. Exceptions prevailed in the Hudson River valley of New York and in much of the region south of Pennsylvania, where comparatively large manors and plantations existed.[8]

Beyond its connection to personal fortunes, land formed the territorial foundation of preindustrial states. Their wealth depended heavily on expanding the spatial extent of the realm and encouraging its utilization. The powerhouses of Europe in the seventeenth and eighteenth centuries used their armies and navies to guard their homelands and their colonial territories from foreign encroachment. Land and history were integrally entwined in North America, where Britain confronted French, Spanish, and Dutch contestants and sometimes unaligned Native Americans. Colonial officials and residents saw the abundant, fertile land as an opportunity for expansion. The maps and atlases circulating in England and the colonies that displayed the vastness of the North American continent fed this vision.[9]

The land had a profound influence on the political outlooks of notable colonials such as George Washington, Benjamin Franklin, Thomas Jefferson, and John Adams. All four paid close attention to cartography. Atlases, almanacs, and geographies, largely printed in Britain, were widely available in mid-eighteenth-century America, where a high rate of literacy promoted geographic literature. Washington, Franklin, and Jefferson had extensive cartographic collections. Adams urged the study of geography, and Jefferson had an avid interest in the geography of North America. The trans-Appalachian West was central in Jefferson's vision of an "empire of liberty" populated by landowning farmers. With an eye on their own personal futures, Franklin, Jefferson, and Washington invested in western lands, as did most Virginia colonial legislators in the mid and late 1700s.[10]

Colonial maps fed the American fascination with lands west of the Appalachian Mountains. Numerous colonials envisioned an expansive British civilization carved out of virgin forest. Benjamin Franklin had Henry Popple's 1733 map of North America, which depicted the broad trans-Appalachian West, installed in the hall of the Pennsylvania Assembly. John Adams noted that the same map hung over the dais of the Massachusetts Assembly.[11] This map and later cartographic renderings of North America encouraged a mentality that fused land, prosperity, and social stability into a sociopolitical portrait of the future. Franklin summarized the sentiment in a 1763 letter: "Here in America she [Great Britain] has laid a broad and strong foundation on which to erect the most beneficial and certain commerce, with the greatness and stability of her empire." To St. Jean de Crevecoeur, a French cartographer turned New York farmer whose writings were used to promote land sales, the prospect of western agriculture was the basis for the "future glory of the United States." If economic interest did not provide sufficient motivation to pursue these dreams, religion might: the book of Genesis instructed, "The Lord God took man and put him in the garden of Eden to till it and keep it."[12]

Land did not sustain everyone. Shippers, seamen, and artisans worked in seaports such as Boston, New York, and Philadelphia. Shipbuilding was a specialty of New Englanders. Besides importing and exporting goods, some merchants manufactured products, such as rum and iron bars. The colonies supported an impressive iron-making industry, which proved valuable during the American Revolution. Most locally consumed goods, such as cloth, leather, pewter, and milled grains, were handcrafted. Benjamin Franklin was a printer and papermaker, as well as assistant postmaster for the British colonies. John Adams and Thomas Jefferson were attorneys. George Washington hired managers to oversee his Mount Vernon farms and retained a large staff of slaves and indentured servants to make garments, footwear, and metal goods. Planters commonly had side ventures or secondary occupations. Washington shipped agricultural products and fish from his wharf on the Potomac River; many Virginia planters also acted as merchants, attorneys, or public officials. Though nonfarmer occupations engaged only a fraction of the workforce, they provided important synergies for an economy based on the principles of capitalism and oriented around the availability of resources.

Work and culture varied across the landscape of colonial North America. Based on economic orientation, at least six regions are identifiable: household farming, fishing, and shipping in New England; the wheat culture of the middle colonies (New York, New Jersey, Pennsylvania); tobacco fields in the Chesapeake Bay area; rice and indigo plantations of the Carolinas and Georgia; and mixed farming regions in the backcountry, which shaded into a frontier zone of trade with Native Americans. Historical geographer D. W. Meinig adds Canada (Quebec and the Maritime Provinces) and the Spanish mission settlements in southern California to the list of distinguishable regional cultures in North America.

Economic regions tended to overlap cultural distinctions. New Englanders were primarily English transplants rooted in a Puritan-Congregational tradition that distinguished the region's town life. The middle colonies contained a heterogeneous population of English, Scotch-Irish, German, and Dutch settlers, along with a smattering of Swedes. Pennsylvania contained a large German population, although Philadelphia was culturally diverse. Residents of the Virginia-Chesapeake region were largely English in nationality and Anglican in religion; social and economic power was lodged firmly in the hands of the largest planters. A similar social structure was found in the coastal communities of the Carolinas and Georgia, whose residents were largely of English origin. African Americans, nearly all of them slaves, lived primarily south of Pennsylvania. Farther inland, in the backcountry, the population was more ethnically diverse, with Scotch-Irish farmers often in the majority.[13]

Colonial identities tracked closely with the cultural and economic distinctions of North America. Besides their attachments to locality and colony, free inhabitants defined themselves by race, kinship, gender, religion, and class. There was no uniform American; a set of cultural layers sorted individuals into particular reference groups. But in every section of the British

North American colonies, white male property owners were a distinct and privileged group that exercised paternal control over their properties, their children, nonwhites, and women. With the exception of Catholics in Maryland, colonial elites were Protestant. And, of critical significance in view of the geographic dispersion of colonial inhabitants, English was the dominant language of communication in British North America.

One other factor had great bearing on America's future. Most residents of British North America, and especially colonial elites of both genders, considered themselves loyal British subjects, proud to proclaim their allegiance to the king of England. They admired the British Constitution for its limitations on the use of capricious power, considered English law their guiding principle and liberty their birthright, and, if their economic situation permitted, aped the cultural practices of the English aristocracy. Calling themselves British, colonial Americans were proud of their heritage and their membership in the British Empire.[14]

Paradoxically, this close identification with things British sowed seeds of colonial rebellion. As Bernard Bailyn has elegantly written, eighteenth-century British polemists saw politics as a perpetual struggle between power and liberty, laced with the suspicion that rulers would plot "conspiracy against the constitutional guarantees of liberty." The political worldview of the British opposition literature, widely available in the colonies, primed Americans to detect conspiratorial intentions in the actions of royal ministers and to see threats to liberty lurking everywhere. Americans had developed a "frame of mind," Bailyn writes, that made eighteenth-century colonial politics "latently revolutionary."[15]

POLITICAL INSTITUTIONS IN THE COLONIES

In theory, Parliament and the Crown possessed complete authority over the governance of British colonies. In practice, however, control of internal affairs in North America lay principally in the hands of its inhabitants, exercised through local institutions. The centers of this power were the colonial assemblies, which had been created early in the history of each of the colonies. The members of these representative bodies were elected in towns in New England, in counties from New York to North Carolina, and in parishes in South Carolina and Georgia. Although property qualifications limited the franchise, widespread ownership of land meant that a large majority of free adult males was eligible to cast ballots. Voters tended to select their lawmakers from wealthy families, often keeping local elites in office for numerous terms. This was especially the case in the southern colonies, and in Virginia virtually all members of the House of Burgesses considered themselves planters. Though democratic by international standards of the time, colonial politics was deferential to one's economic "betters."[16]

Mimicking Parliament, colonial representatives elected their own speaker, initiated legislation, determined membership qualifications, judged election results, and appointed committees. Over the years assemblies assumed a variety of critical powers, such as the authority to levy taxes and to appropriate monies, including the payment of governors' salaries, as well as the authority to formulate policy over land, paper currency, defense, and other matters. Only the charters of Rhode Island, Connecticut, and Massachusetts specified annual sessions; in the other colonies, governors summoned and dissolved the legislatures. Despite the theoretical power of governors and the English Board of Trade to disallow legislation, colonial lawmakers viewed their institutions as "little parliaments," largely autonomous and free from British interference. Elected by their constituents, armed with important powers, and ready to defend their authority as a birthright of English constitutionalism, the colonial assemblies became "the most important institutions in colonial politics."[17]

Local governments handled most day-to-day civic matters. These tasks fell to towns in New England (Massachusetts had 194 towns in 1765); all freemen were permitted to participate in town meetings and elect selectmen. The county was the local administrative body in the South. In Virginia, which had forty-five counties plus four boroughs in 1752, each county was supervised by a county clerk, sheriff, coroner, surveyor, tobacco inspector, customs collector, and naval inspector; some functions were assigned to Anglican Church officials (vestrymen) and justices of the peace in subcounty units called parishes.

The key tasks of local officials were tax collection, defense, and criminal justice. New England communities imposed poll taxes on free adult males and taxed real estate and personal property based on its value. Sometimes additional revenue was raised by lotteries. Virginia levied poll taxes on both free males and slaves of both sexes, taxed imports and exports, and occasionally imposed a property tax. All colonies charged fees for various services, often paid in kind. In cash-starved Virginia, tobacco functioned as a substitute for monetary compensation. Local governments received the greatest share of tax revenue, which funded the salaries of officials, paid for the maintenance of churches and the improvement of roads and bridges, and provided aid to the indigent. New England used public monies to maintain schools.[18]

American colonists exercised coercive force in two significant ways: for the maintenance of a militia and the administration of criminal justice. Every colony assigned all able-bodied men to a militia unit whose primary function was defense, such as repelling attacks by Indians. But equally important, militias served as manpower pools from which to recruit volunteers for more sustained campaigns. Colonial legislatures appropriated funds to pay these volunteers. Citizen-soldiers, most of whom lacked full employment in a cash-strapped economy, welcomed the income. Local governments relied on sheriffs and justices of the peace to enforce the criminal code, which matched stringent British law. Lacking prisons and defense attorneys, local courts wasted little time in sentencing individuals convicted of theft, forgery, arson, and adultery to the gallows. Designed to emphasize "what the state could do to those who broke the law," hangings were public ceremonies that often attracted hundreds or even thousands of onlookers.[19]

Two additional functions suggest the range of powers exercised by local colonial governments. Children born to individuals of British birth or ancestry were automatically British subjects, but immigrants had to apply for such status. Colonists favored granting this status because it attracted settlers, adding to the workforce. Yet at the same time, colonists adopted a strict ethnocentric sense of identity by excluding slaves and free blacks, Native Americans, Catholics, and women from becoming British subjects. Citizenship, which was the basis for political rights, was confined (outside of Maryland) to adult white male Protestant property owners.[20] Assisting the poor was another local responsibility. In Virginia parishes, Anglican clergy administered aid to poor whites but not to slaves. In New England towns, public support for the indigent was only part of a more comprehensive approach to community well-being. Massachusetts towns, for example, "warned out" nonresident males in an effort to protect the local labor force from competition. They also removed "orphans" from families deemed unable or unwilling to properly discipline or educate their children, relocating them to households that, in the opinion of town selectmen, would provide an upbringing that comported with community standards. These policies were emblematic of New England's close scrutiny of communities' social and economic behavior.[21]

CRISIS IN THE EMPIRE

In 1754 Colonel George Washington, just twenty-two years old, led a militia regiment from northern Virginia toward Pittsburgh. Virginia's governor had instructed the young officer to occupy a British fort under construction at Pittsburgh, with the intent of blocking the advance of the French, who sought to gain control of an area around the forks of the Ohio River. But the French beat them to the fort and sent a delegation to negotiate with the approaching Virginians. A firefight resulted, and Washington's group killed twelve French soldiers whose mission had been diplomacy, not battle. Fearing the appearance of enemy reinforcements, the Virginians withdrew to a makeshift barricade ("Fort Necessity"), where a large French contingent forced Washington's surrender. The defeated colonel was allowed to take the remnants of his regiment back over the mountains to Virginia. The skirmish in the wilderness became the opening round of the French and Indian War, known in Europe as the Seven Years' War (1756–1763). This clash between imperial titans, wrote historian Bernard DeVoto, was "a war that changed the world."[22]

The Seven Years' War was the fourth in a series of military encounters between Great Britain and France and their respective allies during the eighteenth century. At stake was control of North America and other colonial outposts and the balance of power among the major European states. Because France fielded a huge army in its continental struggle against Prussia, which was allied with Britain, the Bourbon regime had few troops to defend its North American territory in the 1750s. Britain, in contrast, sent a force to America that vastly outnumbered the French and used its powerful navy to block French and Spanish fleets at strategic locations in the Caribbean, along the coast of France, and elsewhere. The British regular army, aided by regiments of colonial volunteers, defeated the French at Louisbourg (on Cape Breton Island in Canada), took Fort Ticonderoga on Lake Champlain, and defeated the French garrison at Quebec (1759). A year later Montreal fell to the British, crushing French control of the St. Lawrence River–Great Lakes region. In the Treaty of 1763 France ceded its North American holdings (present-day Canada) to Great Britain.

As history would later demonstrate, Britain's triumph in the Seven Years' War was a Pyrrhic victory. Thirteen years after the Treaty of 1763, the thirteen colonies declared their independence. The roots of this separation can be found in the "global war between European great powers" that enlarged British debt and aggravated American irritation over Britain's remedies for its financial burden.[23] The disagreement began over taxation. Britain had borrowed heavily to fund its military campaign in the Seven Years' War. To finance its debt, Britain adopted new revenue measures such as the Sugar Act of 1764, designed in part to force colonists to contribute to the costs of defending them from France. The new levies included customs duties on imports to America, as well as restrictions on exports to England and tighter customs administration, which sought to reduce revenue losses due to smuggling. The Royal Navy was enlisted to catch customs cheaters. This new British toughness was driven in part by resentment over the colonies' minimal contribution to the fight against France and by a severe economic recession, which increased the pressure on British taxpayers. Britain also tightened its ban on paper currency in the colonies, which Americans had issued to ease the economic stress of the recession. Even more galling, in light of past practices, Britain stationed soldiers in the colonies and required the colonies to house them. This new intrusion into colonial affairs was alarming, especially to the Massachusetts Assembly, which created a committee of correspondence that urged the colonies to protest by boycotting British goods.

The second issue that sparked discord between the British and North Americans concerned western lands. After the French and Indian War, Americans ventured over the Appalachian Mountains into the Ohio River valley in search of land. Native Americans resisted this penetration, attacking the "trespassers." The conflict erupted into Pontiac's War (1763–1764), which highlighted the administrative entanglements of managing the frontier. Britain's solution was to prohibit new European settlement west of the Appalachians, announced in the Proclamation of 1763. The order incensed colonials who owned or coveted western lands. George Washington ignored the order, which he correctly predicted would fail. Restrictions on colonial entrepreneurial mobility, coupled with the new tax regime, upset the peaceful coexistence that had characterized British-American relations in the past.

These irritations ignited further conflict. Rather than back down from its new revenue policy, Britain passed the Stamp Act of 1765, which placed duties on ordinary items such as newspapers and legal documents. The Stamp Act triggered the first of three political crises, each of which forged greater intercolony cooperation and provoked philosophic-legal discussions about the relationship between Britain and its colonies. Protesters calling themselves the Sons of Liberty organized in port cities and looted the homes of stamp collectors, many of whom resigned. Delegates from nine colonies met in New York and adopted resolutions that rejected Britain's authority to impose taxes directly on American colonists. Although the delegates pledged allegiance to the Crown and accepted Parliament's authority to set policy for the empire, in the next breath they proclaimed that "his Majesty's liege subjects . . . are entitled to all the inherent rights and liberties of his natural born subjects." Americans, in other words, had the same rights as inhabitants of England and therefore could not be taxed without their consent—an impossibility, given their lack of representation in Parliament. British lawmakers repealed the Stamp Act but used the occasion to reaffirm their authority to make laws for the colonies "in all cases whatsoever."

The abrupt change in British policy provoked coordinated resistance from Americans, which was met in turn by Parliament's assertion that colonists could not second-guess British governance. The events of 1765 initiated a descent into crisis. Parliament enacted the Townshend Duties in 1767, which colonists resisted by supporting nonimportation agreements. Britain repealed the duties in 1770, but not before sending British soldiers to Boston, the hotbed of resistance to British authority. In 1772 Britain decided to pay royal colonial officials directly, so they would no longer be beholden to colonial legislatures for their salaries. The next year Parliament allowed the British East India Company to sell tea in the colonies without paying customs duties, which gave it an economic advantage over colonial importers. A mob of Bostonians raided East India Company ships and dumped their tea into the harbor. New Yorkers held their own tea protest. For the British ministry and a majority in Parliament, the Boston Tea Party was the last straw in what they saw as the breakdown of law and order in the colonies. Parliament responded with the Coercive Acts (the Intolerable Acts, to colonists) in 1774. These laws closed the port of Boston until the dumped tea had been paid for, revoked Massachusetts residents' right to hold town meetings, and protected British soldiers and magistrates from colonial trials. A final act suspended the Massachusetts legislature. British officials had flexed their muscles, terminating citizen governance in Massachusetts.

The more public dimension of this conflict took the form of parliamentary decisions and colonial opposition to them through street protests and organized boycotts of British products. A second and equally influential manifestation of this "cousins' dispute" was a debate over law and constitutionalism. As Jack Greene has shown, the metropolitan government (in England) and colonial publicists—usually lawyers, legislators, and educated observers—produced a flurry of writings that interpreted and illuminated the legal position of the colonies. Each side began with opposing premises and reached different conclusions. The British interpretation argued that Parliament had omnipotent authority over the British Empire. Constitutional authority could not be fragmented among parts of the realm but must be centered in one location—namely, the monarchy and the national legislature. To deny Parliament's authority to tax was tantamount to denying its unicentric control of British governance.[24]

The colonists responded that the British Constitution limited the power of Parliament, which had never been authorized to legislate the internal affairs of each colony. Through usage and custom, the British Constitution had evolved to recognize and accept the rights and practices exercised by colonists in their "little parliaments." Given this history of "directing their internal Government by Laws made with their Consent," Richard Bland, a member of Virginia's House of Burgesses, argued in 1766 that each colony was "a distinct State, independent as to the internal Government," but united to Britain's "*external* Polity." In essence, the colonies had evolved into "pure Republic[s]." To this, British leaders responded that the colonies were bound to "the sovereign power" of Great Britain and that it was "an absurdity" to claim that the Crown had created a series of "independent state[s]." As Greene makes clear, the question of how power was apportioned between colonial peripheries and the metropolitan center raged unanswered throughout the eighteenth century. What changed in the years between the seventeenth century and the Seven Years' War was the rise of parliamentary government in Great Britain and the insistence of American colonists that British subjects possessed constitutional rights.[25]

Little changed in the debate over the reach of Parliament's power between 1763 and 1774, but what did change were events on the ground. In 1774 Parliament enacted the Quebec Act, which extended the territorial domain of French Canada southward to the Ohio River and westward to the Mississippi, retained Catholicism as the established church of the western province, and denied an elected legislature to govern the region. New Englanders were aghast at this embrace of "popery." That same year, a further affront to colonial self-reliance was the assignment of General George Gage, commander of British military forces in North America, to Boston, where he replaced the civil governor and established martial law. In response to this crisis, delegates from twelve of the thirteen colonies assembled in Philadelphia at the First Continental Congress. The group ratified Boston's Suffolk Resolves, which outlined resistance to British martial law, including the recommendation that the colony prepare to counter British militarism with an armed defense. Gage then dissolved the Massachusetts legislature, and New Englanders began stockpiling guns and drilling their militia.[26]

CONCLUSION: THE EMERGENCE OF LITTLE REPUBLICS

The First Continental Congress had little difficulty summarizing the philosophical core of the colonists' constitutional position with regard to their place in the British Empire. It stated that the inhabitants of the English colonies in North American "are entitled to life, liberty, and property," which could not be ceded "to any sovereign power . . . without their consent." Citing the key mechanism for exercising this prerogative, the declaration stated: "That the foundation of English liberty, and of all free government, is a right in the people to participate in their legislative council." The delegates reminded Britain that the colonies held no seats in Parliament and that some of their "little parliaments" had been dissolved and replaced by appointed councils, an action that was "unconstitutional, dangerous, and destructive to the freedom of American legislation." Between 1763 and 1774 Americans had honed their conception of their rights as English subjects and the law concerning the division of power between the center and the peripheries of the empire.

Americans' embrace of their rights should be seen in the context of the colonies' evolution during the eighteenth century. This exercise in self-government transformed each colony into a "little republic" possessing virtually all the powers of a national state, except for diplomacy and foreign trade. Colonial governments levied taxes and appropriated these monies largely at their own discretion. Colonies possessed coercive power through their militias and local officials such as sheriffs and justices of the peace. Their courts heard arguments over property conflicts, including the ownership of slaves, and convicted and sentenced persons for offenses deemed criminal by colonial statute (including imposing the death penalty). Colonies had formulated a legal-philosophical rationale, based largely on British political-legal precedent, that established a constitutional justification for self-government. As Greene characterizes this history, American colonists "engaged in state building."[27]

Neither the majority in Parliament nor British ministers accepted the American argument that Britain's power to rule the empire had limits. To English officials, power held at the center was not divisible. From the vantage point of the twenty-first century, this decision looks like a horrible miscalculation. How could British leaders let such a valuable asset as North America slip through their fingers? Why did they ignore the advice of both members of Parliament and colonists like the respected Benjamin Franklin to accept some sort of compromise rather than cling so dogmatically to a political theory that drove Americans to insurrection?

British intransigence is not easily explained, but one can speculate about the mind-set of British leaders. Perhaps most important, they understood that if the central regime could not impose taxes on all residents in its realm, the state lacked full control over them. Underscoring this axiom was the reality that Britain had fought a costly war against its archenemy France and had invested sizable sums to achieve victory. The evidence also suggests that British officials focused their geopolitical strategy more on the balance of power in Europe than on their relationship with North Americans.[28] Additionally, many in Great Britain resented the colonists' failure to appreciate Britain's costly campaign to drive the hated French from North America. Moreover, British governors had complained for decades about tendencies toward anarchy and independence in the colonies.[29] Contributing to this mix of likely motivations affecting British decisionmaking was a lack of reliable information about conditions in America. British military officers, for example, took a contemptuous view of American military capacity, misunderstanding the tradition of a local militia.[30]

Yet perhaps the root cause of British stubbornness was simply their hubris, which stemmed in good measure from the aristocratic background of the English ruling class. The role of British rulers in the late eighteenth century was to maintain, not reduce, the power of their state. National leaders seldom voluntarily relinquished power, especially to people they regarded as ungrateful and insubordinate. Rather than seeing the dispute with the colonies as a legal-political disagreement that could be negotiated, British leaders saw insurrection and resolved to crush it. Thus a grand paradox ensued, wherein one of history's most liberal states pursued a pathway that led to a separate and more powerful state.

3

Forging a National State

On April 18, 1775, General Thomas Gage, military commander of His Majesty's army in North America and the governor of Massachusetts, launched a nighttime march of troops from Boston to Concord. He was following orders from the secretary of state for the colonies to crush the resistance to British policy in Massachusetts and arrest its leaders. Gage doubted that he could nab the key colonials, but he intended to confiscate whatever arms and munitions the militia had stockpiled. Colonial lookouts spread the word that Gage's men were on the move and alerted the local militia, dubbed "minutemen" for their ability to assemble swiftly. The British first met armed resistance in Lexington, where the redcoats dispersed the colonials, killing eight, and then turned toward Concord. Hundreds of militiamen awaited their arrival, firing on the redcoats as they entered the town and forcing their withdrawal. News of the British attacks spread rapidly across the region, and several thousand militiamen hurried to the area. American muskets rained deadly fire on Gage's soldiers as they retreated to Boston. Seventy-three redcoats were killed and hundreds wounded. With the "shot heard 'round the world," blood had been spilled and lives had been taken, engulfing eastern New England in a deadly crisis.

As planned, the Second Continental Congress assembled in Philadelphia in May. Delegates were confronted with the news from Massachusetts, where thousands of militiamen had ringed Gage's forces on Boston's narrow neck. In June, Gage, now aided by Generals William Howe and Henry Clinton, stormed across the bay to drive off the defenders but suffered unacceptably high casualties in the Battle of Bunker Hill. The Continental Congress's response to the "unprovoked assault" in Lexington and "butchered . . . countrymen" in Charleston was to organize military resistance to the British occupation. Delegates formed a continental army, approved bills of credit to fund it, and appointed George Washington its commander. In its July 1775 "Declaration of Causes of Taking up Arms," Congress stated that "necessity" had caused Americans to repel Britain's "unprovoked" attacks and undertake a "defense of the freedom that is our birthright." In the next breath, Congress denied that the colonies desired to leave the empire.

As Washington arrived in Cambridge, Massachusetts, to take command of the provincial army, the Continental Congress advised the colonies to form temporary nonroyalist governments—a logical step, in view of colonial military preparations. With British rule crumbling in its American colonies during the waning months of 1775, Crown ministers circulated a petition in Massachusetts urging reconciliation. Abigail Adams advised her husband John, a member of Congress, to spurn the offer, writing, "Let us separate, they are unworthy to be our brethren."[1]

THE DECISION FOR INDEPENDENCE

In the fall of 1775 King George III told Parliament that the colonies were in open revolt and denounced its leaders as traitors. If apprehended, they were likely to hang. Parliament supported the king's determination to force the rebels to submit, and it acknowledged Britain's complete authority over all its possessions. Meanwhile, the Americans were keeping Britain's military machine at bay, and Washington's New England army had penned up General Howe's forces in Boston. In March 1776 a daring repositioning of cannon carted from Fort Ticonderoga in New York to Dorchester Heights, overlooking the center of Boston, caused the British to withdraw to Halifax, Nova Scotia. Washington knew they would be back; he guessed correctly that their destination would be New York City.[2]

As Washington moved his army to New York, Congress continued to organize a defense of the homeland, while maintaining hope for reconciliation with Britain. Events, however, undermined this optimism. Word reached Congress of a vast British armada crossing the Atlantic, along with news that the king had hired 17,000 German soldiers as part of an invasion force. These rumors were confirmed in late May when copies of British treaties concerning the mercenaries arrived in the colonies. Congress had already advised colonial assemblies and committees of safety to disarm British loyalists. In April, South Carolina adopted a constitution that established a state government. The next month, Congress warned the colonies that "the whole force" of Britain, "aided by foreign mercenaries," was en route to America. The delegates advised colonists that "any government under the . . . Crown should be totally suppressed" and recommended that the colonies form their own governments.[3]

Still, the Continental Congress hung back from declaring independence. Hope for a peaceful resolution lingered, especially in the middle colonies, where loyalists abounded among seaport merchants, Anglican clergy, recent immigrants, and non-English ethnic groups. Worried loyalists published a flurry of statements arguing the folly of opposing the world's strongest navy and abandoning its protection of seaborne commerce. William Franklin, son of Benjamin and governor of New Jersey, told his assembly, "You can never place yourselves in a happier situation than in your ancient constitutional dependency on Great Britain." Many loyalists agreed that Britain offered the widest protection of rights anywhere in the world. Compromise, they counseled, was possible and preferred.[4]

In January 1776 Thomas Paine published a pamphlet entitled *Common Sense*, and it had a marked impact on colonial thinking. Paine summarized colonial allegations of a Crown conspiracy to subvert American liberties and went on to enumerate "constitutional errors," such as the practice of allowing heredity to select monarchies. In urging Americans to establish an independent republic, he observed that there "is something very absurd in supposing a continent to be perpetually governed by an island." *Common Sense* was a best seller in the colonies and, in the view of numerous historians, was instrumental in swaying people's minds about the conflict. Although Paine did not stampede Congress into a decision for separation, the delegates did appoint a committee in June to write a declaration of independence. The committee asked Thomas Jefferson, known for his literary skills, to draft the document. Still, some delegates hung back, contending that sentiments were not yet sufficiently "ripe" throughout the colonies for a formal separation. Moderate delegates worried that a lack of uniformity could prove fatal to a fledgling state.[5]

Advocates of separation waited for an opportune moment to push for independence. They got it on June 29 when lookouts on the roof of Washington's headquarters in New York spotted forty-five British ships anchored inside Sandy Hook in sight of New York Harbor. Riders galloped off toward New Jersey and Connecticut to spread the news. Word drifted in that more ships and troops would follow. The news reached Philadelphia on July 1, confirming that Britain had resolved to crush the rebellion in America. By July 32,000 British soldiers had encamped on Staten Island, and 400 Royal Navy vessels, many of them heavily armed ships of the line, were anchored nearby. It was the largest expeditionary force of the eighteenth century. Four days after the British armada had been spotted, Congress approved the Declaration of Independence. Hopes for reconciliation evaporated. Resistance had been transformed into revolution. War would decide the outcome of the Americans' defense of their liberties.[6]

The Declaration of Independence was a strategic part of this effort. Its intent was to rally colonists behind a common cause and to give that cause political legitimacy, in part to entice foreign assistance. The document was a synthesis of the theory and charges that colonists had been airing since 1764. It cited the "Laws of Nature and of Nature's God" as authority to form a government "to effect their safety and happiness," a step made necessary by "a history of repeated injuries and usurpations, all having in direct object the establishment of an absolute tyranny over these States." As proof of the last charge, Jefferson listed twenty-seven indictments again the king of Great Britain, including offenses that struck at the heart of republican ideas about liberty: the king had "dissolved representative houses," refused necessary laws, prevented immigration and obstructed naturalization, interfered with the courts, kept standing armies in peacetime, taxed "without our consent," and waged war against the colonies. Parliament had been a party to most of these actions, but Congress blamed the king, to whom colonists and royal administrators had pledged their allegiance. The logical alternative to the royal suppression of liberty, according to Jefferson's proclamation, was the creation of an independent state.[7]

RESISTANCE ON A SHOESTRING

The American rebels had taken on a formidable challenge. They faced a well-trained professional army backed by the most powerful navy in the world. British officers in New York were confident that they could quickly overwhelm Washington's ragtag force of newly recruited continentals and inexperienced militiamen. The prediction proved accurate in the early going, as redcoats landed on Long Island and drove Washington's men from Brooklyn Heights, then from New York City, and finally from White Plains, north of the city. Americans who were not killed or captured in the New York campaign were lucky to escape across the Hudson River and flee through New Jersey to Pennsylvania. As winter approached, the British suspended military activity, as was the custom in the eighteenth century.

From his encampment near Philadelphia, Washington reflected on his retreat from New York and the news of a failed American attack on Quebec, the British stronghold in Canada. He desperately needed a victory to boost deflated spirits, especially among disgruntled members of Congress who were questioning the general's leadership ability. Washington saw his opportunity in Trenton, New Jersey, where a regiment of German mercenaries was garrisoned. On Christmas night Washington led 2,400 continental troops across the Delaware River during a sleet storm and surprised the 1,500 British troops, 900 of whom were captured. It was a critical success for a resistance campaign that had stumbled out of the gate. A much larger triumph occurred at Saratoga, New York, the following fall when Americans stopped a British foray from Canada that had hoped to isolate New England from the middle colonies. British general John Burgoyne surrendered an army of 5,000. Among the fruits of that victory was France's agreement to a treaty that opened the way for overt aid to the American war effort.

Trenton and Saratoga were exceptions to a desultory American campaign in the middle colonies, where the war settled into a stalemate. The British were headquartered in New York and Newport, Rhode Island, and Washington was working desperately to keep an army intact in New Jersey, where he monitored his adversaries' movements. In 1779 British strategists shifted focus to the southern colonies, where they anticipated substantial assistance from loyalists. The Royal Navy landed forces at Savannah and then in Charleston, which surrendered after a five-week siege. Under General Henry Clinton, British forces pushed northward to Virginia, where they nearly nabbed Thomas Jefferson, governor of the state, in 1781. Prodded by the French general who had joined forces with the Americans, Washington agreed to confront Clinton's army at Yorktown, Virginia. Through a sequence of British mishaps and American good fortune—such as bad weather impeding Clinton's attempt to retreat across the James River and the timely arrival of the French fleet, which forced a withdrawal of the Royal Navy—a combined continental and French army forced Clinton's surrender on October 17, 1781. After seven years of a military campaign that saddled the kingdom with a large debt, British officials ended their efforts to suppress the American rebellion. Terms for a peace settlement were signed in November 1782; the Treaty of Paris, which formally recognized the independence of the United States, was announced September 3, 1783.

The Americans achieved their bid for sovereignty, but to say they won the Revolutionary War exaggerates the military reality. A more accurate characterization of the outcome is that the British failed to subdue the patriots. The colonists, in other words, survived the British military storm. The wonder is that the patriots were able to avoid defeat, as they had neither a professional army nor an effective central government. An army had to be formed from scratch and qualified officers had to be found, tasks that proved problematic throughout the war. Washington and his generals periodically called out state militias, but these inexperienced local units, serving short terms of service, were unreliable. Raising money to pay for military supplies was always difficult, largely because there was no central bank and Congress lacked taxing power. The Continental Congress functioned as the national political command post for the duration of the war. Late in 1777 it approved the Articles of Confederation, which gave the colonies' collaboration some constitutional substance, but approval of the plan lingered until 1781. The Articles of Confederation allowed Congress to borrow money but not to levy taxes. Throughout the conflict, congressional committees handled the administrative aspects of war policy, such as securing supplies, issuing paper money, floating loans, and requisitioning financial assistance from state governments. When funds were not forthcoming or goods were priced out of reach, continental troops turned to confiscation.

Given these obstacles, how did the patriots prevail? The answer lies largely in the interplay of six factors, beginning with geography. The Atlantic Ocean played an immense role in the outcome. Britain had to ferry men, food, fodder, and munitions 3,000 miles from England to America, a journey of four to eight weeks by sailing vessel. The Americans were situated along the coast from Maine to Georgia, a distance of nearly 1,300 miles, with some settlements located well inland. The Royal Navy had occupied the major American seaports—New York, Savannah, Charleston, and Philadelphia—for periods during the war but lacked the capacity to blockade every coastal location while also countering the French navy. The American Revolution was principally a land war, but Britain lacked sufficient troops to occupy all strategic locations.[8]

A second factor was leadership, which began with George Washington. The Virginia planter proved to be the right choice at the right time. Washington was not a great strategist, earning criticism for some of his decisions. But he made up for this shortcoming with other attributes. Impressions are important. Washington looked and acted like a leader. Over six feet tall, robust, and always dignified, he naturally commanded respect. Moreover, he treated his officers and troops civilly. Despite Washington's military limitations, David McCullough wrote, he "never forgot what was at stake and he never gave up." He was able to make tough decisions but usually asked his staff for advice. On the battlefield he was fearless. And he was a true republican, committed to the American cause, deferring to the civil authority of Congress, and forswearing an interest in transforming his command into a military dictatorship. But his greatest military contribution was his ability to design and execute a defensive strategy that enabled him to keep his army intact so it could fight another day. American units became adept at small-scale hit-and-run tactics. As long as Washington kept viable military forces in the field, ready to confront the redcoats, Americans had a chance.[9]

Third, American leaders understood the necessity for international assistance, especially from France. The French were eager to strike back at their longtime enemy, and the colonials' victory over Burgoyne at Saratoga spurred the French to commit overtly to the American cause. French soldiers and warships from two fleets were critical in the American entrapment of Clinton at Yorktown in 1781. Spain and the Netherlands also declared war against Britain; Dutch loans were the most important benefit from the victory at Yorktown. Britain had no allies in its American war, as the kingdom watched the actions of Russia, Prussia, and Sweden with a jaundiced eye. George Washington benefited considerably from Europeans who joined his crusade; his favorite foreign officer, the Marquis de Lafayette, helped obtain the French-American alliance of 1778.[10]

Fourth, British strategy was flawed. The London ministers believed that American resistance was unsustainable; they discounted the size and potential contributions of colonial militia and underestimated the difficulties of supplying an overseas army. They expected far more support from colonialists (i.e., loyalists) than materialized. Following a vacillating strategy, British officers came up short in the opinion of numerous historians. Failure to pursue the enemy after an initial triumph was one criticism. The style of eighteenth-century warfare explains much of British hesitancy. Battlefield contests in Europe were fought for limited objectives, not total annihilation of enemy forces. Generals were cautious in committing troops to battle because the customary tactics for soldiers using smoothbore muskets, with an effective range of no more than one hundred yards, meant that sustained head-on charges could produce unacceptably high casualties. Replacing troops was difficult and costly. Moreover, most officers were aristocrats who had purchased their commissions; they were just as concerned with upholding a code of honor as with demonstrating tactical skill in the field. "Gentleman" Johnny Burgoyne was an example of the class. The general brought along his mistress and a personal baggage train of thirty carts containing fine china and wine on his foiled trek from Canada to Saratoga.[11] Communication among military leaders and with the ministry was weakened by distance and personal rancor; these factors and poor judgment prevented the British navy from rescuing Cornwallis at Yorktown.[12]

A fifth factor, admittedly partially speculative, was the socioeconomic makeup of American society. The colonists produced sufficient food during the war, had a substantial iron-making capacity, and manufactured much of their own weaponry and ammunition. Congress and the states took advantage of colonists' experience at sea, commissioning hundreds of privateering vessels (legalized pirates) that preyed on British shipping, a partial compensation for the lack of an American navy. Despite Britain's attempted blockade, Americans continued to trade overseas, including the importation of French weapons. Closer to home, small ships plied coastal waters, some of which were too shallow for Britain's heavy gunships. Given their adequate diet and rural lifestyle, Americans were a healthy people, which arguably helped patriot armies endure long marches and sustained campaigns. Moreover, Americans were farm folk familiar with firearms, including rifles, which were more accurate than muskets.[13]

Last, ideology likely helped the revolutionary cause, although the influence of beliefs and ideas on the behavior of large numbers of people is hard to determine. Still, the historical evidence makes a persuasive case that many colonists saw the fight in terms of preserving their rights—initially as British subjects and then, after 1775, as citizens under their own state constitutions. Certainly they understood that their homes and their lives, as well as the lives of their fellow Americans, would be imperiled by a British victory. The dual motivation of self-preservation and ideological commitment probably stiffened the militias' resolve to muster when called and to stand their ground in the face of trained British regulars. Historian John Shy has argued that the militia "became the infrastructure of revolutionary government," weeding out Tories (loyalists) from their communities and ensuring loyalty to the cause among various locales.[14]

THE IMPACT OF THE REVOLUTION

Success in resisting the British invasion had lasting ramifications for American statebuilding. First and foremost, the peace treaty with Great Britain recognized American sovereignty and secured a huge territorial concession. During the war colonists transformed their colonial governments to semisovereign states based on written constitutions. This process of statemaking set a precedent for defining political authority based on explicit texts. For his role in creating the conditions that allowed these developments to succeed, George Washington was heralded a hero, giving the country its first national figurehead.

The Treaty of Paris (1783), which recognized American sovereignty, emerged from machinations in international politics. The Americans who negotiated the settlement—Benjamin Franklin, John Jay, and John Adams—had taken up residence in Paris. Britain's failure to end the American rebellion, a costly undertaking, had prompted a transition in the ministries in London. Anglo-French enmity continued, which induced the British to make the best of a difficult situation. The treaty ceded to the United States the lands west of the Appalachian Mountains extending to the Mississippi River, running from the Great Lakes in the north to Georgia in the south. Americans were free to navigate the great river "from its source to the ocean." British leaders saw these grants as a way of containing French ambitions in North America. For diplomatic reasons, France turned a blind eye to the American-British settlement, which, according to the American-French Treaty of 1778, required French consent. This territorial transfer was an extraordinary windfall for the United States. The concession allowed the new nation to begin its independence with a geographic expanse larger than western Europe. In so doing, the treaty set in motion the predictions of Benjamin Franklin and others that Americans were destined to occupy western lands as well.[15]

Americans who remained loyal to the English monarch complicated the conduct of the war and the postwar settlement. Somewhere between 80,000 and 100,000 civilians left America during the Revolution, heading primarily for Canada and England. Larger numbers of Tories remained in America, notably in the vicinity of New York and other port cities. Following the recommendations of the Continental Congress, committees of safety, and other organizations, patriots had disarmed loyalists and seized and auctioned off their property, using the proceeds to fund the Revolution. Now, the treaty obligated Congress to "recommend" that the states restore the property of loyalists confiscated during the Revolution and to cease persecution of the opponents of independence. Every state enacted laws establishing loyalty oaths and declarations, forcing residents to confirm their allegiance to the United States. Disloyalty was treason. In reality, state governments provided little restitution or compensation for loyalist property seized or destroyed; the issue lingered in the courts into the nineteenth century. Slave owners did not recover all their human property that fled during the Revolution. A British raiding party helped seventeen of George Washington's slaves escape Mount Vernon. Washington recovered eight of the runaways, four of whom sailed to Nova Scotia with the British when they evacuated New York. The Revolution and the peace settlement, in short, thrust to the forefront the issues of identity and citizenship, matters that principally lay in the hands of the new state governments.[16]

The conflict between the colonies and Great Britain resulted in the dissolution of royal governments and their replacement with temporary provincial assemblies. Acting on the May 1776 recommendation of the Continental Congress, colonists transformed their temporary governments into states by approving written constitutions. Eight states adopted constitutions in 1776; New York and Georgia followed in 1777. Massachusetts voters rejected a proposed constitution in 1778, largely because it had been neither written by a specially elected convention nor submitted for popular approval. Delegates for a new convention were elected in 1779, and Massachusetts voters accepted the revised constitution in 1780. Connecticut and Rhode Island retained their colonial charters, having excised references to the Crown.

These documents have enormous importance in the history of American statebuilding. Unlike the British, who did not base their government on a single written constitution, Americans anchored their governments on explicit rules, which included the enumeration of individual liberties in bills of rights. Equally significant, these new states were semisovereign entities that possessed broad powers that remained largely immune from central interference until the acceptance of a national constitution. This quasi-independent status of the states explains why the name of the new country—the *United States of America*—is expressed in the plural. The transition to statehood and to a union of independent states was primarily the consequence of the crisis of the Revolution. In effect, the years of debate over the powers of Parliament concerning the colonies and their practical governing experience prior to 1776 constituted an incubation period for refining ideas about American constitutionalism, to which the Revolution enabled explicit expression.[17]

The original state constitutions contained several identifying characteristics. First, constitution writers based the authority to form a government on a voluntary association of the people. The Virginia Constitution stated that "all power is vested in, and consequently derived from, the people; that magistrates are their trustees and servants, and at all times amendable to them." The preamble to the Massachusetts Constitution (1780) expressed the principle this way: "The body politic is formed by a voluntary association of individuals: it is a social compact." Section 4 of the Massachusetts Bill of Rights proclaimed, "The people of this commonwealth have the sole and exclusive right of governing themselves, as a free, sovereign and independent State." This principle derived from the philosophy of John Locke, whose influence is visible in the American Declaration of Independence and in the historical development of colonial politics.

State constitutions explicitly listed the rights of citizens. Eight constitutions had separate declarations of rights (as in Virginia); a bill of rights served as the preamble to the Massachusetts compact. Other states embedded similar provisions in the bodies of their constitutions. These statements protected civil liberties, such as freedom of speech, the press, and religion, and prohibited unreasonable searches and seizures of people and property. Criminal procedure operated according to certain limitations on governmental authority, such as the right of the accused to be formally charged with a crime and to be tried by jury and the prohibition against excessive bail, provisions also written into the national Bill of Rights in 1789 (ratified in 1791). States, however, went beyond these well-known protections. Some forbade the granting of titles of nobility; others guaranteed the people's right to form a militia, the right to a speedy trial by a jury of one's peers, and the freedom to emigrate from the state. Americans' understanding of "liberty" meant explicit limitations on the powers of public officials.

The new state constitutions centered the primary power to govern on elected legislators. These representative bodies had broad authority, although some powers were left implicit rather than explicitly enumerated. Taxation, for example, was assumed to be a prerogative of a sovereign government, needing no constitutional recognition. The structure and procedures of these governments, however, imposed limits on the *ways* power could be exercised. Most states created a bicameral legislature (two chambers), and all did so by 1790. State constitutions limited lawmakers to short terms (usually one year for assemblies), mandated frequent elections (annually for most lower houses), and required lawmakers to live in the districts they represented. The new compacts provided marginal expansions of suffrage, but voting privileges remained confined to adult white males who owned property or paid taxes. Some states mandated that lawmakers follow explicit procedures, such as printing bills prior to passage and recording roll-call votes. Suspicious of unlimited grants of power, Revolutionary-era Americans took pains to guard against capricious lawmaking.[18]

States recognized the need for a chief executive, but all imposed strict limitations on their powers. Nine states instructed legislators to elect their governors, usually for one-year terms without the prospect of reelection. Only Massachusetts granted the executive veto power; most states restricted governors' appointment powers. Similar limitations applied to the highest courts, whose jurists were appointed by legislators in nine states. The principle of separation of power among legislators, executives, and judges did not fully blossom until several decades after the Revolution. Recognizing that changes could be warranted, some states provided mechanisms for rewriting their covenants.

The common features of the first state constitutions obscure the different ways the states actually governed. Constitutional actions during the Revolution empowered states to manage their own affairs, subject only to modest cooperation with national officials under the Articles of Confederation (1781–1789). Article II of that document stated, "Each state retains its sovereignty, freedom and independence, and every Power, Jurisdiction and right, which is not by this confederation expressly delegated to the United States, in Congress assembled." Beyond the ability to wage war, conduct foreign relations, and borrow money, Congress scarcely intruded on state governments, other than asking them to support the war with money and men. The semiautonomous condition of the original states has remained a salient characteristic of the American state.

Variations in state policy are visible in terms of their contributions to the war effort. States had the power to tax, but they raised funds in several ways. Some states levied taxes on property, both real estate and personal; some levied poll taxes on individual voters; others levied excise taxes. Virginia sold public lands, and all southern states gave warrants for land to soldiers upon their discharge. Virginia permitted the payment of certain taxes in commodities such as tobacco; tax arrearages in Massachusetts could be paid in cod oil, whalebone, and pearl ash. Maritime states, especially New York, enacted import duties and shipping fees. States auctioned off the confiscated properties of loyalists. Pressed for additional finances, states turned to paper money and borrowing to raise war funds. They also passed laws against profiteering, fixed wages and prices, and sponsored the manufacture of gunpower and firearms. Contemporary critics chastised state lawmakers for failing to comply fully with congressional "requisitions" of funds (more like requested donations) for war purposes. Collectively, the states provided some of Congress's financial requests.[19]

The Revolution prodded colonists to form indigenous civic regimes, but it did not mold Americans into a single homogeneous nationality. Neither a common identity among inhabitants nor a single standard for citizenship had crystallized. The war did not elevate women to equal status with men, nor did it overturn slavery. Some residents continued to give their allegiance to Great Britain, at least in their hearts if not openly after 1776. Many backcountry farmers cared little about the outcome of the Revolution. Yet, as Gordon Wood has argued, Americans tended to think of themselves as distinct from Europeans. To the extent they embraced America's republican values, the majority probably thought their political rights were superior to Old World standards. The Revolution was a politicizing event that imparted widespread pride in the struggle for republican liberty and the right of self-government among residents. The new political collaboration between a national Congress and the thirteen states was staffed by individuals who spoke English. Inadvertently and unplanned, the Revolution had nurtured the seeds of American nationalism.[20]

Independence also produced a national hero in George Washington. As commander in chief of the Continental Army, Washington was the stoic center of resistance to the British invasion, yet he remained deferential to the will of Congress. At the conclusion of the war he relinquished his command and returned to Mount Vernon, signifying his acceptance of civilian over military rule. He chose retirement, not a Napoleonic seizure of power. These achievements made Washington an international celebrity, standing a notch above Benjamin Franklin as the greatest American of his age. The cultivation of national identity requires the popular recognition of individuals who embody the virtues of a nation. Washington fulfilled the role admirably. He championed the cause of republican liberty during the war. He was a committed nationalist who worked for unity in a politically fragmented country whose governmental apparatus was locally oriented, insular, and rent by factional conflicts. "Unreasonable jealousies" among the states, he wrote in 1784, threatened "our downfall as a nation." Conscious of his wide adulation, Washington avoided conspicuous efforts to exploit it, but behind the scenes he worked to forge a more robust central regime. A committed nationalist, his advocacy of a stronger central government was a critical factor in the writing of the Constitution of the United States.[21]

POSTWAR PROBLEMS

The adulation showered on Washington at the conclusion of the Revolution was a bright spot in a country facing formidable problems. The challenges were so extreme during the "critical period," as John Quincy Adams and other contemporaries called the mid-1780s, that some wondered whether the new regime could survive. One difficulty oscillated around foreign relations, particularly the continuing presence of Britain and Spain in North America. The British failed to vacate forts on America's northern perimeter, where they encouraged Native American attacks on settlers. Spain retained territory along the Gulf Mexico, including the port of New Orleans, which it closed to American commercial traffic in 1784. This closure threatened the livelihoods of frontier farmers who used the Mississippi River to transport goods to market. Britain's orders in council banned American ships from the West Indies, where New Englanders had long cultivated a lucrative trade. France restricted access to its markets. "Barbary pirates" sponsored by states in North Africa captured and ransomed American merchant ships in the Mediterranean.[22]

The United States was virtually powerless to resolve these issues. Under the Articles of Confederation, Congress did not possess the power to tax or to regulate commerce. The army had virtually disbanded after 1783, and the few ships in the navy were laid up. When John Adams, America's ambassador to Britain, complained about that nation's failure to send an ambassador to the States, the British queried: shall we send one envoy or thirteen? Equally frustrating was Congress's inability to pay debts incurred during the Revolution. Lacking its own revenue, Congress sent six requisition requests to the states between October 1781 and August 1786, specifying payment in specie (hard currency), as required by creditors. The states filled a portion of the requests but, facing war debts of their own and other fiscal burdens, fell far short of the amounts billed. Not a single state complied with the 1785 assessment.

State lawmakers did raise revenue and retaliate against foreign trade restrictions. Nine states adopted tariffs designed to counter the British orders in council. Under pressure from private investors who had bought depreciated paper currencies (US continentals and state-issued paper), state legislators passed measures to retire war debts, expenditures that were added to normal funding obligations. Massachusetts levied poll taxes (on male voters), property taxes, and estate taxes; placed duties on exports; and adopted excise fees on the sale of liquor, tea, and luxury goods in 1785 in an effort to fund public debts. States allowed sheriffs and courts to seize and sell possessions, including farms and homes, for tax delinquency; some of the debtors were jailed. Many elites were unfazed by hardships imposed on average householders, arguing that citizens had a moral duty to satisfy their creditors and obey the tax laws. Failure to honor fiscal obligations, James Madison wrote to Thomas Jefferson as Virginia wrestled to enforce its tax policy, would "stamp us with ignominy."[23]

Alexander Hamilton, General Washington's principal aide during the war and a rising politician, knew that tax laxity was not simply a moral defect but the result of an "extreme depression" in the mid-1780s. Hard times began in 1784, worsened in 1785, and hit bottom in 1786. That year Madison told Jefferson that "the present anarchy of our commerce" in Virginia had depleted the state's treasury and swept the region clean of specie, creating a currency crunch that generated widespread demands for states to issue paper money and for a "postponement of taxes." The economy had not recovered by January 1790, noted Hamilton in his "First Report on the Public Credit" (1790) as secretary of the treasury. The depreciated price for land, he wrote, "is a serious calamity. The value of cultivated lands, in most of the States, has fallen since the Revolution, from twenty-five to fifty percent. In those farther south, the decrease is still more considerable." Hamilton warned that southern lands might soon be sold at fire-sale prices, a situation the secretary attributed to the "scarcity of money."[24]

The depression exacerbated the decline in national wealth that occurred during the Revolutionary era. During the mid-1780s prices for agricultural goods dropped, especially for tobacco; shipbuilding nearly came to a halt; wages declined perhaps 40 percent for agricultural workers, and artisans went without work; imports at Philadelphia and other ports decreased by half. Foreign credit dried up. The economic downturn spread desperation in many communities. Nearly a third of the male inhabitants of several western Massachusetts counties, including Worcester, had judgments against them for debt, which threatened them with jail, the loss of property, and perhaps even sale into servitude. The chain of debt in the state put stress on eastern merchants, who had imported foreign goods on credit. Indebtedness was just as bad if not worse in New Hampshire, where the number of debtors increased sixfold between 1781 and 1785. As in all depressions in the long nineteenth century, conditions varied substantially by region, subregion, and economic pursuit. Virginia and Carolina experienced significant economic difficulty, but New York recorded less distress than states to the north and south.[25]

The severity and causes of the downturn remain sketchy, largely because of the absence of accurate economic data. But historians generally agree that British imports were the most likely trigger of the collapse; these goods flooded the country when peace returned, resulting in large outflows of specie to pay foreign sellers. Specie had been scarce during the Revolution, and the supply shrank even more as depreciated paper currency circulated in its place. Clinging to their mercantilist mentality, the British closed the West Indies to American traders, which cut off a lucrative market.

The weather probably magnified the severity of the commercial slump. The winters of 1783–1784 and 1784–1785 were among the coldest on record in the United States. Much of Chesapeake Bay froze in early 1784, closing busy ports such as Baltimore for several months and contributing to spring floods in the Tidewater region. Farther south, huge ice floes on the Mississippi passed New Orleans in 1784, a once-in-a-century event. The next year, 1785, brought a drought to Virginia, which stunted crops. George Washington, whose Mount Vernon plantation was located in upper Virginia, had no surplus corn to sell in 1785 or 1786; his crop was even worse in 1787, and rains ruined his corn crop in 1788. Many of his tenants on western lands did not pay their rent; some who did pay offered depreciated paper money, which, to Washington's dismay, tax collectors refused to accept. His financial situation was so bleak that he had to borrow money to pay his taxes. Although he initially declined to accept a salary as president of the United States, he desperately needed the money and did not contest Congress's insistence that he take the stipend.[26]

Exacerbating the economic malaise were the demands of creditors and conservatives to fund the national and state debts, legacies of financing the Revolution. Paying the interest and retiring the principal on these loans were only one aspect of the financial challenges facing many households. They also had to pay local taxes (to the county, parish, or town) and likely incurred private debts as well. Tax obligations placed a heavy burden on landowners during the depression, when most individuals lacked the specie that American governments demanded. The fiscal impasse caused a political crisis in most parts of the United States, leading to violent tax revolts in some places.[27]

Citizen backlash against tax and debt burdens in the 1780s produced demonstrations and local conventions that forwarded petitions to state governments for remedial legislation. All the states acquiesced in some fashion, especially in the most stressed regions, by enacting stay laws that delayed or deferred taxes (in at least nine states), tender acts (which allowed taxes to be paid in commodities, sometimes as land-bank loan arrangements), and bankruptcy laws. The most controversial measures provided for the issuance of paper money. Seven states authorized tax payments by paper currency; conservatives narrowly defeated paper currency proposals in fiercely contested legislative battles in Maryland and Virginia. Throughout most of the country a coalition of financial conservatives, elites, and creditors (e.g., merchants) battled debtors and commoners over public finance. The post-war depression had triggered class warfare in much of the country.

On occasion, civil protests and demonstrations erupted into violence and the destruction of public property, as mobs challenged debtor requirements and tax levies. In at least seven states "regulators" delayed or shut down the local courts, which were responsible for enforcing actions against tax delinquents. The most serious citizen outburst was Shays's Rebellion, a drama that unfolded in central and western Massachusetts in the fall of 1786. A militia force of 4,400 raised in the eastern part of the state, funded by wealthy elites, sent the Shaysites scurrying before a full-fledged "insurrection" developed in January 1787.[28]

ADOPTION OF A NEW CONSTITUTION

The tax revolt dovetailed with the movement to build a stronger national government. Advocates of establishing a more capable central government—nationalists such as James Madison, Alexander Hamilton, and George Washington—had tried unsuccessfully to amend the Articles of Confederation so that Congress could levy taxes. Opponents of the proposal feared the creation of a "consolidated" government that would dominate the states. They were aided by the requirement that all states ratify any amendments to the articles, a very high threshold. The tax revolts offered the nationalists an opportune boost. Madison repeatedly wrote to Jefferson and Washington about misguided efforts in the Virginia legislature to delay tax levies, allow payment in goods rather than specie, and issue paper currency. "These mischiefs," he said, "excite the disgust of all the respectable in America."[29] Largely through Madison's efforts, the nationalists parlayed a conference in Annapolis, purportedly called to consider revising the Articles of Confederation related to trade, into a convention in Philadelphia to discuss broader matters. News of Shays's Rebellion helped tip the scale among individuals who were initially reluctant to attend the conclave. The abortive insurrection in Massachusetts worried Washington, a staunch nationalist who saw the country "fast verging to anarchy and confusion" and bemoaned the "leveling" measures adopted in New England.[30] With insurrection on the horizon, he agreed to participate in the Philadelphia convention, which elected him president in May 1787.[31]

On May 25, 1787, delegates from seven states opened the Constitutional Convention in Philadelphia. Ostensibly gathering to repair the Articles of Confederation, the nationalists designed a whole new government instead. The consensus among the delegates, most of them members of the propertied elite, was that restrictions on the states were necessary and that the national government required greater power.[32] After four months of extended debate and difficult negotiations, representatives from all the states except Rhode Island hammered out a new framework for a national government. Most attendees agreed that the existing Continental Congress was unacceptably weak and that a bicameral legislature was an appropriate way to balance democracy with state sovereignty. Most state constitutions, which served as working models for the architects of the US Constitution, provided for two-house legislatures. Delegates also clung to the eighteenth-century norm that political leadership should remain in the hands of influential citizens and that power should not be too broadly distributed among the common people. Still, putting together a new constitution was a contentious business. Several participants at the convention refused to sign the finished document.

The Virginia delegation, which included James Madison, arrived prior to the opening of the convention and used the time to prepare a set of resolutions to offer for consideration. Called the Virginia Plan, these points set the convention's agenda, shaping much of the product that eventually emerged. During the next four months disagreement flared around four major issues. First, should representation in Congress be proportional to population or distributed equally among the states? Delegates from small states opposed proportional representation, which would allow the five largest states, with 61 percent of the population, to dominate the government. A compromise was struck by creating a legislature consisting of two bodies—a House of Representatives, whose membership would be based on population, and a Senate, whose membership would be apportioned equally among the states (senators would be elected by state legislatures). Selection of a bicameral legislature mirrored the arrangement in both the American states and the British Parliament.

A second sticking point centered on the method of selecting the president. Proposals ranged from popular election by the voters to selection by Congress. Once more, compromise split the difference: state legislatures would choose electors (based on the number of representatives and senators in the state), who in turn would cast ballots for president and vice president. A third controversy arose over the insistence of delegates from the six southern states that the Constitution protect slavery. The compromise struck on this issue prohibited the importation of slaves after 1808, authorized the return of fugitive slaves who fled to other states, and counted slaves (as three-fifths citizens) for purposes of apportioning legislative seats among the states.

The final major disagreement concerned the amount of power to vest in the central government and how many state prerogatives to curtail. Delegates worked out a solution that allotted specific (enumerated) powers to Congress, imposed certain restrictions on state actions, and implicitly designed a federal structure recognizing that both the national and the state governments would act in their respective spheres, with some overlapping (concurrent) powers, such as taxation.[33]

Given the defects of the Articles of Confederation, the chief powers granted to Congress were easily anticipated: authority to tax (including customs on imported goods and excise taxes), borrow money, coin money and "regulate the value thereof," regulate foreign and interstate commerce, establish rules on bankruptcy and patents, punish piracy "on the high Seas," and maintain an army and navy. Congress was also permitted to dispose of and regulate the territory of the United States and admit new states. Debts contracted before the adoption of the Constitution remained valid. The creation of a Supreme Court and of "inferior Courts," as Congress saw fit, established national tribunals to adjudicate disputes relative to the Constitution.

The impact of the depression and tax revolts is clearly visible in the Constitution. In addition to establishing a revenue stream for the payment of national debts, Congress could call forth the militia to "suppress Insurrections." The Constitution stipulated that the national government "shall guarantee to every State . . . a Republican Form of Government," and it promised protection against "domestic violence." States were prohibited from taxing exports and imports; regulating commerce between the states; issuing "Bills of Credit" (paper money); making anything "but gold and silver Coin a Tender in Payment of Debts," a legacy of the fiscal crisis of the 1780s; or impairing the obligation of contracts. Virtually all of the nationalists' critiques of state legislative excesses arising from the depression and the subsequent tax revolts were explicitly addressed in the Constitution.[34]

James Madison, called the "father" of the Constitution, expressed conservatives' alarm about state tax relief laws in *The Federalist Papers* (1788), essays designed to persuade reluctant citizens to support the new plan of government. In the tenth of these famed commentaries, Madison argued that a large republic (one composed of all the states) offered a structure that could block "wicked" legislation, such as "a rage for paper money, for an abolition of debts, for an equal division of property, or for any other improper . . . project." His letters to Jefferson and Washington between 1784 and 1786 expressed his distaste for proposals in the Virginia legislature to delay tax levies and to permit their payment in kind (e.g., tobacco) rather than in specie. A small republic, he wrote, increased the influence of "factions," such as "creditors . . . debtors . . . a moneyed interest," to bend power for their own interests.[35] Alexander Hamilton was the second principal author of *The Federalist Papers*, a project he organized to persuade New Yorkers to ratify the Constitution. He brilliantly argued the benefits of the proposed government while also stressing the limitations on its power.

In *Federalist*, no. 6 Hamilton blamed the "extreme depression" for the crisis over the national credit and for causing "the rebellions in Massachusetts." He referred to Shays's Rebellion and other populist demonstrations in four other essays.[36]

Nationalists had forged a political revolution, at least in the eyes of their detractors. Opponents of the Constitution charged that "young visionary men and the consolidating aristocracy" were plotting to build an entirely new political edifice, despite their avowed intention only to remodel the existing structure.[37] Early in the twentieth century historian Charles Beard amplified this conspiracy allegation by charging that a cabal of delegates at the Constitutional Convention had drawn up a document designed expressly to further their personal economic interests.[38] Most delegates at the Philadelphia convention were affluent elites, and given the norms of colonial politics, such "betters" were expected to rule. The contest over the ratification of the Constitution in 1787 and 1788 turned in part along various economic axes. Nevertheless, the verdict of most historians is that the composition of the Constitution was not exclusively or even primarily driven by the delegates' own financial interests.[39]

Regardless of the intentions of the framers and the motives of the ratifiers, even a casual reading of the Constitution reveals its economic content. The key powers bestowed on the national government with regard to substantive policy concern primarily money and credit, property, commerce, land, and slaves. This list can be broadened by recognizing that the authority to maintain an army and navy and to oversee relations with Indians would be used to protect property and promote commerce. The establishment of courts (which adjudicated disputes over economic matters and property), the restrictions imposed on the states, and the assertion that the Constitution and the laws made under its authority "shall be the supreme Law of the Land" reinforced the explicit grants of financial and commercial power to the central government.

RATIFICATION

Nationalists realized that concessions were necessary to achieve consent for a stronger central government that reduced state sovereignty. The key compromise on this critical issue was the creation of a federal system, which strengthened national authority yet retained most traditional prerogatives for the states. The concept was not novel. The relationship between the colonies and Parliament prior to the Revolution and between Congress and the states during the confederation period embodied elements of the principle.[40] Madison ransacked histories and political philosophy for insight on confederacies past and present. Others who were active in the debate over the proposed constitution, such as Hamilton, were also well read in the classics and history.[41] Limiting the power of government by dividing it was natural to a society steeped in republican political assumptions that viewed the usurpation of power as a tendency of human nature. The key question in 1787 centered on the specific powers to award the central government. On this issue, Madison and pro-constitutionalists fudged a bit, remaining vague on just how much sovereignty would shift to the center. Madison described the new arrangement in Federalist 39 as "partly federal and partly national." At the time, "federal" was understood to mean a "confederacy." The new arrangement, he wrote, was a "compound republic." Conscious of the importance of symbols, the nationalists called themselves Federalists in the campaign to ratify the Constitution. Their opponents thus became Anti-Federalists.

From the vantage point of the Anti-Federalists, the Constitution created a "consolidated" government of frightening power. The new Congress could tax, raise an army, conduct foreign relations, control its territories, and assign significant tasks to an elected executive. The Federalists argued that these powers were necessary for the survival of the nation, which was buffeted by foreign threats and tyrannous majorities in the state legislatures. The Anti-Federalists responded that the Federalists were exaggerating the problems of the 1780s as a strategy to win acceptance of their handiwork. They charged that the movement for a stronger government was an "aristocratic junto" designed to sweep power into its vortex, which would undermine republican government.[42] George Mason, a Virginian planter who attended the Constitutional Convention, thought the plan created a "consolidated government" that would likely "terminate in the annihilation of the state governments."[43]

Federalists countered that the states retained considerable power, including control over the selection of many national officers, such as choosing US senators and presidential electors and setting qualifications for voters in House elections. They argued that the "unruly men" in the state legislatures were a threat to republican institutions and that restricting their powers would protect liberty and guarantee the survival of the union—arguments with which some Anti-Federalists agreed. Pro-constitutionalists also contended that a stronger central government would improve the economy and generate revenue by taxing imports. Improvement of the country's financial credit held out the prospect that the federal government could pay the national debt and perhaps assume the debts of the states as well, which would reduce the need for direct state taxes.

The Federalists' campaign had several advantages over that of their rivals. The pro-constitutionalists were blessed with the extraordinary literary talents of James Madison, Alexander Hamilton, and John Jay, authors of *The Federalist Papers*, which became a monument in American political science. The Federalists brought a distinct model to the debate, while the Anti-Federalists had no common program. The Federalists created a personal network to aid approval in key states, while the Anti-Federalists lacked a similarly coordinated organization. And the Federalists possessed George Washington, the hero of the new republic and likely to become its first president. Yet the campaign for ratification generated intense political tension, especially in Pennsylvania, Massachusetts, Virginia, and New York, where the issue was closely contested. The outcome in all the major states hung on bargains and political cajoling. Virginia's narrow approval, critical to ratification of the Constitution, influenced the vote in New York several days later. Yet with victory uncertain, Hamilton threatened the secession of New York City if New York's Anti-Federalists rejected ratification. Helping to overcome opposition was the Federalists' promise to insert a Bill of Rights in the Constitution.[44]

New York's ratification of the Constitution on July 26, 1788, authorized the election of a president and the gathering of national lawmakers in 1789. Fifteen years had passed between Britain's promulgation of the Intolerable Acts in 1774 and the convening of the First Congress in 1789. The twists and turns in the transition from colonies to a sovereign state, anchored by a new national constitution, surely lay beyond most observers' wildest imagination prior to the deadly confrontations at Lexington and Concord. Blazing this pathway were unpredictable events with far-reaching consequences. A short list of these influential developments would include the Intolerable Acts, the arrival of the massive British invasion fleet, the American military victories at Saratoga and Yorktown, the popular rebellions of 1786, and the emergence of James Madison as an energetic mastermind of a stronger central government during the troubles of the mid-1780s. The crises generated by various anomalous developments required decisions in the moment and stimulated the reconsideration of existing assumptions, establishing new reference points for future actions. Older verities were not wholly abandoned but modified and reshaped as the political context evolved. Out of this remixture of long-term beliefs and short-term crises emerged the initial form of the American national state.

Many historians have concluded that the United States did not look or act like a full-fledged state in 1789. But as the anonymous individual who called himself "Brutus" protested during the ratification debate, Congress possessed the authority to tax and gained a potent grant of power in the "necessary and proper clause" of the Constitution. "He that has the purse will have the sword, and they [the supporters of the Constitution] have both." He predicted that granting these powers to the central authorities would "destroy" the capacity of the states.[45] Though skeptical of the wisdom of the new allocation of powers, the Anti-Federalists acknowledged that the Constitution contained the rudiments for building a powerful state. The Federalists agreed, although they muted this conclusion in their public commentaries.

The 1783 Treaty of Paris and the Constitution established the foundation of the American national state. Compared with other states, nearly all of which possessed centralized authority, America's civic arrangement was fragmented and, on the surface, appeared feeble. During its initial decades of operation, Congress rejected the construction of a large national bureaucracy. Herein lies the paradox. The quotient of power commanded by the new state was deceiving because it rested on two legal platforms—the national Constitution and the constitutions of the states. Both levels of government had the power to tax and to use coercive force. Each had the constitutional authority to regulate a range of behaviors, although much of the federal government's power remained latent—theoretically possible but used sparingly for several generations. Each government possessed wide but not universal popular support. These features embody the criteria of a modern national state.

The irony of this redesign of government was that it was an unintended consequence of crisis. The Americans did not revolt against Britain with the goal of creating a new state. Revolutionary leaders did not follow a clearly outlined plan that delineated a new political structure. Rather, they reacted defensively to provocations that threatened perceived liberties. When crises forced practical decisions between 1774 and 1788, leaders drew on familiar referents for guidance. One was their sociopolitical surroundings, both in their own communities and in the powerful states of Europe. History was another. Jefferson, Madison, Adams, Washington, and others of the Revolutionary generation were familiar with political history and understood the importance of national wealth, taxation, and military capacity to sustain a government. This eighteenth-century inheritance constituted a handbook for creating a new state.

4

Geographic and Economic Expansion

"In the beginning God created the heavens and the earth. . . . The earth brought forth vegetation, plants yielding seeds according to their own kinds, and trees bearing fruit. . . . And God saw that it was good." So reads Genesis 1:1, 12. Religious or not, Americans accepted and understood the sentiment: the land provided sustenance and security. Both objectives were fundamental for the millions of families who earned their keep by tilling the soil. Commercially minded residents of North America saw the value of the land in terms of investment and speculation—buying a choice piece of real estate and selling it for a profit when demand rose. Land was the lingua franca of the American economy in the early decades of the new republic.

Political leaders recognized the power of this fundamental element of preindustrial life. Yet some saw the land from a broader perspective. To Jefferson, the settlement of new lands promoted an "empire of liberty," where property ownership formed the political bedrock of the republic. John Adams used the same phrase in 1786 when he envisioned a nation of "two or three hundred millions of freemen" living in a nation without noblemen or a king. In his first inaugural address in 1801 Jefferson saw "a rising nation, spread over a wide and fruitful land," whose republican form of government was "the world's best hope" to keep Americans free. Later that year he concurred with European onlookers that Americans would spread westward beyond the Mississippi River, observing that "it is impossible not to look forward to distant times, when our rapid multiplication will expand itself beyond those limits and cover the whole northern, if not the southern continent, with a people speaking the same language, governed in similar forms and by similar laws."[1]

The Louisiana Purchase in 1803, which doubled the size of the United States, planted the seeds of the idea that the country would eventually span the continent. Secretary of State John Quincy Adams, who negotiated the 1819 treaty with Spain that gave the United States a toehold on the Pacific, told the cabinet that the world "should be familiarized with the idea of considering our proper dominion to be the continent of North America." Over the next quarter of a century the possibility that the United States would extend from sea to sea gained believers and advocates. The most famous to popularize this vision was John L. O'Sullivan, a magazine editor who wrote in 1845 that it was "our manifest destiny to overspread the continent." If political and cultural factors were not enough to bring about "the inevitable fulfillment of the general law which is rolling our population westward," Sullivan noted, "the projected railroad across the continent to the Pacific" and "the magnetic telegraph" provided additional inducements. A generation later President Abraham Lincoln predicted in 1862 that the "abundant room, our broad national homestead," could support a population as large as that of Europe by the 1920s. The map confirmed, he observed, that the "great interior" of the country "is naturally one of the most important in the world."[2]

The lure of the land was intimately linked to visions of a continental nation that extended America westward from the Mississippi River to the Pacific coast. Some advocates looked north and south as well, eyeing Canada and Spanish territory from Mexico to the Isthmus of Panama. American leaders and writers frequently referred to territory that came under American control as an "empire."[3] Though they seldom clarified their use of the term, several assumptions about its meaning seem reasonable. Few Americans used the expression to refer to a dominion similar to the British Empire, which encompassed subservient colonies in distant lands, or the Roman Empire, which incorporated conquered peoples into the state. The term did connote an entity that occupied a huge area and was composed of distinct parts (states) of equal political standing. The root principle of these governing entities was republicanism, whereby the government derived authority from the consent of its citizens. This principle was apparent in 1845 when President James Polk used his inaugural address to praise the Americans who had trekked overland to Oregon, where they "engaged in establishing the blessings of self government in valleys of which the rivers flow to the Pacific."[4] Presidents echoed this theme repeatedly in the antebellum era: Americans were spreading "liberty" over the North American continent.[5]

What they failed to acknowledge was that American expansion brought numerous peoples under the jurisdiction of the United States without their consent. This incorporation, beginning with the territory gained from the 1783 treaty, included Native Americans, Africans, Mexicans, Spaniards, French, and others of mixed national backgrounds. The country's cultural establishment insisted that eligible newcomers adopt the norms of a society fashioned largely by white Protestants of British and northern European ancestry. Most Africans remained slaves; Native Americans were relegated to the perimeters of their nation. Geographer D. W. Meinig regards this coerced incorporation and segmentation of status as imperialism, a condition that most Americans denied or failed to see.[6] The contradiction between republican ideology and the imposition of American institutions on acquired territories and peoples—that is, the juxtaposition between an "empire of liberty" and imperialism—is a central paradox of American statebuilding.

Between 1803 and 1854 the United States added more than 200 million square miles of territory, which tripled its size and established a national domain that spanned the North American continent. This acquisition satisfied the territorial prerequisite for building an influential state. Even before the purchase of Alaska in 1867, the United States possessed the fourth largest land base among the countries of the world, and this land drew millions of migrants. Immigration and a high birthrate in the young nation swelled its population, so that by 1870 America counted more people than any European country. Between 1789 and 1860 Americans grew more prosperous, ranking behind only Great Britain and perhaps the Netherlands in per capita wealth. Within the span of a single lifetime, the United States had grown into a large and, by world standards, wealthy state.[7]

This extraordinary record raises the question of whether political leaders followed an explicit script for building the American state. The answer is no. There was no officially sanctioned master plan that set a clear course for assembling a continental state. The history of American statebuilding lies in the interplay of contingent events, contextual developments, and a set of widely shared assumptions about society and civic affairs. Europe offered contemporary examples of states whose viability rested on territorial sovereignty, tax authority, and established militaries. The American version of Old World political science was republicanism, whereby the government's authority rested on the consent of its citizens. A second shared element was the importance of land to citizenship and community welfare. A third principle was the protection of the homeland from foreign threats, which, in the antebellum years, consisted of Great Britain, France, and, to a lesser degree, Spain, all of which retained imperial aspirations in North America. American politics generated crosswinds at each step of this history. Regional jealousies and slavery in particular played critical roles in these conflicts.[8] American expansion was neither inevitable nor universally embraced. Territorial expansion was contested, divisive, and decidedly situational.[9]

LOUISIANA AND FLORIDA

The acquisition of territory west of the Mississippi River began with the famed Louisiana Purchase of 1803, a transaction that extended American lands into the broad middle section of the continent. Control of this geography had long interested eighteenth-century leaders, including Thomas

Table 4.1. Statehood, 1776–1861

Original	*North*	*South*	*Trans-Midwest*	*Mississippi*	*Far West*
CT	VT (1791)	TN (1796)	OH (1803)	KY (1792)	CA (1850)
DE	ME (1820)	MS (1817)	IN (1816)	LA (1821)	OR (1859)
GA		AL (1819)	IL (1818)	AR (1836)	KS (1861)
MA		FL (1845)	MI (1837)	TX (1845)	
MD			WI (1848)	IA (1846)	
NC (1789)				MN (1858)	
NH					
NJ					
NY					
PA					
RI (1790)					
SC					
VA					

Jefferson. The context of the acquisition was a steady procession of settlers into the trans-Appalachian West. George Washington noted this westerly migration, writing in 1784 that "the spirit of emigration is great."[10] In the next twenty years the upper Ohio region and the Tennessee River valley filled with thousands of inhabitants, enabling Kentucky, Tennessee, and Ohio to enter the union as new states by 1803 (see table 4.1). The Mississippi River was key to the livelihood of these transplants, who sent agricultural commodities down the tributaries of the mighty Mississippi River to the Gulf of Mexico.

Spain controlled New Orleans, which it occasionally closed, despite a 1795 treaty that granted Americans access to it. Equally alarming, President Jefferson pondered the rumor that France, under the control of the ambitious military leader Napoleon Bonaparte, had secured control of New Orleans and the Louisiana territory in a secret deal with Spain. The prospect of France jeopardizing the livelihood of Americans in the trans-Appalachian region worried the president. He instructed American envoys Robert Livingston and James Monroe to attempt to purchase the "isle of New Orleans," which lay on the eastern bank of the Mississippi. To the Americans' surprise, the French offered to sell their entire domain, which extended to the Rocky Mountains. A slave revolution in Haiti had devastated the French army, persuading Napoleon to abandon plans to reestablish a colonial domain in North America. A fortuitous turn of events thus enabled the Americans to purchase a huge parcel of land for a mere $15 million (excluding later purchases from Native American inhabitants).[11]

The Louisiana prize had immense importance to American statebuilding. As Napoleon mused, "This accession of territory consolidates the power of the United States forever." Despite the hyperbole, the prediction was perceptive. Once the United States was in possession of the center of the continent, the projection of American control to the Pacific seemed feasible, if not likely. Some American interpretations of the Louisiana Purchase had it running all the way to the western coastline. Exactly what territory had been obtained was unclear in 1803, as no reliable maps existed. This informational void had long piqued Jefferson's curiosity, certainly out of scientific interest but perhaps political motives as well. Even before signing the purchase agreement, the president had secretly secured funds for an exploration across the continent to the Pacific. The expedition was commanded by Meriwether Lewis, the president's private secretary, and William Clark. They left St. Louis in the spring of 1804, journeyed up the Missouri River to the foothills of the Rocky Mountains, crossed this barrier on foot, and followed the Clearwater, Snake, and Columbia Rivers to the Pacific coast, which they reached in November 1805. Lewis reported to Jefferson upon his return to St. Louis in September 1806 that no continuous water route to the Pacific existed but that overland trade was possible. Equally important for American statebuilding, the explorers had established an American claim to the Oregon country.[12]

The Louisiana Purchase eliminated the likelihood of a French return to North America. Spain was a weakening state and put up little resistance to American annexations of parts of eastern Florida (1810 and 1812), a strip that extended eastward along the Gulf coast to Pensacola. Americans claimed the region had been included in the Louisiana Purchase. These developments left Britain as the only European power that could block Americans' territorial advances. Britain's chief foreign concern in the first decade of the nineteenth century, however, was not the United States but France, led by the aggressive Napoleon, who had conquered much of Europe. The two European powerhouses became locked in a maritime conflict, each seeking to block trade with its rival. The United States, which had a thriving commerce with Europe, was caught in the middle, as both regimes seized and impounded ships of neutral countries. The Americans' grievance against Britain was accentuated by the practice of impressment, whereby American ships were raided on the pretext that they harbored British deserters (sometimes true), who were then forced into the Royal Navy. Americans denounced the practice as akin to slavery. This anger was exacerbated by the British failure to relinquish forts along the Canadian border, from which the Crown purportedly prodded Native Americans to resist the incursion of settlers into the upper Mississippi valley. Failure to resolve these disputes by diplomatic channels opened the way for Congress to declare war on Great Britain in June 1812.

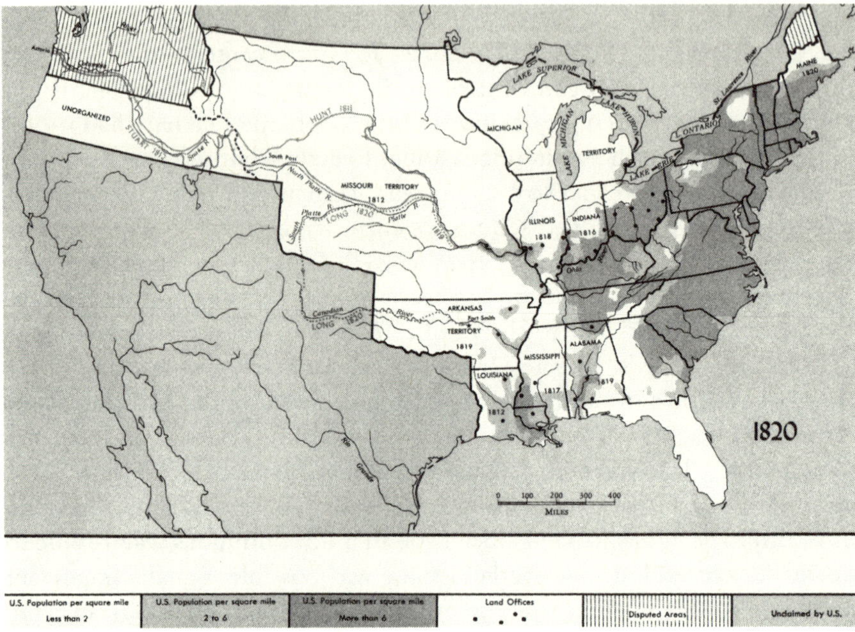

Figure 4.1. Map of expansion, 1820. *Source:* Randall D. Sale and Edwin D. Karn, *American Expansion: A Book of Maps* (Homewood, IL: Dorsey Press, 1962), 9.

The Americans escaped defeat in the War of 1812 by putting up enough resistance to hold off the British, who were preoccupied with their campaign against Napoleon. Lacking a navy capable of confronting the British fleet, Americans attacked the English at the most convenient location—in Canada, which some lawmakers hoped to pry away from Britain. Congress rejected the annexation of Canada, and the Americans failed to defeat British forces there. However, small-scale yet strategically important American naval victories on Lake Champlain and Lake Erie removed the British invasion threat from the north. The last major battle of the war, in which the Americans under Andrew Jackson repelled a British invasion force in New Orleans, took place after the two countries had drafted a peace settlement. News traveled slowly in the preindustrial age.

Although not a victory in a military sense, the War of 1812 had significant ramifications for American statebuilding. The war blunted British capacity to block American incursion into the Great Lakes region, in part by fracturing English ties with Native Americans. Jackson's victory at New Orleans eliminated the possibility that Britain could parlay military success in the Gulf region into an opportunity to reclaim territory in the American

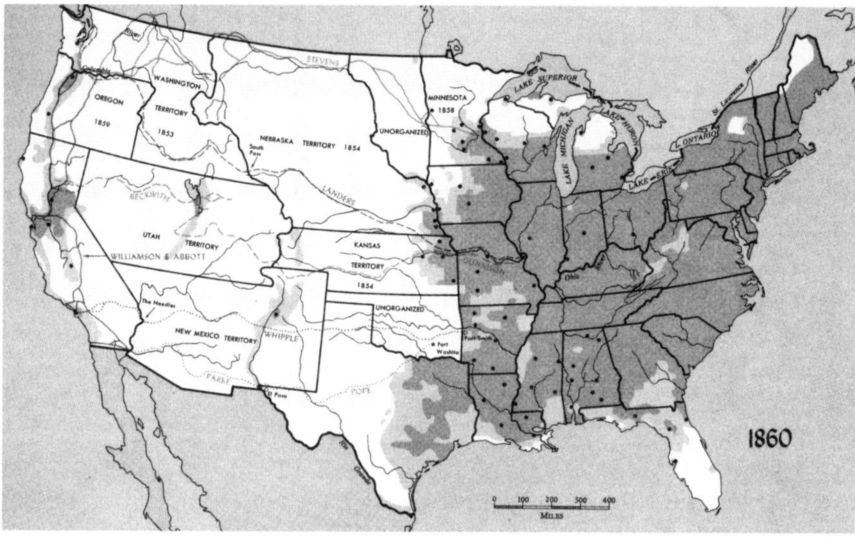

Figure 4.2. Map of expansion, 1860. *Source:* Randall D. Sale and Edwin D. Karn, *American Expansion: A Book of Maps* (Homewood, IL: Dorsey Press, 1962), 17.

heartland. New Englanders, many of whom opposed the war and contributed minimally to it, denounced aspirations to incorporate Canada into the union. The region suffered politically for its unpatriotic posture. Elsewhere in the nation, however, defiance against the world's premier imperial power released a surge of nationalistic pride and allowed Americans to resume their quest for western land.

American pride in standing up to Britain probably mellowed the criticism of Andrew Jackson's invasion of the Florida peninsula in 1818. The general's justification was the pursuit of hostile Seminole Indians and fugitive slaves who used Spanish territory as a base for harassing American settlements. American officials denied giving Jackson the authority to attack, but the geopolitical effect of the raid on Spanish territory was clear. Spain was unable to prevent American encroachment; the territorial consequence of this weakness was the cession of Florida to the United States in 1819, with the Americans paying a small sum to sweeten the deal. Negotiated by Secretary of State John Quincy Adams, the treaty also established a southern boundary to the Louisiana Purchase; the United States conceded the Texas region to Spain in exchange for a border that extended northwest to Wyoming and then west to the Pacific Ocean (see figures 4.1 and 4.2). This pact gave the United States clear title to acreage on the northwest coast. Thirty years after American independence, the United States could claim that it had become a continental state.

ROUTE TO THE PACIFIC

American understanding of the Pacific area had evolved since the 1780s and Captain Robert Gray's penetration of the Columbia River, which he named. In the early 1800s Yankee traders plied the California coast, and John Jacob Astor briefly established a fur trading post at the mouth of the Columbia River. The 1819 treaty with Spain further piqued American interest in the region, especially in California, which possessed a small European population of mainly Spanish descent. The posting of an American consul in Hawaii and the stationing of a US naval presence in the Pacific in the 1820s signaled the emerging attraction of the Pacific basin. Its trade potential increased with the Treaty of Wangxia in 1844, which opened several Chinese ports to Americans.

Meanwhile, fur traders from St. Louis pushed up the Missouri River into the Dakotas and Montana, sponsoring trappers who roamed the streams and "holes" (valleys) of the Rocky Mountains in search of animal pelts. A by-product of their hunting was increased geographic knowledge of the "Stony Mountains," including Jedidiah Smith's discovery of South Pass in 1824, which offered a wagon route through the mountainous terrain. Cartographer John Melish projected early insights from these explorations onto his 1816 map, which was the first to show American territory reaching to the Pacific. Two years later the British and Americans negotiated a northern boundary for Canada along the forty-ninth parallel that reached from the Great Lakes to the Stony Mountains, and they agreed to jointly occupy the Oregon region in the Pacific Northwest.[13]

This boundary extension gave mapmakers another reason to update their gazetteers and geographies, which were popular in the antebellum era. New information about the West came from various sources, including explorers for the US Army, who mapped portions of the West and recorded observations about its topography and resources. The navy sent Lieutenant Charles Wilkes on a scientific reconnaissance of the Pacific, with stops in San Francisco, Oregon, and Puget Sound. In 1841 a trail was blazed from the Rockies to California. Two years later a "great migration" of settlers journeyed overland to the Willamette River valley in Oregon. Transportation innovations stimulated subsequent migrations. By the 1830s and 1840s steamboats were plying the Mississippi River from New Orleans to Wisconsin and up the Ohio River to Pittsburgh, as well as traveling into the western interior via the Missouri River and around the upper Great Lakes. At the end of the 1840s steamships rounded Cape Horn on coast-to-coast journeys.[14]

In the 1830s, when the first American railroads became operational, farsighted prognosticators predicted the construction of a transcontinental rail connection. Congress received a formal proposal for such a route in 1844, but the idea was too visionary for lawmakers at the time, partly because California was not yet officially part of the union. The idea of an east-west rail route had been planted, however, and it remained on the agenda for the next twenty years until the federal government helped fund the project in 1864. The telegraph, in contrast, achieved a cross-continental connection in 1861, just seventeen years after its successful demonstration. These technological developments, coupled with explorations by trappers, army surveyors, and naturalists and the schemes of those who advocated settlement on the Pacific coast, fed the notion that the United States was "destined" to spread over the entire continent. The presumption that the country's "natural" boundaries stretched from the Atlantic to the Pacific was accepted by many Americans—and foreign observers—by the mid-1840s.[15]

OREGON, TEXAS, AND CALIFORNIA

In 1821 residents of Mexico won their independence from Spain. This transition replaced a declining Old World power with an even weaker state on the southern border of the United States. Mexico possessed a huge territorial expanse that stretched from the Yucatan peninsula to western North America up to the forty-second parallel, but it had little capacity to manage this domain, most of which had scant or no fixed settlements. To develop its northern sector and create a buffer along its southern border, Mexico continued the Spanish policy of inviting settlers from the United States into its province of Texas. In exchange for generous land grants, immigrants agreed to become Mexican citizens, accept Catholicism, and relinquish their slaves. But when Mexico attempted to enforce these requirements, tensions escalated. Texans mounted an armed rebellion, defeated Mexican general and dictator Antonio Lopez de Santa Anna, declared their independence in 1836, and then requested annexation to the United States. President Andrew Jackson turned them down, wishing to sidestep a confrontation with Mexico, which did not recognize Texas sovereignty, and to avoid a conflict over adding another slave state to the union during a presidential election year. Martin Van Buren, Jackson's successor and an antislavery northerner, followed suit. Texans then played a waiting game, talking to British agents who saw an independent Texas as a buffer against American expansion across the continent.[16]

The election of 1844 brought the impasse over Texas to a head. Henry Clay of Kentucky, the Whig Party's candidate for president, needed to attract antislavery voters in the North and opposed the admission of Texas. Congressman James Polk from Tennessee, the Democrats' presidential candidate, embraced his party's advocacy of the "reoccupation of Oregon and the reannexation of Texas." Polk won a razor-thin election, partly by capturing New York, where the antislavery Liberty Party siphoned votes from Clay.[17] Between the election and Polk's inauguration, President John Tyler supported a resolution in Congress to invite Texas to join the union. The resolution narrowly passed, and Texas became the twenty-eighth state in 1845, the last that legalized slavery.

With Texas in the union, Polk turned his attention to Oregon. Taking a confrontational position with Britain over the jointly held region, the president claimed that America had rights to territory well above the forty-ninth parallel. Unwilling to risk war over the dispute, he crafted an amicable settlement with the British that extended the forty-ninth parallel to the Pacific shore, a deal that attached a majority of the Oregon territory to the United States.[18]

Polk's larger objective was Mexican territory that lay between Texas and the Pacific. In the mid-1840s expansionists pointed to California as the key to forming a genuine continental nation. The harbor at San Francisco, among the finest on the West Coast, had already attracted numerous Americans. Polk's motivation for supporting western expansion remains obscure, but his willingness to ride the political wave of expansionism, which centered on Democrats, was probably a key factor in his decision.[19] His public statements suggest that he agreed with the widely accepted conviction that establishing American institutions in new lands brought the gifts of self-government and liberty to local residents. Many Americans, perhaps the majority, had little regard for the Spanish speakers and Native Americans who inhabited this borderland region. Initially Polk tried to buy California and northern Mexico. When Mexico rejected the offer, the president asserted that territory between the Nueces River and the Rio Grande in Texas was American ground. He ordered General Zachary Taylor to move US troops into the contested zone and positioned the navy near Mexican cities along the Gulf and Pacific coasts. Viewing these maneuvers as acts of war, Mexico ordered its army to repel Americans who crossed the Nueces River. When several Americans were killed in the region, Polk claimed that Mexico had attacked the United States on American soil. His war resolution sailed through Congress in May 1846. Despite misgivings in the North about a war that could expand slavery, Horace Greeley, editor of the *New York Tribune*, interpreted Congress's decision "as a normal public response to an attack on the flag."[20]

The president expected a brief war that would end with the defeat of Mexican forces in northern Mexico and California. Marching from Fort Leavenworth, Kansas, Colonel Stephen Kearney and American troops occupied Santa Fe and then headed to California to link with the navy, which had already claimed San Francisco and Monterey for the United States. Lieutenant John C. Fremont, who trekked over the Rocky Mountains with a small band of army scouts ostensibly on an exploring mission, helped Americans in San Francisco renounce their fealty to Mexico. Then Fremont, Kearney, and Commodore Robert Stockton combined to pacify resistance in Los Angeles.

The daring resolve of Santa Anna, the exiled Mexican military leader with many political lives, surprised Polk. The Mexican general regrouped his army, prompting the president to order an American assault on Mexico City, located in the heart of the country. He gave the assignment to General Winfield Scott, who orchestrated an amphibious landing near Veracruz and then pushed overland on a six-month campaign to occupy Mexico City. The victory over Mexico was an extraordinary feat in view of the challenging logistics—thousands of miles of supply lines—the inexperienced troops, and the turnover of militia units in the midst of the campaign. A small force (barely 7,500 men at any one time) pulled off a stunning achievement, with immense consequences for American statebuilding.

Opposition to the war grew as Polk's territorial ambitions became clear. Northern members of Congress proposed an amendment to a military bill that would have prohibited the creation of any pro-slavery state on land seized from Mexico. The measure failed in several sessions, as the American victory over Mexico generated nationalist sentiment.[21] Confronting an American occupation of their capital city, and with the scope of Polk's territorial quest unclear, Mexican negotiators made the best of a bad deal. The Treaty of Guadalupe Hidalgo (1848) confirmed US possession of Texas, with a border on the Rio Grande, as well as lands from Texas west to the Pacific and up to the Oregon border, including California. This Mexican cession expanded the United States by 30 percent (counting Texas) and included San Francisco, the "jewel" of the Pacific. The addition of the Oregon territory increased the size of the United States by nearly 10 percent. Polk had wanted to grab more of Mexico, but he nevertheless left an indelible mark on American expansion.

One wonders what would have happened if the Mexican War or negotiations over its settlement had dragged on for several more months, as gold was discovered in California in January 1848. News of the strike reached the East Coast in September, and by the end of the year the gold rush was on, bringing migrants to California from around the world. The territory's non-Indian population catapulted from a few thousand in 1846 to 100,000 in 1850, a total sufficient for statehood.

Two additional pieces of territory rounded out the continental dimensions of the United States. The 1853 Gadsden Purchase involved Mexican land acquired for a railroad route south of the Rockies. The size of this acquisition paled in comparison with Alaska, purchased from the Russians in 1867. Russia saw little of value in Alaska, while Secretary of State William Seward worried that Britain might see Alaska as an opportunity to expand its empire. Few Americans went north to "Seward's folly" in the nineteenth century, but millions were streaming into the West. Meinig called the rapidity and scale of this migration "unprecedented in world history."[22]

INDIGENOUS PEOPLES

Territories added to the United States between 1783 and 1867 incorporated perhaps a million or more indigenous peoples.[23] More than a hundred native groupings (tribes or nations) existed, most with a distinct culture and language as well as traditional residential locales. Some groups were relatively sedentary, while others were migratory, but nearly all were folded into the American jurisdiction. Euro-Americans viewed these "savage" tribes as unfit for amalgamation into American society. But Americans coveted their lands, frequently occupying them prior to obtaining treaty concessions from the native inhabitants. These encroachments regularly sparked resistance, which produced an endless series of Indian wars with white settlers, frontier militia, and army regulars. Military pacification of the natives sometimes employed a scorched-earth policy, destroying homes and crops and sparing no tribal members, including women and children. Some Indians voluntarily moved out of the way of oncoming whites. Groups that suffered military defeat were forcefully moved to new locations on American territory but were denied citizenship. Wherever they were located, the Supreme Court designated them "domestic dependent nations" subject to the legal jurisdiction of the United States.

The innumerable battles with Indians and the hundreds of treaties between the US government and scores of tribes illustrate the piecemeal pattern of US relations with Native Americans. Most of the combat occurred among small groups on the frontier, with sketchy documentation existing about these engagements. But the broad picture of native-white relations can be summarized in three sequential processes: pacification of native belligerence, removal of Indians from the path of white settlement, and attempts to "civilize" Native Americans. Some scholars see this history as tantamount to ethnic cleansing.[24]

Warfare between natives and whites began soon after European settlement in North America. The French and Indian War and the American Revolution included fighting against Indians allied with the French and the British.

Following independence, attention turned to the Ohio River valley, where Americans defeated Indians at Fallen Timbers (1794) near Lake Erie and at Tippecanoe (1811) in northern Indiana. In the Black Hawk War (1832) the US Army and local militiamen chased the Sauk peoples from Illinois into Wisconsin, which removed the Indian threat from the upper Midwest. In the South Andrew Jackson first won fame for his devastation of the Creek nation (1813–1814), an encounter in which his men took no prisoners. Members of the Seminole nation fled to Florida, where they fought US Army regulars for nearly a decade (1835–1840s). By the end of the 1840s Indian resistance had ended east of the Mississippi River.

Indians were excellent fighters, adept at guerrilla tactics, and greatly feared by frontier settlers. But Native American resistance to white incursion was futile in the long run, for reasons that are central to the rise of powerful national states. First, Indians lacked organizational coordination on a scale equal to that of Euro-Americans. Some native confederations existed, but Indians did not formally codify their intergovernmental structures. Americans, in contrast, institutionalized their control over coercive force at all three levels of government. Militias existed in every colony, and American independence gave birth to a permanent national army that was small, to be sure, but controlled by a central administration. Revenue-raising laws were adopted at every level of government, and central authorities maintained arms manufacturing facilities. Historians are correct when they note the small scale of the American military in the antebellum period, but the US Army and state militias were not designed to confront large, well-organized opponents such as the major European states. The primary American military mission was to quell Indian belligerency.

Second, the Indians were outnumbered. Almost from the onset of European colonization, Indian populations were smaller than those of neighboring Europeans. This discrepancy grew greater over time. The population of the United States increased ninefold from 1783 to 1860, while the Indian population declined due to military defeats and disease. Indians lacked immunity to "European" diseases, and countless numbers died of diseases introduced by white settlers, such as the smallpox epidemic on the western frontier in 1837.

Last, Euro-Americans possessed superior technologies. Initially this advantage consisted chiefly of firearms. Indians eventually acquired guns, but virtually all of them came from trade with Europeans. By the early nineteenth century transportation and communication innovations such as steamboats, railroads, and the telegraph provided Americans with a logistical advantage. The invention of the Gatling gun in the 1860s, a weapon that could fire 200 rounds a minute, symbolized this widening technological gulf.

After the Revolution the sentiment that whites could not coexist with Indians crystallized. The solution was to force natives to relinquish their traditional habitats and relocate, usually farther west. The treaties "negotiated" with Indian "nations" designated where they could live and awarded natives economic assistance in exchange for their removal. Considering tribes to be foreign nations, the United States negotiated 377 treaties between 1784 and 1871, when the practice ceased. For example, the Treaty of Greenville (1795), formulated in the wake of the Battle of Fallen Timbers, stipulated that Indians had to vacate the upper Ohio River region. It is important to note that most Native Americans did not speak or read English, and few had a sound understanding of Anglo-American law.

All antebellum presidents faced political pressure to remove Indians from the path of white settlement. The question was: where to put them. The Louisiana Purchase provided an unexpected solution to this problem, as it offered space at a distance from white settlement at the time. Jefferson had envisioned this potential, and President James Monroe began the removal policy in piecemeal fashion. Congress enacted the Removal Act of 1830, which formulated the general policy. At the time the "civilized" tribes in Georgia were the most pressing administrative concern, and the state uprooted them relentlessly. In the 1830s federal troops herded thousands of these natives over a "Trail of Tears" to a region southwest of Arkansas that had been designated Indian "reservations." Federal troops were stationed on the perimeter of these lands to keep the Indians in and whites out.

The rationale for removal was embedded in the Euro-American view of Native Americans as uncivilized, pagan savages. An American history textbook published in the 1870s sums up that assessment:

> [The] Red Man built no cities, no ships, no churches, no school-houses. . . . His highest art was expended in a simple bow and arrow. . . . He knew nothing of books, paper, writing, or history. . . . In war, the Indian was brave and alert but cruel and revengeful. . . . At home, he was lazy, improvident, and an inveterate gambler. . . . If he had any ideas of a Supreme Being, they were vague and degraded. . . . Unless he can be induced to give up his roving habits and cultivate the soil, he is doomed to destruction.[25]

The American solution to the Indian problem was to confine the natives in designated spaces until they became "civilized"—that is, until they were transformed into literate Christian farmers. Learning to master the plow was a critical part of this rehabilitation, given the Anglo-American insistence that only people who worked the soil had a right to possess it.[26] As the 1833 treaty with the Otoes and Missourias put it, they must "abandon the chase for agricultural life." In 1815 the superintendent of Indian affairs established a system of schools for Indians run by Protestant missionaries. Four years later Congress added appropriations for a "civilization fund."

DISTRIBUTING THE LAND

Removing Indians allowed officials to get on with what most white Americans considered the primary benefit of expansion: the transfer of property to private hands. Beginning with the agreement of 1781, when seven states ceded their claims to western lands to the national government, most territorial acquisitions became part of the country's public domain.[27] Congress possessed the authority to dispose of and make rules for "the Territory and other Property belonging to the United States." This prerogative focused attention on three key issues: surveys of acquired lands, rules governing the transfer of land, and the establishment of governments in new territories. In 1785 Congress enacted a land ordinance that required cadastral surveys for the systematic enumeration of acreage parcels. The act created townships composed of thirty-six-square-mile sections, each of which contained 640 acres. This linear mode of denoting boundaries, which frequently became private property lines, was first applied to southeastern Ohio and then widely reproduced. Lawmakers hoped that surveys would precede settlement and that the precise identification of specific parcels would establish clear titles to landownership. In reality, the order of these actions was frequently reversed. However, conceptualized broadly, cadastral surveys represented the central state's imposition of order on land registrations, which facilitated the administration of property taxes.[28]

The terms for distributing the public domain generated intense interest. The land law of 1785 set the minimum price at $1 an acre, with a minimum purchase of 640 acres (one section); total prices were to be determined by auction sales. Revision of the law in 1796 increased the minimum price to $2 an acre. Policymakers expected these terms to result in substantial federal revenue through sales primarily to wealthy investors. The plan was a disappointment, partly because the states had land for sale on better terms. The land law of 1800 began a trend of reducing the minimum price (cut to $1.25 per acre in 1820) and the minimum acreage offered (decreased to forty acres in 1832). In 1820 "preemption" laws were enacted; they initially targeted specific locations and gave individuals who had settled on public land prior to its formal opening the first right to purchase their plots. In 1830 preemption rights were made general, giving squatters the opportunity to purchase 160 acres for $200. This liberalization of land laws, pushed by western members of Congress, helped increase sales of the public domain, which peaked in the "land fever" of the 1830s. Some policymakers advocated "homesteads," which would provide 160 acres of land at no charge if a citizen improved the plot and lived on it for five years. Opposition to that idea centered in the South, whose representatives blocked the legislation. Southerners' withdrawal from Congress during the Civil War opened the way for the enactment of a homestead law in 1862.[29]

Supporters of homesteading were disappointed by the limited redistribution of land to small farmers. Much of the best land had already been claimed by 1862, partly by speculators who hired land agents or bribed federal officials to locate prime properties. Many homestead claims were registered fraudulently. Moreover, the national government allowed other kinds of land transfers, including the continuation of land sales and grants for transportation projects, such as railroad construction. Army veterans from the Revolution through the Mexican War received warrants that entitled them to land in the public domain. Newly admitted states received parcels for education and other civic activities. Some public acreage became Indian reservations.

National officials clearly understood that managing the public domain was important to the viability of the United States, but their policies were riddled with flaws, including the perpetuation of racial and economic inequalities. Despite the many shortcomings, the transfer of land to private individuals allowed a large proportion of the free population to earn a living between 1790 and 1860. The country's rural population, consisting mostly of farmers, increased sixfold during these years. The combination of territorial acquisition and public land policy was instrumental in underwriting the high rate of real estate ownership in the United States.

SETTLING THE LAND

Powerful inducements drove the acquisition of public acreage. Homesteaders and speculators sought land for their private interests; the federal government derived revenue from land sales. The conveyance of public land to private ownership allowed the taxation of real estate, which constituted the largest source of revenue for local and state governments. Encouragement of new settlement, coupled with the formation of new state and local governments, was an integral part of American statebuilding.

The volume of westward migrants after the Revolution surprised many observers. Settlers crossed the Appalachians into Kentucky and Tennessee, inhabited lands around New Orleans (first on the east side of the Mississippi River), and crossed the Ohio River into the upper Midwest. The state land cessions of 1781 led to thoughts about governing the new public domain. An early result was the Northwest Ordinance of 1787 (reenacted by Congress in 1791), which covered the region south of the Great Lakes. Most policymakers assumed that new territories would eventually be integrated into the union on an equal footing with existing states. Although many of the Revolutionary generation doubted that a republic occupying such a huge territory could survive, the principle of reproducing "little republics" in other regions of the "empire" was never seriously questioned. The Northwest Ordinance embodied the core of this principle. It provided for an appointed governor in a territory until its population reached 5,000, at which point it could elect a legislature. When a territory's population reached 60,000, it could apply for statehood, so long as its application included a constitution that provided for a republican government and a bill of rights. Slavery was prohibited in states carved out of the Northwest Territory. The Southwest Territory (Tennessee), created in 1790, omitted the clause concerning slavery.

Tennessee was the first state admitted by Congress under the territorial process, and Ohio was the first state created in the Northwest Territory (see table 4.1). Two more midwestern states and three southern states (all allowing slavery) entered the union by 1819. Statehood was eagerly sought by territorial residents because it afforded control over their local governments and granted them representation in Congress and a vote in presidential elections. In the nation's capital, however, statemaking led to discord. New Englanders worried that new states would diminish their region's influence. Southerners saw expansion westward as a threat to slavery. This issue flared into conflict in 1820 over a proposal to admit Missouri as a state. Southerners blocked the legislation until a compromise allowed slavery in Missouri, admitted Maine as a free state, and ruled that Congress could not bar slavery in territories below a line west of Missouri's southern border. The sectional protocol embodied in the Missouri Compromise (1821) lasted thirty-seven years.

Westward migration and statemaking moved in rough synchronization in the antebellum era. In the 1820s and 1830s settlers flowed into the Ohio and Mississippi River valleys and the Gulf coast. Texas, which controlled its own land, also attracted newcomers. Cross-country treks to Oregon and California began in the late 1840s, but most western migrants eschewed this long, arduous trip and took up residence in the central part of the country. By 1848 all American territories east of the Mississippi River had become states, half of them allowing slavery. Eight years later a tier of states along the western bank of the Mississippi River from Minnesota to Louisiana had become part of the United States. With California entering the union in 1850 and Oregon in 1859, the United States achieved an institutional presence on the Pacific coast. The admission of Kansas in 1861 pushed statehood onto the Great Plains.

The significance of this great migration is hard to exaggerate. In little more than half a century, the population of the United States had overspread an area twice its size in 1790. In 1860 half the country's inhabitants lived west of the Appalachians, creating new regions in the Midwest, the Gulf coast, and the Pacific coast, with a sprinkling of settlements on the Great Plains. Historian Malcom Rohrbough called this westward shift "one of the great migrations in the history of the western world."[30]

Besides its geographic and demographic implications, the western movement had enormous political consequences. At the national level, the redistribution of population and the admission of new states altered sectional representation in Congress.[31] New England lost seats, while the Midwest and the Gulf coast region emerged as powerful legislative blocs. The number of states increased by a factor of two and a half between 1790 and 1860, which changed the regional allocation of Senate seats. Locally, the number of counties multiplied sixteenfold in the antebellum era. Counties were the backbone of local government in many regions; in others, especially in the Northeast and parts of the Midwest, towns and cities oversaw civic functions. And territorial expansion and population growth stimulated another fulcrum of statebuilding: economic development.

POPULATION, RESOURCES, AND ECONOMIC DEVELOPMENT

Population growth constituted a powerful stimulus to the antebellum economy. The country's population increased eightfold between the first national census in 1790 and the enumeration just prior to the Civil War (see table 4.2). Most of this growth was due to natural increase, and 20 percent was attributed to international immigration, which remained relatively modest until the 1840s. Americans maintained a high birthrate in the late colonial and antebellum periods, with large families the rule. This fecundity offset the high mortality rate common in the preindustrial era. Americans were healthy by worldwide standards, however, partly because most people lived in rural surroundings and in climatic zones that tended to mitigate epidemic disease and were favorable for agriculture. Starvation was not a major problem for Euro-Americans.

Although the United States was predominantly a rural nation dotted with thousands of towns, townships, and villages, the number of cities also increased. Twenty-four urban locales existed in 1790; this had multiplied to 392 by 1860. That year, one of every five people lived in an urban setting, eight of which topped 100,000 residents. New York City contained more than a million people (counting Brooklyn, which was then a separate city);

Table 4.2. Territory, Governments, and Population, 1790–1870

Year	Land (Square Miles)	Governmental Entities			Population		
		States	Counties	Cities	Total (Million)	Foreign Born (%)	Black (%)
1790	866	13	283	24	3.9	—	19
1820	1,749	23	762	61	5.2	—	18
1840	1,749	26	1,279	131	17.1	9.7 (1850)	17
1860	2,970	33	2,074	392	31.5	13.2	14
1870	2,970	37	2,295	663	39.9	14.0	13

Sources: Susan Carter et al., eds., *Historical Statistics of the United States: Earliest Times to the Present*, vol. 1 (New York: Cambridge University Press, 2006), tables Aa1, 7, 27, 33; William Anderson, *The Units of Government in the United States: An Enumeration and Analysis* (Chicago: Public Administration Service, 1934), fig. 1.

its population exceeded that of twenty of the thirty-three states. More than half of Massachusetts residents lived in urban locations, including Boston, the nation's fourth largest city in 1860. Urban growth resulted from economic development and migratory inflow from rural America and from Europe. The big and medium-sized cities in the mid-Atlantic states and along the coast between Boston and Baltimore were dynamic centers of economic change.[32] A second tier of cities—New Orleans, Cincinnati, St. Louis, Chicago—anchored economic hubs situated near the periphery of settlement; San Francisco played a similar role on the West Coast.

The growth of cities marks the evolution of a diversified economy fueled by agricultural, manufacturing, and commercial functions.[33] Big cities nurtured entrepreneurial networks where skilled craftsmen, factory hands, operators of retail and wholesale businesses, manufacturers, financiers, and investors circulated. The larger cities, all of which had access to navigable water, functioned as regional hubs for transportation networks, with New York emerging as the largest of these multipurpose centers. Growing urban populations enlarged consumer markets for both America products and foreign imports. Whereas Europe had erected numerous trade barriers between countries, goods flowed freely throughout the United States, an openness that facilitated the expansion of commerce.

Natural resources played a key role in the nation's economic growth. Land provided the basis for farms, extractive activities, and investment in an era before most adults sought nonagricultural jobs. Appraising this natural bounty, economic historian Harold Faulkner notes that "no nation in history has been endowed with natural resources as great as those existing in the United States."[34] The scope of this storehouse defies a brief inventory. Faulkner's review concentrates on topography and terrain, soil types, climate and weather zones, minerals, forests and natural plants, fisheries, and waterways. Most of the lower forty-eight states lay in climate belts favorable to numerous agricultural commodities, which varied by region partially because of differences in the length of the growing season.[35]

This topography included numerous navigable rivers, as well as streams suitable for turning water mills. The Mississippi-Ohio River complex offered 5,000 miles of navigable water, beginning at the Gulf coast (New Orleans) and reaching into Montana via the Missouri River and past Pittsburgh on the Ohio River and its tributaries. Complementing the river arteries were many fine ocean harbors. The 1,500-mile coastline from Portland, Maine, to Miami, Florida, contained a dozen major ports and numerous smaller harbors; others lay along the Gulf of Mexico. The Pacific coast developed five major ocean depots. Russia, by comparison, had a territory larger than the United States yet no conveniently located, year-round ocean port. The Great Lakes supported commercial sites from Buffalo, New York, to Duluth, Minnesota. Water links within America's huge interior facilitated a widening radius of domestic and foreign commerce.[36]

Access to transportation, good land, and hospitable climates created the foundation for a diversified agriculture. Wheat and corn cultivation moved over the Appalachian Mountains in the early 1800s and spread westward into the upper Mississippi River valley. The flat, fertile Midwest lured farmers from New England and the mid-Atlantic region. These migrants settled first in western New York and Pennsylvania and in parts of Ohio and Kentucky; many later pulled up stakes and headed to Indiana, Illinois, Iowa, and Wisconsin. By 1860 the United States had two million farms, with the largest number in the Midwest. The westward movement of the wheat, corn, and meat belts enabled Cincinnati's emergence as the hog-marketing and whiskey-distilling capital of the country at midcentury, a position later held by food-processing enterprises in Chicago, St. Louis, and Minneapolis. As the nineteenth century unfolded, there was great foreign demand for northeastern and midwestern agricultural products, which supplemented local consumption.[37]

Cotton, the great American agricultural export, was cultivated in the South, as it requires a long growing season. Cotton production migrated toward the Gulf coast in a region that stretched from South Carolina to eastern Texas. Tobacco, rice, sugar, and indigo had been the South's chief exports when America won its independence. The invention of the cotton gin in 1793, foreign purchases, and the rise of the cotton manufacturing industry after the War of 1812 changed this equation. Cotton production accelerated, increasing from 200,000 bales in 1815 to 500,000 bales in 1825 and then rising to 4 million bales by the late 1850s. Its cultivation

Table 4.3. Economic Activity, 1800–1860

	1800	*1820*	*1850*	*1860*
Patents issued annually (thousands)	0.04	0.15	1.0	4.6
Post offices:				
Number (thousands)	0.90	4.5	18.0	28.0
Revenue (million $)	0.30	1.1	5.5	8.5
Banks (thousands)	—	0.3	0.8	1.5
Manufacturing establishments (thousands)	—	—	123	140
Prime movers—percentage of horsepower produced by:				
Animals	—	—	70	63
Factories	—	—	13	12
Railroads and ships	—	—	11	19

Source: US Department of Commerce, *Historical Statistics of the United States, Colonial Times to 1970* (Washington, DC: Bureau of the Census, 1975), series W99, R163, 164, X661, 580, P1, S4, 5, 8–10.

was dominated by large farms (plantations), often run by managers who oversaw slave labor while their wealthy owners resided in one of the South's fashionable cities.[38]

Cotton production was a highly capitalized operation whose commercial success depended on the cost of slave labor, the cultivation of a mixture of crops (some for consumption on the plantation), access to transportation facilities, and international commodity prices. Most American-grown cotton was exported to Britain, but domestic consumption increased as the domestic textile industry grew and consumers developed a preference for cotton over more traditional woolen and flax fabrics. The rising demand for factory-made fabrics in place of those spun and woven at home was a major contributor to making cotton "king" in the economy of the Deep South.

The antebellum economy included other resource-based activities. The largest "manufacturing" industries in 1860 produced cotton goods, lumber, flour, iron, woolen goods, and leather (from cattle hides). All these commodities were created by processing raw materials. Among the top ten industries, only boots and shoes, men's clothing, machinery, and carriages and wagons represented more extensive manufacturing processes. The 1860 census counted 140,000 manufacturing establishments; more than 20,000 of them were lumber mills, most of which were small businesses that catered to the local community (see table 4.3). As the timber industry moved into the upper Midwest and then to the Far West, some lumbering operations grew, such as the Weyerhauser firm in the upper Mississippi basin.

The second largest manufacturing industry in 1860 consisted of 14,000 flour and meal producers, most of which were local millers with an average of two employees. As grain production gravitated westward into the upper Ohio River valley, so did supportive entrepreneurs such as Cyrus McCormick, who devised a workable wheat-cutting machine (reaper). McCormick moved this manufacturing business from Virginia to Chicago in 1848, selling his machines to prairie farmers.

Raising animals produced food, a power source (horses and oxen), and leather. Tanneries purchased much of the hide output, which they processed and sold as leather to more than 12,000 boot and shoe manufacturers in 1860.

Valuable resources were taken from the sea, on which New Englanders were heavily dependent. Oysters were harvested off New England and Long Island, fishing craft plied the shallows off Georges Bank, and whaling was a major occupation for seamen from Nantucket and New Bedford. The numerous harbors and dense forests encouraged New Englanders to build vessels of many sizes and to pilot them to coastal and foreign destinations.

The United States held a variety of minerals such as copper, nickel, lead, zinc, and clay, as well as stone such as granite. Iron was used in 2,252 iron-making operations in 1860. The western migration shifted the center of the iron industry from the mid-Atlantic states, especially Pennsylvania, to the Ohio valley and the upper Midwest. Coal emerged as an important commercial commodity in the 1820s, when transportation innovations linked mines in eastern Pennsylvania and Ohio to consumers in northeastern cities. The growth in urban populations and the advent of the cast-iron stove increased the demand for coal for heating and cooking. Improved transportation was instrumental in the evolving commercialization of the country's natural resources.

THE TRANSPORTATION REVOLUTION

Robert Fulton's successful navigation of a steamboat up the Hudson River to Albany, New York, in 1807 launched a new era in transportation. Steamboats proliferated rapidly because of their utility—they were not dependent on wind or favorable river currents. By 1816 a steamboat made the upstream journey on the Mississippi and Ohio Rivers from New Orleans to Pittsburgh. By 1830 several hundred steamboats were operating on western waters, principally out of cities on the Ohio River; other vessels plied the Great Lakes. At sea, steamboats initially hugged the coasts, but by the late 1840s they were making regular transatlantic voyages. Steam-powered ships reduced the sailing time from Liverpool to New York from forty to fifty days

Fig 4.3. Map of railroads, 1860. *Source:* George Rogers Taylor, *The Transportation Revolution, 1815–1860* (New York: Harper & Row, 1951), 87.

in 1815 to ten days in 1860. Soon thereafter craft with iron hulls driven by screw propellers reduced the crossing time by several more days.

The steamboat boom overlapped with a canal craze inaugurated by the opening of the Erie Canal between Albany on the Hudson River and Buffalo on Lake Erie in 1825. Shorter American canals had been built earlier, but the Erie was a moneymaker from the start, encouraging other states to emulate New York. In 1816, as New York lawmakers were considering the construction of a water route across the state, Virginia allowed state investment in private transportation companies. In 1826, cognizant of the competition from New York's Erie Canal, Pennsylvania began its main-line canal and railroad system between Philadelphia and Pittsburgh. Whereas steamboats were private ventures, these major canals were public infrastructure projects, requiring substantial capital outlays. State governments took up the task of financing these endeavors, borrowing in domestic and foreign markets or purchasing stock in canal projects.[39] Canals and steamboats initiated closer commercial ties between regions, such as linking New York's port with the Great Lakes and the Ohio-Mississippi River systems.

By the 1840s farsighted investors saw railroads as the transportation of the future. First appearing in the 1830s, railroads picked up steam by the mid-1840s as promoters in East Coast cities such as Boston, New York, and Philadelphia, aided by state and local governmental subsidies, invested in rail ventures. By the 1850s the laying of 20,000 miles of track had established a relatively dense pattern of rail lines in the Northeast and breached the Midwest; several lines had reached Chicago and crossed the Mississippi into Missouri (see figure 4.3). The rapidity of rail expansion testifies to its commercial utility and, for some, profitability. Europeans saw America's "iron horse" as a particularly attractive investment.

As railroads overcame early obstacles, such as varying track widths (gauges), unbridged rivers, and underpowered locomotives, rail improvements reduced transportation costs. The combination of water and train transportation linked East Coast markets with western products, encouraging the shipment of midwestern wheat to New Orleans and New York. Interregional connections spurred regional specialization: the Midwest became a grain and meat center, the South concentrated on cotton, and the Northeast, especially the urban core between New York, Boston, and Philadelphia, emphasized commerce and manufacturing. No region depended solely on these commodities, but their economic specialization emphasized their regional advantages.

The transportation revolution, especially railroads, stimulated technological and entrepreneurial developments. Engineers and inventors designed more powerful locomotives, stronger metals, and devices such as the screw propeller for ships. Competitive rivalry for transportation connections, as occurred among cities in the Northeast, spurred new business ventures. Railroads, the telegraph, and mail routes (a service of the US government) moved information further and faster. Envisioning the future, nation boosters predicted that railroads would make the country a more integrated community.[40]

THE BIRTH OF INDUSTRIALIZATION

The transportation revolution, territorial expansion, and population growth were catalysts for American economic development. These factors interacted with a societal culture that encouraged business enterprise and welcomed immigrant labor. Nurtured by this open environment, entrepreneurs melded new technologies with organizational innovations to initiate factory manufacturing. Making things was not new to Americans, who produced a wide variety of products ranging from clocks and bells of casted metal to jewelry and mousetraps in the 1790s.[41] Two hundred master shoemakers in Lynn, Massachusetts, turned out 400,000 pairs of footwear in 1800. Know-how attained at the workbench as apprentices (Benjamin Franklin had been one) and jack-of-all-trades experience gained on the farm produced artisans with a variety of skills throughout rural America. Technology also flowed from abroad. Samuel Slater, for instance, emigrated from England to Rhode Island with the blueprint for a water-powered loom committed to memory. Slater's mills along the Blackstone River introduced mechanized cotton manufacturing in the United States, an event generally recognized as the dawn of American industrialization.

Government was a partner in this transition, with its principal contribution being a relaxation of rules that impeded enterprise and investment in certain ventures, such as canals and ocean port facilities. Federal courts promulgated rules that removed local barriers to commercial transactions. The federal system, which contained numerous semisovereign states and autonomous cities, introduced a competitive factor into the American political economy. Political leaders promoted their home economies, especially where commercial rivalries between urban centers, such as New York and Philadelphia, flourished. Besides subsidizing infrastructure projects, states aided capital formation by permitting the creation of manufacturing and banking corporations. The extension of credit, however, depended heavily on private transactions. Historian Thomas Cochran contends that the rise of corporations after 1815 was a key trigger for economic growth in subsequent decades. Numerous historians have emphasized the "get-ahead" attitude in America, where personal enterprise and a propensity for speculation and risk-taking were part of the culture's DNA.[42]

Many Americans eagerly took advantage of new technologies. The cotton gin, steam engine, cast-iron stove, and McCormick's improved wheat reaper were widely adopted. The assembly of products from interchangeable parts owes much to Eli Whitney (inventor of the cotton gin and later a gun manufacturer) and the rise of the firearms industry, which the federal government promoted through its own armories. The 1840s saw the birth of the sewing machine, the rotary printing press, and the safety pin, inventions of lasting importance. Inventions tell only one side of the technological story, however. The gradual adaptation and refinement of existing devices and the rational organization of the manufacturing process were equally important. The development of the machine tool industry, for example, allowed for greater tolerance in crafting interchangeable parts. Improvements to steam engines after 1787 raised their horsepower and lowered their fuel consumption, thereby reducing operating costs. Dams on waterways, however, remained the major power source for stationary machinery such as grain mills and sawmills and for the textile industry through much of the nineteenth century.

The War of 1812 between Britain and the United States marks the birth of American factory manufacturing. The Lowell cotton mill in Waltham, Massachusetts, is usually cited as the first large factory in the United States. The Lowell operation thrived, encouraging replication. For the next two generations, water-powered spinning machines and looms to make thread and weave cotton and woolen fabrics were used throughout New England and the mid-Atlantic states. The Lowell factory relied on rural New England women to tend the mills, working under male foremen. Eventually, Irish immigrants and French Canadians dominated New England's textile workforce. Railroad equipment created another entrepreneurial opportunity. The manufacture of locomotive engines attracted craftsmen with traditional skills such as iron making and metal mechanics to specialized manufacturing centers such as Philadelphia; Paterson, New Jersey; Lowell and Taunton, Massachusetts; Manchester, New Hampshire; and Schenectady, New York.

Every large industrial sector spawned a host of smaller satellite enterprises, a development that broadened manufacturing. The antebellum era recorded an increasing number of products made with interchangeable parts, including firearms, clocks, and cast-iron stoves. Grants of patents on new devices and manufacturing techniques accelerated as the nineteenth century proceeded, suggesting a growth in entrepreneurial innovation (see table 4.3). Merchants (e.g., wholesalers), financial institutions (e.g., banks and insurance companies), and information industries (e.g., publishing) became increasingly important adjuncts to the success of the manufacturing establishment. The combination of commerce and manufacturing enlarged the urban workforce, which drew on migrants from the countryside and from abroad. The densest concentration of industrialism was situated in lower New England and the mid-Atlantic states, usually near water transportation. Other nodes of manufacturing existed further afield, such as in cities along the Ohio River, the port and rail center of Chicago, and a few areas of the upper South.[43]

Factory production was a transformative development in economic history. Yet the United States was not an *industrialized* society on the eve of the Civil War. In 1860 only 20 percent of the population lived in cities; the vast majority of the workforce still toiled on the land; horses continued to supply more horsepower than steam engines; agriculture accounted for a larger portion of national income than manufacturing; and American exports were predominantly agricultural in nature. Although legal changes made it easier to incorporate businesses, most firms were still family owned and managed. The antebellum era saw the dawning of an industrialized economy, not its maturation.[44] Nor did the economy grow in a steady, linear fashion. Severe commercial depressions followed financial panics in 1819, 1837, and 1857. Despite these setbacks for businesses and workers, the economy became larger and Americans generally became richer between 1790 and 1860.[45]

European leaders had scoffed at the idea that a federal republic could survive as a unified state. In America some doubted that such a large republic could withstand the centrifugal forces trying to tear it apart. Yet the republic not only survived assorted stresses but also grew larger and more affluent in its first seventy years. During these decades the United States became the fourth largest territorial state in the world, establishing a domain that spanned the continent. Some of its constituent parts contained as much space as states elsewhere in the world: Texas is larger than France, and California is bigger than Japan. Territorial expansion opened a pathway for population growth. The United States counted more residents in 1860 than lived in Great Britain, and among European states, only France had a larger population. Territorial expansion and population growth constitute formidable pillars of statebuilding. America's expanding economy added a third leg to this foundation. National states begin with territory and people, but they require a robust economy to satisfy private needs and fund public endeavors. The pre–Civil War decades witnessed the expansion of conditions conducive to economic development. At the end of the period, America ranked third globally in wealth on a per person basis, despite its skewed distribution caused by slavery. Within a single lifetime the United States had acquired the critical ingredients for statebuilding.

5

Nationalism and Public Policy

George Washington waited at his Mount Vernon estate in April 1789 for the arrival of the messenger who would confirm his election as the country's first president. Even though Washington was the consensus (and only) candidate for the office, the outcome of the election worried him. Besides being reluctant to leave his "peaceful abode" in Virginia, he harbored doubts about his fitness for the job. At fifty-seven, he had already logged years of service to his country. But friends had persuaded Washington that he was the logical choice and perhaps the only person who could successfully steer the new ship of state.

Washington also dreaded the fawning and ceremony to come. The eight-day journey to New York confirmed his expectations, as he was feted at each stop along the way. In the words of biographer Ron Chernow, the trip was "the republican equivalent of the procession of a royal coronation." A special barge was constructed to carry him across the Hudson River from New Jersey to New York City. The huge flotilla of boats that joined the procession included musicians who serenaded the excursion. The streets of the city were lined with spectators; ladies threw flowers from windows and "shed tears of joy." The pageantry continued over the next several days until his inauguration, when Washington stated that his foremost objective was the "triumph of national unity over 'local prejudices or attachments.'"[1] He repeated his hope for national unity eight years later in his farewell address as president.

Washington was America's foremost hero. He was the only political notable who received unreserved adulation from all sections of the United States. Paradoxically, he left the presidency under a cloud of vitriolic criticism. Political division, not national unity, emerged during his tenure as the nation's chief executive. And yet, time would heal these political wounds and restore his stature among Americans, eventually elevating him to unrivaled heroic figure in the history of the United States. The history of American nationalism in many ways paralleled the Washington parable.

GOVERNANCE AND NATIONALISM IN THE ANTEBELLUM ERA

Governance embodies the legal powers granted to civic officials and how they exercise this authority. In its simplest expression, this responsibility reduces to the adoption of rules for the community (laws) and the application of these rules (administration and litigation). In democratically based polities, and in the United States in particular, these actions are publicly phrased in varying degrees of concordance with constituent thinking. The actions of government evoke various responses, often negative, especially when taxes, wars, or cultural mores are involved. Thus, the survival of a political community requires popular acceptance of its underlying foundations that transcend political conflicts of the moment. Without acquiescence to its sustaining principles, support for the state can erode and even collapse. The legitimacy of the regime, in short, requires the consent of the citizenry. Patriotism—loyalty to the national state—is a critical factor in this equation. The development of personal identification with the nation (i.e., nationalism) provides this bonding between constituents and the state.

By its nature, nationalism is difficult to define and even harder to reconstruct historically. The concept refers to sentiments manifest within a national territory and the psychological identification with the symbols of a state. Hans Kohn has defined nationalism as a "state of mind, in which supreme loyalty of the individual is felt to be due the nation-state." These feelings spring from a "deep attachment to one's native soil, to local traditions and to established territorial authority." Nationalism, he states, is a living and active corporate will, "inspiring the large majority of the people and claiming to inspire all its members."[2] National identity rests on a collective sentiment shared by the inhabitants of a locale; this sense of peoplehood identifies individuals as members of a distinct society. The evolution of national identity transforms a national state into a nation-state, in which cultural identity becomes fused with loyalty to a country's civil apparatus. Although people may share identities through language, ethnicity, and a common history, a nation is a fictive congregation and not an explicit political entity.

The nation, Benedict Anderson suggests, is an "imagined community," and its traditions are invented, according to Eric Hobsbawm. Yet German historian Heinrich von Treitschke believed that, "again and again, it has been proved that it is war which turns a people into a nation."[3] In America, however, other factors were influential in cultivating a national identity. David Waldstreicher has made a convincing case that nationalism in the early decades of the republic was shaped by rival visions of an American nation and that active participation in civic festivities, such as parades and holiday pageants, interacted with ideological declarations to construct an American nationalism. Susan-Mary Grant argues that the development of American nationalism was forged in a sectional dialectic between the North and the South.[4]

Individuals possess several identities. Race, religion, gender, and family are important personal referents; so too are attachments to place, such as one's neighborhood, town, and region, and an individual's status (class) in society. The overlapping nature of personal identities has produced complex configurations that were difficult to untangle historically, especially before the advent of polling techniques. This is especially the case for the antebellum era, when sentimental attachments to an American "nation" evolved slowly, displayed divisive strains, and remained largely nonexistent in places. Fogginess about the substance of nationalism is a major reason why writers have questioned the existence of an American state in the antebellum era.

We do know that America was a nation of joiners. Societies and associations multiplied among professionals, merchants, artisans, military corps, ethnic brotherhoods, and other voluntary groups, especially in the cities. Independence Day, Washington's birthday, and memorable events such as the opening of the Erie Canal and the victory over Mexico led to public celebrations, luring myriad groups to parade the city streets and listen to patriotic rhetoric delivered by local notables.[5] Presumably these public exercises reinforced bonds to the American state.

THE EVOLUTION OF NATIONAL IDENTITY

M. Walzer wrote that "the state needs to be personified before it can be seen, symbolized before it can be loved, imagined before it can be conceived."[6] George Washington fulfilled much of this requirement in the long nineteenth century. He was indelibly linked to the American Revolution, the birth of the republic, the writing of the Constitution, and the inauguration of the federal government. Partisan animus over the French Revolution and other issues during Washington's presidency (1789–1797), however, dimmed some of this adulation.

Time restored Washington's venerated status among Americans. By the 1830s his reputation had undergone a revival that took many forms. His likeness adorned homes, public buildings, and folk art. The nation's capital had already been named in his honor, but 300 counties and towns later bore his name. Parson Weems's 1800 biography (revised and republished many times) cast Washington in a saintly light, while Chief Justice John Marshall provided a longer but less fanciful narrative of his life. Jared Sparks, Harvard College's first historian, published a twelve-volume collection of Washington's correspondence between 1834 and 1837. Construction of a monument in the capital in Washington's honor began in 1848 and was completed in 1885. Henry Brown's equestrian statue of Washington was unveiled in New York's Union Square in 1856, the city's first commemorative monument to the Revolution. The Mount Vernon Ladies Association purchased Washington's estate from his descendants in 1858 and turned it into a national shrine. In later years admirers continued to add reminders of Washington's contribution to the forging of the nation.[7]

Washington's role in the Revolution and the Constitution personified the fusion of "Liberty and Union, now and forever, one and inseparable," as Daniel Webster phrased the axiom.[8] This ideological synthesis became the ideological heart of the American republic. The principle was repeated time and again during the long nineteenth century at Fourth of July celebrations where local luminaries delivered orations to the assembled throngs. Independence Day became the "national Sabbath." American nationalism was, as geographer D. W. Meinig observes, "connected first of all to a set of principles rather than a place."[9] The union and the republican principles it embodied were key to preserving freedom, a refrain that echoed across generations of politicians. They added that this civic covenant made the United States unique among nations and posited that God had directed a "mission" to extend American liberty. When the expansion of territory was linked to this providential mandate, it was called "Manifest Destiny." Protestantism, republican political institutions, and optimism about material progress were folded into a recurring motif of America's special civic culture. The removal of property qualifications for white male voters represented a logical development of this civic vision. Congress and Washington designated Thanksgiving Day to commemorate the blessings of citizenship and opportunity.

Numerous factors promoted a sense of America's civic uniqueness. Language and heritage were important. Most Americans were native English speakers of British ancestry. An even larger proportion accepted the moral imperatives of Protestantism, even if they were not active churchgoers, as was the case for large numbers of Americans. Protestant morality was diffused in the schools, which were often run by charitable and religious organizations but increasingly by local governments. The 1850 census counted nearly 81,000 public schools, sustained largely by tax dollars. The American passion for education produced the most literate nation in the world; the 1850 census identified only 9 percent of white adults as illiterate.

In addition to the basics of reading, writing, and arithmetic, schooling fused a mixture of Protestant piety and American patriotism, attributes that were conspicuous in Jedidiah Morse's *Geography Made Easy* (1784 and later editions), a popular schoolbook, and McGuffey's readers (1836–1837 and later), some of the most widely read books in America at the time. A literate population encouraged the establishment of a growing number of newspapers; the formation of the Associated Press in 1849 forged an expanding network of news gatherers. The publication of newspapers and books and the creation of libraries and historical societies all contributed to an American national ethos.[10] The US Post Office, which underwrote the cost of mailing newspapers, played a major role in "spreading the news" around the country.[11] Along with schooling and religion, literacy promoted a sense of Americanism.

The expansion of the country added a material basis to the rise of nationalist sentiments. The lure of the land was viewed as a limitless opportunity for individuals to start anew and become property owners. Orators envisioned that America's expansion across the continent was destined to make it "a great and unified Nation." The surge of settlers to the frontier pushed republican institutions westward, as newcomers established towns and counties to anchor the new states added to the union. Historian Frederick Jackson Turner argued in his famous essay "The Significance of the Frontier" (1893) that "the frontier promoted the formation of a composite nationality." More than other regions, he credited the West as being a breeding ground of American nationalism.[12]

The extent to which the frontier environment promoted distinct American attitudes is still being debated. From the vantage point of many mapmakers, however, geography was a handmaid to American nationalism. Beginning in the 1820s cartographers depicted the United States as a country with both an Atlantic and a Pacific coast, which offered visual proof that a great new "empire" had been formed. The East provided environmental inspiration for pride in America. American artists, especially painters in the Hudson River school (1820s–1850s) such as Thomas Cole (*St. John in the Wilderness*, 1827) and Frederick E. Church (*Niagara Falls*, 1857), envisioned landscapes in the Northeast as a fusion of nature, Christianity, and American identity. For a new society that lacked traditional relics of national identity, the celebration of nature was a substitute for Europe's ancient castles and kingly epics.[13]

Technological progress also substituted for more conventional symbols of national identity. "Steam and electricity," wrote Gordon Bennett, editor of the *New York Herald*, "have made and are making, this country the greatest . . . the sun ever shone upon." The railroad was repeatedly depicted as an engine of progress that would forge national unity. A transcontinental line, promoters argued, would bind the union together by building a great commercial highway. In 1846 a midwestern member of Congress marveled how the iron horse and the telegraph had conquered distance and would allow remote places like Oregon to join "this great temple of freedom."[14]

The transportation-communication revolution overlapped two important political changes: the expansion of the electorate and the development of modern political parties. Debate over Alexander Hamilton's financial policies during the Washington administration and differing views about the French Revolution in the 1790s keyed the formation of the Federalists and the Jeffersonian Republicans, partisan groupings that continued through the War of 1812. During these early years of the republic, political leadership remained largely in the hands of elites, a feature that undermined the survival of the first parties. Political parties reappeared during the presidency of Andrew Jackson (1829–1837) and evolved into a primary vehicle of popular politics in the 1840s. This development was cued largely by the legal expansion of the electorate, achieved via state constitutional and statutory changes (circa 1800–1840) that removed property qualifications for voting, although suffrage remained limited to adult white males. Other reforms made offices formerly filled by appointment open to election, such as county officials in the South, city mayors in the North, and judges in many states. The admission of new states expanded the geographic reach of these electoral changes, reinforcing the logic behind constructing a national network of party organizations. From the late 1830s through the mid-1850s, two partisan groups—the Democrats (initially the Jacksonian Democrats) and the Whigs—engaged in vigorous competition and influenced the management of government.[15]

The rise of this "second party system" was instrumental in American statebuilding because it integrated individuals of diverse backgrounds and geographic locations into the electoral democracy, albeit within partisan groupings. The enlargement of the voter base increased the ranks of political citizenship, a civic development that numerous historians see as a kernel of early American nationalism. Historian Robert Wiebe argues that America and democracy were synonymous, resulting in a fusion of sentiments that produced a "romantic nationalism."[16] The Democratic and Whig Parties manipulated this association between democracy and citizenship in their electioneering. The cumulative effect of partisan competition contributed to a growing sense of membership in the American nation until sectional stresses in the 1850s ripped it apart.

IMPEDIMENTS TO NATIONALISM

Although political parties and economic factors influenced national identity in the antebellum years, various conditions blunted its development. One set of restraints concerned citizenship and social status. Women, free blacks, and many immigrants, especially Catholics, were denied full political rights. Slaves were defined as property, not people, and Indians were regarded as culturally incompatible with Euro-American society. Non-English-speaking and Catholic immigrants faced widespread ostracism, especially in New England, where white Protestantism set social conventions. Some people on the periphery of citizenship, such as women and Protestant immigrants, shared patriotic sentiments through family ties and identification with the dominant culture. But the strongest sense of national identification was centered among white males, the group that occupied the top rung of society's social and political ladder.[17]

Americans were also segmented by geographic location. The identities of most inhabitants included a locational attachment based on their town or village, as well as their county and state. Clusters of states and even parts of states formed the geographic basis of regional cultures.[18] Turner saw sections as regional aggregations of states. "Each section," he wrote in 1922, "has its own special geographic qualities, its own resources and economic capacities, and its own rival interests." In addition, "There is a sectionalism of culture." The country's history and geographic size made it "impossible" to understand American politics, Turner wrote, "except through sectional spectacles."[19] Virtually every historian of antebellum America uses the South, the North, and the West as referencing markers.

Distinctive sectional and regional characteristics are visible in the artwork of the age, which took everyday life, western migration, and natural landscapes as its subjects. The artists of the Hudson River school have already been noted, but others also interpreted American culture in the mid-nineteenth century. Emmanuel Leutze was perhaps the most well-known artist to depict heroic moments in American history. Leutze's fame grew with his rendition of *Washington Crossing the Delaware* (1852) and his mural painted on the dome of the Capitol (*Westward the Course of Empire*, conceived in 1854 and completed in 1862). Artists such as Karl Bodmer, John Mix Stanley, and Albert Bierstadt painted idiomatic images of the Far West that evoked pride in Americans' advance across this idyllic countryside. The art of the period fused themes of progress, Christianity, and the triumph Anglo-Saxon civilization over heathen natives and untamed natural geography.[20]

Many of these renditions were reproduced as lithographs. The best-known vendors of affordable images were Currier and Ives, printmakers located in New York City. Consciously attempting to appeal to middle-class tastes, Currier and Ives depicted people and places that suggested the role of class, gender, and race in American culture. Their lithographs also captured sectional differences, such as fall apple picking and winter sledding in the North, plantation manors in the South, and wagon trains heading toward the Rockies in the western frontier.[21]

New England furnished the model for American nationalism. New Englanders possessed a prideful sense of their town-based communities, which they heralded as the cradle of liberty and the embodiment of their Puritan-Pilgrim heritage. More ethnically homogeneous than residents of other regions, New Englanders were predominantly of English background prior to the inflow of Irish and French Canadian immigrants at midcentury. The region produced much of the nation's literary output and embraced a culture that venerated hard work and moral rectitude. This quest for self-improvement explains why illiteracy in the region was substantially lower than in the southern states.[22] New England's politicians condemned slavery and the three-fifths clause of the Constitution, which gave southerners additional seats in Congress and control of the presidency from Washington through Jackson (except for John Adams and his son John Quincy Adams). As Joseph Conforti explains, New Englanders considered their region the "American homeland" and had no doubt that their values should constitute the heart of the nation.[23]

Many southerners took offense at northern definitions of Americanism. Differing in various ways from most of the North, the Deep South was a cotton-growing agricultural region with few cities or industries, relatively few modern transportation facilities, a poorly developed school system, and low literacy rates. Northern stereotypes depicted southern society as dominated by a patriarchal hierarchy of planter elites (cavaliers), a small minority among more numerous poor white farmers. The evolving northern conception of American nationalism fed off a negative view of the South as "feudal, aristocratic, and backward." Whereas northerners generally welcomed innovation, the South showed less interest in technical and intellectual growth, with the exception of the cotton gin. The southern "middling" strata were considerable smaller than those in the North. Ralph Waldo Emerson spoke for many of his northern contemporaries when he called southerners "haughty, selfish, willful and unscrupulous men." Increasingly, those in the North saw slavery as a national problem, not simply a sectional peculiarity.[24]

In reality, "there were many Souths," as Daniel Boorstin has observed. The region was not a cultural or geographic monolith, although northerners increasingly perceived southerners as arrogant, slave-owning aristocrats intent on controlling national policy. Partly because of these perceptions, leading white southerners defined their homeland in distinctive sectional terms, especially after 1830. William Taylor attributes the development of the cavalier myth embedded in antebellum literature as an attempt to contrast southern planters' noblesse oblige with the heartless acquisitiveness of Yankee northerners. Susan-Mary Grant sees the development of southern sectional conceptions of Americanism as a defensive response to northern cultural chauvinism. These contrasts dichotomized into sectional nationalism by midcentury in the view of some historians.[25]

The mid-Atlantic, which extended from New York to the upper Ohio

River basin and abutted settlements around the Great Lakes, represented the most heterogeneous region. New York City was a multiethnic urban center with influence throughout the "core" area of the country, challenging Boston as the nation's cultural capital. The city also anchored the socioeconomic "nuclear area" of the United States between Boston, Philadelphia, and Washington. Migration of native-born Americans and immigrants across the Appalachians brought Ohio and then Indiana and Illinois into the rapidly settled "west." This region contained a variety of cultural nodes and influences, with New England Yankees settling in northern areas (Ohio and Michigan) and southerners flowing into locales along the Ohio River and up the Mississippi River into Missouri. Scandinavian and German immigrants mingled in between, with many favoring the northern reaches of the Midwest, especially Wisconsin and Minnesota. Notwithstanding this swirl of peoples in the nation's midsection, Turner saw the "west" as the most nationalistic region in antebellum America.[26]

Sectional, regional, and community attachments impeded the development of an unqualified nationalism. Economic development failed to instill modern values in all places in the expanding national state. The sectional cleavage that resulted in the Civil War demonstrates the shortcomings of a common national identity through 1860. Yet conversely, northern willingness to suppress southern secession from the union provides evidence that patriotic devotion to an American nation was broad, powerful, and sustained outside the South. This cohesiveness is probably what Turner meant by the existence of an "American spirit" in the midst of sectional divisions.[27]

FEDERALISM AND AMERICAN GOVERNANCE

In 1833 Congressman Thomas Dickens Arnold from Tennessee rose on the floor of the House to advocate the distribution of "the laws of Congress" to every court of record in the nation. "It is true," he said, "that the every-day concerns of the citizens of the country are entrusted to the legislation of the State Governments, but still there are many matters, coming under the legislation of Congress, in which the whole people have an important interest."[28] Arnold's remarks touched three elementary truths about the antebellum polity. First, he pointed to legislatures, not executives, as the primary locus of lawmaking authority. During Arnold's time, representative bodies, not presidents and governors, were viewed as the foundation of republican government. Second, he noted the allocation of responsibilities between the states and the national government. This delegation of powers is the foundation of the American federal system. And third, he noted the states' prevalence in dealing with "every-day concerns."

Federalism constitutes the structural arch of governmental authority in the United States. This political-legal arrangement had immense significance for how Americans managed civic affairs. The system arose from the colonial experience, when American assemblies exercised extensive powers while remaining within Britain's imperial jurisdiction (see chapters 2 and 3). The decisions made at the Constitutional Convention in 1787 preserved state prerogatives. The Constitution delegated explicit "enumerated" powers to Congress and contained some explicit restrictions on state authority, including the ability to break contracts, coin money, and declare war. Beyond these limitations, states could govern as their officers saw fit, so long as they observed their own constitutions and did not directly contravene federal authority. In addition, both governments shared "concurrent" powers, most notably the ability to tax, preserve law and order, and create new governing units. However, the US Constitution's vagueness on certain provisions, and competing legal interpretations, spawned ongoing controversy about the boundary between state and national powers. These disagreements roiled politics throughout the antebellum era.[29]

Federalism is a prism for viewing American political history, for three basic reasons. First, the federal allocation of responsibility instructs us to track both national and state actions. And one must remember that state action includes the acts of local governments, whose authorities were outlined primarily by state lawmakers. Counties, towns, townships, villages, and cities were the workhorses of public administration in the long nineteenth century. More than 10,000 local general-purpose governments existed in the United States in 1850.[30] Any political history that excludes state and local government cannot capture the scope and scale of American governance.[31] In the nineteenth century, local governments, the states, and the federal government performed relatively distinct tasks.

Second, federalism provided mechanisms for interactions between state and national arenas. States, for example, selected the electors who cast ballots for the nation's president, and state legislatures chose US senators until 1913. States designed the districts for representatives elected to the lower house of Congress and specified who could vote in *all* elections. Because staffing of the national government ran largely through each state, federalism created a political conduit for the expression of local constituencies at the national level of government and for sectional alliances in congressional policymaking. Changes to the Constitution had to win the approval of three-fourths of the states. Federal courts, however, could disallow state actions if they violated the US Constitution. Federalism, in short, provided a central forum for the representation of local and regional interests. In the language of the late eighteenth century, the union was a confederated polity.[32]

Third, federalism was plastic and pliable, as the relationship between the national government and the states changed during the nineteenth century and even more so in the twentieth. A variety of factors prompted these alterations, in part because federalism offered a platform for politicians to challenge political practices. The addition of new states to the union altered the political dynamics, such as by recasting coalitions in Congress. The replacement of justices on the US Supreme Court and a steady stream of new laws and court rulings in the states continually revised the political-legal context in which the relationship between state and national authority was discussed. Federalism evolved over time yet remained the critical platform for statebuilding in America.[33]

STATE AND LOCAL GOVERNANCE

Local government played the most conspicuous role in the everyday lives of Americans. The most dynamic governmental entities were the cities, especially the biggest cities, whose commercial activity and increasingly dense populations created a variety of dislocations and political demands. Cities derived their authority from state governments through charters and statutes that created civic offices and outlined their responsibilities. Technically, cities were legal creatures of the state; in practice, a power granted or denied to a municipal government usually represented a behest from city officials and residents. Regardless of who initiated an action, state legislatures frequently intervened in urban affairs, often by statute on specific matters, but sometimes by the wholesale revision of municipal charters.[34]

Boston illustrates the patterns of governance in the largest municipalities. Massachusetts elevated the town of Boston to a municipality with a charter in 1821, effective in 1822. The new city brought a long civic history to its mandate, having already established public schools, including a high school; street improvements; a police force (constables and a night watch); fire protection; and care for paupers. Actions of the city legislature and the mayor, frequently based on the new authority granted by the state, expanded these functions and added new ones over the next four decades (see table 5.1). The city redeveloped Faneuil Hall into the Quincy Market (which the city rented to vendors), established a permanent police force under the command of a marshal, inaugurated a public water system, created salable land from the waters of Bay Back, appointed a single marshal to command the volunteer firefighters, constructed a public library, issued regulations for the use of horses on city streets, constructed sewers (although not yet a citywide system), and sponsored a city hospital. In 1854 the city established a police department; police officers were required to wear uniforms five years later,

Table 5.1. Boston Governance, 1821–1863

Year	Policies Enacted
1821	High school established
	House of Industry (almshouse) established; transferred to Deer Island, 1849
	City of Boston incorporated by state legislation
1823	Almshouse established
1824	Boston Garden authorized, next to Boston Common
	House of Corrections (South Boston) established
	Quincy Market project authorized (redevelopment of Faneuil Hall area)
	Health Commission appointed
1826	House of Reformation (for children) established
1832	Bridge to South Boston acquired
1838	Police officers authorized
1846	Water system authorized (Cochituate Reservoir)
1847	Hospital (Deer Island) established
1851	City engineer appointed
1852	Commissioners on Boston Harbor and Back Bay appointed
	Boston Public Library approved; Boylston Street facility constructed, 1855–1857
1854	Police department established; uniformed police authorized, 1859
	Charter revised to provide veto power for mayor
1856	Milk adulteration prohibited; inspector appointed, 1859
	Hack drivers licensed; horse traffic regulated (codified)
1857	Commissioners authorized to fill and sell Back Bay land
	Sewer construction on Boston Neck authorized
1858	City hospital authorized; completed, 1864
1863	Police allowed to be armed

Sources: Richard H. Abbott, "Massachusetts: Maintaining Hegemony," in *Radical Republicans in the North: State Politics during Reconstruction*, ed. James C. Mohr (Baltimore: Johns Hopkins University Press, 1976); Dale Baum, *The Civil War Party System: The Case of Massachusetts, 1848–1876* (Chapel Hill: University of North Carolina Press, 1984); Charles J. Bullock, *Historical Sketch of the Finances and Financial Policy of Mass. from 1780 to 1905*, 3rd ser., vol. 8:2 (New York: Publications of the American Economic Association, 1907); Ronald Formisano, *Transformation of Political Culture: Massachusetts Parties, 1790s–1840s* (New York: Oxford University Press, 1983); Oscar Handlin, *Commonwealth: A Study of the Role of Government in the American Economy; Massachusetts, 1774–1861, 2nd ed.* (Cambridge, MA: Harvard University Press, 1969); Albert B. Hart, ed., *Commonwealth History of Massachusetts*, vol. 4, *1820–1889* (New York: States History Co., 1930); Charles P. Huse, *The Financial History of Boston, 1822–1909* (Cambridge, MA: Harvard University Press, 1916); John Koren, *Boston, 1822 to 1922: The Story of Its Government* (Boston: City of Boston Printing Department, 1922); Roger Lane, *Policing the City: Boston, 1822–1905* (Cambridge, MA: Harvard University Press, 1967); Robert H. Whitten, *Public Administration in Massachusetts: The Relation of Central to Local Authority* (1898; reprint, New York: AMS Press, 1969).

and in another four years, they were permitted to carry guns. Hard-core criminals could be sent to the state prison, which was located in town. Boston controlled real estate development by selling city land, issuing building permits (an early form of zoning), and regulating stables that housed the city's growing population of horses ("living machines"). It licensed numerous trades and businesses, such as saloons, and could close them down if they were deemed "nuisances."[35]

Boston levied taxes to pay for these civic tasks. In 1854–1857 Boston's financial outlay equaled $16.90 per person. Overall, the most expensive activity (at $5.71 per person) was maintaining the "streets," a category that included sewers, lighting, bridges, ferries, public lands, and the Board of Health (which oversaw street cleaning). The other most expensive functions were schools ($2.39 per person), water ($2.19), institutions such as the House of Industry and the House of Reformation ($1.52), and police ($1.24). The remaining outlays were earmarked for the county (government), fire protection, the library, public grounds (e.g., Boston Garden), and general government. This last category covered the salaries of city officials, such as the mayor. Members of the City Council and the Board of Aldermen, the city legislature, and most committees that supervised numerous administrative activities served without compensation. Despite this donated labor, Bostonians' share of city costs increased from $4.61 per person in 1828–1831 to four times that amount by the end of the 1850s.[36] These increasing expenditures reflected the expanded scale and scope of Boston's civic activities.

Not every municipal government mirrored Boston's civic history, of course, but the Massachusetts capital did typify governance in the big eastern cities. All the large cities maintained streets, bridges, and lighting; supported education; established a police presence; protected against fire; and developed public water systems—the major municipal responsibilities at midcentury.[37] Some also invested in transportation projects. This expanded role in the provision of services and the development of infrastructure is suggested by a comparison of fiscal activities in 1860 (see table 5.2). The per capita expenditures of Boston, New York, Baltimore, and other major cities were roughly six times larger than federal outlays; city spending dwarfed the financial activity of state governments.

Paying for these amenities required localities to levy taxes and fees. Because local revenue rested primarily on the taxation of property, developing new real estate was a rational urban strategy. In the hope of adding properties to the tax rolls and attracting new commerce and industry, cities competed for business, people, and prestige. Offering up-to-date services for burgeoning populations furthered this goal. Large projects such as supplying fresh water and building bridges, which had years of potential utility,

Table 5.2. Governmental Expenditures, 1860

Governmental Entity	*Per Capita Expenditures (Current $)*
Federal government	2.08
State and local governments	4.54
States:	0.89
Massachusetts	0.97
New York	1.23
Illinois	1.05
Georgia	1.11
North Carolina	3.89
Texas	1.37
Cities:	
Boston	20.14
New York	12.14
Providence	8.04
Baltimore	13.56
San Francisco	16.18
Large cities (sample)[a]	11.46

Sources: US Census Bureau, *Historical Statistics of the United States: Colonial Times to 1970* (Washington, DC: Government Printing Office, 1975), series Y457; John Legler, Richard Sylla, and John Wallis, "U.S. City Finance and the Growth of Government, 1850–1920," *Journal of Economic History* 48 (1988): 347–358; Secretary of State, *Illinois Blue Book, 1929–1930* (Springfield, IL: Office of the Secretary of State, 1930), 587; Richard Sylla, "Long-Run Trends in State and Local Finance: Sources and Uses of Funds in North Carolina, 1800–1877," in *Long-Term Factors in American Economic Growth*, ed. Stanley L. Engerman and Robert E. Gallman (Chicago: University of Chicago Press, 1986), 819–868; Peter Wallenstein, *From Slave South to New South: Public Policy in Nineteenth Century Georgia* (Chapel Hill: University of North Carolina Press, 1987), 106–107; Edmund T. Miller, *A Financial History of Texas* (Austin: University of Texas Press, 1916), appendix, table 8; Charles J. Bullock, *Historical Sketch of the Finances and Financial Policy of Mass. from 1780 to 1905*, 3rd ser., vol. 8:2 (New York: Publications of the American Economic Association, 1907); New York State Constitutional Convention Committee, *Problems Relating to Taxation and Finance*, vol. 4, *State and Local Government in New York (1938)*; Andrew C. McLaughlin and Albert Bushnell Hart, *Cyclopedia of American Government*, vol. 1 (New York: Appleton, 1914), 697 (New York City); Paul Studenski and Herman E. Krooss, *Financial History of the United States* (New York: McGraw-Hall, 1963), 197 (Providence); Alan D. Anderson, *The Origins and Resolution of an Urban Crisis: Baltimore, 1890–1930* (Baltimore: Johns Hopkins University Press, 1977), 34; Charles P. Huse, *The Financial History of Boston, 1822–1909* (Cambridge, MA: Harvard University Press, 1916); Terrence J. McDonald, *The Parameters of Urban Fiscal Policy: Socioeconomic Change and Political Culture in San Francisco, 1860–1906* (Berkeley: University of California Press, 1986).

[a] Sample of thirty-five large cities in Randall G. Holcombe and Donald J. Lacombe, "The Growth of Local Government in the U.S. from 1820 to 1870," *Journal of Economic History* 61 (2001): 188, based on regression estimates of data in Legler, Sylla, and Wallis, "U.S. City Finance and the Growth of Government," 347–358.

necessitated loans. By 1860 city debt was roughly equal to state government indebtedness. City fathers in the large eastern metropolises realized that officials in smaller and newer places looked to them for inspiration and advice. Philadelphia was the leading urban model early in the century but increasingly relinquished this position to New York. The combination of urban rivalry and emulation elevated big-city governance from a local activity to national significance.[38]

State governments aided and abetted these activities in various ways, principally by creating local governments and specifying their powers. Beginning in the 1820s states expanded their promotion of economic development, driven in part by economic rivalry among states and cities. The most famous state ventures concerned transportation projects, then called "internal improvements." The headliner among these endeavors was the Erie Canal, an immediate financial success when it opened for business in 1825. Financed and operated by New York State, the Erie Canal sparked other states in the mid-Atlantic region and Ohio River valley to invest in canals (see tables A.2 and A.3 in the appendix). By the 1830s several states and numerous cities were involved in the financing of railroads.[39]

From 1790 through the 1830s state economic policy took the form of mercantilism, whereby states used various techniques, including grants of monopolies to private firms and governmental operation of public facilities, to benefit the commonwealth. By the late 1830s a new pattern—an egalitarian era—began to replace earlier state practices. During this next phase, states withdrew from direct sponsorship of economic projects and opened commercial ventures to private enterprises, following principles of entrepreneurial competition and open access to the incorporation of businesses. This trend was partially the consequence of the political democratization of the electorate, as well as a heightened distrust of legislators, whom critics charged with favoritism for elites.

The Panic of 1837 inflicted a jarring shock on states' economic promotion. The downturn in business that followed in the late 1830s and early 1840s cut direct state investment in infrastructure ventures, opening new opportunities for private entrepreneurs. By the 1840s states turned to general incorporation laws that specified administrative criteria for the formation of private businesses, which replaced the older practice of enacting a separate charter for each venture. This revised approach led to regulations that imposed legal obligations on corporate owners. These new incorporation policies, along with supportive state and federal court rulings, represented a "release of energy" that facilitated economic development.[40] In some states the new incorporation principle was extended to private banks (so-called free banking acts); by 1860 the nation counted 1,500 banks operating under state laws, some of which were run by state governments. A few states, notably New York and Massachusetts, created commissions in the 1850s that initiated the regulation of banks and insurance companies. To compensate for revenue losses from state-run ventures caused by the depression, many states levied taxes on businesses and banks; in other cases, legislatures imposed licensing fees on commercial activities. States revised their approaches to commercial activity during the egalitarian era but did not wholly withdraw from economic involvement.

Law and order concerned both state and local officials, who could impose death sentences for numerous crimes in the late eighteenth century. Public pressure to reduce the number of capital offenses swept through the states in the early decades of the nineteenth century. By midcentury northern states had reserved capital punishment for murder and treason and had outlawed public executions (which often drew massive crowds). Southern states clung to a longer list of capital offenses, used in part to control slavery. Fewer death sentences—the result of changes in the law and juries that were reluctant to condemn a person to death for nonlethal offenses such as theft or arson—stimulated the establishment of state prisons, which Pennsylvania, Virginia, and New York pioneered after the Revolution. An "institutional movement" created asylums to incarcerate individuals deemed wayward, incompetent, or in need of public supervision. Beginning in the 1820s lawmakers authorized state-operated facilities for juvenile offenders, the insane and feebleminded, and the blind, as well as almshouses for paupers.[41]

Local officials were tasked with maintaining order in their communities. In the cities, police forces evolved from part-time constables and night watchmen to salaried and uniformed officers under the command of a chief marshal or superintendent. New York City established a salaried police force in 1845; in the following decade it armed its officers and required them to wear uniforms. As police functions crystallized, officers concentrated on preserving law and order and relinquished tasks such as maintaining the streets and caring for the poor. Sheriffs and constables policed counties and rural areas. If local law enforcement could not handle public disturbances, which erupted regularly in large cities, governors called in the state militia. The 1849 Astor Theater riot in New York City, where militiamen killed thirty-one people, documents the extent to which local authorities could exercise lethal force. A notable parallel was the 1844 Kensington riot in Philadelphia, where militiamen fired into the crowds, causing numerous fatalities.[42]

State and local officers' maintenance of community mores increasingly relied on education. Schooling had been a special concern in New England communities since the colonial era, a tradition that expanded with national independence. First Massachusetts and then other states mandated publicly funded schools between the 1820s and 1860s. States provided financial aid to local communities for education, established normal schools for the education of teachers, and founded several state universities (e.g., Virginia, Wisconsin) prior to the US Land Grant College Act of 1862. Northern states far outstripped the South in the support of education.[43]

Besides providing instruction in reading and writing, public schooling was intended to instill moral values. Lawmakers took steps in that direction, especially in the North, by enacting social regulations, such as licensing saloons and requiring that they close on Sundays; in some places the sale of alcoholic beverages was prohibited altogether. Some authorities limited lotteries. Massachusetts and California banned racial segregation in public schools, while Virginia (1836) and Illinois (1820s) adopted laws that maintained a racially segregated society. States reformed marriage law by broadening the grounds for divorce and loosening the tradition of fathers' custody of children. Several northern states protected married women's property rights. The myriad state and local jurisdictions were custodians of public morality during the antebellum years.[44]

FEDERAL POLICY IN THE ANTEBELLUM ERA

President George Washington got down to business in May 1789, working with twenty-six US senators and sixty-four members of the House of Representatives. The First Congress worked for 519 days during three separate sessions, much longer than its subsequent meetings in the early republic. During the eight years of Washington's presidency, legislators passed 324 public acts. Historian–political scientist Leonard White sorted these actions into forty-five separate "functions or activities." The second act on his list, adopted in 1790, levied duties on scores of imported goods ranging from coffee and pickled fish to silk slippers and distilled spirits from Jamaica. In succeeding decades the national government also collected revenue from the sale of public lands and other miscellaneous items, including excise taxes adopted during the War of 1812. The land boom of the 1830s directed a flow of dollars into the federal treasury until the Panic of 1837 and the ensuing business depression ended the speculative scramble. But customs taxes (tariffs) accounted for the largest share of federal receipts during the antebellum era (see table 5.3). The central government's revenue therefore depended on international trade. Most of these tax dollars were spent on defense, which consisted primarily of a small regular army and an equally minuscule navy. Aside from the wars against Great Britain (1812–1815) and Mexico (1846–1848), campaigns that necessitated federal borrowing, US military operations concentrated on subduing and relocating Indians.[45]

Table 5.3. Public Finance and Administration, 1800–1860

	1800	*1820*	*1840*	*1860*
State and local government expenditures (per capita):				
Holcombe-Lacombe estimate	—	$1.15	$2.67	$4.54
Boston	—	$3.97	$6.78	$20.14
State and local government revenue (per capita):				
Wallis estimate	—	—	$2.11	$3.89
Federal expenditures:				
Per capita	$2.16	$1.89	$1.43	$2.00
Percentage for defense	87	67	55	49
Federal revenue:				
Percentage from customs	84	84	69	95
Federal employees:				
Number (thousands)	3	7	18	37
Ratio to population	1,914	1,373	944	838
Postal (thousands)	2.87	4.8	14.3	30.3
Active-duty military (thousands)	6.5	15	21.6	28

Sources: Randall G. Holcombe and Donald J. Lacombe, "The Growth of Local Government in the U.S. from 1820 to 1870," *Journal of Economic History* 61 (2001): 188; Charles P. Huse, *The Financial History of Boston, 1822–1909* (Cambridge, MA: Harvard University Press, 1916), 351; Wallis estimate in Susan B. Carter et al., eds., *Historical Statistics of the United States: Millennial Edition*, vol. 5 (New York: Cambridge University Press, 2006), table Ea-A; US Bureau of the Census, *Historical Statistics of the United States* (Washington, DC: Government Printing Office, 1975), series Y457–459, 463, 335, 353 (federal expenditures and revenue), series Y308–317, Y904 (employees); James Sterling Young, *The Washington Community, 1800–1828* (New York: Harcourt, Brace & World, 1966), table 1, p. 30 (data for 1802).

Revenue is essential for the viability of government, largely to pay public debts. Honoring these obligations was an axiomatic principle for civic officials, as it was for the elites in the early republic. The federal government began its history with fiscal obligations resulting from the Revolutionary War. Alexander Hamilton, the secretary of the treasury and George Washington's chief economic adviser, designed a plan to manage this responsibility. He proposed to repay the federal government's debt at its face value at the time of its issue (not at the lower rates at which the notes later traded in private markets) and to add the states' war debts to this total. Congress adopted Hamilton's scheme in 1790, over objections from the states that had already paid their war debts.

Hamilton also proposed the creation of a national bank, both as an instrument to manage federal finances and as a stimulus to commercial development. Uncertain whether the Constitution authorized such as institution,

Washington asked Hamilton and Secretary of State Thomas Jefferson for their opinions on the matter. Jefferson said it did not, as the Constitution made no explicit provision for a national bank. He charged that Hamilton's financial schemes were "calculated to undermine the Republic," largely by expanding national power at the expense of the states. He added that it was likely that banks would reward mercantilist interests in the North to the detriment of agrarian interests in the South. Hamilton responded that the "necessary and proper" clause of the Constitution (Article I, section 8, clause 18) granted Congress the authority to adopt measures that facilitated the implementation of enumerated powers (those explicitly mentioned in the Constitution). He argued that a bank was integral to the government's fiscal operations. Like Washington, Hamilton was a staunch nationalist who believed that his financial proposals would promote the stability of the central government, in part by encouraging elites to assume a financial stake in its survival. Congress created a Bank of the United States in 1791.[46]

The Jefferson-Hamilton disagreement was just the opening round of a dispute over a national bank and, more broadly, the scope of national power that unfolded over generations. Congress did not renew the bank's charter when it expired in 1811, at which time Jefferson supporters controlled Congress and another Virginian, James Madison, occupied the presidency. The fiscal stress of the War of 1812, coupled with hyperactive state banks that flooded the country with paper banknotes of dubious value, persuaded lawmakers to create a second national bank with regulatory powers in 1816. The debate over banks, most of which were formed by close-knit groups of elites, grew after the depression of the early 1820s, and it became a leading issue in Andrew Jackson's political rise and his election to the presidency in 1828. Jackson vetoed a bill to extend the life of the second Bank of the United States in 1832, claiming that it was unconstitutional, a monopoly controlled by American and foreign elites, and disposed to issue paper banknotes that undermined the economy. Following his reelection in 1832, Jackson restricted the federal government's acceptance of state banknotes (instead of hard money, or specie) and transferred federal deposits from the national bank to selected state banks.

Jackson, his successor Martin Van Buren, and most Democrats embraced a hard-money policy (reliance on specie and a ban on small-denomination banknotes) by the 1840s. Their Whig Party opponents saw banks in general, and a national bank in particular, as essential props for an emerging commercial economy. But the Whiggish outlook remained the minority position until the Civil War, when Congress reestablished national banks. By this time, state-chartered banks—some private, some joint ventures with the government—had proliferated.

Collecting revenue, managing federal finances (including the minting of coins), adding territory to the republic and admitting new states, distributing the public domain, fighting Indians, delivering mail (to post offices, not yet to individual addresses), and maintaining a diplomatic posture that avoided entanglement with the major European powers constituted the primary functions of the national government between 1789 and 1860. Congress did, however, undertake other activities that collectively assumed significance.

Waterways played a critical role in the nation's early development, which Congress acknowledged by voting for programs that facilitated ocean, harbor, and river transportation. The Light House Service, originally assigned to the Treasury Department, represented an important aid to coastal shipping. Surveying and offering technical advice for the improvement of harbors and removing impediments on major rivers were ongoing endeavors usually assigned to the Army Corps of Engineers, founded in 1802. Between 1824 and James Polk's veto of a rivers and harbors bill in 1846, Congress regularly allotted money for the improvement of navigable inland rivers. Subsidies paid to marine contractors for carrying the mail added another dimension to federal assistance for water transportation. The government began to inspect steamboat boilers in 1838 and added teeth to the law in 1852, when it required the annual licensing of pilots and engineers and improved enforcement. Congress regulated space on passenger vessels and provided for the inspection of imported drugs. National lawmakers invested in canals and funded hospitals for seamen.[47]

National policymakers also assisted in the development of land transportation. They subsidized the construction of a "national road" from Maryland to the Midwest and, beginning in 1850, gave grants of public land to facilitate the construction of privately owned railroads, a practice that continued until 1871. The US Army built military roads in both territories and states. Since 1803 Congress had allocated between 3 and 5 percent of receipts from the sale of public lands to the states for internal improvements. Although legal and political views placed rigid limits on the extent of federal involvement in internal improvements, the federal government's contribution to this endeavor was important. Other significant actions that aided the economy included minting coins, patenting inventions, negotiating trade treaties, chasing down pirates, manufacturing weapons (at arsenals in Springfield, Massachusetts, and Harpers Ferry, Virginia), and transferring millions of acres of land, largely to private individuals. The army encouraged settlement of the public domain by exploring and mapping the West, performed by the Army Corps of Topographical Engineers. The navy undertook coastal surveys, providing a valuable service for a seafaring nation. The navy's exploration and mapping of the Pacific (1838–1842) under the command of Lieutenant Charles Wilkes rendered valuable geographic information. The US Military Academy at West Point, authorized in 1802, was among the first colleges to train engineers; the War Department loaned some of them to act as consultants on private transportation projects, especially railroads, until 1838.[48]

The Naval Observatory at Annapolis, opened the year before the US Naval Academy was established there, was an important site of scientific activity. Army and navy explorations and surveys, plus the creation of the Smithsonian Institution (1846) to serve as a sponsor of and repository for scientific information in the nation's capital, put the federal government in the forefront of the promotion of science in the antebellum period. If one expands the interpretation of science to include education and publication, the national role in learning and science was even broader. The decennial census of the United States, first conducted in 1790, was the nation's largest single data collection project through most of the long nineteenth century. Beginning with the admission of Ohio to the union in 1803, the United States granted public lands for the support of public schools in the states. The expansion of the postal system greatly widened the distribution of printed information in the form of books, pamphlets, and newspapers. Postal policy, in effect, subsidized the publication of newspapers, giving the United States the largest circulation in the world by 1810. In 1851 Congress mandated a flat fee of 3 cents for a stamp that would send a letter anywhere in the United States. Contracts to serve as mail carriers constituted a steady revenue stream for private transportation companies. A survey of the national uses of power would be incomplete without emphasizing federal support of slavery, especially via national court rulings.[49]

Though administratively small by modern standards and constricted by ideological controversies, the federal government was hardly impotent during the antebellum years. Its wide range of activities was politically possible in large part because, as historian Brian Balogh argues, they were performed primarily "out of sight," unlike the more visible presence of state and local governments. But behind the cloak of unpublicized actions, national officials played an important role in the development of the American state. The inventory of federal actions here and in chapter 4 documents the numerous ways the national government influenced society in the antebellum era. When state and local governments are included in the civic equation, the antebellum era hardly looks like a "night-watchman state," doing little of consequence. Governments exercised a plenitude of powers over life and property in the early nineteenth century, albeit in a style wedded to communal associations, voluntarism, and reliance on private enterprise.[50] Rhetorical genuflections to the tenets of America's civic ideology, uttered so predictably in public ceremonies, obscure the governmental side of this dichotomy. Therein lies the paradox of American statebuilding. Democratic theory heralded individual freedoms, but in practice, officials increasingly used the powers of government.

6

The Dynamics of Antebellum Governance

Late in 1807 President Thomas Jefferson signed a bill that forbade American vessels from transporting goods to foreign countries. This "embargo" was Jefferson's solution to a dispute with Great Britain and France. Locked in combat during the Napoleonic Wars, both Britain and France had seized and impounded Americans ships purportedly destined for one of the combatants. After the British destroyed much of the French navy at the Battle of Trafalgar, Napoleon resorted to impounding foreign vessels in European ports, while the Royal Navy roamed the sea freely. The British also snatched seamen believed to be British nationals from American vessels, sometimes within sight of American shores.

Jefferson saw three options to address this quandary: war, economic pressure, or nothing. War went against a fundamental tenet of Jeffersonian philosophy, which regarded the maintenance of a large military force as a step toward executive tyranny and a cause of fiscal hardship. But a more immediate impediment was Britain's possession of the world's strongest navy, while the United States had hardly any navy at all. Likewise, Napoleon had the world's largest army on the continent of Europe, and Jefferson would have had to field a military force almost from scratch. Thus, an armed confrontation with France would have been disastrous. But to do nothing perpetuated the humiliating interference by foreign powers. An embargo, however, could be ordered with the stroke of a pen.

Congress granted the president formidable powers to implement the embargo. Its immediate direction was in the hands of Jefferson and his secretary of the treasury, Albert Gallatin. Their principal assistants were customs collectors, who numbered around eighty-five and were scattered at ports up and down the East Coast. Their instructions were to review the cargo on vessels and deny departure certificates unless the ship intended to stay within coastal waters. Cheating by ship captains led to a tightening of enforcement powers, whereby collectors were authorized to seize ships and their cargoes on the *suspicion* that a vessel was bound for an illegal destination. In the larger ports, such as New York and Philadelphia, collectors had a few assistants and some revenue cutters. US marshals, district attorneys, and federal courts were called on when legal disputes arose. The country's small navy was authorized to stop American merchantmen at sea. And, if push came to shove, both the regular army and the state militia could be called to discipline scofflaws, as occurred along the New York–Canada border.

These were extraordinary administrative powers under any circumstances. In Jefferson's case, they made a mockery of his pledge to limit federal powers and to protect states' rights. In a technical sense, the policy was successful, as American exports dropped 80 percent; however, it did not stop English or French depredation of American shipping. Moreover, what had seemed like a good idea to the president won few political points in Federalist New England, where maritime commerce provided a livelihood for many.[1]

ADMINISTRATION

The contention that there was no state in America during the nineteenth century rests largely on the absence of a rationally ordered, centralized national bureaucracy. There is truth to this claim, but it is misleading when considering the entire polity. Fiscal parsimony, fragmented jurisdiction, and antipathy to bureaucracies with full-time career employees were prevalent during the period. But these impediments did not prevent officials from exerting authority or performing numerous tasks. For instance, a small staff of federal employees oversaw the distribution of millions of acres of the public domain, albeit in a process laced with flaws and scandals (see chapter 4). Native Americans were pushed westward—forcibly, when treaty negotiations failed. Natives were uprooted by the thousands in Georgia and surrounding areas and deported to the Indian Territory west of the Mississippi River in an operation assigned to the US Army. Congress adopted a variety of regulations concerning the collection of customs duties on imported goods, a function handled by collectors in the Treasury Department. The United States also inspected steamboat boilers, levying fines and imprisonment for violations. In these and other instances, the federal government pursued a variety of objectives, despite an underdeveloped administrative establishment.

The Federal Workforce

Notwithstanding congressional penny-pinching, the federal civil workforce expanded in the antebellum years. The national government hired 3,000 civilian workers in 1800; this number grew to 18,000 in 1840 and 37,000 in 1860. The vast majority of these civil servants were local postmasters, most of whom worked part time (retaining their jobs as storekeepers or newspaper editors) and were compensated by fees. Most localities had at least one post office, and many had two or more. Most deputy postmasters lived in small communities.[2] The other sizable group of federal employees worked in customhouses collecting tariff duties. New York's customhouse, the nation's busiest, had 861 employees on the payroll in 1858. Only 1,000 federal employees worked in Washington, DC, in 1841—a number that doubled by 1861.[3]

Fear of a standing military force, a reluctance to spend public funds, and the great oceanic barrier that separated the United States from the powerhouses of Europe kept America's regular army and navy tiny. As the country edged toward war with Great Britain in 1812, it had an army of 6,000; when Polk considered war with Mexico in 1846, the military establishment consisted of 20,000 members, less than half of them army personnel. Both wars required military leaders to rely on militia units (poorly organized, partially armed amateurs) and volunteers (new recruits) to field a creditable army. Andrew Jackson's force that smashed the British attack at New Orleans in 1815 numbered roughly 4,500 men drawn from the Tennessee and Kentucky militia, two battalions of free African Americans, Choctaw Indians, and a battalion of followers of the Louisiana pirate Jean Laffite. General Winfield Scott, who led the American expeditionary force from the port of Veracruz to Mexico City in 1847, was halted midway because his volunteers decided to return home when their one-year enlistments expired. Even with their replacements, Scott's contingent that stormed the city numbered only about 6,000. A combined American force of just hundreds routed the Mexican defenders in California.[4] Except for some engagements against Indians, who were highly skilled in small-scale encounters, the American military compiled a surprisingly successful record in view of Congress's budgetary stinginess.

The federal administrative establishment limped along in the antebellum era with an approach that produced only modest improvements in organizational capacity. The emphasis at the presidential level was to pick administrators of known talent and good character to head departments over which they were given wide managerial discretion. Federal department secretaries and bureau chiefs could keep an eye on their staffs in Washington, but much of the government's work was spread across far-flung places. This complicated the supervision of land offices, post offices, and customs collectors—functions that offered opportunities for fraud and scandal. Land office officials sometimes helped speculators obtain the best acreage. Private vendors schemed to win contracts to transport the mail. Customs officials enforced revenue laws that imposed fines on merchants for violations, a portion of which was retained by the collector. Postmasters, customs collectors, and law enforcement personnel were compensated by fees, a system inherently prone to abuse. The rise of political parties in the 1830s put pressure on presidents to reward loyal supporters with patronage jobs in government, leading to some regrettable appointments. The federal administrative apparatus grew larger as the nation and its business expanded, but it underwent only minimal administrative rationalization. In the Jacksonian era (1828–1850s), good administration rested on choosing individuals of "good character," not on improving the efficiency of governance.[5]

Administrative Capacity

Why did administrative capacity remain underdeveloped in the antebellum era? Three factors tell much of the story. First, prevailing ideology did not support a robust bureaucracy. In fact, Jeffersonians of the early nineteenth century and many politicos during the Jacksonian era saw executives as a potential threat to liberty. Congress questioned virtually every item in appropriations requests, becoming even more parsimonious during depression years. Antebellum America at all levels of government, but especially in the states and localities, relied heavily on part-time administrators, most of whom were volunteers who served without compensation.

The norm of amateur, part-time public servants rather than career politicians was reflected in the schedules of Congress and the state legislatures. Congress stayed in session for about 300 days out of each two-year cycle; most House members served a single two-year term. They got along without any personal staff assistance, but with the emergence of permanent "standing" committees by midcentury, the House did hire a clerk. Committee members developed close relationships with administrative department heads. State legislative sessions lasted, on average, a couple of months each year—until constitutional revisions in the 1840s inaugurated the trend toward biennial meetings. Most state lawmakers served only a single term. Committees of legislators at every level, from towns and city councils up to Congress, handled a large portion of administrative business. Ideology reinforced the conventional practice of relying on these elected amateurs and nonelected citizens to attend to public matters.[6]

Second, the technologies associated with modern administrative practice had not been invented or perfected by 1860. Government workers throughout the antebellum era copied documents by hand using quills and inkwells. Until midcentury, offices were heated by wood-burning fireplaces and illuminated by candles or whale oil lamps. Indoor plumbing and electric lighting were developed after 1870. Typewriters, adding machines, telephones, reliable fountain pens, and modern filing cabinets were advances of the late nineteenth century. Record keeping was haphazard if not nonexistent for certain activities, and there was inadequate safe (e.g., fireproof) storage space for documents. Three generations passed before government employees of the 1830s worked in modern-looking government offices. Their field offices were many miles away from Washington, DC—3,000 miles in the case of the Pacific coast states. A transcontinental telegraph was not operational until 1861. During the Jacksonian era, efforts were made to beef up inspections of field administrators. Still, geography and technology created barriers for the monitoring of administrative activities.[7]

Third, most civic tasks and the bulk of public administration were handled at the local level, with minimal assistance and oversight from state governments. Few studies of state-local administration exist for the pre–Civil War period, which complicates an assessment of the antebellum polity. What is clear is that the 10,000 or so general-purpose governments at midcentury relied on elected officials and appointed volunteers to oversee various civic functions, from law enforcement and education to care of the poor and road maintenance. Many if not most of these positions were part time and uncompensated. This amateur, citizen-based system fit comfortably with the rising democratic tide that swept the nation during the first half of the nineteenth century.

Nonetheless, a trend toward salaried, full-time administrative personnel for specialized functions (e.g., engineers) was under way in the larger cities by midcentury. The four largest municipalities maintained police forces of more than 2,600 men in the mid-1850s, a figure that equaled the total number of federal employees in Washington. The 1850 census recorded 91,000 public school teachers, exceeding the number of federal employees.[8] The city workers who maintained the streets and the rural residents who performed roadwork probably exceeded the number of federal workers as well, including the mechanics and laborers hired for particular projects, such as in navy shipyards. This fragmentary evidence points to a sizable and growing administrative presence at the local level by midcentury.

Foreign Policy and Domestic Security

The lack of a full-time, salaried bureaucracy in most areas of governance in the decades before the Civil War constrained government but was not a fatal handicap. The handling of foreign affairs illustrates this point. The Constitution assigned management of the diplomatic and military establishments to the president of the United States, who delegated oversight of most foreign matters to the Department of State, created in 1789. During Thomas Jefferson's tenure as its first secretary, the State Department had five ministers (now called ambassadors) and sixteen consular officers, plus several clerks in the home office. In Jefferson's first term as president, the State Department had nine employees in Washington, including the secretary, who oversaw ten ministers, sixty-three consulates, and thirty-four treaty commissioners and agents. In 1842 the Diplomatic Bureau of the State Department under Daniel Webster (who served from 1841 to 1843) had thirty employees grouped into four areas of responsibility, twenty-one missions (now called embassies), and 160 consulates. Ten years later, the State Department had fifty-seven US-based employees, some of whom were ordinary office workers. Chief clerks of sections in the Diplomatic Bureau were akin to middle managers in today's world; some had considerable experience in the State Department. The consular service consisted of 121 persons, including twenty ministers, each of whom was granted a one-person secretarial staff in 1855.[9]

The number of staff assigned to the State Department and its Foreign Service clearly grew between 1789 and 1860. Numeric and geographic expansion, however, does not necessarily mean more effective policy, but this line of reasoning is misleading for diplomacy. Foreign policy is formulated by presidents, sometimes alone but usually in consultation with the secretary of state and, from time to time, other department secretaries and members of Congress. All the presidents between Thomas Jefferson and John Quincy Adams (1801–1829) had been secretaries of state; a number of subsequent secretaries, such as Henry Clay, John Calhoun, and Daniel Webster, were prominent members of Congress. President James Madison, a former secretary of state and member of Congress, used his secretary of state, James Monroe, to communicate with the House and Senate Foreign Relations Committees. President James Buchanan, who had been a secretary of state as well as minister to Russia and Great Britain, handled important foreign policy matters himself. Besides their authority to manage diplomacy, presidents also commanded the armed forces, which enhanced their personal control of foreign relations.[10]

Prior to 1815, France, Spain, and Great Britain represented the principal international threats to American security. France seized American ships in the Caribbean in the late 1790s, in conjunction with Napoleon's campaign in Europe. John Adams's administration strengthened the navy, which countered French depredations, but the president negotiated a settlement in 1800 that sidestepped a larger war. Aside from its bungled intervention in Mexico during the 1860s, France lost interest in North America after the slave revolt in Haiti and its sale of Louisiana. Great Britain was a more durable threat, both along the Canadian border and in the Atlantic, where its ships preyed on American vessels and hindered commerce with Europe until 1815. Unable to negotiate a solution to British impressment of American seamen or the impoundment of American ships, and amid charges that Britain had encouraged Indian attacks in the Great Lakes region, President Madison asked Congress to consider war in 1812. Despite the country's lack of preparation, Congress voted for a military confrontation. The United States was fortunate to achieve a standoff during the War of 1812, largely because Britain's primary opponent was Napoleon in Europe.

There was a reduction of diplomatic tensions after 1815. In the first half of the nineteenth century, the world contained far fewer national states than it did after decolonization following World War II. Lacking strong states, Africa and Asia posed no immediate threat to American security. The Napoleonic Wars had sparked independence revolts in Latin America that drove Spain from most of its colonies, leaving weak states in its wake. Mexico, on America's southern border, lacked the military capacity to repel the comparatively small American invasion force that captured its capital in 1847. The American navy was tiny during the pre–Civil War era, but it had sufficient resources to blockade Mexico along its Gulf coast and along the Pacific coast as far north as San Francisco during the Mexican War. American naval vessels also subdued hostile North African principalities that preyed on US commerce, as well as pirates on dozens of occasions in the early nineteenth century. Commodore Matthew Perry's eight-ship armada apparently convinced the Japanese in 1854 that it would be better to negotiate a treaty than to take on the US Fleet moored in Tokyo Bay.[11]

American foreign policy's success in keeping the ship of state afloat has often been attributed to the country's geographic isolation from the powerhouses of Europe. There is some truth to this conclusion, but it can also be argued that presidents and secretaries of state made decisions at critical moments that deflected threats and protected the national interest. Thomas Jefferson, James Madison, John Quincy Adams, and James Polk were instrumental in the expansion of the United States, increasing the country's land area severalfold. All things being equal, more territory meant more wealth and, from an international perspective, greater security.

The most persistent threat to domestic security during the antebellum era came from Native Americans. Pacification of belligerent Indians was the principal activity of the regular army and state militias. Indians were dangerous, but they did not threaten the stability of the republic. Time and again, until 1871, Amerindians were coerced or bribed to enter into so-called treaties in which they relinquished their traditional lands. Thereafter, relations with individual tribes settled into a bureaucratic phase. The nerve center of these transactions was the Bureau of Indian Affairs in the War Department, until it was shifted to the Department of the Interior in 1849. The bureau's small staff doled out minimal assistance to relocated tribes and attempted to turn Native Americans into literate, Bible-carrying farmers.[12]

The Courts

Besides adjudicating conflicts, courts also served as administrative units before the Civil War. The tempo of this workload increased as the antebellum era progressed and the statute books expanded. Most of this activity took place at the state and local levels, not only in courts but also in legislatures, county councils, and aldermanic bodies, which had certain judicial powers in the early nineteenth century. In New York and Philadelphia, for example, aldermen functioned as magistrates who dealt with minor criminal offenses. It is also important to note that extralegal justice at the hands of vigilante groups prevailed in the West on occasion.[13]

Several developments reflect the reliance on law as a tool of administration at the local level. States and municipalities adopted a variety of regulations in the antebellum era, and as the range of these actions increased, so did the legal challenges to them. Many of these actions were upheld by courts under a doctrine known as "state police powers." Emerging in the early nineteenth century, the concept of police powers held that state governments (and their municipal agents) possessed broad authority to adopt measures that protected the health, safety, morals, and welfare of the community. Clearly, the term "policing" encompassed a much wider scope of activity in the early nineteenth century than it does today. Whereas the modern expectation is that policing involves essentially patrolling to reduce street crime and investigating crimes when they occur, police activity in the antebellum era ranged from maintaining the streets and removing nuisances to restricting offensive behaviors (e.g., cursing) and regulating economic activities (e.g., issuing trade licenses or setting commodity prices). Not directly outlined in constitutions, the police power emerged from state and federal court interpretations of the common law (traditional law) and practical experience, as in the case of the "law of nuisances" and the "rights of necessity." City officials relied on the latter concept, for example, as a justification to destroy private residences to contain fires. The US Supreme Court acknowledged the concept in several cases between 1824 (*Gibbons v. Odgen*) and 1850. In *Cooley v. Board of Wardens of the Port of Philadelphia* (1851), the Supreme Court explicitly accepted the doctrine as a valid state power to regulate the community.[14]

A second strand of state law was oriented around property rights and economic development, areas in which judges and legislators sparred. Out of these actions and negotiations emerged statutory and legal standards for the incorporation of businesses, guidelines for eminent domain, torts (civil wrongs involving negligence and liability), and contracts. Torts and contracts were concepts developed primarily by state jurists.[15]

As state and municipal regulations, services, and taxes grew, so did legal challenges. Increasingly, state courts examined the constitutionally of these actions during a process called judicial review. State judges upheld most of these state actions, often based on the police power, but an increasing number of statutes and ordinances were overturned at the century's midpoint. In New York, for example, sixteen laws were challenged during the 1820s, and one was struck down as a violation of the state constitution; in the 1850s, 127 laws were challenged, and thirty-four were disallowed. In Massachusetts, sixty-two laws were reviewed by the state court through 1860, and ten were declared unconstitutional. In Virginia, by comparison, only two laws failed on grounds of constitutionality. These judicial contrasts reflect the diversity of state actions. Nonetheless, state courts seemed increasingly willing to hold municipalities liable for certain actions that harmed property owners. For instance, in 1842 New York State's chief justice ruled that New York City was liable for damages to a plaintiff whose mill along the Croton River, which supplied water to the city, was demolished when a dam burst. This case put the city on notice that its efforts to promote the public interest could be deemed harmful to private interests.[16]

State actions became subject to double legal scrutiny when the US Supreme Court assumed the prerogative of negating statutes as unconstitutional, a power not explicitly expressed in the Constitution. The key event in this judicial development was *Marbury v. Madison* (1803), in which the court held that section 13 of the Judiciary Act of 1801 gave it the power to rule on the constitutionality of an executive action. This decision arose in the aftermath of a tense political period, as the United States confronted France in an undeclared war (1798–1800) and President John Adams and the Federalists in Congress enacted the Alien and Sedition Acts (1798), which allowed the deportation of "dangerous" immigrants and jail time for critics of administration policy. Thomas Jefferson and James Madison, leaders of the opposition, responded to the Alien and Sedition Acts with resolutions adopted by the legislatures of Kentucky and Virginia (1798) that condemned attempts to stifle speech and asserted that states had the right to judge the constitutionality of *national* actions. Similar charges of misconduct by President Adams continued during the campaign for the presidency in 1800, which Jefferson won. In 1802 the new president and his congressional supporters repealed the Judiciary Act of 1801.

In the last days of his administration, Adams had appointed John Marshall, a Federalist and a strong nationalist, as chief justice of the Supreme Court. Marshall shaped his decision in *Marbury* to avoid the political pitfalls lurking in the supercharged partisan atmosphere. In a clever move, Marshall held that section 13 of the Judiciary Act violated the principle of the separation of powers between the legislative and executive branches and was therefore unconstitutional. This concession reduced the taint of partisanship, yet Marshall went on to assert the Supreme Court's authority to declare an act of Congress unconstitutional. Despite Jefferson's refusal to accept the ruling, *Marbury* legitimized the independence of the Supreme Court and elevated the judiciary's stature as a coequal branch of the national government.

The reach of the Supreme Court expanded into state statutes in *Fletcher v. Peck* (1810), which held that Georgia had violated the clause of the Constitution prohibiting states from "impairing the obligation of contracts." During the remainder of his tenure as chief justice (1801–1835), Marshall reviewed numerous state actions, issuing opinions that defined the legal boundaries of federalism and enhanced national authority. Roger B. Taney, a southern slaveholder who served as chief justice from 1835 to 1864, took a less nationalist stance than his predecessor but continued to clarify the relationship between state and national power. Before the Civil War, the high court struck down only two federal laws but negated thirty-five state laws, mostly between the 1820s and 1860. The Marshall court aggressively expanded the Supreme Court's authority, ruling that it had jurisdiction in all cases involving the Constitution (1816), including those in state courts (1821). Marshall struck down a Maryland tax on the Bank of the United States (1819) as an unconstitutional intrusion on a legitimate federal activity.

In *Gibbons v. Ogden* (1824) Marshall ruled that New York's charter granting a monopoly to a steamboat company navigating across the Hudson River to New Jersey violated a national law that licensed coastal vessels. Monopoly charters were common in the early republic, and the *Gibbons* decision was read as an encouragement of private commercial activity. Taney expanded this line of thinking, most famously in the *Charles River Bridge* case (1837), in which he disallowed an injunction that would have prevented a second company from bridging the Charles River. The same year, the Supreme Court rejected a complaint that banknotes issued by the Bank of Kentucky violated the Constitution's restriction on states to "emit Bills of Credit." In *Swift v. Tyson* (1842), announced in the midst of a severe depression, the justices held that state courts need not be bound by decisions involving disputes between citizens of different states. That ruling opened the way for federal courts to formulate "general principles . . . of commercial jurisprudence," a doctrine later used to remove state impediments to a national commercial market. The high court questioned state restrictions on slavery as well. In 1826 Pennsylvania adopted a personal liberty law designed to hamper slave catchers' efforts to retrieve runaways. The Supreme Court ruled the law unconstitutional in 1842 (*Prigg v. Pennsylvania*), indicating that Pennsylvania's action conflicted with the national fugitive slave law enacted in 1793. Once again, the Supreme Court had limited state jurisdiction, in this case involving a subject that would continue to cause political and legal tension.[17]

State and Local Governance

Although the "capacity" of government in the antebellum era has been questioned, it is clear that many jurisdictions, notably large cities, broadened their administrative activities, particularly with regard to police, jails, education, streets, water supply, and fire protection. Boston, for example, appointed superintendents (also called marshals and commissioners) for streets, sewers, health, fire, police, water, and engineering between 1827 and 1851. Cities substantially increased expenditures on these services. Differentiation of administrative units also took place in the states. Between 1827 and 1857, for example, Illinois created boards for the state penitentiary, school for the deaf, hospital for the insane, school for the blind, geology, and education. New York opened Castle Garden in Manhattan to process immigrants in 1855. How much these steps improved states' administrative effectiveness is unclear, but the enactments themselves indicate that officials were attending to a widening set of civic concerns. A rough parallel exists for the national government, which established the Library of Congress, US Military Academy, Coastal Survey, General Land Office, Bureau of Indian Affairs, Patent Office, US Naval Academy, Smithsonian Institution, and Government Printing Office between 1800 and 1860. One student of federal administrative units documented a tripling of federal agencies between 1792 and 1860.[18]

THE EVOLUTION OF ANTEBELLUM GOVERNANCE

Assessing the contours of nineteenth-century governance in the United States must consider all three levels of government, which encompassed nearly three dozen states and thousands of local governments by 1860. Given this array of civic forums and the lack of any comprehensive documentation related to their performance, conclusions about antebellum governance remain partially conjectural. The available evidence, however, points to an incremental expansion of the public sector during the antebellum era, with policy additions accelerating after the early 1840s. This record may look minuscule from the perspective of the twenty-first century, but with 1789 as a base point, this expansion was substantial.[19]

What drove this evolution? Locating the causes of historical development is a speculative enterprise, given the challenge of weighing the influence of critical factors amid the unpredictable course of historical events. The approach here is to review the dynamics of the most important factors driving civic development. On the short list of key determinants are socioeconomic change, economic depression, the rise of political parties, war, and political structures.

Socioeconomic Change

The United States underwent an extraordinary territorial expansion in the antebellum era, which helped fuel population growth, economic development, and the creation of thousands of new political units. In the early decades of the nineteenth century the nation was filled with young people who were restless and on the move. More than half the population was younger than twenty years old in 1830 and 1850; white males in their twenties and thirties were twice as numerous as older men in both years. The generation that came to maturity in around 1830 experienced the opening of the Erie Canal, the advent of steamboat travel on inland and coastal waters, and the United States' expansion to the Pacific. Young white men who came of age in around 1850 could have ridden the railroad, likely heard talk of building a transcontinental line, may have seen telegraph wires, and perhaps considered searching for gold in California. Most did not push that far west, yet at midcentury, 45 percent of the population lived outside the boundaries of the original states.[20]

These changes had two important consequences. First, social and economic development bred new outlooks that were increasingly at odds with the assumptions of pre-Revolutionary America. Religious revivals, new views about personal responsibility and character, and eagerness to participate in the country's economic progress altered both attitudes and behavior. The proliferation of institutions such as churches, schools and colleges, reform societies, publishers, artisan associations, and political parties helped disseminate new ideas. Charles Sellers, who argued that a "market revolution" spawned competitive commercial activity, saw a host of social consequences following this transformation, especially the erosion of family and communal traditions. In Robert Wiebe's estimation, early nineteenth-century America created a world of nontraditional "choices" flowing from socioeconomic change, which opened up numerous opportunities in life.[21]

The benefits of this new sociocultural milieu were largely restricted to white Protestant men and, through family ties, white women. Social reforms forged by legal changes and cultural practices during the middle of the century undercut the traditional male patriarchy, creating separate gender spheres of domesticity, especially in the North. African Americans (most of whom were slaves), Indians, and non-Protestant immigrants remained largely outside these webs of change. But for white males, most of whom became eligible to vote by the 1830s, swirls of nonconventional thinking eroded older civic habits, especially deference to elites who commanded most positions of power through 1815.

Second, socioeconomic change spawned new problems for society. With territorial expansion, officials assumed responsibility for governing a huge landmass that spanned the continent, a task that Europeans thought was impossible in a republic. New technologies generated their own hazards, such as boiler explosions on steamboats and fires ignited by sparks flying out of locomotive smokestacks. People poured into cities, creating difficulties related to increased population density (e.g., sewerage) and conflicts due to ethnic antagonism (e.g., riots).

Economic Depression

The antebellum economy was buffeted by three economic depressions popularly identified as the Panics of 1819, 1837, and 1857. Each financial crisis was followed by an economic slowdown manifested by steep declines in agricultural prices and real estate values, rising unemployment, mortgage foreclosures, business failures, and social turmoil. Sharp, sudden shocks to the economy always have political repercussions; for instance, "tax revolts" can disrupt and redirect the patterns of politics, and their effects can last for years. Generally, the popular reaction to depression is a discrediting of the prevailing political ideology and incumbent officeholders, especially with regard to public finances.[22]

The depression that following the Panic of 1819 was partially a reaction to the economic consequences of the Napoleonic Wars, very unusual weather in 1816, and the boom-bust cycle in agricultural production that followed. Signs of economic distress were apparent in the decline of agricultural exports, plummeting land sales, banks' suspension of specie payments, and real estate foreclosures. Numerous state governments enacted "stay laws" that delayed property foreclosures and relief laws that loaned paper money, easing the financial sting of indebtedness. Resentment of paper money and bankers' cliquish favoritism in issuing loans fueled antibank policies in parts of the country. Cotton production in South Carolina's Piedmont region never recovered from falling prices, a decline that some southerners blamed on the tariffs of 1824 and 1828. The economic slump, along with the experiences of the War of 1812, generated support for government sponsorship of transportation improvements as a way of regenerating commercial activity. Hard times spawned a backlash against the use of banknotes and appeared to foster the trend toward greater democracy, especially in the West.[23]

The economic recovery under way by the mid-1820s became an expansionary boom in the 1830s, which lasted until a devastating banking collapse swept across the country in 1837. A mild recovery in 1838 was cut short by a second financial crisis in 1839 that ignited a deep and prolonged economic depression. Urban workers, businesses, banks, and farmers were caught in the grip of a severe commercial contraction. The suspension of specie exchange for banknotes provoked riots. By 1842 roughly half of American banks no longer existed. Agricultural commodity prices stayed low through the middle of the 1840s. Consequently, the depression cut sharply into state governments' revenue, and as a result, nine states defaulted on their debts, incurred largely to finance transportation projects. The political reaction to what was widely considered fiscally imprudent behavior produced a "revolution against internal improvements." Most states stopped construction on uncompleted projects, turned to budgetary retrenchment, and amended their constitutions to prohibit state investment in and ownership of corporations. Constitutional limits were imposed on state indebtedness. Because legislators were thought to be complicit in these fiscal crises, states began to substitute biennial for annual meetings of their legislatures.[24]

These restrictions on the states suggest that public promotion of the economy met an impenetrable roadblock, but that was not quite true. Some states (e.g., Massachusetts) escaped draconian limits on their legislatures, while others found loopholes around constitutional limitations. Moreover, state constitutional changes did not affect most municipalities or Congress. Public assistance to private corporations continued over the next several decades, albeit at lower levels, in part because railroads relied primarily on private sources of capital after the depression lifted. The backlash against state investment in internal improvements was a conspicuous impact of the depression, but it was not the only one. Taking a cue from Horace Greeley, the New York newspaper editor who advised the unemployed to go "to the Great West," streams of migrants headed to Texas and the Pacific coast. The lingering hard times and the flood of westward migrants during the early 1840s influenced the election of President James Polk, who provoked a war with Mexico over the annexation of Texas.[25]

Political Parties

The depressions that followed the Panics of 1819 and 1837 had a significant impact on political parties. During the 1790s, Federalist supporters of the

Washington and Adams administrations and their Jeffersonian Republican opponents in Congress had battled over financial policy and foreign affairs. After Jefferson's election as president, this partisan division limped along through the War of 1812. During these years, gentleman elites dominated leadership positions and discouraged a broadening of popular democracy. The depression of the 1820s, which was widely seen as caused by elites' control of banks and their irresponsible speculation, fanned popular resentment of the privileged classes. This animosity was a factor in undermining the traditional fear of political parties, which had historically been regarded as disloyal factions that threatened the viability of the state. The expansion of eligible voters (through legal changes and population growth), the trend toward popularly elected presidential electors, and the admission of new states fed a growing acceptance of parties as an essential component of electoral politics. Andrew Jackson—Indian fighter, hero of the Battle of New Orleans, slave-owning planter from Tennessee, and bitter foe of banks—took advantage of these trends to win the presidency in 1828. His veto of the bill to renew the charter of the Bank of United States (1832), his hard-money policy (restricting loans that circulated as paper currency), and his aggressive defense of depositing federal revenue in selected state banks galvanized an opposition that coalesced into the Whig Party.[26]

By 1838 Democratic (Jacksonian) and Whig Parties existed in most states. Unlike the first set of parties, the second party system evolved into competitive electoral organizations that circulated party platforms, held nominating conventions, and sponsored gala electioneering rallies. The impact of this new style of politicking is demonstrated by dramatic increases in voter turnout, especially for national elections. The Panic of 1837 dropped a bombshell on this new political arrangement, and the recovery in 1839 lapsed into depression in the early 1840s. Democrats lost badly in 1840, when Whigs won a majority in Congress and in many state legislatures and defeated incumbent president Martin Van Buren. Then voters punished the Whigs for failing to produce satisfactory remedies to the malaise. The party's delegation in the House of Representatives was reduced by half, and its majority status in the state legislatures was cut by an even larger proportion. Whig fortunes sank further when the Mexican War and proposals to limit the expansion of slavery in the late 1840s posed stiff challenges to party cohesion.[27]

Although sectional conflict in the mid-1850s doomed the Whigs, their competition with Democrats over two decades influenced public policy. Democrats opposed a national bank and local banks in many states, supported hard-money policies that favored specie over paper banknotes, and advocated low tariff rates, a position favored in cotton-growing regions. Viewed in broader terms, the Democratic mind-set resisted the development of a market economy that rested on financial credit, governmental promotion of internal improvements, and free public education, positions the Whigs supported. Northern Whigs were hostile to the expansion of slavery in the new territories, advocated restrictions on immigrants and immigration, and favored the regulation of liquor and social reforms, goals that were anathema to Democrats. The party of Jackson consistently supported budgetary parsimony and constitutional restrictions on state fiscal authority.[28]

In 1857 another financial panic shocked the economy, triggering a commercial slump that lasted until 1860 in the North and influenced party performance. The depression arrived during the birth of the Republican Party, which had replaced the northern Whigs when they fractured over slavery. Initially formed to block the expansion of slavery into new territories, the Republican Party added economic measures to its agenda—namely, free public land (homestead allotments), more flexible banking and credit, and a protective tariff—programs promoted as depression remedies. President James Buchanan and the Democrats hunkered down around Jacksonian proscriptions, opposing all three measures. Republican victories in 1860 and the resignation of southern Democrats from Congress opened the door to the new economic program.[29]

Political parties, in short, influenced economic policy. But the contributions of the Democrats and the Whigs to statebuilding may have been equally significant. Political parties were the only secular organizations in the United States that bridged the federal system, at least in terms of sharing a common affiliation in elections for Congress, president, and state offices. Parties thus contributed to the national integration of a noncentralized polity. In their electioneering capacities, parties welcomed all white males (certainly for their votes, and usually for their participation in party activities such as electioneering parades) and embodied egalitarian qualities. And in their articulation of common values, such as the connection between the union and liberty, the acceptance of legal constitutionalism, and the characterization of America as a land of opportunity and progress, parties promoted national identity. The tonality of each party's nationalism differed, but sufficient common ground existed to make political participation a key element of American citizenship.[30]

War

The United States fought two declared wars in the antebellum era, as well as many engagements against Native Americans. Despite the relatively small scale of battlefield encounters during the War of 1812, the conflict left a significant mark on the new republic. The most important military event was

Andrew Jackson's victory over the British force at New Orleans. Jackson's victory blunted the possibility of Britain reestablishing a foothold in the center of North America, with an outlet on the Gulf of Mexico. The war's outcome also led to the demilitarization of the northern border, thereby reducing the probability of repeated conflict with Great Britain. Victory in New Orleans forecast the end of Spain's control of Florida, which resulted in the 1819 treaty that gave the United States a legal foothold on the Pacific. Finally, New Orleans made Jackson a hero, which he parlayed into a successful run for the presidency in 1828. Jefferson's embargo and the economic disruptions caused by the war stimulated American manufacturing. Federalist opposition to the war, centered in New England, spelled the death knell for the party. The war also sparked an upsurge in nationalist pride, although this patriotic glow soon faded.

Victory in the Mexican War also had reverberations beyond the modest scale of battlefield operations. The United States reaffirmed its acquisition of Texas and obtained a massive territorial concession from Mexico. Despite a penny-pinching Congress, the American navy was able to mount a blockade of Mexico on two oceans. The war allowed the transfer of Mexican real estate to the United States, which set up a fateful debate over the extension of slavery into the newly acquired territory. Military pacification of hostile Indians, many of whom were resettled west of the Mississippi River, added to the impact of war on American statebuilding.

Political Structures

The Constitution created a governmental framework that reflected ideological axioms of the early United States. The document affirmed the principle that the states and the national government formed a political union in which each component retained the authority to govern in allotted fields of activity. President George Washington saluted this exceptional division of power in his farewell address "as a main prop of your liberty." Upon his departure from the presidency, Andrew Jackson noted, "in the union of these states there is a sure foundation for freedom." Antebellum presidents invariably repeated the maxim that the federal union underwrote American liberty. A second axiom emphasized the limited authority of the national government and the semisovereign competency of the states, subject to limitations outlined in the Constitution. Time and again, presidents and political commentators stressed the necessity of carefully observing the limits on national authority so as not to intrude on the sovereignty of the states. As Jackson put it in his 1837 farewell address, citizens had to be on guard against the expansion of federal powers to prevent the creation of a "consolidated" government. While the principle of dual governance was accepted, disagreements repeatedly arose about the precise allocation of this diffused power. This constitutional pact contained one of the central paradoxes of American governance—power was divided and distributed functionally and geographically in an arrangement that obscured the actual aggregate application of sovereign authority.

A third political axiom pledged equal treatment of citizens and condemned favoritism for special interests. This principle reflected the growing embrace of egalitarianism and the influence of democratization in American society during the antebellum era. In Jackson's words, citizens must be on guard against any "corrupting influence," by which he meant the "army of powerful interests" that sought to gain public support for private enrichment. At the top of Jackson's list of political offenses were cabals between government and banks, a theme that Jacksonian Democrats reiterated for decades. Some Democrats and most Whigs regarded paper banknotes and the incorporation of private businesses as useful devices for economic growth. Nonetheless, virtually all political participants concurred that special-interest favoritism offended the public good. The Democratic version of this axiom stressed minimal federal action and the maintenance of a "plain and frugal government," as President Polk phrased the sentiment. Democrats were the most hawkish party in terms of keeping the lid on government spending and debt. Yet the mantra of no special favoritism and stringent fiscal control formed an ideological penumbra that restrained the use of power, especially among policymakers in Washington.

The principles of diffused power under constitutional federalism and equal treatment before the law established boundaries for policymaking. But rhetorical genuflection before common political axioms and the practical task of governance represented two sides of the governmental coin. Political maxims and actual uses of power coexisted. The rise of new problems and unexpected crises within an increasingly democratized political arena created pressure to use public power. Disagreement over how governments should address these irritants was inevitable in a multilevel representative democracy.[31] The political structure eased much of this decisionmaking dilemma by leaving a great array of issues to the states and localities to resolve. This functional duality allowed the federal government to concentrate on a few key activities often undertaken far from the centers of population, thus keeping national governance largely "out of sight," in Brian Balogh's formulation.[32] States and cities operated under less rigorous legal restrictions and faced competition for people and business from other jurisdictions. America's political structure allowed the paradoxical situation whereby governments devoted to liberty could use and amplify their powers.[33]

The political structure's interactions with socioeconomic change, economic depression, political parties, and war were the primary factors that fostered a modest expansion of the public sector in the antebellum era. The nation's territory increased severalfold, states and municipalities used their authority in new ways, and a sense of national identity developed, especially outside the South. The national government played an instrumental role in this evolution, particularly in relation to the nation's borders and in maintaining an independent national state. Collectively, these facts point to America's central paradox: a nation schooled in the principles of limited government, individualism, and legal constitutionalism actually used its governmental power frequently, and often with significant consequences for statebuilding. Situations that prompted lawmakers to address problems with civic interventions could trump ideology.

The War of 1812 and the Mexican War demonstrate the United States' willingness to use coercive force to assert American sovereignty. These two conflicts, however, represent only the best-known uses of coercive force during the antebellum period. When lawlessness prevailed or danger threatened, Americans responded with organized force. George Washington and Alexander Hamilton formed a federal military force of 12,500 militiamen to quell a tax rebellion in western Pennsylvania in 1794. The US Navy confronted pirates, including the piratical Barbary States in the Mediterranean, in the early nineteenth century. State and local militias repeatedly drove off Indians, sometimes in collaboration with the US Army. Governors and mayors often summoned militias to suppress urban rioters; some of these encounters resulted in numerous fatalities, as occurred in the Astor Place Opera House riot in New York in 1849. Vigilante justice prevailed in the 1850s in San Francisco and in western mining camps. State and local governments retained capital punishment, including public executions, and allowed city police to carry firearms. In the South, state laws institutionalized slavery and maintained a legal culture that seldom convicted whites for killing Africans.

Viewed collectively, these actions demonstrate the widespread use of coercive instruments in the years between 1789 and 1860. A key characteristic of a state is a monopoly on coercive force.[34] This power was used regularly and was an accepted part of civic life in antebellum America.

7

The Civil War Builds New States

On January 1, 1863, President Abraham Lincoln signed the Emancipation Proclamation, which freed slaves held in the areas of rebellion against the United States. The edict was one of the most significant federal actions in American history, but also one of the most perplexing to explain. Shortly after the announcement of Lincoln's election as president in November 1860, putting a northerner in charge of the national government, South Carolina and six other states seceded from the union. By February 1861 they had formed a breakaway government and had seized federal facilities, including most forts located in the Deep South. The South Carolina militia trained its cannon on Fort Sumter in Charleston Harbor and demanded its surrender.

Confronted with this hostile action, Lincoln denounced secession as "legally void" and an "insurrection" against the United States in his inaugural address on March 4. "The Union of these States is perpetual," he said, and his responsibility was to administer the union intact. At the same time, the president implied that he would not invade the South and disclaimed any intention of abolishing slavery where it already existed. Yet paradoxically, less than two years later, President Lincoln issued an executive order that stripped Confederates of their slaves, wiping out $2 billion of their wealth. The president had undergone an extraordinary transformation, moving from acceptance of the traditional compromise over slavery to a decision that smashed the institution. What explains this change of heart?

Lincoln defended his proclamation as "a fit and necessary war measure" derived from his constitutional authority as commander in chief of the American military. The president was conscious of critics who complained that slaves were contributing to the Confederate war effort and that freedmen were fleeing to Union military lines. Historians have pointed to additional factors that may have influenced Lincoln's decision: pressure from Republicans in Congress (especially the antislavery radicals) and from the Democratic Party, which was still politically powerful in parts of the North and opposed to Lincoln's war policies; a flagging war effort and drooping morale in the North; unresolved diplomatic tensions with Great Britain; abolitionists' demands; and bitter northerners who yearned for revenge for their fallen sons. Lincoln never unveiled his full thinking about the proclamation. That story went to the grave following his assassination in 1865.

Yet the Emancipation Proclamation does reflect an explanatory truth: circumstances can alter prior positions. The war, with its mass killings, widespread suffering, and deep social angst, changed the decision-making landscape in a realm on which previous generations had compromised. A train of events—some deadly—recast the context in which a decision about slavery was reached. The Emancipation Proclamation stands as one of the most conspicuous instances in which the turn of events—in this case, secession and war—can reshape political decisions.

FEDERALISM, SECTIONALISM, AND DISSOLUTION OF THE UNION

The causes of the Civil War have engaged some of the best scholarly minds for generations. The origins of the crisis are devilishly difficult, if not impossible, to pin down, and that is not the task of this book. Rather, its objective is to analyze the Civil War in relationship to American statebuilding. To begin, it is useful to specify the broad context of the union's division.[1]

Four factors were instrumental in the breakdown of the union: federalism, socioeconomic change, geography, and political capacity.[2] Federalism is the logical place to start because it formed the structural arch of American governance. There was wide agreement that an intimate bond existed among the union, the Constitution as its legal foundation, and the preservation of republican liberty. Virtually every president articulated the axiom, beginning with George Washington, who coupled union with liberty, and continuing through Andrew Jackson, who saluted the states as the foundation of constitutional liberty.[3] But disagreement persisted about the balance between national authority and state autonomy. This debate was frequently expressed as opposing views on the origin of the constitutional union. Some claimed the federal government was created by "the people" of the nation; others held that the Constitution was a compact among states that had bestowed specific powers on Congress. At midcentury, Whigs and Republicans in the North tended to accept the former interpretation, while southerners and Democrats favored the latter.[4]

There was nearly universal agreement that the federal government lacked the authority to overturn slavery in the states where it existed. Slavery was viewed as a domestic institution under the purview of state law. Lincoln ran on a Republican Party platform in 1860 that pledged "the maintenance inviolate of the rights of the States, and especially the right of each State to order and control its own domestic institutions according to its own judgment exclusively." He repeated this stricture in his inaugural address and mentioned it again in his message to Congress on July 4, 1861. Congress's power to regulate slavery existed only at the seams of the federal system, that is, on the high seas, in cases in which fugitive slaves crossed state borders, in the District of Columbia, and in federal territories. This last arena was the subject of impassioned debate, as slave owners contended that the Fifth Amendment of the Constitution protected private property in the territories from deprivation without due process of law. Complicating the debate was the concentration of slavery in contiguous states, a geographic reality that accentuated the power of the slaveholding South and maximized its political position in Congress.

Socioeconomic change over the course of the antebellum period fostered sectional tensions, which had profound political ramifications. Population growth steadily advantaged the North. In 1790 the slave states held a slight majority in the House of Representatives; by 1860 they occupied a little over a third of the House seats, and this proportion was significantly enhanced by the large increase in slaves. Slave states controlled half the seats in the Senate until the admission of California as a free state in 1850. During this period the South remained a rural region and became more dependent on growing and exporting cotton, its chief staple, while the North underwent a socioeconomic transformation, especially in the urban Northeast. In addition to the rise of steam transportation, the commercialization of economic transactions, and urbanization, the North innovated public schooling and developed a robust communications and publishing capacity. The number of daily newspapers increased from 42 in 1820 to 387 in 1860, with circulation doubling in the 1850s alone. While the theoretical attributes of "modernization" have been questioned, the concept is suggestive in drawing a connection between individuals' aspirations for personal fulfillment and support for nationally uniform values.[5]

Modernization theory helps explain the behavior of abolitionists, whose campaigns are conventionally tied to the appearance of William Lloyd Garrison's newspaper the *Liberator* in 1831. The rise of evangelical Protestantism is similarly linked to the antislave campaign, which grew over subsequent decades. To some opponents of slavery, keeping territories free of blacks and slave labor competition was probably just as important as condemning an immoral institution. Whatever the mixture of motivations, abolitionists were a small minority, favoring a degree of equality for African Americans that was repulsive to most southerners and many northerners. The historical significant of the abolitionist movement was its continuous campaign of publicity and protest, including the formation of small political parties after 1840 that sought to limit if not eradicate slavery. Southerners responded with a robust defense of their "peculiar" institution. Viewed through a wider lens, southern justification of its slavery–cotton plantation complex and northern distaste for the South's aristocratic society crystallized into divergent cultural images by the late 1840s.[6]

Geography complicated the unfolding of these sectional contrasts. On two occasions during the Mexican War the House of Representatives passed the Wilmot Proviso, which prohibited slavery from any territory that might be taken from Mexico. The Senate squelched both measures. The acquisition of Mexican territory in 1848 set the stage for further conflict over slavery in the newly acquired lands, an issue that remained on the national political agenda until the onset of the Civil War. Actual and contemplated settlement of the West, coupled with the national government's authority to make rules for the territories, set up repeated clashes between sectional leaders. Geography also figured in the formation of the Confederacy, which encompassed an area equal to western Europe and contained hundreds of miles of ocean coastline, important ports, and the lower portion of the Mississippi River. The South's territorial expanse made its bid for nationhood creditable and its government a formidable enemy.

Finally, political capacity directs attention to volatile components of the governmental system. As the polity advanced, electoral reforms enfranchised virtually all adult males of European ancestry for elections at every level of government by midcentury. By the late 1840s political parties were the principal managers of these canvasses. No office, including the presidency, was filled by a national tally of popular votes. Place (geography and political jurisdiction) and politics were intimately connected. The combination of party politics and procedural mandates of the Electoral College gave Lincoln the presidency. Party politics was highly competitive and often engendered viciously derogatory characterizations of opponents. In light of the unbounded nature of many contests, some historians have blamed partisan politicking for the breakdown of the political system.[7] Party rhetoric could be inflammatory, which accentuated the implications of the Republican presidential victory. Southerners did not wait for Lincoln to take office to secede.

THE CRISIS OF THE 1850S

A procession of provocative events buffeted American politics between the Mexican War and Lincoln's inauguration, a chronology that is integral to the breakdown of the union.[8] It is useful to note that the debate over slavery had three broad dimensions: legal-constitutional, political-legislative, and cultural. In a general sense, arguments over slavery engaged judges, lawyers, and theoreticians; candidates for public office and lawmakers; and members of society, such as clergy, editors, and organized antislavery advocates. Recognizing the societal location of the debaters helps track the connections between each set of actors.

The Mexican cession set the stage for this argument. The gold rush in California, which dramatically swelled its population, supported its demand for statehood—as a free state. A deadlock between pro- and antislavery legislators in the territories was broken by the Compromise of 1850, which admitted California as a free state, abolished the slave trade in the nation's capital, and allowed populations in the territories of New Mexico and Arizona to decide the status of slavery themselves. The most controversial part of the compromise was the Fugitive Slave Act, which permitted slave catchers to apprehend virtually any African American by swearing that the person was a runaway slave. Apprehended individuals had no legal right of self-defense; federal marshals could command bystanders to "aid and assist" in the arrest or risk up to a $1,000 fine. An egregious denial of civil liberty, the law brought the reality of slavery into nonslave communities.

A succession of polarizing events unraveled the compromise. Harriet Beecher Stowe, daughter of a well-known abolitionist, published *Uncle Tom's Cabin* (1852), a novel that dramatized how decent people become corrupted by the evils of slavery. The book became an instant best seller, reinforcing northern images of southerners, who in turn saw the book as Yankee meddling with the southern way of life. The Kansas-Nebraska Act of 1854, which organized lands west of Missouri into the territories of Kansas and Nebraska, largely to facilitate a transcontinental railroad, overturned the Compromise of 1850. The new policy was the brainchild of Stephen Douglas, Democratic senator from Illinois, who agreed to repeal the Missouri Compromise (1820–1821) in return for southern Democratic support for this plan. Political reaction in the North was swift, with various segments of the electorate converging into anti-Nebraska coalitions in the 1854 elections. With the Whig Party dissolving over slavery, the anti-Nebraska groups coalesced into the Republican Party for the 1856 election.

Rival settlers poured into Kansas, forming pro- and antislavery governments preparatory to a bid for statehood. Violence between the two factions—leading to the epithet "Bleeding Kansas"—kept the battle over slavery alive for years both in the territories and in Congress, working to the advantage of the Republican Party. In 1857 the Supreme Court announced its *Dred Scott* decision, which invalidated the prohibition against slavery in any federal territory. Most northerners probably saw Chief Justice Roger Taney's opinion as further evidence that southerners had fastened their grip on the federal establishment. That year also recorded a serious business slowdown, which prompted Republicans to add economic measures, such as a protective tariff and a Pacific railroad, to their agenda, which had initially centered on opposition to the expansion of slavery. The recession cost the Democrats control of Congress.[9] By this time many southerners had concluded that the Republicans were bent on squeezing slavery to death. People of this mind-set could find confirmation in John Brown's unsuccessful raid on the federal arsenal at Harpers Ferry in 1859.

The election of 1860 took place in the context of these provocations. The Democratic Party split into northern and southern factions, with southerners insisting on constitutional protection for slavery in the territories. Douglas headed the northern Democrats, whose position was popular sovereignty (local voter decisionmaking) in the territories. Extremist southerners threatened secession if a "Black Republican" won the election. Some surviving Whigs in the border states formed the Constitutional Union Party, devoted to preserving the union. Lincoln and the Republicans gained the presidency by winning the electoral vote in fifteen of the eighteen free states, without capturing a single slave state. Although Lincoln received just 40 percent of the total popular vote, 55 percent of the voters in the free states supported him. Republicans won control of most northern state governments but failed to win a majority in either chamber of Congress.[10]

SECESSION AND LINCOLN'S DECISION FOR UNION

The announcement of Lincoln's election triggered the secession of seven southern states and the formation of the Confederate States of America by early February 1861.[11] Secession presents a curious puzzle. By seceding, the South triggered the very result it feared: the abolition of slavery and the destruction of southern society. Why did southern leaders take such a big risk? Precedents dating back to 1787 demonstrated that workable compromises on slavery could be achieved. Republicans would have held a minority of seats in Congress in 1861 had southerners not withdrawn from that body. The Supreme Court was dominated by southerners, including Chief Justice Roger Taney. Democrats remained a viable political presence in the North. A temporary truce might have been achievable, which would have bought time to recapture power in Washington. Moreover, southerners did not know that Lincoln would use military force against the Confederacy.[12]

Unraveling the thinking of southern leaders is speculative, of course, but charges of conspiracies afoot help explain the decisions of both sides in 1860 and 1861.[13] Conspiratorial thinking, common to the age, led to the belief that conclaves of individuals were plotting in secret to gain self-serving goals. Although conspiracy scenarios can have factual foundations, predictions of plotters' intentions open up an unbounded spectrum of possible outcomes, including unlikely fantasies. Both southerners and Republicans accused their sectional opponents of secretive schemes to undermine the republic.

The core of Republican Party ideology after 1854 was the existence of a "slave power" conspiracy, whereby southern aristocrats plotted to control the national government in order to protect slavery. William H. Seward, a senator from New York, argued that the Democratic Party had become the tool of southerners pushing a "nefarious schedule of slaveholding designs." Conscious of racist attitudes among many northerners, Republicans attacked the "slaveocracy," emphasizing the efforts of a minority of southerners who allied with "doughface" northern Democrats to control the national government. Evidence existed that gave credence to such allegations, such as the Kansas-Nebraska Act and the *Dred Scott* decision. After 1854 southerners pressed for a legal guarantee of slavery in the territories, but some Republicans contended that they planned much more. In his debates with Stephen Douglas during their 1858 campaign for the US Senate, Abraham Lincoln said, "put this and that together," and before long the Supreme Court will allow slavery in the free states.[14]

Secessionists responded with far-fetched allegations concerning the intentions of the "Black Republicans," a party that they averred was under the sway of abolitionists. Historian James McPherson has succinctly summarized their charges: "secessionists conjured up frightening scenarios of future Republican actions." Notwithstanding Republican leaders' promise not to interfere with slavery in the South, secessionists contended that the party's real agenda was to squeeze slavery into extinction. Other horrors would follow, such as interracial marriage and murderous hordes of freed slaves in their midst.[15] Lincoln's election raised the possibility that the president would appoint antislavery judges to federal courts in the South. No one knows how much of this alarmist rhetoric was an attempt to gain constituents' support for the secessionist cause. What is apparent is that both Republican and secessionist conspiracy theories were consistent with and probably reinforced by stereotypes prevalent in the 1850s. Given that politics entails making decisions based on the available information within an atmosphere of cultural belief, it is reasonable to suppose that allegations of conspiracy persuaded some people to foresee the opposition implementing worst-case scenarios.[16]

Southern secession presented Lincoln and the Republican Party with a difficult predicament. Lincoln had stated in his inaugural address his intention to administer the union intact, but he offered no specific plan of action or timetable. He waited for events to develop, perhaps thinking that radical southerners had pitched another power play to force concessions from Congress. Lincoln and the Republicans refused to be blackmailed and hoped that unionist sentiment throughout the slave states would lead to reunification. Reports that the federal garrison at Fort Sumter could not hold out without supplies forced the president's hand. He announced to the Confederacy that he would send nonmilitary aid to Sumter. Lincoln realized that his decision was likely to result in war, but he was unwilling to fire the first shot. After the South Carolina militia forced the fort's surrender, Lincoln called on the governors to deliver 75,000 militiamen for federal service to suppress an "insurrection."

Lincoln could have followed another path. He could have accepted secession as a fait accompli and allowed the southern states to form their own national state; their withdrawal would have cleansed the United States of the aristocratic slave-based culture. He could have agreed to southerners' demand for an iron-clad constitutional guarantee of slavery, but he and congressional Republicans rejected that proposal. Although there is no persuasive evidence that Lincoln thought war was necessary prior to the firing on Fort Sumter, he had addressed the issue of preserving the union on several occasions, offering clues to his thinking.

Like other Americans, Lincoln saw an indivisible link between the union and the republic. Several generations of Americans had lived under the Constitution and its federal system, an arrangement repeatedly heralded as the civic solution for preserving liberty. The ideological commitment to this axiom transcended the legal-constitutional basis of the political system and embraced a cultural understanding of the union. It may be that the awakening of nationalist sentiments in Europe and the frequent use of military force to achieve political goals at midcentury influenced Lincoln's course of action. His second annual message to Congress (December 1862) displayed elements of a mystical, philosophical vision of the political community. Referring to the great midsection of the country, Lincoln's homeland, the president said, "a glance at the map shows that territorially speaking it is the great body of the Republic," one of the most important regions in the world, but a pivotal part of "our national homestead."[17] It would be unthinkable to bisect America's sociocultural heartland. In other words, the United States was more than a collection of states; it was a community of people spread over a massive landscape. As Lincoln expressed the sentiment in December 1862, "A nation may be said to consist of its territory, its people, and its laws." The territory of the United States, he said, "is well adapted to be the home of one national family." Lincoln may well have considered it his duty to safeguard this view of republican liberty.[18]

CREATING A WARTIME STATE

The Civil War lasted four years, beginning with Lincoln's call for volunteers on April 15, 1861, and ending with the formal capitulation of Robert E.

Lee's Confederate army on April 12, 1865.[19] By extending this chronology through Reconstruction, when US (Union) military forces occupied parts of the South, the Civil War era covered roughly fourteen years. The armed forces of the United States expanded from 28,000 in 1860 to over 1 million in 1865; 2,667,000 people served in the US military during the war. A total of 900,000 individuals enlisted with Confederate forces, although the Confederate army seldom exceeded a quarter million men at any one time. This massive mobilization of manpower equaled one-third of the nation's male workforce.[20] Men in uniform fought in 237 named battles. More than 700,000 of them did not survive the conflict. The North spent about $3.3 billion to subdue the South, a figure that exceeded all previous federal expenditures and left the national government with a debt of $2.6 billion, dwarfing previous fiscal obligations. The number of federal employees ballooned from roughly 30,000 in 1860 to nearly 200,000 in 1865. These data attest to the massive scale of the war, which occasioned the national government's largest intervention into society up to this point in US history.

Lincoln's first major task as commander in chief was to raise an army. His April 15, 1861, communication asking governors to provide 75,000 volunteers generated more men than requested, as did the president's call in May for three-year volunteers. By the time Congress assembled in July, a quarter million men had been mobilized; lawmakers authorized a million more. The War Department relied primarily on governors to form units, and as a result, most Union regiments bore the name of their state. As the war settled into a prolonged and bloody struggle, volunteers dwindled, and recruitment became more difficult. The Union then turned to conscription. The draft attracted additional volunteer enlistments, particularly in congressional districts with unmet quotas. Volunteering was sweetened by state and federal bounties, which eventually cost northern governments as much as soldiers' regular pay. By the middle of the war Congress and the president accepted black troops, previously barred from joining the regular army or state militias. Eventually, 186,000 African Americans served in the Union army.[21]

Supplying these troops with arms, uniforms, footwear, housing, and food was a monumental task. The War Department had on hand only a fraction of the supplies needed to outfit tens of thousands of soldiers. Initially the states outfitted most units, until the War Department's Quartermaster Corps improved its acquisition procedures. By 1862 the War Department had instituted centralized procurement, which became more efficient as the war progressed. In 1864 the Quartermaster Corps had nine specialized units that acquired materials and food destined for dozens of Union supply depots around the country. Some goods, such as small arms, ammunition, and uniforms, were made at federal arsenals; by the end of the war the US arsenal at Springfield, Massachusetts, could make 200,000 rifles a year. Other items were procured from private firms via contractors. In addition to ships and other vessels that were built or refitted by commercial vendors, the US Navy operated five yards, employing between 2,500 and 5,000 workers to construct vessels. By any scale of measurement, the wartime procurement program dwarfed any prior efforts by the national government.[22]

The Peninsula Campaign in the spring and summer of 1862 suggests the magnitude of the job facing the War Department. Prodded into action by Lincoln, General George B. McClellan, commander of the large Army of the Potomac, ordered an amphibious expedition from his base in Alexandria, Virginia, to Fort Monroe on the James River, with the objective of capturing Richmond, the Confederate capital. Three hundred vessels were employed to transport 70,000 troops to the strip of land bounded by the James and York Rivers. The entourage included hundreds of wagons and thousands of animals to pull them. Three hundred wagons were needed just to haul food for the horses and mules. Despite the magnitude of this operation, McClellan failed to defeat the Confederate armies defending Richmond. In addition to water transportation, railroads proved invaluable for moving armies between locations, but the US military was still dependent on horsepower. The Union purchased a million horses and mules during the war. General Joseph Hooker's 1,159-mile rail trip to rescue trapped Union forces in Chattanooga, Tennessee, in September 1863 included 3,000 horses and mules, along with 20,000 troops.[23]

Feeding, outfitting, and compensating a million-man Union army cost an unprecedented amount of money. The military buildup was sudden, but few thought the war would last very long. The unexpected financial shortfalls put Treasury Secretary Salmon P. Chase and Congress under pressure to secure additional funds. The basic fiscal solution was to borrow, accounting for about 78 percent of wartime costs. This approach was consistent with the general pattern of financing major wars in the United States and elsewhere. The Treasury issued a variety of bonds, which became harder to sell as the war progressed. To address the reluctance to purchase these bonds, Congress created national banks (the law was passed in February 1863 and amended in June 1864), which were allowed to issue paper notes in exchange for accepting one-third of their capital in US bonds. The national government, in other words, created a subscriber for its own debt. To overcome bankers' hesitancy to join the new system, the 2 percent tax levied on state banknotes was raised to 10 percent in March 1865. The creation of national banks during the Civil War was the third time since the Revolution that the central government had authorized a banking system, each in the wake of war.[24]

Pressure to bolster funds in early 1862 moved Congress to issue $150 million in paper currency (greenbacks), which was convertible to specie. Banks' suspension of specie payments resulted in the elimination of the convertibility provision in two subsequent greenback authorizations, both for $150 million. Congress approved a variety of new tax measures, in part to provide assurance that the government could pay the interest on its borrowing. The most lucrative source of funds was a traditional one—customs duties on imports, for which rates were raised. A direct tax was apportioned among the states. Numerous excise (indirect) taxes were approved, which imposed levies on manufactured items, occupations, liquor, tobacco, and documents. A graduated income tax was adopted, and by 1865 it competed with the tariff as a source of revenue. A sense of the scale of these fiscal innovations can be obtained through simple comparisons: in 1861 Washington collected $41 million in revenue and spent $66 million; in 1865 the government received $333 million and spent $1,297 million. These numbers illustrate how the crisis of war magnified the fiscal operation of the national government.[25]

Congressional Republicans demonstrated a firm commitment to funding the war effort, despite considerable intraparty differences over the design of these measures. Republicans also used their majority status to promote economic development, principally by using land grants to aid the construction of a transcontinental railroad, establishing state agricultural colleges, and passing a homestead act that provided 160 acres to qualified recipients. Congress created the Department of Agriculture, the Comptroller of the Currency, and the Internal Revenue Service, and it initiated free mail delivery in cities. The election of 1860 and the departure of southern congressmen had opened the legislative gate for Republicans to enact most of their economic agenda.[26]

The states, largely under Republican control, contributed substantially to the funding of the war. At its outset, northern states outfitted newly formed regiments and built facilities to accommodate them before their departure to fields of deployment. State and local governments provided bonuses for the recruitment of volunteers, a policy that continued through the war. They assumed the major burden of caring for wounded veterans and the families of soldiers, some of whom lost their male breadwinners. Boston, for example, spend a third of its 1862 budget on the war, which occasioned the adoption of new taxes but still left the city with an enlarged debt. Chicago and Cook County shared fiscal responsibilities for recruiting soldiers and caring for their families. These state and local contributions to the northern war effort demonstrated cooperative federalism in action.[27]

MILITARY STRATEGY AND EXECUTION

The Confederacy's objective was to defend its territory until the North tired of war. In the meantime, the Confederacy hoped to win foreign aid and recognition, goals that were never realized. The elevation of Robert E. Lee to commander of the Army of Virginia in 1862 during the Peninsula Campaign brought an aggressive military mind to Confederate strategizing. Lee hoped that a military foray into the free states would reduce Union morale and enthusiasm for continuing the conflict and induce a negotiated settlement. Confederate attacks took place at Sharpsburg, Maryland, site of the Battle of Antietam (September 1862), which turned out to be the bloodiest day of the war, and at the Battle of Gettysburg (July 1863) in southern Pennsylvania. Both were repulsed and may have strengthened, not diminished, the North's commitment to subdue the South.

The shock of the Union retreat at the Battle of Bull Run near Washington, DC (July 1861), the first major fight between the two armies, convinced Lincoln and Union officers that suppression of the rebellion would be more difficult than anticipated and would require broader strategic thinking. From the outset, Lincoln was adamant about keeping the border states, Kentucky and Tennessee in particular, out of the Confederacy; this objective included controlling the river systems that flowed through them, as well as the Mississippi. Lincoln declared a maritime naval blockade of the South at the beginning of the war and worked to keep Great Britain neutral, which thwarted Confederate efforts to win foreign support. As the war dragged on and casualties rose, Lincoln's hope to force a rebel cease-fire evolved into a strategy of relentless pressure to destroy the enemy's capacity to wage war. Prospects for success appeared dim in the summer of 1862: McClellan's Peninsula Campaign had not succeeded, and Confederate resistance in the border states was stiff. Abolitionists were pressuring the administration to take action against slavery, and Congress passed a confiscation act in 1862 that stripped rebels of their property, including slaves. Aware of these developments and worried about the upcoming fall elections, Lincoln looked for an opportunity to boost Union morale and pressure the rebels to desist. The Union's successful but costly repulsion of Lee at Antietam afforded Lincoln an occasion to announce his intention to issue the Emancipation Proclamation on January 1, 1863. By this point he had committed to an "unlimited war" that sought the South's unconditional surrender and the banishment of slavery.[28]

Executing Lincoln's strategy was another matter. The president was repeatedly disappointed by his generals' inability to pursue and destroy rebel forces. McClellan was the epitome of an overly cautious commander. The military situation brightened in 1863 when the Union stopped Lee's northward probe at Gettysburg, followed by Lincoln's conclusion that Ulysses S. Grant, William T. Sherman, and Philip Sheridan were the kind of military leaders he needed. Still, lagging morale and a stalemated war led Lincoln to anticipate defeat in the presidential election of 1864. Sherman's capture of Atlanta helped Republicans prevail in that election. By the end of the year Sheridan had driven the rebels out of the Shenandoah Valley; Sherman had started his March to the Sea in Georgia, bringing "the hard hand of war" to the South by destroying property; and Grant had begun his siege of Lee's forces at Petersburg, Virginia. Under continuous Union pressure, Lee's army dwindled until his capitulation near Richmond in April 1865.[29]

It had taken the Union four years to get to this point. Why so long? Many factors affected the conduct of the war, with geography ranking as a primary influence. The Confederacy covered a huge area but had only one major city: New Orleans. With rivers that emptied into the Atlantic honeycombing the eastern coastal plains and mountains running north and south in the region's midsection, the Confederacy's terrain posed logistical difficulties for armies that lacked modern transportation and accurate (or any) maps.[30] Within this huge landmass the Confederacy waged a defensive war and displayed a fierce élan to uphold southern honor and pride. The adoption of the rifle, which quadrupled the effective range of the older smoothbore musket, advantaged the defenders, subjecting the massed formation of attackers to deadly lines of fire. The use of cannon could increase the suicidal nature of a close-formation attack, which was still the standard tactic. The extraordinarily high casualty rates at Shiloh, Antietam, and Gettysburg attest to the juxtaposition of new killing technology and conventional fighting techniques. The notable exceptions to the South's defensive posture were Lee's advances into Union territory, which produced little more than a dreadful number of Confederate casualties.[31]

These deadly realities made Union commanders cautious. The classic manifestation of offensive timidity was General George McClellan, whom Lincoln relieved of command in late 1862. Many officers from the regimental level to the division and army level were political appointees, but this was not much of a liability, given the minimal military understanding of offensive warfare with armies numbering in the tens of thousands. It took time for officers to obtain on-the-job training in tactics and for Lincoln to find commanders who understood that the North had to win a "complete conquest," as Grant put it. Some of the caution exhibited by military leaders was mimicked on the political front. Considerable opposition to Lincoln's military course came from the Democratic Party, which favored a negotiated settlement and opposed emancipation. McClellan headed the Democratic ticket in the 1864 presidential election.[32]

Given these constraints, how did the North win? First and foremost, the Union had overwhelming population and economic advantages. There were four times as many white males living in the North than in the South. The North also enjoyed a large numerical edge in the female population, an imbalance that worked to the Union's advantage. Women in the North took on numerous important tasks—working as nurses in military hospitals, seamstresses in army arsenals and for private clothing manufacturers, clerks in the federal government, and welfare workers in local communities, as well as running their family farms in the absence of their husbands. The North's manufacturing base, established before 1860, strengthened during the war, while the South's limited industrial sector did not. Most railroad mileage, canals, and telegraph connections were located in the North. Overall, the North's assets gave it a decisive edge in a war of attrition.

The Union's economic advantage extended to public financing, the lifeblood of war. The South's fiscal system was teetering on the brink of collapse by 1865, caused in part by the Union's ocean blockade, which had shut down most Confederate ports by 1864. Unable to import (or, for that matter, export) goods, the Confederacy collected minimal customs duties—the chief source of government revenue in the antebellum era. Inflation sucked the blood out of the South's fiscal capacity. Besides building, buying, and refitting oceangoing vessels, the US Navy acquired hundreds of gunboats that allowed the Union to dominate the interior rivers, such as the Mississippi. The Union had captured New Orleans in 1862; Grant's capture of Vicksburg on July 4, 1863, the South's last stronghold on the Mississippi, isolated the western portion of the Confederacy.

The last factor that enabled the Union victory had to do with government and politics, especially the leadership of Abraham Lincoln. In effect, the president functioned as the army's chief of staff, outlining strategy and instructing generals himself until he found a military man who shared his goals, at which point Grant became the army's top commander. Lincoln also played an instrumental role politically as the nation's chief executive. Caught between conservative Democrats, some of whom were slaveholders in the border states, and radical Republicans who urged a vindictive approach to the South, the president proceeded cautiously yet adroitly. He remained the leader of his party, working cooperatively with Republicans, who controlled most state governments in the North. Lincoln's decision to issue the Emancipation Proclamation (both the preliminary and final versions) was a military and political masterstroke, adding a moral objective to the war that satisfied antislavery Republicans. Although the Confederacy's constitution was nearly a carbon copy of the US Constitution, conflicts over states' rights impeded the capacity of the South's central government. Whereas Lincoln withstood criticism with humor and self-control, Confederate president Jefferson Davis was sensitive to political slights. As a mechanism for channeling political activity, the northern version of federalism worked better than its southern imitation.[33]

RECONSTRUCTION AND NATIONAL POWER

The Confederate surrender in April 1865 ended the confrontation between armies but did not eliminate armed conflict. Resistance to the federal presence in the South continued during the years of Reconstruction (1866–1877), when white southerners undermined Yankee attempts to reform local governance and blocked assistance for former slaves. The Northern response to these developments occasioned unprecedented federal intervention in southern society. Reconstruction represents a critical stage of American statebuilding.

Planning for the occupation of former Confederate territory raised complicated questions about the nature of citizenship, the protection of civil liberties, and the conditions under which southern states could rejoin the union. Lincoln took a lenient approach to the latter issue during the war, presumably to induce Confederates to cease military hostilities. Moderates in his party supported this approach, but Republican radicals demanded the eradication of slavery and the destruction of southern aristocratic rule. Lincoln's assassination, which occurred just days after Lee's capitulation at Appomattox, and Andrew Johnson's elevation to the presidency changed the political calculus. Johnson was a former slave owner and Democrat from Tennessee who had accepted the vice-presidential nomination by the Republican-Union coalition in 1864 in an effort to win the support of border states. As president, Johnson showed his regional prejudice by supporting southern whites, many of them ex-rebels, who attempted to block the extension of political rights to African Americans. This defiance was embodied in the so-called Black Codes (1865–1866), state laws that restricted former slaves with regard to working conditions, landownership, and political rights.

These developments convinced many Republicans that ex-Confederates intended to reinstate slavery and negate the sacrifices incurred in suppressing the rebellion. The Republican-controlled Congress responded with support for the Freedmen's Bureau (created in 1865) to aid ex-slaves and a civil rights act (1866) that explicitly extended citizenship to African Americans and authorized federal protection of their right to the "full and equal benefit of all laws." Congress refused to admit senators and representatives from states that Johnson claimed had been reconstructed. The bitter dispute between the president and Congress on these issues prompted Republicans to craft the

Fourteenth Amendment, which placed the provisions of the 1866 civil rights statute in the Constitution. The first section of the amendment clarified the muddled question of citizenship by stating, "All persons born or naturalized in the United States, and subject to the jurisdiction thereof, are citizens of the United States and of the State wherein they reside." American citizenship, in short, spanned the levels of federalism. The second section eliminated the three-fifths clause related to congressional representation and penalized southern representation in Congress for denying the right to vote for any federal or state office to "any male inhabitants" twenty-one years old and US citizens. Section 3 barred individuals who had supported the rebellion from holding state or national office, unless Congress removed this disability. The amendment gave Congress the power to enforce these provisions—a formidable expansion of federal authority.

To counter southern defiance of the war's outcome, Congress enacted the Reconstruction Acts (1867) over Johnson's veto. These laws placed southern states under military supervision and stipulated conditions for their return to the union, beginning with revised constitutions that provided for black suffrage. Readmission also required that each southern state ratify the Fourteenth Amendment. Johnson used various tactics to try to impede these objectives. Incensed by his disregard of congressional mandates, particularly his removal of army generals who sought to uphold federal law in the military occupation zones, Republicans in Congress impeached the president. Johnson avoided removal by one vote in the Senate trial in 1868, the year Ulysses Grant was elected president. As these events unfolded, Democrats vehemently denounced Reconstruction policy, censuring Republicans for "centralizing" power and promoting an "Africanization" of southern society. Claiming that America was a white man's country, Democrats argued that the federal government lacked the authority to overturn states' rights or "meddle with the rights of the people."[34]

Southern terrorism against black voters in 1868 helped persuade Republicans to approve the Fifteenth Amendment to the Constitution, which provided that citizens could not be denied the right to vote "on account of race, color, or previous condition of servitude." Its ratification in 1870 expanded the reach of federal power, but the amendment's prohibition against state interference with voting rights applied only to males, to the disappointment of supporters of female suffrage.[35]

Congress readmitted the former Confederate states to the union between 1868 and 1870, under governments composed of southern white unionists, Republicans who had relocated to the South, and blacks. But readmission intensified rather than diminished racial harassment and intimidation, which included the murder of white unionists, federal soldiers, and blacks, as unrepentant Confederates strove to recapture control of their state governments. A reign of terror swept through the South from the end of the 1860s to the mid-1870s as conservatives drove pro-unionists from power to "redeem" southern society. Congressional Republicans responded to civil rights violations with three enforcement acts that authorized federal marshals to arrest individuals who conspired to interfere with the right to vote. The third statute, the so-called Ku Klux Klan Act, was aimed at the suppression of night riders who terrorized citizens (both white and black), and it authorized the president to use the US Army to punish offenders and restore order. President Grant dispatched troops to southern states on more than a hundred occasions.[36]

Protecting African Americans in the former Confederacy was beyond the capacity of the national government. Only 6,000 US soldiers were assigned to southern duty, far too few to police the hundreds of communities where illegal activities occurred. Yet even hundreds of thousands of Union bluecoats probably could not have overcome southern racism, hatred of federal dictates, and embitterment at the Yankee invasion. The problem confronting the federal government was massive and beyond Washington's political and fiscal means, given the prevalence of racism and anti-Yankeeism embedded in southern culture and the increased opposition in the North to national intervention that overrode "local self-government."[37] Faced with this reality, a growing number of northern Republicans disengaged from policing southern society. The political costs of pursuing the civil rights goals of the 1860s became too high for most northerners by the early 1870s.[38]

The Panic of 1873, which threw the country into a deep depression that lasted until 1878, was instrumental in this shift of sentiment.[39] Hard times brought high unemployment, a sharp rise in bankruptcies, and finger-pointing by both parties claiming that the other had caused the crisis. The depression cooled Republican support of Reconstruction even before an "electoral tidal wave" swept the country in 1874, netting Democrats ninety-three additional seats in Congress. This massive partisan turnover, in which fifty-four Republican incumbents were defeated, gave Democrats a solid majority in the House. The Republican majority in the Senate was reduced, as victories in state legislative elections allowed the Democratic Party to pick US senators. The economic downturn was not the only cause of this electoral carnage. Still, 1874 was a classic case of depression politics whereby voters vent their frustrations by turning against the party in power.[40]

When Congress convened in late 1875, the Republicans were more attentive to economic matters than to Reconstruction. Yet neither party was unified on key subjects, such as monetary policy and railroad regulation. The economic and political repercussions of the depression, plus the new

Democratic majority in the House, undercut the motivation to continue an aggressive campaign against southern racial terrorism. Republican Rutherford B. Hayes, who became president in 1876 after a special committee awarded him disputed southern electoral votes, withdrew the last contingent of federal troops from the South.[41] The federal courts put an exclamation point on this transition with rulings between 1874 (*U.S. v. Cruikshank*) and 1883 (*Civil Rights Cases* and *U.S. v. Harris*) that stripped the teeth from federal civil rights law. Subsequent violations reverted to southern courts, where white juries seldom convicted whites of abusing blacks.

Some historians have argued that the Civil War had little effect on the fundamentals of government in the United States.[42] This claim is true to the extent that a primary goal of the Civil War was to preserve, not dismantle, the federal structure, a point the Supreme Court affirmed during Reconstruction.[43] Yet the contention that the war had a minimal impact on governance sidesteps the outcome of the conflict, which settled the question of where ultimate authority rested. The surrender at Appomattox confirmed that this power resided in the national government. Moreover, the three so-called Civil War amendments to the Constitution (1865–1870) gave the national state significant legal authority with regard to citizenship and rights, although this authority was more potential than actual for several decades. The establishment of a national banking system linked the US Treasury and the financial community in new and important ways, such as the functioning of the currency system and debt operations.[44] During the early years of Reconstruction the federal government intervened politically and militarily in southern governance in unprecedented ways. This expansion of federal power during the wartime crisis provided a model for further national activism in later years.

After Appomattox the Union army was largely disbanded, and the massive wartime outlay of federal monies was drastically reduced. But these contractions were normal reactions to the return of peace, at least in the United States. Every major war in American history has been followed by the rapid demobilization of the military and the reinstatement of a peacetime fiscal mentality. Federal expenditures in 1865 and the federal debt level of 1866 were not equaled until 1917. But federal outlays in the 1870s were five times higher than in the 1850s; controlling for inflation and population growth reduces the interdecade comparison to a tripling of expenditures, which was still a significant jump.[45] The wartime experience ratcheted up the national government's financial activities, and a similar phenomenon occurred at the state and local levels. Boston's expenditures averaged $16.90

per capita between 1854 and 1857, compared with $40.97 between 1868 and 1871; wartime inflation explains only part of the increase. Other large cities registered similar spikes in spending, as did northern states. The war, in other words, recalibrated public finance. These fiscal changes also made government a more tempting target of corruption, as witnessed in the Grant administration and in New York City in the 1870s.[46]

Federal employment also underwent significant growth, doubling between 1851 and 1871 and nearly tripling between 1861 and 1881. Fifteen hundred civilians worked for the federal government in Washington, DC, in 1851; this number rose to 6,000 in 1871 and then doubled during the 1870s. Some of the additional federal workers joined the new federal agencies created between 1861 and 1871, such as the Department of Agriculture, the Internal Revenue Bureau, the Commission of Immigration, the Office of Education, and the Justice Department.[47]

Comprehensive employment figures for state and local governments are not available, but it is reasonable to suppose that the number of civil servants increased in these governments as well, given their policy actions. Boston, for instance, constructed the Chestnut Hill Reservoir and built a pleasure drive around it, opened a city hospital, provided aid to the families of veterans (partially reimbursed by the state), undertook health inspections in conjunction with the Tenement House Act (1868), expanded the size of its police force, and established a Department of Health (1873). New York State adopted a number of new policies between 1861 and the mid-1870s, when the state oscillated between Democratic and Republican regimes. A sampling of these actions includes the establishment of state normal schools and institutions for the blind and insane, the creation of a board of health and tenement house regulations for New York City, the regulation of saving banks, the establishment of free schools and compulsory education, and steps toward the creation of Adirondack State Park.[48] Notwithstanding the difficulty of gauging the extent to which the Civil War and Reconstruction influenced these developments, the evidence shows that a notable expansion of governance occurred between 1861 and 1877.

Equally significant for statebuilding was the war's impact on nationalism. Expressions of nationalist sentiments were visible in various settings, such as in the orations of clergy, some of whom became military chaplains; in campaign rhetoric; and in the display of the American flag on the battlefield. Lincoln articulated feelings of patriotic unity in his Gettysburg Address, in which he referred to the United States as a "nation" five times, but not once to the "union." The Grand Army of the Republic (GAR), a fraternal organization of former Union soldiers, kept alive the memory of wartime sacrifices and persuaded Congress to recognize Memorial Day as a national holiday, in addition to lobbying for veterans' pensions. Battlefields were recognized as sacred places, and Gettysburg became a national park. These sentiments reached into Congress, where veterans from both sides served during the Gilded Age and later. Ties to the nation strengthened by the war, the martyrdom of Lincoln, and the struggles during Reconstruction reinforced more concrete actions that fostered American statebuilding. America's defense of the national union may have influenced nationbuilding elsewhere, such as in Canada, Germany, Italy, and Japan. Statebuilding was in the air in various parts of the world in the 1860s and early 1870s.[49]

The expansion of the national government during the Civil War slowed in its aftermath, but the identities produced by the conflict lingered for generations, providing a baseline from which later expressions of patriotism developed. Nationalism was not embraced in every part of the nation. The sectional bifurcation that characterized American political culture before 1860 deepened after the war. Spurred by bitter memories of Union troops ravaging parts of the South and Yankee reforms afterward, the majority of white southerners doggedly resisted federal intervention during Reconstruction and used terrorism to build their own conservative alternative. Based on racism and opposition to federal centralization, the South developed a one-party polity of Democrats that lasted a hundred years. This unique sectional politics had an immense influence on subsequent governance in the United States.

PART II

The Gilded Age through World War I and the 1920s

8

Social and Economic Transformations

Theodore Roosevelt opened his reminiscence of his days as a cattle rancher with this portrait of the borderlands between the Dakota Territory and the plains to the west:

> The great middle plains of the United States, parts of which are still scantily peopled by men of Mexican parentage, while other parts have been but recently won from the warlike tribes of Horse Indians, now form a broad pastoral belt, stretching in a north and south line from British America to the Rio Grande. Throughout this great belt of grazing land almost the only industry is stock-raising. . . . The northern cattle plains occupy the basin of the Upper Missouri, that is, they occupy all of the land drained by the tributaries of that river, and by the river itself, before it takes its long trend to the southeast. They stretch from the rich wheat farms of Central Dakota to the Rocky Mountains, and southward to the Black Hills and the Big Horn chain, thus including all of Montana, Northern Wyoming, and extreme Western Dakota.[1]

Roosevelt's book was a best seller. Written when he was only twenty-six years old, it revealed his keen eye for topography and for flora and fauna, despite being a "dude" from the East. He relished shooting game, such as deer, elk, and waterfowl—a somewhat surprising passion, given his interest in birds. He wandered for days in search of buffalo, which had already been virtually eradicated from the West. But Roosevelt did not begrudge his days stalking the plains' largest beast because he firmly believed that emersion in the outdoors fostered a "manly" character.[2]

Roosevelt particularly admired the rugged lifestyle of the cowboys of the middle plains, which was the primary motivation for his 1883 purchase of two cattle ranches on the Little Missouri River in the western Dakotas. A cattle boom was in progress on the northern plains, and Roosevelt hoped to cash in on what looked like a sure thing, as did many other eastern and European investors. But then disaster struck. It began with dwindling grasslands caused by overgrazing and a summer drought, followed by a record cold winter in 1886–1887, accompanied by monstrous blizzards. The severe weather wiped out three-quarters or more of the livestock that roamed the open range; Roosevelt estimated that he lost two-thirds of his herd.[3] The financial wreckage prompted cattlemen to change their livestock practices on the plains. As miners, farmers, and cattlemen learned while chasing their fortunes in the West, the unpredictable environment and the volatile commercial markets made stern taskmasters. Roosevelt sold his ranches and shrugged off his financial losses, looking back on his Dakota days with fondness. He took away from the experience a heightened appreciation of the great bounty of America's wilderness, as well as a sense of its fragility in the face of relentless pressure from settlers and entrepreneurs. These sentiments influenced his performance when he became the twenty-sixth president of the United States in 1901.

Born in 1858, Theodore Roosevelt lived through the great transformation of American society between 1870 and 1919. A series of dramatic changes swept the United States during these years, when the western half of the country was integrated into the union and the nation's economy recorded an extraordinary expansion. A dual burst of economic development—a vast increase in the country's agricultural capacity and the rapid growth of industrial manufacturing—was responsible for one of the most remarkable stories in modern history. The results of these two linked economic pathways substantially increased the standard of living for most Americans during the Gilded Age and the Progressive Era (1870–1917). The number of farm owners and homeowners increased markedly during these decades, giving millions of people a property stake in America.

An increase in the nation's population, which grew from 40 million in 1870 to 106 million in 1920, helped fuel these developments. The attraction of America drew 26 million people from Europe and elsewhere. Many of them settled in the countryside, including new farms in the West, but even more headed for the cities, where factories and other employers welcomed workers. The foreign-born proportion of the population hovered at 13 to 14 percent, but it was much higher in the industrial cities, which lured Americans as well as immigrants. A quarter of the nation's population lived in cities in 1870; slightly more than half were city dwellers in 1920. Chicago, one of the nation's commercial powerhouses, grew from 299,000 residents in 1870 to 2,702,000 in 1920 (see table 8.1).

Socioeconomic change substantially altered the context in which government operated. Although the form of governmental entities (e.g., representative bodies) and ideological principles (e.g., individual rights) continued essentially unchanged, the consequences of social and economic changes during the Gilded Age and Progressive Era altered the direction of governance. Theodore Roosevelt's career illustrates how an attentive citizen saw

Table 8.1. Population of Major Cities, 1870–1920

City	Population (Thousands)		
	1870	*1900*	*1920*
Northeast/Mid-Atlantic			
Boston	250	561	748
New York[a]	942	3,437	5,620
Philadelphia	674	1,294	1,824
Pittsburgh	139	452	588
Baltimore	267	509	734
Midwest/Central			
Chicago	299	1,699	2,702
St. Louis	311	575	773
Detroit	80	286	994
Kansas City, MO	32	164	324
Kansas City, KS	—	52	101
Southeast			
New Orleans	191	287	387
Atlanta	22	90	201
Jacksonville	7	28	92
Tampa	0.8	16	52
Southwest			
Dallas	—	43	159
Denver	5	134	256
West/Northwest			
San Francisco	149	345	507
Los Angeles	6	102	577
Seattle	1	81	315
Spokane	—	37	104

Source: US Bureau of the Census, *Census of Population 1960*, vol. 1, *Characteristics of the Population, Part A: Number of Inhabitants* (Washington, DC: Government Printing Office, 1961).

[a] Originally included only Manhattan; Brooklyn and the Bronx were added as of 1899. By 1920 Queens was also included.

the rise of new problems and proposed solutions for them. These developments are the subject of chapters 9–12. Here, the task is to sketch the social, geographic, and economic transformations that occurred between Reconstruction and World War I.

INTEGRATION OF THE WEST

James Bryce, the famous British interpreter of American politics, was enamored by the American West. "There has been nothing in the past resembling its growth, and probably there will be nothing in the future," he wrote. "A vast territory, wonderfully rich in natural resources of many kinds; a temperate and healthy climate . . . a soil generally, and in many places, marvelously fertile . . . our planet contains no such other favored tract of country."[4]

In his adoration of the American West, Bryce gave no indication of the near extermination of its original inhabitants. From the conclusion of the Civil War to 1890, the US Army, with the occasional assistance of state militias, subdued Indian resistance to white incursion in the West. From the Sand Creek massacre in eastern Colorado (1864) to the massacre at Wounded Knee in South Dakota (1890), Indians suffered defeat after defeat in the Great Plains. Between 1865 and 1898 there were more than 900 combat actions between the US Army and natives, mainly in the western Great Plains and the foothills of the Rockies. Engaged in vicious guerrilla warfare, the army searched for hostile Indians, occasionally attacking entire villages and killing women and children as well as warriors. During the Red River campaign against the Kiowa, Comanche, and Cheyenne in the Palo Duro Canyon of the Texas panhandle, the army took the Indians' best ponies and killed 1,000 others after burning native lodges.

Horses were critical to the Plains Indians for hunting buffalo as well as for engaging in mounted warfare. Railroad construction accelerated the decimation of vast herds of buffalo, depriving many tribes of their main food source. Although limited in manpower, the army operated out of scores of forts across the western frontier that relied on railroads and steamboats for logistical maneuverability. Seldom taking more 2,000 soldiers into combat, the army possessed a level of coordination and organization that the separate Indian tribes lacked. Despite their skill as mounted warriors, the Indians were outgunned by the soldiers, especially after the revolver became standard equipment. Troops used field artillery against the Sioux at Wounded Knee, killing 300.[5]

After years of war, the Sioux had agreed in 1868 to settle on a reservation in western South Dakota. The allotted territory included the Black Hills, where gold was discovered in 1875. Thousands of prospectors flocked to region, ignoring treaty protections for the Indians. The federal government's failure to restrain "the avarice of the white man," as President Ulysses S. Grant characterized the trespassers' penetration, along with other grievances, spurred the Sioux to flee their homes. A large aggregation of refugees camped on the Little Bighorn River in Montana, where Colonel George A. Custer and his troops stumbled upon them and were annihilated. The Sioux victory at Little Bighorn was short-lived. Within the year, the army had forced the group back onto the reservation. This scenario was repeated numerous times: Indians were forced at gunpoint or lured by liquor and promises of government subsidies to accept life on reservations, which were usually located on wasteland. Grant's effort at a humane "peace policy" failed.[6]

In 1887 the Dawes Severalty Act capped generations of efforts to acculturate the natives to Anglo-American ways, including the abandonment of their tribal structure. The law offered tribesmen small plots of land to which they would receive title after twenty-five years of cultivation. Citizenship was possible if individual Indians rejected tribal membership and "adopted the habits of civilized life." As President Grant phrased it, the goal was to get Indians to "live in houses and have schoolhouses and churches."[7] Reservation land could then be opened to white settlement. In 1889 Congress purchased Creek and Seminole reservation land in Oklahoma, which was the site of a land rush by 100,000 people. Indian reservations there and elsewhere in the West were whittled down by various subterfuges over the next fifteen years.

Military pacification of the Indians was a key step in opening the West to white settlement. The extension of railroads was a second catalyst for moving people into the interior and beyond. Railroads had bridged the Mississippi before the outbreak of the Civil War and pushed across the first tier of states west of the river by 1870. The so-called Granger Roads, such as the Burlington, crisscrossed the upper Midwest with spurs that directed traffic onto the main lines to Chicago and eastern cities. In 1869 the Central Pacific and Union Pacific completed a rail link between Omaha, Nebraska, and Sacramento, California, with connections to cities on San Francisco Bay, creating the first "transcontinental" railroad (see figure 8.1). The following year the Kansas Pacific reached Denver from Kansas City. Construction during the 1870s pushed the rails into the Dakota Territory, Montana, and New Mexico as far as Santa Fe. By 1887 the Santa Fe Railroad was connected with Los Angeles; this connection, along with the Southern Pacific Railroad, stimulated a land boom in southern California reminiscent of the land rush in Oklahoma. The Northern Pacific Railroad, running from Minneapolis, Minnesota, to Portland, Oregon, forged a second transcontinental line in 1883. Nearly 70,000 miles of track was laid west of the Mississippi River between 1865 and 1890.[8]

Railroads were instrumental in facilitating the settlements that stretched from the Dakotas south to central Texas and west to Colorado and elsewhere along the Rocky Mountains, as well as down the Pacific coast from Seattle to San Diego. By 1920 the West's nine million inhabitants constituted 9 percent of the nation's population. Sizable migrations also populated the upper reaches of the Midwest and the Gulf coast. Like those who were drawn to the West, people flocked to the country's middle zones largely to access natural resources, with agricultural land being a prime objective. The number of farms increased from 2.7 million in 1870 to 6.5 million in 1920;

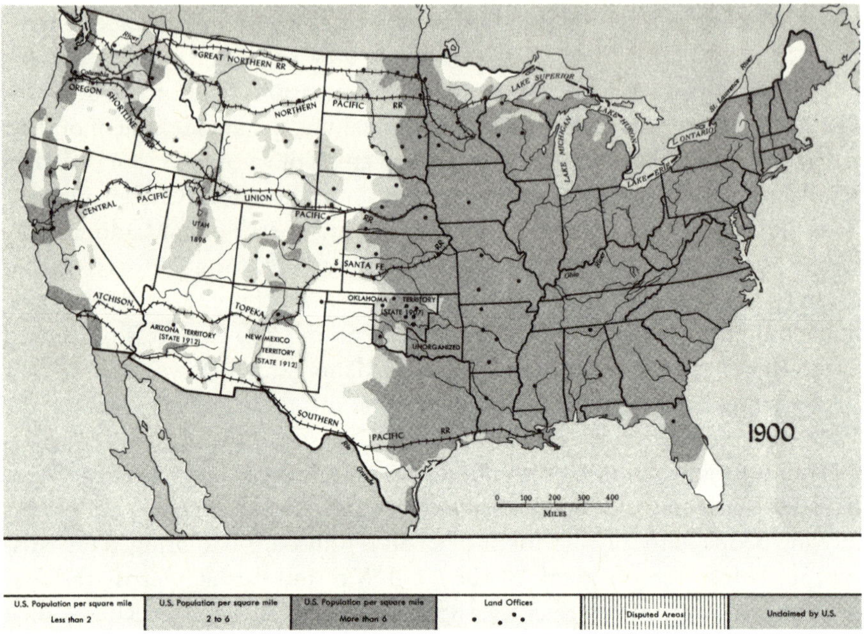

Figure 8.1. Map of expansion, 1900. *Source:* Randall D. Sale and Edwin D. Karn, *American Expansion: A Book of Maps* (Homewood, IL: Dorsey Press, 1962), 25.

farmland more than doubled during this period. With greater acreage devoted to farming and ranching, the output of wheat, corn, cotton, and beef soared. Most farms were located in the Midwest and South, but many new homesteads were established in the Great Plains and in the valleys between the Pacific coast mountains. New England and the mid-Atlantic region lost population during this transitional era. Some migrants from the Northeast took up wheat cultivation or cattle ranching on the Great Plains. Citrus groves and vegetables sprouted in southern California and central Florida. With the exception of New England, American agriculture underwent a surge of growth in the two generations following Reconstruction.

The West held a special fascination for transplants. Reminiscent of the California gold rush, opportunists swarmed to the Comstock lode in Virginia City, Nevada; its silver output boosted San Francisco's economy in the early 1860s. The West yielded a variety of industrial metals, such as iron ore in Minnesota, copper in Montana and Arizona, and coal in Wyoming, although most coal mining occurred between Pennsylvania and Illinois and in the southern Appalachians. Oil, which was first pumped in Pennsylvania and the Midwest, was later discovered in Texas, Oklahoma, and California. The northern Midwest was a locus of the timber industry during the Gilded Age, until lumbermen migrated to the Pacific Northwest and the piney woods of the South; however, lumberjacks continued to work Maine's north woods.

Water was a critical commodity in the arid West, and there were fierce battles over this scarce resource. California took the lead in formulating water policy for urban growth and farm irrigation. Los Angeles's growth was enabled by the Owens River aqueduct project, completed in 1913, which brought water from the mountains more than 200 miles away. The construction of a dam in the Hetch-Hetchy Valley of Yosemite National Park to supply water to San Francisco, proposed in the 1880s, was bitterly opposed by environmentalists; it was authorized by Congress in 1913 and completed in 1934. Western cities were dependent on access to water and, after electrification arrived, coal.[9]

Economic opportunity in the West did not rest solely on access to natural resources. Cities were also economic magnets. San Francisco, with its magnificent harbor, became a gateway to the Pacific coast and was the region's commercial center, supplying goods such as mining supplies to western locations. By 1900 San Francisco contained numerous businesses, including transportation facilities, mercantile outlets, manufacturing, and banking, providing jobs for thousands. Seattle, with its protected harbor, developed similar synergies, while Spokane became an inland emporium of western wheat after the railroad arrived. Most large Pacific cities had both railroad and ocean access, whereas inland cities such as Denver were dependent on the railroad for economic linkages. Positioned on the fringe of the Great Plains, Denver occupied a relatively favorable location in comparison to other cities in the Rocky Mountains. Dallas, another city that blossomed as a result of rail connections, offered commercial services for the southern Great Plains.[10]

The urbanization of the West was part of a national trend. The Pacific coast region became as urbanized as the Midwest, while the Great Plains was more urbanized than the South, the nation's most rural region. The largest cities, located in the Northeast and upper Midwest, dwarfed municipalities elsewhere. By 1880 New York City (then including only Manhattan) had 1.2 million people, which exceeded the population of twenty-three of the thirty-eight states. After Manhattan was consolidated with Brooklyn, Queens, and the Bronx, New York City counted 5.6 million inhabitants in 1920. By then, Chicago had become the nation's "second city," with 2.7 million people. Once railroads reached northern Florida in the 1880s, city building began in that state, starting with Jacksonville and later Tampa. Railroads extended down both coasts of Florida, mimicking their impact on western destinations such as Los Angeles and Phoenix, where transportation connections and a mild climate lured newcomers.[11]

GOVERNMENT AND WESTERN DEVELOPMENT

Governments were established as people flowed into the West. With the admission of New Mexico and Arizona to the union in 1912 (the last of the twelve new states admitted since 1867), state governments covered the continental United States, with the exception of the District of Columbia. Territorial residents eagerly sought statehood, which promised economic and political benefits. Each new state added seats to the US House and Senate, electoral votes for the presidency, and federal aid. Statehood was viewed as a prerequisite for attracting eastern capital for development.[12] Given these stakes, proposals for new admissions sparked partisan conflicts in Washington.

Political contests also swirled around the creation of local governments, especially the designation of county seats, which were administrative focal points in the nineteenth century. County officers in Wisconsin included the sheriff, district attorney, judges, registrar of deeds, treasurer, surveyor, coroner, county clerk, and county superintendent. County tax assessors existed in some states.[13] Municipal, county, and state governments numbered close to 3,000 in 1870 and increased to 5,700 by 1920 (see table 8.2). With the addition of minor civil divisions, mainly rural districts such as townships, the number of governments in 1900 increased to more than 13,000. A more accurate national census of governments taken in 1933 found close to 40,000 civil units. These surveys excluded public school districts, which usually had their own governing boards and sometimes separate revenue mechanisms. There were 125,000 school districts in 1870, and the number had doubled by 1933. The spread of people into the West and other parts of the country expanded the geographic matrix of civic entities. Cities were a major element in this spatial radiation. Municipal jurisdictions increased more than threefold between 1870 and 1920; "big" cities recorded a fivefold increase. The expansion of subnational governments between end of Reconstruction and World War I added hundreds of thousands of policymakers and administrators, underscoring the geographic fragmentation underpinning American governance.[14]

An important congressional task was designing new territories, appointing their administrators, and admitting new states. The West presented a different geographic canvas for this process than the East. The West was a massive region, and Congress relied more heavily on surveyors' lines than natural features to determine state boundaries. Montana was twice the size of all six New England states. Wyoming's dimensions, like those of Colorado and New Mexico, were strictly rectangular. The army removed Indians from the path of settlers; then federal officials surveyed the public domain

Table 8.2. Governments in the United States, 1870–1933

	1870	*1900*	*1920*	*1930–1933*
States	37	45	48	48
Counties	2,295	2,713	2,927	3,053
Cities[a]	663	1,737	2,722	3,105
Total	2,995	4,495	5,697	6,206
Rural territories/minor civil divisions	—	8,931	12,855	11,667
Total governments[b]	—	13,426	18,852	39,730
Big cities[c]	14	38	70	93
Towns/townships[d]	—	—	—	20,262
School districts	—	—	—	127,108
Public schools	125,000	—	—	262,000

Sources: William Anderson, *The Units of Government in the United States: An Enumeration and Analysis* (Chicago: Public Administration Service, 1934), fig. 1; US Department of Commerce and Labor, *A Century of Population Growth . . . 1790–1900* (Washington, DC: Government Printing Office, 1909), 71; US Bureau of the Census, *Historical Statistics of the United States to 1970* (Washington, DC: Government Printing Office, 1975), series A43–56, table II, 1086.

[a] Based on the census definition of incorporated places with populations of 2,500 or more.

[b] General-purpose governments, consisting of United States, states, counties, and rural territories in 1900; United States, states, counties, incorporated places, towns, and townships in 1933. The 1900 and 1920 figures are estimates, using rural territories as a proxy for minor civil divisions; both figures probably underestimate the number of local minor political subdivisions.

[c] Cities with populations of 100,000 or more.

[d] Excluding federal territories.

and recorded land transferred to individuals.[15] The government in Washington sponsored explorations of the Yellowstone and Colorado River regions. Some of the public domain was transferred to states to support schools (embedded in the acts that created the states) and colleges (Morrill Act of 1862).

Congress generously granted public land to railroads between 1850 and 1871, initially using states as conduits and then transferring land directly to railroad companies in 1862, chiefly for lines that would traverse the central and western portions of the country. Land grants were important inducements to railroad companies that were considering building lines in advance of settlement, as was the case for the transcontinental lines. Counties and municipalities from Maine to Missouri, anxious to attract feeder routes that linked with trunk lines, bought railroad securities. Southern states and localities invested enthusiastically in new railroad ventures during Reconstruction. Widespread rail bankruptcies and unsustainable government debts arising from the depression of the 1870s largely ended these subventions and spawned restrictions on local governmental subsidies for railroads.[16]

The Homestead Act of 1862, which initially allotted 160 acres to individuals who improved their plots over five years, symbolized the liberalization of federal land policy in the late nineteenth century. Additional acts granted large tracts of desert land, mineral rights, and permission to graze on the public domain. National lawmakers assisted agriculture in the arid West through the Newlands Reclamation Act of 1902, which funded the construction of reservoirs and irrigation ditches. In 1891 the president gained the authority to set aside public forest reserves, which expanded in subsequent years. The creation of Yellowstone National Park in 1872, a region seen as unfit for agriculture or grazing, inaugurated federal retention of areas of unique beauty. Yosemite, which Congress had granted to California, became a national park in 1890. Other national parks included Sequoia in California (1890), Glacier in Montana (1910), and Grand Canyon in Arizona (1919). The National Park Service was created in 1916 to manage the growing list of scenic reserves. Collectively, these decisions document Washington's significant role in the development of the West. In 1890 the US Census Bureau put an exclamation point on these decisions by announcing that a frontier line no longer existed.[17]

TRANSPORTATION AND COMMUNICATIONS REVOLUTIONS

The Centennial Exposition held in Philadelphia in 1876 commemorated the first hundred years of American independence. The Pennsylvania Railroad and the Philadelphia and Reading Railroad pulled out all the stops for this celebration, creating special tracks to transport visitors to the fairgrounds. The Pennsylvania Railroad built new stations for the event; Centennial Station, the finest on its system, reached Chicago and St. Louis. The Penn transported five million of the nearly nine million people who attended the Centennial Exposition during its six-month run. It also contributed exhibits to the fair, which displayed the latest products and inventions related to mining, manufacturing, agriculture, and machines. Best-in-class medals were awarded to Sharp rifles, Otis elevators, Gatling guns, and Pullman railroad sleeping cars. Penn's engineer of buildings and bridges designed Machinery Hall, where "machines in motion" were displayed, including the giant Corliss steam engine that supplied power to the exhibits. President Grant opened the exposition by turning the handle that activated the forty-foot-tall dynamo. The inventions and machinery showcased at the exposition reflected the country's economic advances during the 1870s.[18]

The railroad connections to the Centennial Exposition heralded the beginning of a second transportation revolution. In 1860, 30,000 miles of railroad

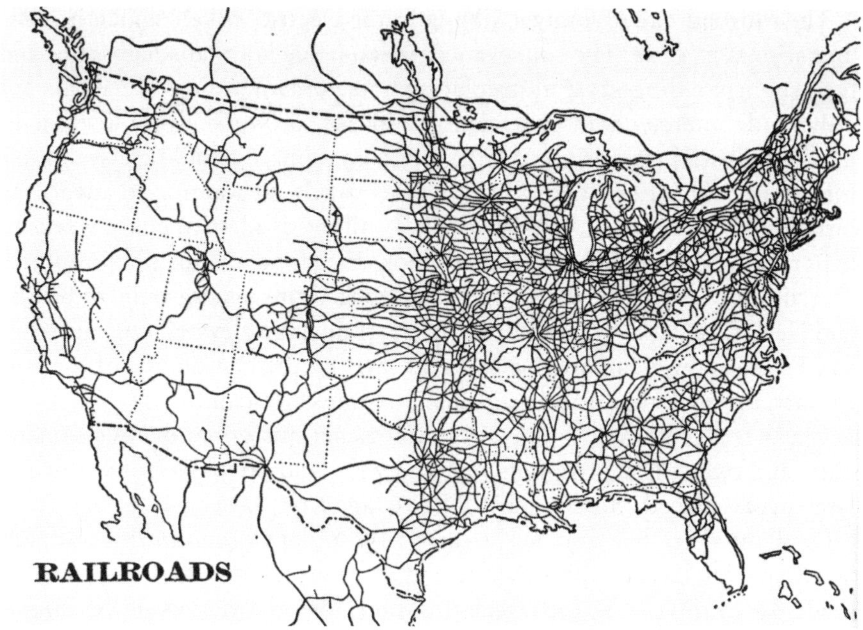

Figure 8.2. Map of US railroad network, 1900. *Source:* D. W. Meinig, *Transcontinental America, 1850–1915* (New Haven, CT: Yale University Press, 1998), 254, reprinted from Jacques Redway and Russel Hinman, *Natural Advanced Geography* (New York: American Book, 1901).

track had crossed the Mississippi, reaching eastern Iowa and St. Joseph, Missouri. The rails spread rapidly in the late 1860s and early 1870s and again in the 1880s; by 1916 track mileage peaked at 254,000 miles (see figure 8.2). Few counties in the agriculturally rich Midwest lacked a rail connection; by the turn of the century lines extended into northern Maine and deep into Florida. Critical to the emerging national rail network was the standardization of track gauge in 1886. Until this occurred, freight and passengers had to be off-loaded and reloaded at many junctions. The consolidation of numerous railroad companies into larger corporations, the opening of "union" stations that served several roads, and the inauguration of limited express service between distant destinations assisted in establishing a national railroad network. Additional contributions came from technological improvements in locomotives (more powerful), the substitution of steel for iron rails (more durable), the shift to coal for fuel (more British thermal units per pound), the introduction of air brakes, more reliable bridges, and similar refinements that allowed trains to pull more weight (and cars) and to travel faster and more safely—all cost-saving developments.[19]

The railroad had a younger sibling in the electric trolley, which became operational in 1888. The conveyance spread like wildfire through cities and their suburban fringes, rapidly replacing horse-drawn trolleys. Streetcars not only made intercity transportation affordable for workers but also facilitated the spatial expansion of large cities, enabling the middle class to live further from the urban core and its dense crowds. In addition to advancing intracity transportation, *intercity* trolleys allowed riders to enjoy weekend trips to rural parks and beaches, excursions the transit companies promoted. The subway, initiated in the 1890s, put electric trains underground in Boston and New York; Chicago ran its intraurban train as an elevated railway, while San Francisco was famous for its cable cars. By the first decade of the new century, urban America had reinvented its transit system.[20]

Ocean travel also underwent a technological transformation, as steam engines and twin screw propellers replaced wind and sail power, and iron and later steel replaced wooden hulls. The voyage from Liverpool to New York took about thirty-five days in the early 1850s; that same journey was cut to less than eight days in 1879. Wireless signal transmission, available in 1901, made ocean travel safer, although it did not save the victims of the *Titanic* in 1912. Two years later the Panama Canal opened, significantly cutting the transit time between the Atlantic and Pacific Oceans. These improvements, however, did not stop the decline of the American maritime industry.[21]

The advent of motor vehicles drove the transportation revolution to another level. The automobile debuted in the 1890s, and commercial production was under way at the turn of the century. Henry Ford led the new industry, developing simple, durable, and inexpensive vehicles, beginning with his Model T. Using an assembly-line production technique, Ford made nearly 600,000 Model Ts in 1916, offered at about one-third the price charged in 1909. In the early days of auto manufacturing, Ford faced numerous competitors, including Will Durant, who organized General Motors in 1908, lost control of the firm in the recession of 1910, and regained control in 1916, largely based on the success of his newest line, Chevrolet. Initially seen as a novelty for the wealthy, auto ownership grew rapidly after 1910, with a third of urban families owning a vehicle by 1920. By then, horses were largely absent from downtown areas, which had become snarled with motorized traffic. Motor vehicles ranked second in value among industrial products in 1919. With the expansion of a national grid of highways in the 1920s, another transportation network had emerged.[22] Air travel was slower to get off the ground following the Wright brothers' successful flight in 1903. Passenger service awaited aircraft capable of sustained flight and infrastructure such as airports. The appearance of the DC3 in 1936 was instrumental in turning passenger flights into a paying proposition.

Innovations in communications forged another kind of network. Five years after the telegraph spanned the continent in 1861, an underwater cable was laid to Europe. The telephone arrived in 1876, and long-distance connections were possible by 1884. Six million telephones were in use in 1906, and a coast-to-coast telephone hookup was in place by 1915. By 1891 Americans could listen to recorded music on phonographs. In the 1910s they could watch films shown in large, ornate theaters; these venues were wired for "talkies" starting in 1927. *Birth of a Nation*, released in 1915, is conventionally cited as the first feature film and established the cinematic genre. Newsreels of national and world events were part of each theater performance. Commercial radio began in 1920 and rapidly entered homes throughout America.

The typewriter was in wide use by the 1880s. This, along with innovations in printing (e.g., photoengraving in 1873 and Linotype machines in 1886), enabled major advances in print communications. As early as 1884, Chicago morning newspapers reached Monmouth, Illinois, 180 miles away, by 7:00 a.m. A few years into the twentieth century, trucks began to replace horse-drawn carts to deliver newspapers to street vendors. By then, the US Postal Service's rural free delivery was bringing letters and the Sears Roebuck catalog to rural residents; by 1912 buyers could receive their purchases via parcel post. Businesses used these new communications technologies to advertise to customers and to contact other firms. As Robert Gordon observes, "isolation was replaced by communication."[23] Technologies that advanced printing, film, and radio greatly increased the volume of information and the speed of its dissemination.

The transportation and communications revolutions had major impacts on economic development, and the railroads were most influential. Transportation costs fell as trunk through-lines were expanded. The operation of a rail network—first in the Northeast (1870s) and then throughout the United States (1890s)—opened up national markets for various commodities and increased competition, both of which tended to lower prices. The organizational skills required to run a railroad encouraged executives to adopt cost accounting, a technique that spread through the corporate world. Because capital investment was mandatory to build a railroad, their construction stimulated financial markets, especially the bond market. Western railroads received millions of acres of land from government grants as collateral to entice investors.

Railroads purchased a substantial portion of the economy's output. They consumed large quantities of coal, wood, and oil and ordered equipment ranging from steel rails to locomotives and rolling stock. Rivers were bridged, real estate was purchased, and stations and maintenance facilities were built. Railroads hired mechanical engineers, managers, accountants, statisticians, and attorneys, as well as an army of workers that included locomotive engineers, brakemen, conductors, station managers, and baggage handlers. In 1920 railroad employment peaked at two million workers. Railroads were clearly the engines of economic growth.[24]

The auto industry offered similar synergies. Automakers bought materials such as steel, as well as specialized parts ranging from ball bearings to rubber tires and eventually radios. Henry Ford's production facilities, first at Highland Park (1910) to mass-produce Model Ts and then at River Rouge (1919), which manufactured steel in addition to assembling cars, heralded the emergence of massive manufacturing complexes.[25] As motor vehicles hit the road, secondary industries arose in response, such as gasoline refineries, service stations, road builders, and travelers' services such as A&W root beer stands.

THE INDUSTRIAL TRANSITION

Cars, locomotives, and communications equipment became the banner products of America's expanding industrial output. No single index kept track of industrial companies over the long nineteenth century, but the number grew substantially after the Civil War. Census takers recorded 140,000 "factories and neighborhood industries" in 1859 and half a million in 1899, of which 205,000 were "manufacturing establishments." During this period, John D. Rockefeller produced oil, Andrew Carnegie manufactured steel, Thomas Edison made lightbulbs, George Pullman produced railroad sleeper cars, and Kodak introduced its Brownie camera. Lesser-known firms turned out chemicals, fabrics and apparel, fabricated metal products (e.g., razor blades, iron stoves), and mechanical devices such as typewriters, cash registers, and threshing machines. By 1919, 270,000 manufacturing firms existed, with double the number of production workers employed twenty years earlier.

Other industrial manufacturers processed mineral resources such as copper, coal, and iron; food and beverages (e.g., Swift meats, Quaker oats, Coca-Cola, Anheuser beer); tobacco products; lumber; paper; and publications. Procter and Gamble advertised Ivory soap and Crisco shortening, products aimed at the growing retail market. Much of the bounty that poured forth from the nation's workshops was sold by mail-order firms such as Montgomery Ward and Sears Roebuck; the latter's 1909 catalog listed more than 100,000 items. Both these retail giants were headquartered in Chicago, where railheads sped products around the nation.[26]

This pace of industrial expansion propelled America to global leadership. The US manufacturing establishment, largely situated within a parallelogram bounded by Milwaukee, St. Louis, Baltimore, and Boston, accounted for one-third of the world's industrial output in 1900. The value of its output matched that of Great Britain in 1870 and doubled it in 1913, when US manufacturing was four times larger than that of either France or Germany. Expansion of the economy lifted the national income from $152 per person in 1869–1878 to $287 in 1909 (in 1860 prices), signifying an increase in the average American's income. With millions of farms, resource extraction industries, manufacturing establishments, and service firms, the United States was the world's largest economy by World War I. American incomes were among the highest in the world. And because indexes of national income do not measure all aspects of human existence, the rise in the standard of living between 1870 and 1920 was greater than quantitative indicators implied.[27]

Several factors drove this economic growth. Most scholars acknowledge the contribution of America's abundant natural resources and favorable climates for diversified agriculture. A second stimulus was population growth, which increased 2.5-fold between 1870 and 1920. Immigrants, largely young males, were a major component of this increase. More people meant more labor in the newly opened territories. Other Americans gravitated toward cities, which spurred the purchase of American goods and services. Urban residents were especially important consumers because they produced a limited range of goods at home. Given that the United States relied less heavily on exports than did European nations, the country's domestic market was a key stimulus to economic growth.[28]

Wherever they settled, both native-born and newcomers were immersed in a culture of acquisitiveness. Capitalism, protection of private property, entrepreneurship, and individualism were fundamental components of popular American ideology. The country's historical tradition denigrated landed aristocracy and prohibited state-sanctioned nobility. The national self-image heralded the opportunity for self-advancement, as expressed in the hugely popular children's novels by Horatio Alger, and accepted the notion that wealth conveys social status.

Besides producing a high rate of literacy, education, especially publicly supported grammar and high schools, imparted basic skills that were increasingly important to a commercially oriented workplace, such as arithmetic, diction, and typing. Schools also socialized children to American norms, teaching them the importance of punctuality and manners and emphasizing the notion that success is the reward for hard work.[29] Still, earning a living was never easy or assured. Many new city dwellers felt lucky to hold a job at a time when steady employment throughout the year was rare for the working class. African Americans, immigrants from outside northeastern Europe, and women faced innumerable economic barriers.

Economists emphasize technology as a critical factor in American economic growth. Americans had an affinity for adopting new technology, regardless of its origin. In fact, many important devices, such as the electric railway, wireless radio, and internal combustion engine, were invented in Europe. The late nineteenth century witnessed a succession of transformative inventions and productive processes. Steam power, the telephone, electric power plants, and the Bessemer process of steelmaking were important innovations of the latter nineteenth century. Agriculture benefited from these advances, which led to the introduction of steel plows, barbed wire, and machinery such as reapers and threshers. Improved horticulture and husbandry techniques increased agricultural output, allowing farmers to grow more crops per acre and breed cows that gave more milk. These transformations were well under way before the widespread use of the gasoline tractor in the 1930s.[30]

The greatest engineering achievement of the twentieth century, according to the National Academy of Engineering, was electrification, followed by the automobile, the airplane, water supply and distribution, and electronics—all of which appeared between the 1870s and 1903. Right behind these top-ranked inventions were the radio, agricultural mechanization, and the telephone.[31] Technological progress embodies not only seminal inventions but also continual refinements and adaptations. The end product of all this tinkering and improvement was increased productivity, or getting more output from less labor. For consumers, it meant a stream of new products, and for many workers, it meant higher wages.[32]

Technological innovations were instrumental in the expansion of some businesses, from small family-owned firms to large corporations. Incorporation of their enterprises offered owners limited financial liability and greater flexibility in managing their investments. These attributes were attractive to firms involved in large-scale operations, such as railroads, which pioneered corporate management. Likewise, incorporation was attractive to manufacturing companies that emphasized continuous-process production techniques, such as Standard Oil. Firms of this nature generally organized as corporations, hired professional managers, and expanded in size and market influence. The Pennsylvania Railroad hired 50,000 workers in the 1880s, Carnegie Steel employed 20,000 in 1900, and General Motors had 49,000 on its payroll in 1918. By this date, corporations were responsible for the lion's share of the value of manufactured products. The increase in corporate size resulted from efforts to take advantage of economies of scale and improve product marketing. Until the 1880s corporations received charters that permitted them to operate only within their home states. Firms such as John D. Rockefeller's Standard Oil devised a trust arrangement to circumvent this restriction. When state courts began to block this scheme, New Jersey (1889) and New York (1892) enacted laws that permitted multistate holding companies, allowing corporations to go national.

Worried about the effects of big business, Congress enacted the Sherman Antitrust Act of 1890, which made it illegal to monopolize commerce. The law spurred some corporations to merge with their competitors (rather than try to put them out of business) as a tactic to avoid prosecution. The Panic of 1893 and the ensuing depression, which put severe financial strain on some firms, accelerated these consolidations. A wave of mergers between 1897 and 1904 reduced more than 4,000 firms to just 257 corporations, essentially laying the foundation for big business in America. Reorganization produced the American Tobacco Company, Pillsbury, Heinz, and Procter and Gamble—all corporate giants in their fields. Although corporate expansion made considerable sense to managers in terms of reining in costs, the public tended to see big business as the mother of monopolies and higher prices. The dominance of large corporations in numerous industries by the early twentieth century touched a raw political nerve.[33]

Government had a hand in the nation's economic growth. At the federal level, the distribution of land to individuals and corporations continued a century-long practice. National policy encouraged labor recruitment by keeping the gates to immigration open, protected American firms from foreign competitors through tariffs, and nurtured an imperfect currency system through national banking legislation and the monetization of silver. Federal court decisions struck down state impediments to the development of national markets, thus fostering a legal climate favorable for interstate businesses. State and local governments stimulated economic development through tax exemptions, stock subscriptions, and incorporation laws. Government at all levels fostered transportation connections through municipal harbor improvements, railroad rights-of-way, and, late in the period, road and bridge construction. Public education, from the primary level through high school, assisted economic growth. State universities conducted research in agriculture and mining, work that was partially supported by federal funds. Favoring business over workers, government at all three levels countered strikes and repeatedly suppressed labor violence during the late nineteenth century and into the next (see chapter 9).

These policies document public contributions to economic development. Since independence, political leaders had recognized the importance of a successful economy to a viable polity. Consequently, they offered governmental assistance where they could, justifying these actions as supportive of private enterprise and an economically robust society.

ECONOMIC FLUCTUATIONS AND SOCIAL CLASSES

Viewed in the long run, the American economy recorded extensive growth between 1870 and 1920. In the short run, however, entrepreneurs, workers, and families were buffeted by repeated economic slumps. Several of these depressions were severe and prolonged and had wide ramifications, causing bankruptcies, unemployment, and social violence. As in earlier eras, major depressions put significant pressure on government, as leaders faced reduced revenue, financially stressed families, and public protests, some of which degenerated into riots. Depression was experienced differently in particular regions of the country and among the various social classes—from the very affluent and business owners to the middle class, farmers, and industrial workers. Examination of the worst of these crises underscores how situational conditions affected the performance of the American state.

Three major depressions slowed the economy between Reconstruction and the onset of World War I. Each depression had its own narrative, yet they shared some common features. The pre–World War I slumps were preceded by financial panics (1873, 1893, and 1907) in which leading brokerage firms or banks failed. On each occasion, stock prices and interest rates fell. Each slowdown had links to events in Europe, either as causes, such as the tightening of central bank policy and fewer foreign purchases, or as consequences, such as reduced American sales and investment abroad. These connections testify to the United States' integration into the world economy by the late nineteenth century.

Major depressions caused a decline in national income, resulting in business bankruptcies, worker layoffs, and wage cuts. Massive worker strikes rocked communities during each downturn. Individual consumption slowed; revenue collection at each level of government declined, leading to fiscal (budget) deficits. In the throes of these financial crosswinds, conservatives demanded the reduction of public spending, while distressed groups pushed for measures that slowed mortgage foreclosures and lowered property taxes. Numerous voices called for the reform of tax and financial policy.[34]

The collapse of Jay Cooke and Company, a brokerage firm that marketed bonds for the Northern Pacific Railroad, triggered the Panic of 1873. Investor caution about the durability of the railroad boom of the early 1870s was instrumental in causing the crisis, but other factors also strained the financial markets, such as the repercussions of the devastating fires in Chicago (1871) and Boston (1872); revelations about the Credit Mobilier bribery scandal in Congress (1872–1873), which involved stock in the Union Pacific Railroad; and financial crises in Austria and Germany. In 1877 New York governor Lucius Robinson bemoaned the hardships facing state canal operations due to "the great depression in every branch of business." Railroad revenue dropped annually between 1873 and 1877. Rail companies defaulted on a quarter of their debt, even after cutting wages, which sparked the massive railroad strike of 1877. By the time recovery set in (1879), hundreds of banks had closed their doors, and savings and loan institutions had seen their assets contract.[35]

The bankruptcy of the National Cordage Company, a twine-making firm, triggered a financial panic in 1893. Wall Street traders were already nervous about a European depression, which had led Britain to liquidate investments in the United States. The ensuing depression pushed one-fourth of American railroads into bankruptcy and idled about one-fifth of the industrial workforce during the worst of the slowdown. Businesses cut wages, provoking work stoppages and public demonstrations, the largest of which was the Pullman strike, which shut down rail traffic in Chicago and other northern cities for weeks. Declining prices for agricultural commodities caused numerous farmers to lose their land. Businesses searched for solutions to these uncertain conditions by reducing costs and pursuing mergers with rival firms. Renowned financier J. P. Morgan was a leading figure in reorganizing the troubled railroads, which accounted for two-thirds of the country's mileage. Seven major rail systems emerged from the consolidation of scores of lines. Recovery was under way by 1897, helped by the Spanish-American War in 1898.

Another financial meltdown on Wall Street in 1907 provoked a sharp recession in 1908. Trouble began when an attempt to corner the stock of the United Copper Company led to the failure of the Knickerbocker Trust Company, a New York firm. Its collapse triggered a crisis in the stock market, which was largely unregulated at the time. Once again, J. P. Morgan's intervention prevented a complete financial collapse. The devastating earthquake and subsequent fire in San Francisco in 1906 apparently caused a liquidity crisis in New York and Europe, as foreign banks tightened interest rates in the face of rising insurance claims. Outflows of gold, which anchored the American dollar, led to higher interest rates and a slowdown in industrial production. The 1908 depression was short, but recovery was incomplete, as business slowed in 1910 and 1911 and dipped again in 1914 with the outbreak of World War I. Joblessness peaked in 1915, then declined as the war fueled recovery. Although the slowdowns between 1908 and 1915 were milder than the depressions of the 1870s and 1890s, a second problem—rising consumer prices—overlapped the economic stagnation. Prices had been increasing since 1898 and jumped higher in 1910–1911, even though the economy remained sluggish. The combination of the rising cost of living and a languishing economy contributed to the adoption of reforms during the Progressive Era.[36]

Economic slumps did not have a uniform effect throughout the country, partly because a fully integrated national market had not yet developed. Regional economic differences continued to exist in the United States. Besides well-recognized sectional tendencies, such as the agricultural South, the industrializing Northeast, and the corn and hog belt of the Midwest, numerous locally distinct economies existed in every region. The manufacturing belt was concentrated in lower New England, the mid-Atlantic, and the lower Great Lakes region of the Midwest. New York and Chicago, each with a distinct urban persona, anchored this industrial sector. New York became known for its banks, financial brokerages, insurance companies, and a variety of manufacturing firms, as well as a busy international port. Chicago anchored a railroad hub that made it the gateway to the West, and it hosted a number of heavy industries, making it a "city of broad shoulders." The geographic expansion in these years brought additional subregions into this socioeconomic matrix. Smaller cities and single-industry regions lacked the economic diversity of the larger urban areas, rendering them particularly vulnerable to commercial slowdowns. Urbanization, ethnic and racial makeup, and class differences within specific locales produced microstriations in economic circumstances.[37]

Millions of workers and their families lived on the edge of poverty in the industrializing era, even in the absence of economic depression. During the hard times of the 1870s, many tramped from town to town in search of work; in the early twentieth century, these unemployed wanderers were called hobos. Even when they found work, their pay was stretched thin because food consumed nearly half the family budget around the turn of the century. Most semiskilled and unskilled laborers experienced unpredictable work shortages and layoffs, which contributed to high rates of poverty. Employers often cut wages during depressions, which sparked violent strikes, such as the Pullman strike of 1894. The 1908–1915 recessions provoked wage cuts and strikes in the Massachusetts textile mills and shoe factories and among garment workers in New York and Chicago; steelworkers walked off the job in Pennsylvania.[38]

Labor unions made little headway in cushioning the effects of these cyclical crises or in persuading employers to reduce hours, raise wages, and accept collective bargaining. Strike leaders and union organizers were vulnerable to blacklisting, which barred them from employment in their industries. Factory and mine foremen could fire workers for numerous reasons, including age. Industrial accidents were a common occurrence among workers engaged in metalworking, mining, construction, and railroading; these mishaps, as well as diseases related to cotton and stonecutting dust, could bring financial devastation to a laborer's family. Economic circumstances for Blacks, most of whom skimped along as tenant farmers in the South or as unskilled urban workers, and for women who worked outside the home were worse than for white men. Employers commonly hired blacks, some of whom were recruited in the South, to replace striking miners and factory workers in the North.

Worker compensation improved over time. Available data indicate that the per capita "real" gross national product (GNP) increased 88 percent between the 1870s and 1909. Nominal income more than doubled when the data are extended into the 1920s. Moreover, these figures understate gains in the standard of living because measures of GNP do not take into account product improvements; better working conditions; the health benefits of improved water and sewer systems; the availability of gas, electric, and telephone hookups; greater longevity; and other amenities. Both quantified and nonquantified advances in social and economic conditions indicate that most Americans achieved a higher standard of living over the course of the industrial transition.[39]

Some workers were able to join the middle class. Entrance into this group usually required a salaried income or ownership of a business, although some skilled workers and successful farmers qualified. Industrialization created numerous occupations that provided steady, salaried employment, such as managers of businesses, banks, or railroad divisions. Members of the learned professions, such medical doctors, attorneys, college presidents, accountants, and engineers, usually commanded middle-class incomes. So did some government administrators, such as the head of the Smithsonian Institution in Washington, or high school principals in larger cities. Although no precise measurement of middle-class status exists, a rough guess is that 15 percent of urbanites achieved middle-class status in the 1870s, and perhaps 25 percent did so by the early 1920s.[40]

Entrance into the middle class generally enabled the purchase of a home. Available evidence for urban locations shows considerable variation in homeownership, with the lowest rates in the largest cities, such as New York, and considerably higher levels in smaller cities, such as Muncie, Indiana. Census data show that homeownership increased nationwide, accounting for 37 percent of nonfarm housing units in 1890 and 41 percent in 1920. Although the proportional gain seems small, the *number* of homes occupied by owners more than doubled during these thirty years. Moreover, middle-class homes received significant upgrades between 1870 and 1920, acquiring indoor plumbing (running water), sewer connections, electricity, central heating, and gas and telephone connections. Forty-seven percent of urbanites had electricity in 1920, and one-third owned a motor vehicle. The vast majority of city homes had flush toilets by 1930.[41]

Income left over after paying housing costs allowed the middle class to buy a widening array of consumer products, perhaps at downtown department stores. Increased manufacturing productivity reduced the price of many goods; the branding of products, which implied consistent quality, attracted repeat customers. Rural residents could order items from catalogs they received in the mail. The postman also brought newspapers and magazines, which proliferated during the Progressive Era. By the early twentieth century manufacturers and advertisers sought to expand their markets by inserting women's sections into newspapers, based on the assumption that women were the primary consumers in their households. Middle-class affluence allowed parents to keep their children in school rather than sending them into the labor market; a high school diploma was a key credential for getting a middle-class job by 1920.[42]

Economist Robert Gordon has called the rising standard of living between 1890 and 1930 a "unique achievement."[43] His conclusion is persuasive, yet there were limits to this improvement. Many Americans continued to face significant difficulties, ranging from reduced income during depressions to the barriers encountered by groups pushed to the social periphery. Nonetheless, from a macroeconomic view, the United States developed a more prosperous economy in the half century after Reconstruction.

This growth had important ramifications for the development of the American state. First, the industrial transition produced a host of new problems. Some maladies took the form of random events, such as fires ignited by sparks from railroad locomotives or ruptured gas lines, as occurred in San Francisco following the 1906 earthquake. Depression-related disruption of business, labor, and consumers came to be recognized as a cyclical problem. Each economic downturn raised the pressure to reform public finances. Other quandaries grew out of structural changes in the economy, such as the rise of corporate monopolies, a flawed banking system, dangerous urban tenements, and no safety nets for workers. Economic change, in short, altered the socioeconomic landscape. These changes spawned new problems that commanded attention from politicians.

Second, although rising incomes were welcomed, the trend was relative. Millions of people experienced little or no gain in their economic situation. Improvement in the standard of living was more apparent after 1900 than before. Nonetheless, long-run trends such as rising wages, expansion of the middle class, increased homeownership, and declining infant and child mortality—key elements of an improving standard of living—held out hope of personal advancement. A reasonable speculation is that these advances bolstered support for the political regime and diminished the prospect of revolution, numerous labor strikes notwithstanding. Most Americans seemed willing to accept the political arena as the appropriate place to debate their grievances.

Third, greater wealth in the United States led to increased tax revenue, enabling more investment in public goods. Few people enjoy paying taxes, yet the historical record suggests that people are willing to share their affluence with the government if they think the benefits are worth the price tag. Evidence lies in the expansion and reform of taxation during these decades. Conversely, when hard times stressed people's pocketbooks, there were demands to cap taxes, reduce expenditures, and limit indebtedness. These interconnections are examined in the following chapters.

9

Nationalism, Parties, and the Coercive State, 1870–1917

In August 1870 James Bryce stepped off the SS *Scotia* at Battery Point in New York Harbor. The thirty-two-year-old Englishman had come to see America. A newly appointed professor of law at Oxford University, Bryce already knew a lot about the United States. Nonetheless, he wasted no time on his first day, taking in Broadway's theater district and visiting E. L. Godkin, the Irish-born editor of the *Nation*, one of America's most influential magazines. The next day he visited Long Branch, New Jersey, a favorite summer haunt of affluent New Yorkers and Philadelphians.

Armed with introductions, Bryce headed next to New England, where he called on some of America's most celebrated intellectuals. He chatted with poet Henry Wadsworth Longfellow and dined with Oliver Wendell Holmes of Harvard Law School (and later a US Supreme Court justice). He traveled to the White Mountains in New Hampshire, where he encountered philosopher Ralph Waldo Emerson. Then Bryce set out for the Midwest, first by railroad and then by steamer across Lake Michigan to Milwaukee. He took a train across Wisconsin to La Crosse, where he rode a paddle wheeler up the Mississippi River to Minneapolis and St. Paul. After touring the Twin Cities and glimpsing the great prairies to the west, he returned via Chicago, which he called "the handsomest city we have seen in America."

En route east he stopped to observe the New York State Democratic Party convention, over which William Marcy Tweed, the notorious boss of New York City's Tammany Hall, presided. Bryce never forgot the scramble for "place and power" he witnessed there. Returning to Massachusetts, he spent the weekend on an island off Cape Cod owned by railroad financier John Murray Forbes. In the last days of his nine-week tour he visited Yale and Columbia Law Schools. Upon his departure he reflected, "There is a sort of freedom and spirit about the place and the people which one doesn't get in England."

Bryce visited again in 1881, arriving amid speculation about President James Garfield's chances of surviving the recent assassination attempt (he died that September). Anxious to see the West, Bryce took the Santa Fe Railroad from Chicago to San Francisco and then sailed up the coast to Seattle.

He visited Yosemite in California (then a state park) and later toured the South. Last on his itinerary were lectures at Johns Hopkins, the new university in Baltimore that had inaugurated a Ph.D. in history in the United States, and a visit to Washington, DC. Now a member of the British Parliament, Bryce felt quite at home conversing with US senators and representatives at the Capitol.

Bryce visited the States a third time in 1883. He attended a lavish celebration in Idaho commemorating the completion of Henry Villard's Northern Pacific Railroad. Bryce then sailed to Hawaii, not yet officially part of the United States, and climbed Kilauea to view the volcano's eruptions. His return to the mainland took him through the Southwest and New Orleans en route to Baltimore, where he conducted a seminar at Johns Hopkins. One of the young scholars in attendance was Woodrow Wilson, a budding historian and future president. Bryce had previously met Theodore Roosevelt and William Howard Taft, also destined to occupy the White House. These eminent figures and Bryce's other well-educated hosts influenced how he viewed America. As the Englishman sailed home, he was already gathering his thoughts for a book about American government.

Drawing on his experiences in the United States as well as research in documents, contemporary publications, and correspondence with Americans, Bryce published *The American Commonwealth* in 1888. Several editions and many reprintings followed over the next several decades. A work of extraordinary breadth, the book painted a panoramic portrait of American government and society. Reviewers showered the author with praise. Theodore Roosevelt, a competent historian, gave it high marks. Woodrow Wilson, a professor of history and government, called it "a great work." Bryce admired much about the way Americans conducted their civic affairs and marveled at the influence of public opinion in politics. In New England town meetings, "No better school of politics can be imagined," he wrote. Yet Bryce was sharply critical of other elements of American governance. He saw state governments as administratively inept and heaped scorn on "the extravagance, corruption, and mismanagement" of city governments, which he called America's "one conspicuous failure."[1]

NATIONALISM

Bryce's travels gave him clues to Americans' feelings about their homeland. Nationalistic pride is a critical component of statebuilding yet one of the hardest to reconstruct. We know a lot about the outward prompts for patriotism but less about the extent to which most people based their identities on them. There is abundant evidence of efforts by famous elites, prominent groups (e.g., veterans' organizations), and the government to foster devotion to the country. The circulation of national banknotes, which replaced unreliable state banknotes, gave Americans a uniform currency. In all likelihood, these efforts reinforced emotional ties to the nation and its symbols, which differed among social groups and regions. James Bryce remarked that European visitors to America were surprised at the amount of national pride they observed. A generation later, Woodrow Wilson accentuated the observation, contending, "We have come to full maturity with the new century and to full self-consciousness as a nation." Theodore Roosevelt, a lifelong cheerleader for American patriotism, began his 1910 speech titled "The New Nationalism," which advocated federal action to tame corporations, by recalling the sacrifices of Washington and Lincoln.[2]

The 1876 Centennial Exposition in Philadelphia was also a celebration of America's emergence as an industrializing nation. Subsequent world's fairs—Chicago in 1893, St. Louis in 1904, and San Francisco in 1915—boasted similar themes of American industrial, technological, and national advances. President Ulysses Grant took part in opening the 1876 exposition, which was attended by a young Woodrow Wilson. Grover Cleveland traveled to Chicago for the opening ceremony of the 1893 fair, where he turned on the lights; Wilson flipped a switch to initiate a wireless transmission from New Jersey to San Francisco to open that city's world's fair. These presidents clearly saw the connection between the celebration of American materialism and the development of the nation.

By the late 1870s a turn toward historical memory leavened this materialist conception of the country's essence. Congress used the 1876 centennial as the occasion to assume responsibility for completing the Washington Monument, a project initiated by private citizens before the Civil War but not finished until 1885. The celebration of older American virtues and its heroes was interwoven with the "colonial revival" that thrived during the last quarter of the nineteenth century. The movement spawned a proliferation of Washingtonian fervor in the form of calendars, magazine art, advertising, and portraits, including on national banknotes. The famed general and first president was the most popular image among Currier and Ives prints.[3] He was seldom ignored in Fourth of July orations. Memorial Day, which commemorated the sacrifices of the Civil War, arose simultaneously in northern and southern communities in 1866; by 1891 every northern state had made it a legal holiday. In 1911 Congress authorized the construction of the Lincoln Memorial, which was dedicated in 1922. The Washington Monument and Lincoln Memorial became must-see landmarks in the nation's capital for generations of schoolchildren.

The Grand Army of the Republic (GAR), formed immediately after the

Civil War, worked assiduously during the Gilded Age to keep the memory of the Union cause alive. The organization lobbied to make Memorial Day a holiday (in each state, as Congress did not address the matter), pushed for the display of the American flag at public schools, and urged the teaching of American history and civics. It encouraged local communities' efforts to erect statues and monuments to Civil War soldiers. Congress responded to the movement by establishing several national battlefields in the 1890s, places that had already hosted reunions of veterans' groups. Gettysburg, designated a national military park in 1895, attracted thousands of visitors each year. The GAR's campaign to fly the flag at schoolhouses became linked to the Pledge of Allegiance, which was first published in *Youth's Companion* in 1892. The magazine spearheaded the Columbian Public School Celebration, which commemorated the 400th anniversary of Columbus's landing in the Americas. State laws requiring public schools to display the American flag were enacted beginning in 1889; seventeen states had done so by 1903 and twenty-nine by 1916, none in the former Confederacy. In 1919, in the wake of the upsurge in patriotism during World War I, Washington State inaugurated the movement to require children to recite the Pledge of Allegiance in schools. These efforts to promote patriotism pinpointed local governments as the incubators of American nationalism.[4]

Compulsory education tightened the link between schooling and patriotism. Laws requiring school attendance first appeared in the 1860s and had spread to all the states outside the South by 1900. Besides displaying the flag, schools taught American history, which in the Gilded Age was written largely by Protestant New Englanders, who emphasized national politics (supplanting state-based orientations) and patriotism. The authors of one school history text, originally written in 1871 and revised through 1900, expressed the hope that America's story would inspire "a love for our common country" and that, through the "wonderful history of their native land," American youths would "learn to prize their birthright . . . their patriotism must be kindled." Thirty states required the teaching of US history by 1903. The writers of popular histories during the Gilded Age, when college-based academic history became a discipline, were nationalists who championed both conservative politics and national unity. The American Historian Association, organized in 1884, called for a synthesis of national history, which materialized as a multivolume series published in the first decade of the twentieth century. Most volumes were written by academic historians, with the word "national" appearing in many of their titles. The legacy of this nationalization of American history was the "presidential thesis," in which the nation's evolution was traced within the framework of presidential administrations. This orientation became the standard for American history textbooks.[5]

Geography was once called the "mother of all sciences." By the turn of the twentieth century, when the subject was widely taught, it had become nationalist in tone. Atlases of the period were explicitly oriented around national states and their political subdivisions. A more proactive prompt for nationalism was the requirement that English be the official language of instruction in the common schools. Lawmakers and editors who touted the Edwards law in Illinois (1889), which mandated instruction in English and the teaching of American history, stressed the need to inculcate patriotism among the children of immigrants. Many parents in immigrant communities saw the law as a cultural affront. In most communities, the majority likely shared a general set of values that venerated individualism, a morally based view of the polity, an economy built on private initiative, and primacy of the English language. Some scholars argue that high enrollment of school-age children in rural communities reflected their embrace of these firmly held principles.[6]

Private organizations were instrumental in cultivating national sentiments. Arguably no entity rivaled the railroad in welding parts of the country together, at least in a physical sense if not an emotional one Train travel enabled people from far and wide to visit the 1876 Centennial Exposition in Philadelphia, the Chicago World's Fair in 1893, and the national monuments in Washington, DC. Railroads increasingly encouraged travel for leisure and recreation. Prior to the Civil War, only the very adventurous or the very rich traveled long distances for pleasure. In later decades, many in the growing middle class joined the affluent in touring scenic locations and summering at resorts. New England and the mid-Atlantic states, where the well-heeled were concentrated, developed scores of vacation destinations such as Bar Harbor, Maine; Newport, Rhode Island; Cape Cod, Massachusetts; Oyster Bay (Theodore Roosevelt's hometown) and the Hamptons on Long Island, New York; the New Jersey shore; upstate New York; and the White Mountains of New Hampshire. President Grant made Long Branch, New Jersey, his summer White House; President Cleveland vacationed at Buzzards Bay on Cape Cod. The railroad connected northeasterners to Florida in the 1890s and sponsored grand hotels on the Atlantic coast. Artist Winslow Homer was one of the first snowbirds to flee Maine winters for Florida and the Bahamas. Inventor Thomas Edison and automaker Henry Ford built vacation homes in Fort Myers, Florida, while John D. Rockefeller wintered on the state's Atlantic coast.

Railroads aggressively promoted the American West. Aided by travel agencies and guidebook writers, railroads advertised their western routes and built fancy hotels to accommodate travelers lured by the grandeur of the Rockies and the California coast. Yellowstone, designated a national park in 1872, was within a carriage ride of the Northern Pacific line in 1883. The Santa Fe Railroad build a lodge at the edge of the Grand Canyon, which was designated a national forest reserve in 1893 before being upgraded to a national park in 1919. Several lines promoted the California coast's stunning vistas and healthy air and put Yosemite's spectacular beauty within reach. Much of what James Bryce described in *The American Commonwealth* he saw through the window of a railroad car or learned in conversations along the way.[7]

Western travel had a marked impact on Americans' patriotism. The Rocky Mountains and the national parks, especially Yellowstone, Yosemite, and Grand Canyon, were advertised as just as spectacular as Europe's famed rivers and mountains. Paintings that romanticized western landscapes were widely reproduced, and by the 1870s photographers provided realistic confirmation of the West's natural wonders. In William Goetzmann's opinion, the artists and photographers of western landscapes enlarged "the American vision of itself and its own continent to proportions beyond that of any other nation." The West became "an emblem of America's pride in itself." The western movie, a genre originating in the 1910s, fused the vastness and rawness of the western landscape with mythical masculine qualities, turning that imagery into a staple of American self-definition. Much like Daniel Boone and the mountain men of an earlier era, film stars like Tom Mix and John Wayne became icons of American values, displaying resolute individualism, enormous courage, and an unflinching sense of fair play.[8]

The movies thrived on conflict and aggression, qualities that were clearly on display in international politics. During the latter half of the nineteenth century, European powers engaged in a new surge of imperialism, seizing colonial possessions in Asia and Africa and broadening their commercial footholds around the globe, all stimulated by heightened expressions of nationalism. Great Britain led this international race, followed by France, the Netherlands, and Germany. Japan caught the fever by the end of the century. Atlases of the day conveyed the new political geography, depicting each country's territorial possessions in the same color. The British Empire, embracing 390 million people in 1900, was usually shaded pink. International competition and conquest had changed the map by 1900.[9]

The color coding of maps offered a visual confirmation of western Europe's commercial and military power. Trade routes, underwater telegraph cables, and coaling stations around the world certified the role of Great Britain's powerful navy. Internationally minded Americans like Theodore Roosevelt were keenly aware of the link between technological advances (e.g., steel-plated battleships with rapid-firing guns) and status among the world's great powers. Many Americans, Roosevelt in particular, saw national competition for economic and military dominance as part of a Darwinian struggle for survival and mastery. The inauguration of a modernization program for the US Navy in 1882 and the declaration of war against Spain in 1898 occurred in the context of this global competition and Darwinian thinking. America's decisive 1898 victory in the "splendid little war" (Spanish-American War) confirmed the utility of possessing a modern navy and resulted in the acquisition of the Philippines and Puerto Rico. The United States annexed Hawaii the same year, five years after marines helped resident Americans overthrow the native government. Despite the denials of American expansionists, the United States was an imperial power. The Spanish-American War spiked a surge of patriotic fervor at the end of the century that was probably unmatched until America entered World War I. Early in the twentieth century, President Theodore Roosevelt proudly asserted, "We have become a great nation."[10]

PATRIOTISM ON THE CULTURAL PERIPHERY

Despite technical advances and military victories, Americans' patriotic identification around the turn of the century remains blurred. By most reckonings, nationalist pride was most widely disseminated among white males of northern European, Protestant backgrounds—that is, white Anglo-Saxon Protestants (WASPs)—who resided in the North and the West. Opinion leaders, such as authors, newspaper editors, and clergy, as well as most Republican Party officials and leaders of big business, usually had WASP-ish lineages and decidedly patriotic leanings. With the memory of the Civil War still burning, white southerners maintained a much lower identity with national symbols, at least until sectional reconciliation was fully under way in the 1890s. But even with varying degrees of civic healing, many southerners remained indifferent about patriotic unity, seeing their region as distinct and separate.[11] African Americans, women (especially in the working class), unnaturalized immigrants from non-English-speaking places, individuals of Mexican birth or lineage, and Native Americans were also on the periphery of the white Protestant culture. A reasonable conjecture is that most of these groups were less likely than WASPs to feel patriotic toward the national state.

African Americans, most of whom resided in states where slavery had been legal, held Abraham Lincoln in esteem as the Great Liberator. But after Reconstruction, most southern blacks were systematically reduced to rural peonage, and beginning in the 1890s, they were stripped of the right to vote. This racist subjugation was reinforced by lynching, an extralegal form of execution that had de facto approval of southern white officials (see "The Coercive State" later in this chapter). Mexicans, Chinese immigrants, Native

Americans, and labor radicals experienced similar outbreaks of violence in the West.[12]

Women in America possessed a truncated form of citizenship. Most were barred from voting in general elections before the twentieth century. How disfranchisement influenced female attitudes toward the nation and the state is unclear. Women, especially middle-class WASPs outside the South, were active in numerous social and charitable organizations, including an entity linked to the GAR, and many joined clubs that campaigned for political candidates. After women's failure to be included in the Fifteenth Amendment, which prohibited the use of race but not gender as a criterion for voting, leaders of the female suffrage movement emphasized their cultural links to white males and gravitated toward a race-based conception of republican ideology. In a more applied setting, women who became schoolteachers assumed a position in which an emphasis on citizenship and patriotism was common. In all likelihood, women, especially those from WASP families, followed the male head of household in identifying with the national community.[13]

Attitudes among immigrants varied considerably, depending on when they arrived in America, their homeland culture, and their employment circumstances. Protestants from the British Isles and northern Europe assimilated rapidly into the general culture. Some states (mainly in the Midwest and West) allowed unnaturalized (male) immigrants to vote if they declared their intention to become citizens, a concession that probably served as an incentive to embrace American norms. Yet ethnic hostilities flared between core and peripheral cultures, as evidenced by conflict between Yankees and Germans in nineteenth-century Wisconsin. A public campaign in the 1880s to require all schools, including institutions sponsored by Catholics and Lutherans, to teach basic subjects only in English reflected resentment of nonnative cultures.[14]

Newcomers from southern and central Europe who arrived after 1890 and Mexicans who immigrated during World War I faced greater hurdles to acculturation. The welcome mat for immigrants got smaller after 1900. Calls to restrict immigration from Asia, especially China, began in the 1880s; later, immigrants from southern and central Europe, particularly Poles, Italians, and Russian Jews, faced mounting intolerance. Most of these newer immigrants entered the industrial and agricultural working classes. The majority retained emotional and social ties to their ethnic communities yet tried to fit into their new homeland. Employers, social welfare organizations such as settlement houses and the YMCA, and some labor unions provided instruction in navigating American society by teaching English and the essentials of American democracy.[15]

The rising tide of immigrants from nontraditional countries sparked a campaign to restrict admission to the United States at the turn of the twentieth century. This intolerance fed pressures to raise the bar on certain legal privileges, particularly the right to vote. Adoption of the Australian ballot, which states prepared and local governments administered, made it difficult for non-English readers to vote. Numerous states retracted the franchise from nonnaturalized immigrants and passed stricter voter registration laws; a few jurisdictions made literacy a criterion for suffrage. The national immigration law of 1891 allowed federal officials to bar admission on moral, economic, and physical grounds, such as insanity or the likelihood of becoming impoverished. The 1903 act excluded anarchists. The 1906 naturalization law made it much more difficult to attain citizenship and authorized federal officials to oversee this administrative process. Washington, however, left the job of preparing newcomers for citizenship to local governments. Beginning with New York at the start of the twentieth century, cities began to sponsor classes in English, civics, and American history. State governments joined the Americanization effort in 1907, expanding their programs in cooperation with the US Bureau of Naturalization.[16]

How these carrot-and-stick policies affected immigrant identity before World War I is unclear. The evidence suggests that most immigrants accepted the ideological premises of American republicanism, such as equality and justice for all, as well as middle-class norms such as thrift and hard work; they looked forward to citizenship, if only for practical reasons. Native-born children of immigrants (second-generation Americans) latched onto national values more readily than their immigrant parents. According to immigration historian Marcus Lee Hansen, most newcomers in the upper Midwest were "capitalist at heart" and stood firmly behind the concept of political democracy.[17]

The restrictions on naturalization and suffrage reflected middle- and upper-class outlooks that linked "new" immigrants with political radicalism. Worker strikes and protests in the late nineteenth century, such as occurred during the depressions of the 1870s and 1890s and the 1886 Haymarket Square riot in Chicago, fanned the flames of anti-immigrant nativism. Officials during the Gilded Age and the Progressive Era commonly pushed a law-and-order response to strikes, which often pitted recent immigrants, many of whom did not speak English, against employers that had the backing of local politicians and law enforcement officials. An outgrowth of this backlash was the Immigrant Restriction League, founded in 1894. The league advocated a literacy test for admission to the country, a proposal that was enacted in 1917.[18]

Segments of the immigrant population, therefore, had legitimate reasons to express indifference toward if not actual rejection of patriotic loyalty.

A small cadre of workers aligned with the Socialist Party preached international solidarity but not outright disloyalty to the United States. The Industrial Workers of the World (whose members were known as Wobblies) was an avowedly anticorporatist organization, denouncing capitalism as an economic system. Yet Socialists and Wobblies were small, marginal groups in American politics, and most of them rejected violent revolution. Workers' resentment in the United States was directed at employers and corporations rather than the state, although some radical labor leaders saw little difference between these groups when the government took employers' side.

For most residents, the American version of revolution involved the ballot box rather than the barricade, despite frequent violence at strikers' picket lines. The electoral record is suggestive on this point: voter turnout reached an all-time high during the last decades of the nineteenth century. With the exception of the South, where official intimidation of voters (blacks and poor whites) was effective in depressing turnout, 80 to 90 percent of the eligible electorate voted in national and state elections, considerably higher than twentieth-century rates. The close competition between the Republican and Democratic Parties in national elections and in some northeastern and midwestern states—sometimes animated by third parties that could act as spoilers—accounts for some of this surge. Attention to federal issues in party platforms for both state and national elections suggests how partisan competition fed national identity. Despite being an imperfect indicator of political sentiment, turnout data suggest widespread acquiescence to the American national state. The decline in voter turnout during the Progressive Era apparently reflected stricter regulations and the inflow of migrants from places with weak or nonexistent democratic traditions, as well as weakening bonds of partisanship, not a slump in nationalism.[19]

THE COERCIVE STATE

A key attribute of a national state is its legal monopoly on the use of coercive force. This power can promote a state's stability and influence attitudes about it. Officials at all levels of government regularly exercised coercive power in the late nineteenth and early twentieth centuries and frequently acquiesced when private citizens took the law into their own hands. Reliance on court orders to cease an activity; deployment of the army, militia, and police; and extralegal intimidation are tools of a coercive state. The application of coercion is commonly justified in nationalist terms, especially when "foreign" groups are targeted. Coercive actions may dampen patriotic sentiments of harassed populations, especially when violence is directed at specific ethnic groups or striking workers.

Deployment of the US military represented the chief form of national coercive force in the Gilded Age. The army remained an occupying presence in the South during Reconstruction. It invaded Cuba, Puerto Rico, and the Philippines in 1898 during the Spanish-American War, while the navy defeated Spanish fleets off the coast of Puerto Rico and in Manila Bay. A large American ground force remained in the Philippines, where anticolonial resistance lasted until 1902 and cost ten times more US fatalities than the fighting in Cuba. American armed forces occupied several Central American countries during the Progressive Era, including forays into Mexico between 1914 and 1916. Campaigns in the Caribbean and Asia that engaged indigenous natives were sometimes justified in racist (nonwhite) terms. The army also launched numerous expeditions to pacify Indians in the trans-Mississippi West in the late nineteenth century.

Regular troops of the US Army were summoned to suppress rioters and maintain law and order during labor disputes. President Rutherford B. Hayes ordered the army to help state militiamen quell rioting at numerous locations during the great rail strike of 1877. The largest deployment of the US Army between the Civil War and the Spanish-American War occurred during the Pullman strike of 1894, when railroad workers and others blocked rail access throughout the Northeast, the Midwest, and portions of the West. All rail traffic in and out of Chicago was halted. President Grover Cleveland authorized the intervention of federal troops, under the guise of protecting the mail. At the height of the conflict, 14,000 federal troops and marshals, state militia, and local police patrolled the streets and rail yards of Chicago. Up to thirty-four demonstrators, none of them strikers, were killed; Eugene Debs, the railroad union leader who purportedly led the uprising, was convicted in federal court and sentenced to prison. Policing of a different order occurred in connection with federal immigration enforcement in the early twentieth century, resulting in the deportation of aliens, sometimes on the basis of their alleged subversive beliefs.[20]

State militias (increasingly called the National Guard) were mobilized on hundreds of occasions during the Gilded Age and Progressive Era to quell strikes and riots, often using lethal force to do so. Theodore Roosevelt's charge up San Juan Hill in Cuba during the Spanish-American War won him national notoriety and aided his election as governor of New York. Known as a staunch law-and-order man, Roosevelt called out the militia (which had been uniformed at his instruction) to intervene when Italian construction workers walked off the Croton Dam project in a dispute over wages. The New York militia arrested the Italian labor leaders, protected the workers who had been hired to replace the strikers, and suppressed the strike. This was one of many instances when business elites persuaded elected officials to use organized force (militia, police, sheriffs, and sometimes deputized private contractors such as Pinkerton guards) to break strikes and protect business interests. Accusing the "riotous Italians" of assassinating a militiaman, Governor Roosevelt justified his intervention with the statement that "order must be maintained." Labor violence worried elites and many in the middle class. Shaken by the great rail strike of 1877, middle-class New Yorkers built a massive new armory for the city militia. Similar efforts occurred around the country over the ensuing decades.[21]

The most frequent use of coercive force occurred at the local level, frequently at the hands of city police who were called upon to monitor the "dangerous class" and control worker protests in an era when picketing and boycotting were illegal. In the Tompkins Square "riot" (1874), New York City police, some on horseback, attacked a crowd of workers who had assembled in support of public works projects during the 1870s depression. Police dispersed the demonstrators in a bloody melee. Another clash between police and demonstrators that had enormous political reverberations occurred during the Haymarket Square riot in Chicago (1886). Workers and social activists had gathered in the square to protest police brutality and the killing of six workers during a strike in support of an eight-hour workday. After an anonymous person threw a bomb at the police, officers fired on the crowd, killing several people. Officials convicted local labor radicals of conspiracy and hung several of them. The Illinois legislature enacted antiriot laws that criminalized conspiracy to cause violence to human life or property and held cities and counties responsible for the destruction of property by mobs. Most policing action, however, occurred on an individual level and was characterized by the use of the billy club, usually in working-class neighborhoods. Police arrested people without jobs as vagrants, as well as those operating illegal saloons. African Americans were hounded regularly by police in the South.[22]

States invested heavily in prison construction in the last decades of the nineteenth century. The 1,800 cells in the prison at Columbus, Ohio, made it the largest jail in the world in the 1890s. Before authorizing the construction of its own prisons in 1891, the federal government rented space in state facilities or county jails. By the early twentieth century approximately seventy-eight state prisons and 3,000 city and county jails housed more than 100,000 individuals, including those confined to juvenile institutions, according to the US census. But a much larger number, perhaps half a million, spent some time in local, state, or federal lockups in 1910. This count excludes convicts who were leased to private contractors in the South. Incarceration was a growing dimension of statebuilding in the post–Civil War decades.[23]

State prisons were the usual sites for executions, which numbered in the thousands during the Gilded Age and Progressive Era. Although the use of capital punishment declined after the 1870s, illegal executions probably increased during the latter half of the nineteenth century. Commonplace in the West and the South, lynching was an extralegal death sentence at the hands of a mob, frequently with the tacit support of local officials. Blacks, labor activists, immigrants from central Europe and Asia, and Hispanics were the most likely victims. In the South, blacks were executed at a much higher rate than whites, both within the justice system and by mob action. Rates of capital punishment in the South were the highest in the nation and far exceeded the number of executions in Europe.[24]

Coercion and incarceration were part of a governmental endeavor to suppress behaviors believed to be immoral or dangerous. There were two major efforts at social control: shuttering saloons and limiting the availability of alcoholic beverages, and enforcing compulsory education, a task assigned to truant officers. Numerous statutes made vagrancy a crime; these laws were used in the South to force African Americans into legally sanctioned peonage. Although the regulation of cultural mores was primarily a local function, the federal government was authorized to suppress certain obnoxious behaviors, such as polygamy in federal territories (1869 and later) and among immigrants (1891). US marshals took action against Mormons in the West who violated the law prohibiting multiple marriages; Congress stripped Mormon offenders of the right to vote. Postal officials restricted the use of the mails to disseminate obscene materials, such as pornography, and lotteries.[25]

National control of immigration and naturalization tightened during the late nineteenth century. The immigration law of 1891 authorized officials to expel aliens who had violated the rules for admission to the country. Congress added anarchists to the barred list in 1903 and prostitutes in 1907. The 1917 codification of the immigration statute specified thirty-three qualitative and physical attributes that barred newcomers. Thousands of aliens were deported, often without full judicial review, during the first two decades of the twentieth century. The US Treasury Department maintained a fleet of vessels with armed crews to enforce customs collections and immigration and quarantine laws and to suppress mutinies on ships. In the early 1890s James Bryce concluded that the forces maintaining order in the United States were as strong "as anywhere else in the world."[26] These laws and their application demonstrate that the American federal state acquired and exercised greater coercive power at home and abroad in the decades after Reconstruction.

POLITICAL PARTIES

The principles underlying American politics, many have said, constituted the nation's civic religion. At the center of this ideological vision was republican liberty, which allowed the popular election of officials at all levels of government. Short terms in office meant a constant churning of officeholders for thousands of jurisdictions. At the national level, only candidates for the House of Representatives were directly elected. US senators were chosen by state legislators until 1913. Elections abounded at the state and local levels. All forty-five governors and 6,600 state legislators were elected directly by voters in 1900, as were constitutional officers such as attorney generals and treasurers, as well as judges, in most states. The penchant for democracy was most visible at the local level, where tens of thousands of candidates ran for mayor and city council positions, as well as for township offices and school boards in rural areas. Besides selecting their mayor, Boston voters chose twelve aldermen and seventy-two city councilors; Philadelphia's city council had 143 members. Reference to a "national" electorate in America is a literary euphemism; the foundation of participatory politics rested at the local level.

The presidency was the only office that could claim a national constituency. The seven presidential canvasses between 1876 and 1900 elected five individuals: four Republicans—Rutherford B. Hayes, James Garfield, Benjamin Harrison, and William McKinley—and one Democrat—Grover Cleveland, who was elected in 1884, lost as the incumbent in 1888, and returned to the White House after the 1892 election. Cleveland was the only president during this period who had not served in the Civil War. Three of the elected Republicans plus Chester Arthur, who replaced Garfield (assassinated in 1881), had risen to the rank of general; a young William McKinley had left service in the Union army as a brevetted major. Theodore Roosevelt, who assumed the presidency following McKinley's assassination, had been a colonel in the army volunteers during the Spanish-American War.

Gilded Age presidents have received low grades from historians, who tend to describe them as undistinguished personalities who exercised little influence on policy. This characterization is part of the indictment thesis that has long labeled Gilded Age governance as corrupt and tone-deaf to societal needs. But it bears noting that none of the Gilded Age presidents was involved in a major political or personal scandal while in office. It is also true that they largely supported the status quo and accepted existing constitutional limits on national power, which goes a long way toward explaining why they gained their party's nomination and perhaps why voters supported them. They largely deferred to Congress concerning administrative reform.

The idea that executives should exercise policy leadership by laying out a comprehensive agenda and pressing for its enactment had not yet taken hold. Nonetheless, by the 1880s American presidents and governors had signed legislation that expanded the federal government's public role. Beginning with Theodore Roosevelt's ascension to the White House in 1901 and continuing with William Taft and Woodrow Wilson, presidents became more active policy advocates.[27]

The partisan makeup of the House of Representatives provides a rough index of national electoral trends, although the winner-take-all system of selecting a victor in single-member districts magnified the partisan proportion of seats won in relation to the party distribution of the national vote. The House contained 293 seats in 1871, 391 in 1901, and 435 in 1913, as it still does today. State legislatures draw up congressional district lines. Affiliation with one of the two major parties is the most conspicuous characteristic of House members. The southern states' reintegration into national politics in the 1870s helped Democrats become a competitive factor in control of the House between 1870 and 1894, when they held a majority of seats in eight of fifteen sessions. Democrats' sweeping defeat in the congressional elections of 1894 inaugurated an eighteen-year Republican reign as the majority party (see figure 9.1). Democrats managed to control the Senate in only five sessions between 1871 and 1919.

Several factors drove these partisan patterns. The dismantling of Reconstruction-era governments in the South launched Democratic political dominance in the region, which greatly increased the party's chances of winning a majority in the House. Republicans had a solid foothold in the West, benefiting from the admission of new states, which helped the party control the Senate. A second influence on elections was the condition of the economy. The business slump following the Panic of 1873 cost Republicans nearly half their seats in the House of Representatives in 1874, producing substantial losses in all sections of the country.[28] Outsider third parties, principally the Greenback Party, lured Republican defectors, partially on the basis of economic appeals. The GOP regained the majority in the House in 1880, only to lose badly in 1882. A mild economic downturn during the mid-1880s helped Democrats regain seats, and various political factors catapulted the party to a large congressional majority in 1890. Democrats controlled both chambers of Congress and the White House following Cleveland's election in 1892, only to suffer a sweeping loss (116 House seats) in 1894, largely due to the worst industrial slump of the nineteenth century. Republicans retained majorities in the House until 1910, when a combination of economic stagnation and the defection of insurgent Republicans fueled a Democratic resurgence.

Figure 9.1. Republican seats (%) in the US House of Representatives and the Illinois and New York Assemblies, 1870–1928. *Sources:* Author's data collections; for the House, Harold W. Stanley and Richard G. Neimi, *Vital Statistics on American Politics*, 5th ed. (Washington, DC: Congressional Quarterly, 1995), table 3-16.

Partisan fortunes in the states roughly corresponded to national trends. Figure 9.1 compares lower house seats held by Republicans in the Illinois and New York Assemblies with Republican seats in Congress. The rise and fall of Republican victories in New York followed a similar but not identical pattern. In Illinois, Republicans' hold on seats shadowed the trend in the US House but with much less volatility, largely because of the Prairie State's system of three-member districts, which essentially guaranteed a seat for the minority party candidate in each district. Other northern states' legislative races ranged from close to faint correspondence with congressional races, indicating that state elections were not wholly coordinate with national elections. Some regions and states, such as New England, Iowa, and Oregon, habitually returned large Republican majorities to their legislatures. The fate of Republican gubernatorial candidates in the northern states mimicked the surges and declines in electoral outcomes for Congress, with the GOP normally winning a majority of state contests.[29] The parties also ran candidates for mayor and municipal legislators (councilmen and aldermen) in large cities, although it is unclear how closely those results corresponded to state and national trends. The evidence suggests that local circumstances could have a decisive influence on local elections. Young Theodore Roosevelt, for instance, the Republican candidate for New York City mayor in 1886, came in third behind the Democratic winner and Henry George, a critic of unregulated capitalism who ran on the Labor Party ticket.[30]

Generally, most voters stuck with a single party during the Gilded Age, which raises the question of how each party wooed its supporters. Republicans emphasized their devotion to the Union during the Civil War, a refrain known as "waving the bloody flag." The GOP was also willing to use governmental power to promote economic development, principally through the support of high tariff rates that "protected" American manufacturers and supposedly boosted wages. The party favored measures of social control, such as restricting liquor-related businesses and embracing puritanical standards of personal morality. Republicans pushed for laws that mandated English as the language of instruction for basic subjects in schools; this triggered a backlash in Illinois and Wisconsin that cost the party control of these states in 1890. Republicans won the support of most Yankee voters (Americans of English descent), as well as recent British, Scottish, and Swedish immigrants. The majority of the urban middle class and business owners voted Republican, except in the South. Southerners moved steadily toward the Democrats, particularly after the farmer-based Populist surge in the mid-1890s.

Democrats were the party of small government and white supremacy during the late nineteenth century. The Democratic Party opposed Republican efforts to protect the rights of African Americans and to impose cultural regulations, calling itself the party of personal liberty. Democrats emphasized respect for states' rights as the proper approach to federalism and urged an economic policy that provided no special benefits; this included high tariffs, which, according to President Cleveland, rewarded selfish interests. Cleveland's party was more insistent about low taxation and frugal spending than the Republicans were, although both parties preached the virtues of fiscal discipline. The Democratic agenda appealed to whites in the South and to southern transplants in the Midwest, Catholics, large segments of the German community (immigrants and their American-born descendants), and a majority of big-city residents, most of whom were working class but also included a small segment of business elites.

Democratic and Republican agendas did not appeal to all Gilded Age voters. Dissenters bolted to smaller third parties throughout the period. The Greenback Party, which complained about a restricted money supply, won seats in Congress and in state legislatures in the 1870s. In the 1890s the Populist Party attracted voters from the major parties in the South and

West with its critique of the constricted money supply, corporate monopolies, and inattention to the needs of rural America. Prohibitionists worked to control if not eliminate the "liquor interests," but they also advocated other moral reforms throughout the late nineteenth century. Small worker-oriented parties appeared during these years as well, centered largely in cities. Independents disturbed by self-serving partisanship defected from the Republican Party in the 1880s—notably, the mugwumps, who supported Grover Cleveland in 1884. Given the close competition in many jurisdictions and nationally, each party wrestled to keep its coalitions intact; even small voter defections could doom a candidate's chances.[31]

Unexpected events could upset the conventional electoral calculus, as illustrated by William McKinley's victory over William Jennings Bryan in 1896, in the face of a lingering depression. A Nebraskan, Bryan attacked eastern-based business and supported agrarian interests, currency inflation, and prohibition. These positions resonated poorly with urban workers, who wanted a more rapid economic recovery. The Republican surge in 1896 anchored the party's majority position in Congress and the presidency for the next fifteen years. Bryan lost again in 1900, and in his final run for the presidency in 1908, voters preferred William Howard Taft as Theodore Roosevelt's successor. By 1910, however, the GOP faced a rebellion by reform-oriented Republicans, a development that blossomed into the Progressive Party. Progressives encouraged Theodore Roosevelt to return to politics, giving him the party's presidential nomination in 1912. His candidacy siphoned votes from President Taft, the Republican incumbent, and handed the victory to Woodrow Wilson. Governor of New Jersey and a southerner by birth, Wilson had been assured of capturing all the electoral votes of the South, virtually eliminating Republican and third-party chances in the region. Wilson narrowly won reelection in 1916 but saw Democrats lose control of the House, largely due to the recession triggered by the outbreak of World War I.[32]

Electoral dynamics in the Progressive Era shifted incrementally away from the straight party-line voting and close partisan competition that had characterized the Gilded Age and animated high voter turnout. Split-ticket voting became more common, especially in state and municipal elections. Growing complaints about excessive partisanship discredited legislatures and increased the appeal of executives, who were seen as more likely to restore honest and efficient government and stop collusion between special interests and corrupt politicians.

The rising resentment over political corruption and corporate monopolies was accentuated by a faltering economy. A financial panic struck the country in 1907, causing a sharp recession in 1908. The Republican Party largely weathered this downturn because voters apparently considered Taft and the Republicans more likely to restore prosperity than Bryan and the Democrats. But the shoe was on the other foot in 1910 and 1912, when a stalemated recovery was exacerbated by rising consumer prices, a combination now called stagflation. The increased cost of living discredited Republicans' support of high tariff rates, the party's main panacea for economic growth. A rash of labor strikes in 1909 and 1910 reflected the strain on family budgets. The 1910 elections catapulted Democrats into the majority in the House of Representatives and boosted the party's fortunes in the northern states. Democrats widened their control of the House and state legislatures in 1912, put Woodrow Wilson in the White House, and gave him a Democratic majority in the Senate. This shift in party control was instrumental in enacting Progressive Era reforms between 1911 and 1916.[33]

The condition of a democratic state depends largely on the inhabitants' acceptance of the legitimacy of their leaders. During the Gilded Age political parties were the primary tool for marshaling popular support for governing regimes, with private groups such as religious organizations, commercial interests, labor and farmer groups, and publishing entities playing important supporting roles. After 1900 parties lost some of their hold on voter loyalty, while nonpolitical interests such as business groups, labor organizations, and citizens' reform-oriented groups, as well as more assertive executives at all levels, assumed more influential leadership roles. These post-1896 shifts were evolutionary and incremental, however, and did not disturb the basic cultural and structural foundations on which the American national state rested.

The historical evidence suggests that a substantial majority of residents (adult citizens and aliens) accepted the principles that formed the nation's ideological foundation. Clearly, the vast majority of Americans remained loyal to the national regime, in the sense that no violent (i.e., unconstitutional) revolution or palace coup occurred during the Gilded Age and Progressive Era. Support for the federal state rested heavily on a popular embrace of classic American tenets—individual rights, equality, and economic opportunity—as frayed as these principles were in practice. Numerous cultural groups and disgruntled labor activists were relegated to secondary status by white Protestant males. Where persuasion failed, power holders wielded coercive force to extract compliance from dissidents. Behind the celebration of political rights and individualism lurked the reality of American insistence on law and order, particularly for people of color and those with marginal incomes. The American state consisted of a noncentralized structure held together by popular consent for its democratic principles as articulated by the core cultural establishment, the competitive arrangement of its party system, and leaders' willingness to force compliance from social and political deviants.

10

The Federal State during the Gilded Age

"Mr. Speaker! Mr. Speaker!" yelled the impetuous young lawmaker as he stormed the rostrum seeking recognition. The high-pitched voice with a patrician New York accent belonged to Theodore Roosevelt, just twenty-four years old and two years out of Harvard College. He now represented the Twenty-First Assembly District in New York City. Within weeks he made his presence felt, bringing youthful exuberance and brash moralism to the chamber. One of his fellow lawmakers described him as "a ball of dynamite" with the fuse burning, which annoyed some colleagues and puzzled others who were accustomed to the more sedate cadence of legislative business. Roosevelt's biggest target in 1882 was the impeachment of a sitting state supreme court judge, a campaign launched through his membership on the Committee on Cities. He accused the judge of illegal use of funds and complicity in Jay Gould's efforts to acquire the Manhattan Railway Company on the cheap. The committee majority refused to recommend impeachment, a decision rumored to be leveraged by bribes. Roosevelt's attack on the purported connivance between a public official and a notorious entrepreneur was the cause célèbre of the session and won accolades from his Republican colleagues, who supported him for the speaker's chair in the next session.[1]

A Democratic majority in the New York Assembly in 1883 blocked Roosevelt's chances of gaining the speakership, but he spearheaded the enactment of a civil service commission for state employees, the first among the states. Democratic governor Grover Cleveland rallied a sufficient number of his party to join the Republicans in passing the measure. Roosevelt returned to the assembly in 1884 for his third consecutive term. This was unusual at the time. Rotation of legislative representation was the norm, and roughly three-quarters of state representatives were first-termers.[2] Although Republicans regained the majority in the 1884 assembly, Roosevelt lost his bid for the speakership. He settled for chair of the Committee on Cities, which gave him a platform to push for reforms. For weeks he commuted from the capitol in Albany to New York City, where he headed an investigation of its administrative practices, probing unauthorized fees collected by officeholders and the police. This highly publicized fact-finding venture paid off, as the legislature adopted most of his recommendations, which included greater appointment power for the mayor as well as restrictions on taxes and indebtedness for the city.[3]

Roosevelt's crusade against the spoilsmen—politicians allied with businessmen who preyed on the government for personal financial benefit—was frequently cited as evidence of political corruption during the Gilded Age. Roosevelt's published accounts of ethical lapses that he saw or suspected during his legislative career reinforced the indictment of Gilded Age politics, a view prominent among the well educated and well heeled. English scholar James Bryce drew on Roosevelt's articles to profile local politicians. "The State legislatures," Bryce opined, "are not high-toned bodies." Though he conceded that some New England and midwestern states had a tradition of sending "good men" to their legislatures, this was not the case for big-city states like New York, where, Bryce wrote (quoting Roosevelt), the "worst legislators . . . are usually foreigners of little or no education, with exceedingly misty ideas as to morality." A standard interpretation of American politics for several generations, Bryce's *American Commonwealth* reiterated a belief widely held among pundits of the time and historians thereafter: that state legislatures were sinkholes of bribery and extortion, under the thumb of party bosses, and composed of inexperienced, unqualified lawmakers. This toxic mixture allowed corruption, badly drafted laws, and "too much legislation." Article titles such as "The Blight on Legislatures" and "The Menace of Legislation" illustrate how contemporary writers propagated the theme. Urban politics was thought to be even worse.[4]

The ethical quality of legislative politics in New York was regarded as among the lowest in the country.[5] Yet behind such stinging indictments lay some contravening realities. Writing about his experience in the legislature, Roosevelt acknowledged, "there is at Albany a little home rule parliament which presides over the destinies of a commonwealth more populous than any one of two-thirds of the kingdoms of Europe." Its business affected "a magnitude of interests" in the state.[6] During Roosevelt's stint at the capitol in Albany, the state created a railroad commission, inaugurated bank inspections, established a bureau of labor statistics, formed a state civil service commission, took the first step toward creating Adirondack State Park, established a dairy commission to set milk standards, enhanced the administrative authority of New York City's mayor, and imposed debt and tax limits on the city. Later in the 1880s New York enacted an inheritance tax, required the inspection of factories on behalf of workers, created a board of labor arbitration, regulated trust companies, mandated that firms pay employees' wages in money (rather than credit at a company store), and required state exams for the licensing of physicians.[7] Putting aside, for a moment, the question of the administration of these enactments, the record clearly shows that New York exercised its civic authority broadly. This juxtaposition between the indictment of Gilded Age politics as tone deaf to societal problems and the incremental expansion of state capacity is the central paradox of governance during the late nineteenth century.

GOVERNING AMERICAN CITIES

A reading of the platforms of the major political parties only hints at how America was governed during the Gilded Age. Describing this process requires an examination of lawmaking, administration, and judicial adjudication across the three levels of government, but especially local government, which shouldered responsibility for most public functions. Summarizing this record poses challenges, not only because of the great number of jurisdictions in the United States but also because of the evolving scale and scope of their activities. Here we must be content with a condensed summary of these trends. Policymakers at all levels during the Gilded Age expanded civic involvement in society, spent more public money, and initiated improvements in public administration. This history contradicts the traditional claim that government acted as little more than a night watchman in the late nineteenth century.

The public workhorses in the Gilded Age were the local governments, especially the cities, which grew faster than rural areas. Between 1870 and 1900 the urban population increased more than 200 percent, adding 20 million people. The number of big cities (with at least 50,000 inhabitants) more than doubled to 78 major municipalities; by 1920 the count had risen to 144. The expanding urban population, much of it made up of recent immigrants, raised the population density in cities, a situation that bred an array of problems that were minor or nonexistent in rural areas. The crowding of urban environments elevated the difficulty of providing fresh water, disposing of sewer waste and garbage, maintaining usable thoroughfares, and ensuring reliable intracity transportation. Additional obligations included providing police and fire protection, schools, and recreational areas; assisting the infirm and indigent; and implementing policies for the development of real estate. How well a city addressed these challenges affected its ability to attract and maintain businesses and taxpayers.

The *Chicago Tribune* editorialized in 1889, "The two great needs of this city are pure water and pure air."[8] Ample clean water, the editors recognized, was critical to urban life. At the household level, water was used for drinking, cooking, and washing, while at the municipal level, water flushed away horse dung and urine from city streets and extinguished fires, a constant hazard in nineteenth-century cities. By the 1880s bacteriologists had discovered that toxic microbes bred in polluted water, offering a new inducement to supply clean water and to discard wastewater in a sanitary manner.

Boston illustrates the evolution of urban water policy. The city embarked on a program of publicly supplied water in the 1830s and expanded its availability in subsequent decades. The city created Chestnut Hill Reservoir in 1871 and connected it to Wachusett Reservoir in 1898 in one of the largest water projects in the nation. The discharge of pollutants into rivers, which were a source of drinking water, concerned the Massachusetts Board of Health, which was established in 1869. In 1875 the state legislature instructed the board to institute antipollution procedures. The Boston Health Department (created in 1873) became the administrative arm of the state board. The outbreak of cholera and smallpox epidemics in the 1880s led the legislature to give the state board additional authority; it hired a bacteriologist to test water sources and required cities that were planning sewer systems to file reports with the board. In 1895 the state created a metropolitan water district for the Boston area, with the authority to issue bonds for the construction of water facilities. In 1890 Boston spent a third of its budget on water, streets, and sewers, suggesting that state and urban governments had recognized the connection between water quality and public health.[9]

New York established a city board of health in 1866, an agency that became a model for the nation. It was among the first to hire a bacteriologist, who reported in 1889 that tuberculosis (TB), a scourge of working-class residents, was caused by a bacterium and was preventable. The New York Board of Health mandated the inspection of dairy herds for the TB bacillus in 1896, and the following year it required doctors to report cases of the disease. By 1910 the city's TB rate had fallen substantially. The New York and Massachusetts city-state partnerships in public health influenced local jurisdictions elsewhere in the country. By 1900 most large and midsized cities and thirty-nine states had boards of health. Garbage collection had begun in many cities, and they increasingly turned to engineers to oversee these activities or to consult about methods of keeping the urban environment clean.[10]

Progress in creating a healthy city was slow, however, as boards lacked sufficient enforcement powers and fiscal pressures limited their budgets. Some groups, particularly immigrants and physicians, resisted the imposition of health regulations; antistatist thinking and racism hindered reform in the South. Despite these countervailing pressures, most cities had public water facilities by 1900 and had embarked on sewer and storm drainage projects. Water infrastructure and public health campaigns, along with regulations concerning food adulteration, street paving, and garbage collection, produced positive dividends for urban health. Mortality rates, especially for infants, dropped substantially in the first decades of the twentieth century, well before the medical profession had a major impact on extending longevity. By 1900 America's large cities were at least as healthy as Europe's.[11]

The legal doctrine of state police powers enabled local governments to protect the health, safety, and welfare of their citizens. Efforts to ensure clean water clearly fell within this purview, as did policing and firefighting. Police departments, the primary units charged with protecting city neighborhoods, enlarged their forces during the late nineteenth century, although policing practices changed only incrementally and remained a highly politicized arena of municipal government. State lawmakers in Massachusetts transferred the management of Boston's police department to a commission appointed by the governor in 1878. Fire protection evolved in a different context, as a burning building constituted a clear and dramatic danger. Pressured by insurance companies and city businesses, fire departments became more professional and better equipped to extinguish fires, thanks to mobile steam engines, alarm systems, fire hydrants, and building codes. Losses due to fire damage fell during the era.[12]

Education was the other major function of local governments. Public support of education was decentralized in more than 100,000 schools, whose student populations doubled between 1870 and 1900. The number of teachers, who were increasingly female, kept pace with the surge of students, who generally stayed in school longer in 1900 than in 1870. Three policy trends marked the direction of public education: state laws requiring compulsory education (in seventeen states by 1900), the creation of high schools, and state-based requirements for teacher certification. Statewide coordination of education policy was accomplished by establishing boards of education (in twenty-eight states by 1900). Despite these steps toward state oversight, education remained firmly lodged in local hands.

Funding for schools, police and fire protection, water and sewer infrastructure, and other urban functions raised the cost of municipal government. Borrowing to finance infrastructure projects saddled some cities with large debts. Figure 10.1 plots city spending for Boston and Cleveland during the Gilded Age; expenditures rose over the long run but dropped or slowed during depression years, notably in the mid-1870s and 1890s. The downturn following the Panic of 1873 had a large impact on financial outlays, as city after city retrenched its spending in response to declining revenue. Middle-class residents, who were property owners and thus the principal taxpayers for urban governments, blamed fiscal imbalances on improvident financial management, including corruption, and demanded restraint. The depression of the 1870s spurred a wave of state constitutional revisions and statutes that limited cities' borrowing capacity and imposed tax limits. By

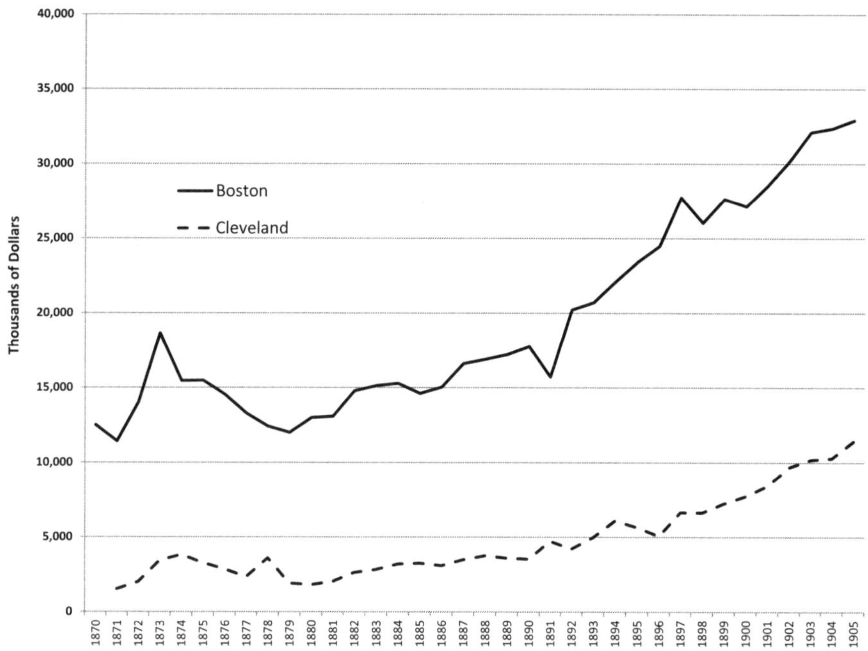

Figure 10.1. Boston and Cleveland expenditures, 1870–1905. *Sources:* Charles Phillips Huse, *The Financial History of Boston, 1822–1909* (Cambridge, MA: Harvard University Press, 1916), 351; Charles C. Williamson, *The Finances of Cleveland* (New York: Columbia University Press, 1907), 243, appendix C.

1881 fifteen states had set debt ceilings on local governments, and twenty-four had restricted their investment in railroads. Constitutional revisions limited New York City debt to 10 percent of the assessed value of property, the chief source of urban revenue, and limited property tax rates to 2 percent of assessed value. In 1894 New York State extended these limitations to all its cities and counties. Fiscal restrictions helped municipalities weather the economic downturn of the 1890s better than they had in the 1870s. Over time, however, local restrictions increased the pressure to expand the fiscal role of the state government.[13]

Despite conflicts over taxation, urban governance progressed during the Gilded Age. Contrary to Bryce's conclusion that city government was a "conspicuous failure," historian Jon Teaford titled his comprehensive study of municipal governance *Unheralded Triumph.* Compared with their European counterparts, American cities were superior or equal in areas such as water systems, streetcar service, fire protection, public parks and libraries, and education. But US cities, Teaford wrote, fell short on support of the poor, slum clearance, and, until the last years of the period, police professionalism.[14] Wrestling with formidable challenges during the late nineteenth century, city officials managed to improve urban environments.

EXPANSION OF STATE GOVERNANCE

City governments operated under rules adopted by the state legislature. Before the Civil War most of these bodies convened annually. Beginning in the 1840s a movement to restrict meetings resulted in legislative sessions that convened in alternate years and were limited to a certain number of days. No state that entered the union after the Civil War scheduled annual legislative sessions. By 1900 only six state legislatures met every year. Twenty-one states convened their lawmakers biennially and limited meetings to sixty days or less. Virtually all these states paid their lawmakers a daily rate. Most New England, mid-Atlantic, and midwestern states, which included nearly half the nation's population, convened their legislatures annually or biennially, without limits on session length, and all paid their legislators a salary. Massachusetts, New York, and Illinois, whose policies influenced lawmakers elsewhere, were in this category. Empire State lawmakers met annually for four months on average and received a salary of $1,500. At the other end of the spectrum, Wyoming's legislators stayed in Cheyenne no more than forty days every other year and received $5 a day.[15]

Despite their more permissive schedules, some northeastern states—notably, Connecticut, Rhode Island, and New Jersey—had the most malapportioned legislatures in the country. New York City was shortchanged in its allotment of seats in Albany. Boston and Chicago, however, received more equitable treatment. Urban growth after the Civil War skewed the apportionment of representation among legislative districts. This inequity was especially prevalent in state senates, many of which allotted at least one lawmaker to every county, regardless of its population. Rural advantages in malapportioned chambers probably blocked numerous proposals, especially those concerning industrial workers.[16]

Most state lawmakers were elected as either a Republican or a Democrat, came from a middle-class background, and served one term. The majority party selected the leaders and committee chairs in each chamber. Only a rudimentary staff, mainly clerks for selected committees, assisted lawmakers. Many state lawmakers were attorneys, which helped resolve the technical problems of drafting legislation, although critics complained about poorly written bills. Despite operating under tight schedules, receiving minimal compensation and little staff assistance, and being subjected to close scrutiny by newspaper editors and lobbyists, America's citizen-based legislatures produced an abundance of laws—far too many in the eyes of some critics. On a select number of issues, political party served as the reference for lawmakers' decision-making, but the majority of issues were settled by nonpartisan voting alignments, often by unanimous consent.[17]

State lawmakers reviewed a plethora of proposals, many of which were routine and some of which blazed new pathways. Classifying significant policy decisions into several broad domains suggests the uses of state authority during the Gilded Age.[18] Two such domains concerned governmental processes and public finance. Conspicuous in these categories were provisions that limited taxing and borrowing by local governments (see table A.3 in the appendix). Related to these restrictions was the veto power that allowed governors and mayors to prune specific appropriations from spending bills. Massachusetts was the first state to create a tax commission, and its first assignment was to ensure fair property assessments across the state. Election procedures were reformed, principally through laws that mandated secret ballots (printed ballots, marked in private), voter registration, and regulation of campaign finances. Proponents of female suffrage argued that granting the ballot to women would reduce political corruption, but that argument failed to convince most male lawmakers.

State-mandated social policies included compulsory education, mainly in the North and West, and racial segregation in the South. Numerous statutes set moral standards, such as restricting the availability of alcoholic beverages. Some states let localities decide whether to allow the sale of liquor (local option laws), a compromise that permitted state legislators to avoid taking a definitive position on prohibition. Some laws extended benefits for specific groups, such as veterans and the physically impaired, or for specific purposes, such as the creation of recreational areas. New York's Adirondack State Park (1883) and Revere Beach in Massachusetts (1896) pioneered the development of state recreational spaces.

Acting under the advice of medical experts and pressure from civic reformers and urban officials, legislators established state boards of health (in most states before 1900) and gave them the authority to set water standards and direct the construction of new water facilities, including the installation of sewers. Statutes that made it illegal to adulterate foods were common by the 1880s in the northern states, although their scope and enforcement remained rudimentary during the Gilded Age. Building codes and tenement regulations adopted during these decades were similarly weak. More effective was the licensing of health care providers such as doctors, pharmacists, and dentists. Professional organizations used these licensing panels to establish quality standards, which afforded their members occupational protection.

Public demands for security stoked support for better police and fire protection, mainly in cities. The depression of the 1870s and ensuing labor conflicts produced statutes that restricted vagrancy (directed in part toward unemployed tramps) and revitalized the militia. Illinois enacted an antiriot and anticonspiracy statute in the wake of the 1886 Haymarket Square riot in Chicago; the city responded by enlarging its police department. Laws providing for parole addressed the number of inmates in state prisons, which was growing faster than the population as a whole.[19]

Conscious that blue-collar workers made up an increasing proportion of their constituents, legislators in northern states established bureaus of labor statistics and boards of arbitration, the latter designed to mediate labor disputes. Laws limiting the number of hours worked by women and children in factories appeared by the mid-1880s; other statutes mandated the payment of wages in money (rather than company scrip), the regulation of sweatshops, and the adoption of standards affecting mine safety and pay. Illinois, New York, Massachusetts, and California adopted regulations concerning factory workers by 1889. The catch was a shortage of inspectors to ensure compliance with the law. A second hurdle was the hostility of some state courts.

Numerous scholars have argued that legislative actions in the Gilded Age tended to bestow benefits, sometimes labeled "distributive policy." To the extent the states enacted policies that helped businesses and producers, the concept has merit. State law allowed corporations to establish holding companies (so they could legally do business in more than one state) and eased the rules for the incorporation of banks. Lawmakers helped farmers, dairymen, and stockmen by creating dairy and cattle commissions and setting standards for the marketing of agricultural commodities. States authorized agricultural experiment stations (essentially research bureaus, usually located at state colleges) and created state departments of agriculture. Federal financial grants to agricultural experiment stations beginning in 1887 stimulated additional legislative action on this front. Helping farmers and real estate developers was good politics, especially for land reclamation promoters in Florida and on the West Coast. Merchants welcomed laws that improved water transportation, such as harbor development in Boston and in Portland, Oregon. A number of states enacted laws for forest management.[20]

Legislation that assisted private enterprise, often written by the beneficiaries themselves, seldom generated widespread criticism. In contrast, legislation that regulated industry tended to rub the raw nerves of members of the affected sector. However, there was wide support for state action on some commercial subjects, especially concerning railroads and banks. Banking standards were approved by many northern state legislatures. Railroad laws swept through the country in the 1870s and 1880s, resulting in oversight commissions; some had the power to regulate rates (e.g., Illinois), and others merely collected data and used publicity to police the industry (e.g., Massachusetts). Some states adopted antimonopoly laws beginning in the late 1880s, when the issue of trusts and big business appeared in the public consciousness. Other measures regulated insurance companies to ensure general standards of operation. Thus, although the legislative record contained numerous instances of distributive policy, states also regulated commercial enterprise, albeit often with a gentle hand. Regulation of business generated furious pushback from middle-class legislators, well-heeled lobbyists, and the courts. But many members of these groups stood behind laws that regulated social behavior and dictated uniform community values.

NATIONAL GOVERNANCE

Congress was the primary policymaker in the national government. Most members of the House of Representatives were part-time lawmakers with minimal legislative experience. Between 1875 and 1890, 48 percent of House members were first-termers. As late as 1883, a majority of representatives were serving their first terms. Offsetting congressional inexperience was the fact that a large majority of House members had served in some other government position prior to their election. More than half the representatives had practiced law before arriving in Washington. Legal knowledge was helpful because members of Congress had minimal staff assistance before the 1890s; the congressional Legislative Reference Service was authorized in 1914.[21]

Political parties had the greatest influence in preparing Congress for business. The majority party selected the leadership positions in each chamber, including the chairs of committees.[22] Party leaders also had the means to keep the legislative mills working if the minority party proved obstructive, a frequent occurrence during the Gilded Age. Party cues provided policy positions on some issues, particularly civil rights, tariffs, the admission of additional states, and procedures for operating Congress. Party had a lesser impact on railroad regulation, money and currency, and the administration of government, including territorial offices. Lawmakers filed four times more bills at the end of the century than in the 1870s, yet the number of days in session remained constant, averaging 360 through each two-year congressional cycle. Handling this increased business without lengthening the congressional calendar prodded lawmakers to consider making the legislative process more efficient.[23]

Despite periods of obstructive partisanship, legislator inexperience, meager staff assistance, and powerful antistatist bias, Congress enacted important laws. Some of these decisions concerned traditional functions such as territorial organization, relations with Native Americans, the distribution of land, taxation and tariffs, overseas commerce, the postal service, and the army; a web of actions revised many statutes during the late nineteenth century. At the same time, Congress carved out new areas of activity. Every administration from Grant's through McKinley's expanded the national agenda (see table A.4 in the appendix).

The construction of a "new" navy illustrates how one of the traditional functions evolved. Tethered to sails and wooden hulls, the US Navy became outmoded after the Civil War. By the early 1880s the United States' ranking among the world's naval powers, which had adopted steam-powered vessels, steel hulls, and modern rifled guns, had dropped conspicuously. European imperialism and the expansion of overseas commerce convinced some Americans that the nation had to keep pace with Europe. Beginning in 1883 President Chester Arthur (who had replaced the slain Garfield) and the secretary of the navy persuaded a cost-conscious Congress to fund the construction of three steel-hulled cruisers. National lawmakers approved eight more "protected" cruisers between 1884 and 1889, one of which was the *Maine*, later designated a second-class battleship. In theory, the new vessels were limited to a defensive range close to the American coastline. During the first Cleveland presidency, lawmakers approved the construction of full-scale battleships and allowed them to steam in most waters. Naval modernization continued through the administrations of Harrison, Cleveland (second term), and McKinley. By 1898 the US Navy, with four modern battleships (and more under construction) and several fortified cruisers, easily overwhelmed Spanish defenders in Manila Bay and around Cuba. By 1900 the US Navy ranked fourth in the world. America's victory in the Spanish-American War led to the annexation of the Philippines as a colony, a case of how the "march of events" produced an unintended consequence.[24]

Legislation on internal subjects also added new policies to the national agenda. Expanded benefits and new services were approved, including pensions for Union Civil War veterans and their widows (which became the largest category of federal expenditures in the 1890s) and postal delivery to urban addresses (1863) and rural homes (1896). The US Department of Agriculture (USDA) sponsored a variety services, including seed distribution, research on the eradication of crop and cattle diseases, and, beginning in 1887, extension of subsidies to state agricultural experiment stations. As settlers moved west, lawmakers established the US Geological Survey (1879) to inventory natural resources and permitted presidents to set aside forest reserves. Congress had already created Yellowstone National Park (1872), and it added several more preserves before 1900. It established the Bureau of Labor in 1885, approved cash grants to state universities in 1890, and created the Coast Guard. The United States also assumed control of immigration, first by banning Chinese entrants (1882) and then by supervising the admission of all immigrants (1891).

The national government took tentative steps to regulate commerce. Taking a cue from state oversight of railroads, Congress created the Interstate Commerce Commission (ICC) in 1887. The Sherman Antitrust Act (1890) authorized the Justice Department to prosecute firms that deliberately restrained commerce. Both areas engendered extensive litigation, which initially hamstrung regulation. In 1891 the United States inaugurated the inspection of imported meat. Currency and the money supply followed a zigzag path throughout the Gilded Age, with fiscal liberals advocating inflation, largely through the monetization of silver. Conservatives sought to drive federal paper currency (greenbacks) out of circulation but not notes issued by the private national banks, and they wanted to base the country's currency solely on the gold standard. This complex matter produced divisions among lawmakers, sometimes along regional lines.

Although broad managerial intervention into the economy lay in the future, Washington established significant precedents in this direction during the Gilded Age. Its actions touched five major functions: national security and immigration control, resource management, economic services and individual benefits, commercial regulation (including business monopolies and railroads), and the governmental process. The last category included legislation that created an appeals court system, established the Department of Justice, and passed the Civil Service Act of 1883, which eventually brought the large majority of federal employees under a nonpartisan merit system. Judicial impediments were among the reasons cited by contemporary critics who faulted the national government for not acting more boldly, especially with regard to business and labor. Despite its modest efforts to control the private markets, Congress did enlarge its statutory intervention into society during the late nineteenth century. These steps raise the question: how well did officials administer these new responsibilities?

ADMINISTRATION

Assessing administration is handicapped by a scarcity of pertinent records and scholarly studies, especially for state and local governments. Nevertheless, the available evidence allows some rough generalizations. All cities and most rural areas supported schools and a police presence, the two functions that accounted for about half of all public employees in the United States in the late nineteenth century. Schoolteachers and staff (the vast majority hired by local governments) outnumbered all federal employees by fourfold in 1870 and nearly twofold in 1900. These differences may have been even larger because of undercounts; many teachers, particularly women, were part-time employees, while others taught in one-room schools that may have escaped notice. States established boards of education and state superintendents' offices that assisted teacher preparation and designed criteria for obtaining teaching certificates. Cities funded free high schools. High proportions of school-age children were enrolled in public schools, and the school year got longer during the late nineteenth century. America's public schools, supported primarily by local taxes, were among the best in the world and were instrumental in producing a highly literate population.[25]

Policing, especially in large cities, warrants a mixed assessment. The challenges facing municipal police rose as populations increased and urban space became denser. To cope with these changes, Boston's police force expanded from 500 in 1870 to 1,241 in 1900; the cost of the city's policing rose sevenfold during these decades. With this expansion came organizational reforms such as pensions for retirees, starting in 1878. New York City had taken this step a decade earlier. Chicago's force totaled 4,000 in 1913. Depressions taxed the capacity of urban police because economic slowdowns increased unemployment. Some of the jobless turned to petty crime and, occasionally, organized protests; others turned up at the local police station for a bowl of soup and a roof overhead for the night. Economic stress and fear of the "dangerous classes" among more affluent residents fueled demands for greater control over workers and minorities, groups accustomed to police brutality. After 1900 police turned their attention to solving crimes rather than merely maintaining social stability. Formation of a national organization of police chiefs facilitated a discussion of common problems across various jurisdictions.[26]

City administrators also managed streets, health policy, building inspections, public works such water service, public libraries and parks, transportation facilities and other utilities, taxation, audits of public spending, and debt management. All these functions required staff, whose numbers grew during the last decades of the nineteenth century. Cynics sneered that more city workers simply showed that political bosses were inflating the public payroll with sinecures, perpetuating the "extravagance, corruption, and mismanagement" of American cities, as James Bryce put it.

Graft and fraud enriched some urban (and county) political machines around the turn of the century, but Bryce's indictment is exaggerated. As Rebecca Menes has argued, most city bosses were careful not to alienate middle-class taxpayers and businesses—the groups that made their livelihoods possible. Structural factors limited the range of options available to city bosses. Open borders allowed capital to migrate out of a city to the suburbs or some other urban location. Voters could oust urban officeholders; the bond market could cut off funding for infrastructure projects. Moreover, state lawmakers placed constitutional and statutory limits on city taxation and indebtedness, which constrained fiscal possibilities. Despite these restraints, city bosses got things done, responding to the needs of the poor and immigrants as well as middle- and upper-class urbanities.[27] Both the bosses and elitist reformers turned to professionals and experts when dealing with technical matters such as health, engineering, education, libraries, firefighting, and park landscapes. Many city administrators gained decades of experience in their jobs. Despite ethical lapses and the tendency for civic improvements to proceed incrementally, America's cities registered substantial achievements by the end of the century.[28]

State governments also expanded their administrative activities. An indicator of this trend was the creation of boards, agencies, and commissions to monitor and in some cases regulate social and economic activities. The pattern began at midcentury and accelerated after 1870. By 1900 New York had eighty-one administrative boards, Oregon sixty-two, Massachusetts fifty-six, and Illinois thirty-four. Most important were boards of health (thirty-five states), railroad commissions (thirty-two states), and bureaus of labor statistics, all of which had regulatory functions. The Massachusetts Board of Health, for example, had numerous responsibilities, including ensuring clean water and proper sanitation, enforcing the food and drug laws, and inspecting dairies and slaughterhouses. It also licensed physicians and medical schools, collected health data, and promulgated health standards. Many boards of labor statistics were charged with enforcing factory laws and investigating employee issues, such as the garnishment of wages for debt. Railroad commissions had a wide variety of oversight missions; the Illinois commission claimed it was responsible for enforcing 294 laws. Some railroad commissions set rates, even after the federal Interstate Commerce Act (1887) went into effect. Other commissions were essentially fact-finding agencies, although their findings could have regulatory effects.[29]

The effectiveness of state administration varied. Some states failed to create administrative agencies; for example, few bureaus of labor statistics existed in the South. Managers of most regulatory bureaus complained of understaffing and underfunding. Courts undercut the force of statutes designed to protect workers, especially in New York and Illinois.[30] Some social regulations were widely ignored by both the public and law enforcement officials. Carrie Nation's famed destruction of saloons indicates that the prohibition of alcohol was not working in Kansas. The campaign to eliminate the liquor business was the Achilles' heel of law enforcement in the Gilded Age.

These shortcomings must be measured against the trend of greater state intervention into community affairs after the Civil War. The creation of administrative boards represented an important step toward state administrative centralization, a process that continued into the twentieth century. Board members, many of them leaders in their fields, drew on their expertise to advocate solutions for emerging problems. Adding to their creditability was their affiliation with national organizations of civil engineers, public health officials, firefighters, teachers, and librarians, bodies that were active by the 1880s.[31] National officials tapped the experiences of state agencies when the federal government expanded its supervisory agenda.[32]

Washington has traditionally received poor grades for its administrative efforts before 1900. Some agencies, especially the General Land Office, Bureau of Indian Affairs, and Pension Office, were riddled with inefficiency and scandal. Staffing of these offices was dominated by partisanship and patronage appointments, which, according to reformers, impeded effective policy management. A prime example was the New York customhouse, noted for financial mischief and kickbacks. Congress perpetually resisted division heads' requests for more staff, confident that better administration could be achieved by working more efficiently without spending more money. Nevertheless, as national functions grew, so did the federal workforce, which increased from 51,000 in 1870 to 239,000 in 1900. Twenty-one thousand federal employees worked in Washington, DC, at the end of the nineteenth century.[33]

About half of all federal employees worked for the postal system, which maintained offices at virtually every jurisdiction in the nation. The military accounted for another quarter of the federal workforce. A large fraction of the remaining federal workers handled routine assignments, which led Daniel Carpenter to call the national establishment in the nineteenth century a "clerical state." The Washington-based workforce grew slightly faster than federal employees elsewhere, as officials hired more clerks, messengers, and laborers. The pace of their work slackened in the summer, when offices closed early and many managers escaped the capital's oppressive heat and humidity. Theodore Roosevelt spent the summers at his Long Island home and sojourned in the Rocky Mountains when he was a federal civil service commissioner. While serving as assistant secretary of the navy, Roosevelt was put in charge of the department while his boss summered on Cape Cod in 1898, as the Spanish-American War unfolded.[34]

Political practice and theoretical know-how constrained efficient administration. Because patronage jobs were the lifeblood of partisan electoral organizations, members of Congress bombarded executives with requests for appointments. Whether Democrat or Republican, lawmakers kept a close watch on executive departments, meddled in policy minutiae, and jealously guarded their oversight prerogatives over administration activities. Both parties disliked bureaucracies, holding to the notion that any citizen could perform administrative duties. Congress followed through on this thinking by underfunding administration requests for more staff. Even if Congress had been open to advice from best-practices literature, there was hardly any available: research and theory in public administration did not appear until the twentieth century. Conversely, concepts derivative of laissez-faire economics, pervasive among judges and many entrepreneurs, inspired a set of federal court decisions that stripped the ICC and the Sherman Antitrust Act of their regulatory teeth. The fee system of compensating certain public officials lingered throughout the nineteenth century, a practice that worked against administrative neutrality.[35]

The pace of administrative action was also slowed by premodern office conditions. At the start of the Gilded Age, electric lights, telephones, duplicating machines, vertical file cabinets, and calculating and tabulating machines did not exist. The typewriter was not widely used until the end of the 1880s. Compounding these technical obstacles was insufficient building space in Washington. The commissioner of the General Land Office reported in 1880 that its records were stored in the corridors of buildings scattered around town, requiring that documents be carried to places with sufficient lighting to read them. Administrative buildings lacked central heating and indoor plumbing. It took years for all the offices to be connected by telephone (invented in 1876). Arguably, the premodern office that relied on handwritten documents and the personal delivery of messages conveyed by telegraph or mail was just as responsible for blunting administrative efficiency as were fraud and corruption.[36]

Modern policy implementation (and evaluation) relies on the collection and processing of pertinent information. This critical dimension of governance was in its infancy during the Gilded Age, when the first data-processing devices became available. The Hollerith tabulating machine (which sorted and counted punch cards) first tallied the numbers from the 1890 federal census. Electric power (which drove the Hollerith tabulator and illuminated work spaces) became available by the end of the period. Administrative advances by large corporations impressed some political leaders, and President Cleveland called for the "application of business principles to public affairs" in his first inaugural address (1885). The Cockrell Committee, a congressional body charged with investigating administrative practices, recommended in 1888 that the federal government adopt office techniques used by businesses and banks. Although blocked in their efforts to apply modern economic thinking to railroad regulation, ICC commissioners campaigned for data collection and uniform accounting, advancing a program begun in the states. By the end of the century the US Census Bureau was a model for massive data collection.[37]

These innovations produced incremental improvements in federal administration, which grew in managerial complexity as Washington took on more responsibilities. New federal agencies were formed, including the Department of Justice (1870), Coast and Geodetic Survey (1871), Civil Service Commission (1883), Bureau of Labor Statistics (1885), Immigration and Naturalization Service (1891), and Office of Road Inquiry (1894). The USDA (awarded cabinet status in 1889) created divisions for National Forests, Chemistry, Animal Industry, Dairy, and Entomology. All these units had regulatory assignments. The USDA also housed the Office of Experiment Stations, which administered federal grants for agricultural laboratories in the states, as well as the Weather Bureau. By 1899 most positions in the USDA and 45 percent of all federal employees were subject to civil service regulations.[38]

Both the USDA and the US Postal Service, which launched rural free delivery in 1896, worked to build their reputations as efficient organizations and nurtured a cadre of governmental experts that advocated policy enhancements. The diffusion of administrative units occurred in the Foreign Service, which maintained 300 consuls and thirty consuls general who coordinated international commercial relations by the turn of the century. The Pension Office sent checks to nearly a million Union military veterans and their dependents in the 1890s, an outlay that accounted for two-fifths of the federal budget. This proliferation of governmental units documents the development of federal organizational specificity between 1870 and 1900 (see table A.5 in the appendix).[39]

Federal administrators turned to experts in certain fields to fill many of these positions. The USDA, which became known as a client agency (especially for farmers), acquired a reputation as a science center, hiring PhDs in an age when advanced degrees were a rarity. Dr. Charles W. Stiles, a physician educated in Germany and France, was hired as a consulting zoologist in the USDA's Bureau of Animal Industry; he went on to discover that hookworms were the cause of lethargy among southerners. Cleveland Abbe, who joined the Army Signal Service in 1871 as a meteorologist, headed the Weather Bureau for forty-five years and lectured at Johns Hopkins University. Harvey W. Wiley, who headed the USDA's Chemistry Division between 1883 and 1912, led the battle for national food and drug regulations. In addition to the USDA, experts were employed by the Naval Observatory, Coast and Geodetic Survey, Patent Office, Smithsonian Institution, and Office of Education, among other agencies.

Many of these talented individuals stayed in federal service for decades, bringing expertise and a long institutional memory to their agencies. Alevey Adee, who began as a clerk drafting state papers and eventually became chief of the Diplomatic Bureau, worked for the State Department for forty-seven years. The head of the Library of Congress held his position for forty years. The top officer cadre of the navy and army were careerists, retiring with pensions.[40] Federal judges also achieved long tenures. The median length of service as a justice of the US Supreme Court in 1887 was ten years; Stephen J. Field and John Marshall Harlan sat on the high court for thirty-four years, and Samuel Miller served for twenty-eight years. Many state supreme court jurists also held their seats for many years.

Assessments of Gilded Age administration that go no further than Boss Tweed's misdeeds in New York City, the Whiskey Ring scandals in the Grant administration, or corruption in the General Land Office distort history. Scandal and inefficiency clearly marred the era, but administrative improvements inched forward as the century closed. Even before theories of public administration had been formulated, the public sector had registered some important achievements, such as improved health in the nation's cities and applications of science in the USDA. Ideas and inspirations arising from the influence of corporate organizations and university experts, technical innovations that aided office work, and pragmatic experimentation at the state and local levels nurtured the administrative reforms that blossomed during the Progressive Era.

WAS THE GILDED AGE LAISSEZ-FAIRE?

The traditional interpretation of Gilded Age politics leveled a stern indictment. Three charges constitute the heart of this unflattering assessment. First, critics stressed corruption, epitomized by city officials' and legislators' shakedown of corporations for favors. As journalist Henry Demarest Lloyd expressed it, Standard Oil "has done everything with the Pennsylvania legislature except refine it."[41] Corruption dovetailed with a second theme, excessive partisanship, wherein political parties pursued power and advancement for their own advantage, not the public interest. And third, critics faulted policymakers for embracing laissez-faire. Broadly construed, laissez-faire is a philosophy that advocates minimal exercise of civic power, particularly with regard to the regulation of business and the protection of workers. The intertwining of laissez-faire theory with a corrupt and partisan politics produced a governmental regime that Henry Adams opined was "poor in purpose and barren in results."[42]

Was Adams right? The answer depends on one's angle of vision. The case for laissez-faire can be found in the Jeffersonian and Jacksonian interpretation of American republican principles, in the prominence of classical economic theory, and in judicial decisions. The classic rendition of American republicanism embraced limited government, the protection of individual rights (liberty), equality of treatment and the avoidance of special legislation for favored groups, suspicion of bureaucracy, and restriction of national action to the enumerated powers in the Constitution. Among prominent late nineteenth-century politicians, Grover Cleveland came closest to embodying these precepts, although all presidents gave them lip service. The Democratic Party stood closer to the Jeffersonian-Jacksonian credo than the Republicans did, yet most citizens accepted the general tenor of nineteenth-century republicanism.

Classical economic theory grew in influence during the late nineteenth century. The essence of this view was that natural laws drove commercial markets, which worked best when left in the hands of private enterprise and when there was competition among businesses. Honoring these principles produced the greatest social and economic progress. Governmental intervention was counterproductive because it interfered with the operation of natural laws—divinely prescribed, according to some—and thus hindered the social good. Firm support of property rights and individual liberty, the theory held, would expand the public good. Wide segments of elite opinion makers and judges subscribed to both classical economic theory and traditional liberalism, which decried "class" legislation that conferred benefits on selected individuals. These ideas helped create a mentality that opposed protection for workers, regulation of business, and welfare measures for nonveterans.[43]

Corporate attorneys and judges frequently drew on classical economics to frame their legal briefs and court rulings. Although the US Supreme Court rejected most constitutional challenges to federal legislation and state statutes, by the mid-1880s the justices displayed increasing hostility to business regulation and taxation. The Supreme Court struck down an Illinois law that regulated railroad rates in the state (1886), declared the income tax portion of the 1894 tariff act unconstitutional (1894), invalidated the federal antimonopoly case against the nation's largest sugar manufacturer (1895), and prevented the ICC from setting rates for railroads (1897). The high court also upheld the federal government's prosecution of Eugene Debs, leader of the Pullman strike, for violating a court injunction (1895), a decision that sent him to prison. And in one of the most famous (infamous) cases of the age, *Plessey v. Ferguson* (1896) upheld racial segregation by southern state governments.[44]

These and other rejections of federal laws in the 1890s earned sharp rebukes from critics, who labeled judicial laissez-faire "conservative" and out of date. Some state supreme courts received similar rebukes. Illinois and New York had reputations for striking down regulatory, pro-labor, and tax laws. Massachusetts and Virginia, by contrast, displayed no judicial hostility to state action. But delegates in numerous states proceeded in the spirit of leading legal theorists such as Thomas M. Cooley and John F. Dillon, curbing state and city budget powers by constitutional provisions that set debt limits and prohibited the repudiation of debts. Although Americans have often written their political complaints into state constitutions, it warrants repeating that state courts upheld the vast majority of laws whose constitutionality was challenged.[45]

Courts did disallow some legislation, especially business regulations, pro-labor laws, and tax measures. Several dynamics were responsible for this judicial negativity. For one, the output of statutes increased during the 1880s and 1890s, with numerous provisions affecting economic activity and finance. In addition, third-party challenges to the political establishment, notably by Greenbackers, Populists, and assorted labor parties, worried conservatives. Mainly composed of WASP elites, the legal establishment cast a jaundiced eye on third-party "radicals." Finally, as legal historian Michael Les Benedict has theorized, the legal profession became alarmed at legislators' tendency to enlarge the powers of bureaucrats, a step that threatened traditional judicial prerogatives. American courts operated largely on the basis of the common law, which had built up a complex case-by-case legal artifice designed and interpreted by lawyers and judges. Attorneys were prominent among the critics of too much legislation and badly drafted statutes. Motives are difficult to untangle and, to some extent, are irrelevant in the face of explicit actions. Whatever the causes, the US Supreme Court gained a reputation in the 1890s and the Progressive Era for limiting the reach of government. Corporations played a role in this trend, as entrepreneurs had both the incentive and the funds to hire talented attorneys to challenge policies they disliked.[46]

Although courts displayed laissez-faire tendencies and legislators exhibited hesitancy on controversial subjects, these actions represent only one side of the story. Conversely, the actions of cities, states, and the national government document an incremental expansion of civic intervention. Government regulated more, spent more, hired more employees, and launched new administrative agencies between 1870 and 1900. State and federal courts usually consented to statutes if their legal foundations rested on state police powers. By these criteria, the era should be regarded as a transitional period during which the increased use of political power spurred pushback from conservatives and traditionalists.

James Bryce, the scholar who was so influential in establishing the template for the Gilded Age, recognized this transition. Americans may not have a "theory of the state," he wrote, yet the states were engines of policy innovation. Laissez-faire was given lip service, but "economic theory did not stop" governmental invention because American lawmakers were "practical men." To document his contention, Bryce included a table in the first edition of *The American Commonwealth* that recorded the legislative actions of six states, the United States, and Great Britain in seven policy areas ranging from public health to labor laws. The American states, he observed, exceeded Parliament in the scope of their actions in four categories. Bryce conjectured that most lawyers and economists missed this development because it had been so gradual.[47]

Nonetheless, the minimalist image of the Gilded Age survived long after Bryce's death. Historians are largely responsible for the longevity of the laissez-faire thesis. During the Gilded Age influential historians adopted a nationalist perspective on the nation's history, celebrating the emergence of the national state and slighting the states and cities. An alternative perspective arose in the early twentieth century with the advent of "progressive" history by scholars such as Frederick Jackson Turner and Charles Beard, who traced the political influence of environment and economic class. From the 1930s through the 1960s, leading American historians were New Deal liberals who applauded robust governmental action. They agreed with the Progressive historians who castigated the Gilded Age for corporate domination, boss rule, and disregard for farmers' and workers' interests. Charles and Mary Beard called the Gilded Age the "age of negation" that awaited Progressive Era reform. Samuel Eliot Morison and Henry Steele Commager's *Growth of the American Republic*, one of the most successful college textbooks on American history, rehashed classic indictment themes. Richard Hofstadter embellished the political horrors of the period in "The Spoilsmen," a chapter on the Gilded Age in his influential classic *The American Political Tradition*. The "captains of industry," Hofstadter wrote, "bought legislatures." Castigating the Gilded Age was a convenient jeremiad to discredit laissez-faire approaches to American governance.[48] Little if any space was devoted to the positive uses of power.

A second reason that historians misread the Gilded Age stems from their style of history. The progressive and liberal historians who wrote about the period relied heavily on the writings of elites and civil service reformers such as Theodore Roosevelt and Edward Godkin, the conservative editor of the *Nation*. Contemporary critics were fond of depicting state and local governance as inept, tarnished by corruption, and stymied by partisanship and laissez-faire mentalities. Nonnational history was demoted to second-rate status, resulting in a political portrait oriented largely around presidents. So, while it is true that economic management under national supervision remained minimal until the 1930s, it is false to conclude that the power of the American state as a whole did not grow during the Gilded Age.

11

The Progressive State

In 1907 the Knickerbocker Trust Company, a banking institution in New York City, went bankrupt, triggering a financial panic that sent shock waves around the country. Knickerbocker's collapse caused a sharp drop in stock values, closed dozens of banks, and induced national banks in the major cities to suspend the redemption of customer deposits. This freeze on financial assets triggered a severe depression in 1908, a slump that was not fully corrected until World War I. The demise of Knickerbocker, the ensuing panic, and the economic slowdown jarred the nation's banking system, whose weaknesses were widely known. The country possessed a decentralized array of 25,000 national banks, state banks, and trust companies, plus state-chartered savings and loan institutions. No effective mechanism oversaw this disjointed matrix or facilitated the movement of funds between regions when seasonal demands peaked or panic struck.

The Panic of 1907 galvanized a movement to repair the country's financial structure. Congress enacted a stopgap currency act in 1908 that created a National Banking Commission to study banking practices, including those in Europe. The commission submitted its findings in an eighteen-volume report, but its proposed reforms, which kept the control of banking and the issuance of currency in private hands, failed to win congressional support. The legislative logjam was broken by the 1912 election, which elevated Democrats to a majority in Congress and put their presidential candidate, Woodrow Wilson, in the White House.

Pressure for banking reform received a boost from the House Banking Committee (the Pujo Committee), which alleged that the money supply was controlled by a small group of powerful bankers who were closely allied with big insurance companies and corporate trusts. Resisting pressure from the financial industry, President Wilson supported a plan that placed national banks under minimal federal control. Pushed through by congressional Democrats in 1913, the Federal Reserve Act created twelve regional reserve banks that would issue a new national currency called Federal Reserve notes—today's dollar bills. The system reflected the traditional American opposition to a single central bank (the European model) in favor of a decentralized banking scheme, but in this case, some supervisory authority over member banks was granted to the Federal Reserve Board.[1]

Four years later another tragedy struck New York. In March 1911 a fire rapidly engulfed the Triangle Shirtwaist Company, which occupied the top three floors of a ten-story building in Manhattan. The firm manufactured ladies' blouses, relying primarily on young female immigrants to make the garments. Company officials on the tenth floor evacuated safely, and workers on the eighth floor were able to flee as the flames approached. But people on the ninth floor were trapped. Flames from a barrel of oil blocked one stairwell; the other exit had been locked to prevent employee pilfering. The fire escapes on the exterior of the building failed, plummeting to the ground under the weight of the panicked workers. The sprinklers did not activate, and the valve for the fire hose was rusted shut. Neither the fire department's ladders nor water from its hoses could reach the top floors of the building. A few fortunate individuals on the ninth floor used two small elevators to escape, but scores of workers were engulfed in flames, which swept through a workshop strewn with fabric. In all, 146 women died, many by jumping from the ninth-floor windows.

Reported in newspapers nationwide, the Triangle fire was a shocking tragedy that dramatized unsafe working conditions and the negligence of company owners. The New York legislature established a Factory Investigation Commission to gather evidence on workshop safety and recommend reforms. Over the next several years, and after extensive study, the commission recommended numerous measures to improve the health and safety of factory employees. Republican control of the state government stymied most of the bills in the 1912 session, but Democrats gained the majority in 1913, opening the way for dozens of bills. Lawmakers imposed new fire safety regulations and strengthened the agencies that enforced them, policies that became a model for other states. The commission's recommendations to reduce the hours of work for women and children and to regulate sweatshop manufacturing (in homes) were adopted. The horrific Triangle fire had set the stage for a coalition of Democratic lawmakers, labor leaders, and middle-class reformers to increase the state's responsibility for the health and safety of workers.[2]

The Triangle fire and the economic slowdown following the 1907 panic illustrate the impact of crises in stimulating new civic responsibilities. Neither the Federal Reserve System nor New York's new safety rules were adopted solely because of these unforeseen events. Each issue had been discussed for decades. But political systems tend to settle into inertia, which sustains the status quo. Dramatic events can shock the polity out of complacency and present opportunities for policy innovation, often facilitated by electoral change, as occurred in 1912. Much of the expansion of government during the Progressive Era followed such a historically contingent pathway.[3]

PROGRESSIVISM IN THE NATION

Progressivism is the customary name for a burst of reform activity at all levels of government in the early twentieth century. Narrowly construed, the Progressive Era ran between 1901 and 1916, during the presidencies of Theodore Roosevelt and William Howard Taft and the first term of Woodrow Wilson. Progressivism was also a sentiment and an attitude of distrust of conventional politics and a preference for civic actions to address problems in society. By this latter definition, the roots of progressivism were visible in the Gilded Age, sometimes triggered by economic crises. In the 1890s a deep depression, bitter and brutal labor strikes, business mergers that spawned huge corporations, and political tensions arising from the challenge of Populists and other third parties buffeted the country. The midterm elections of 1894 and the presidential election of 1896 established the Republicans as the clear majority at the national level until 1913. World War I, which the United States entered in 1917, sapped most of the energy from the progressives' domestic reform agenda.

Although reformers were commonly called progressives, no progressive movement existed in terms of a single organization. Individuals supportive of reform could be found in the existing political parties, in public administrative capacities, and in nongovernmental settings. The major exception to this pattern was the Progressive Party, which had a brief history and was created largely as a vehicle for Theodore Roosevelt's run for the presidency in 1912. Progressivism was more a mood than a cohesive body of activists who subscribed to a single credo. As journalist William Allen White put it, "reform was in the air."

What reformers did share was a desire to remedy "problems" in society. At the top of this list was the rigid partisanship that characterized politics, followed by the expanded power of big business. The political challenge of the age, according to Massachusetts governor Eugene Foss, was "the dictatorship by the political bosses and by the special interests"; the latter referred to the "monopoly interest" and the corporate "trusts." The Progressive Party's 1912 platform condemned "the invisible government," which it identified as a "corrupt" alliance between political parties and special interests. White remembered that "the people were questioning the way every rich man got his money." These and other problems demanded "affirmative action" from the government, as President Theodore Roosevelt phrased the solution. Woodrow Wilson said the federal government "must be positive, not negative." Both men used the power of the presidency to highlight social and economic problems, the hallmark of a progressive reformer.[4]

Progressivism also resulted in a substantial expansion of government. Between 1901 and 1916 lawmakers authorized a broad range of new programs and expanded existing policies, primarily through legislative action. Most of these laws concerned four issues: regulation of the political process, including political parties; regulation of business practices; provision of new services and assistance to individuals and economic groups; and rules defining unacceptable social behavior. In addition, the government authorized new sources of public revenue and modernized methods of managing public finance, such as budgets. Out of these actions came a substantial enhancement of governmental power. Moreover, these reforms dovetailed with changes in how the polity operated: elected executives gained greater influence and were expected to be policy leaders; the administrative capacity of government expanded, especially through the creation of nonpartisan agencies and commissions; and shifts in governmental relations produced greater state supervision of local governments and a modest gravitation of power toward the national government. This latter trend increased the centralization of political decisionmaking and administration.

Identifying the wellsprings of progressive reform has long intrigued scholars. This search is likely to continue because of the difficulty of pinpointing the causes of complex historical developments. It is possible, nonetheless, to identify the likely influences underlying progressivism. Socioeconomic change heads this list. Industrialization altered economic life between the 1870s and early 1900s—a period that witnessed a host of important developments: the formation of big businesses (i.e., trusts), urbanization, mass migration, discoveries in science and technology, and the creation of new institutions such as universities and organizations serving particular professions, economic interests, and cultural groups. These and other facets of socioeconomic change not only improved the standard of living but also undermined older assumptions about business, politics, and social behavior.

Changes in the socioeconomic environment also bred new problems and aggravated old ones. The two most publicized maladies were corporate monopolies, which restricted commercial competition and raised prices, and civic corruption, which undercut an equitable and transparent politics. New business management techniques undermined the autonomy of craft workers, stimulating labor union protests over working conditions.[5] Other irritants included tax avoidance, rising consumer prices, threats to morality (e.g., prostitution, dance halls, saloons), child labor, and denial of the franchise to women. The appearance of motor vehicles illustrates how technology and commercialism spawned new threats to public health and safety. Cars and trucks produced traffic jams and were involved in accidents that caused property damage, injuries, and fatalities. One may not see automobile registration, driver's licenses, and the enforcement of speed limits as progressive reforms, yet such laws imposed new constraints on individuals.[6]

The evolution of medical science—particularly bacteriology, which identified microscopic organisms as the source of numerous diseases—represented another significant socioeconomic change. As the germ theory gained acceptance and researchers tracked the dissemination of toxins, pressure grew to ensure the availability of clean water and safe methods of disposing of wastewater. Public health agencies responded to this new knowledge by employing bacteriologists, medical doctors, and sanitary engineers. The increased reliance on expert advice to create a disease-free environment gave health agencies greater authority.[7]

The rise of public health was part of a broader expansion of science and intellectual pursuits. Institutions that nurtured and disseminated knowledge-based subjects included universities, corporate and government laboratories, public libraries, publications such as books and technical journals, and professional associations that represented academics, business interests, civic groups, and government.[8] Lawyers, doctors, teachers, economists, and engineers formed associations around their specialties in the Gilded Age and Progressive Era. Governments hired more professionals, such as accountants, chemists, and food and drug experts, who formed associations to promote discussion and publish research about their specialties. Commercial publishers reached out to the broader public through popular magazines such as *McClure's*, *Cosmopolitan*, and *World's Work*. Some magazines specialized in muckraking, publishing exposés of political corruption and business scandals. Ida Tarbell's claims about Standard Oil's strong-arm tactics against competitors and David Graham Phillips's *Treason of the Senate*, a 1906 book that alleged an unholy alliance between US senators and economic titans, suggest the temper of this type of journalism.[9]

Muckraking journalism was directed largely at the "new" middle class, another strategic factor that shaped the political context of progressivism. The shift away from agriculture to urban and commercial employment enlarged the middle class. Several attributes of middle-class life were particularly relevant to a new political consciousness. Middle-class individuals were increasingly better educated (many had graduated from high school), were homeowners (which entailed property tax obligations), and identified with their occupations as much as (or perhaps more than) they did with their locales and ethnic-cultural backgrounds. And because they bought food and other items rather than producing them, the urban middle class was especially sensitive to consumer prices. They also furnished the lion's share of members of professional associations, such as those for librarians, municipal engineers, bankers, and social workers. Robert Wiebe summed up their role by pointing to the new middle class as "the heart of progressivism."[10]

Women played an instrumental role in middle-class progressivism. Although barred from voting in general elections and largely excluded from holding public office, many women participated in public affairs through volunteer organizations that addressed urban problems such as garbage collection, utilities, education, child welfare, and social morality. Bringing a "materialist" perspective to civic reforms that originated in the "prism of the home," women's view of the urban community was usually broader than that of men, who were more narrowly focused on business. Many female activists worked within the General Federation of Women's Clubs, which advocated improved working conditions, especially for women; mothers' "pensions" (an early form of welfare assistance); minimum wages; improved sanitation; and safer foods, among other issues. The campaign for female suffrage was spearheaded by women. Fourteen states allowed women to vote in general elections by 1914, and eight of them adopted women's suffrage during the peak of progressive reform (1910–1914).[11]

Not all middle-class adults supported progressive reforms, nor were progressives drawn exclusively from the middle class. An important dimension of support for governmental action came from workers, especially "new stock" immigrants (from eastern, central, and southern Europe). Labor organizations were chiefly interested in legislation that improved working conditions and pay. They had less interest in reforming the political process and far less interest in most moral reforms, such as Sunday restrictions. Most urban workers had little sympathy for the Protestant activists who crusaded to board up saloons and ban alcoholic beverages. Working-class voters provided substantial support for progressive candidates by the second decade of the twentieth century. Generally, state and municipal reform lagged in rural areas. Yet members of Congress from the South and other rural regions provided considerable support for the regulation of banking and corporations and aid for rural programs, such as agricultural education and roads. The Democratic monopoly in the South was critical to the formation of a reform coalition in Congress after 1910.[12]

Locating progressive reformers is complicated by the shifting membership in coalitions that formed around specific issues. Sometimes these alignments tracked closely with political party affiliation. The election of Republican governors in California, New Hampshire, and elsewhere in the years around 1910 testifies to the old parties' capacity to rally around progressive issues. In other cases, temporary alliances of Republicans and Democrats carried progressive reforms. The traditional partisan tendencies of ethnic groups did not evaporate, but they were modulated by increased cross-class and nonpartisan alliances in support of progressive-oriented candidates. Progressive Era reform, in short, unfolded within the traditional matrix of partisan competition, but with frequent deflections over specific issues. The precise form of these ad hoc coalitions varied from place to place and over time.[13]

Reform impulses in the United States had important global connections. By the 1890s the United States participated in an international economic arena in which trade, technology and science, and social ideas circulated around the world. Labor militancy and waves of strikes were common throughout North America and Europe in the 1890s and early twentieth century. Policy innovations in Europe, such as social welfare in Germany and municipal transportation in Glasgow, Scotland, captured the imagination elsewhere. Civic developments in Europe, Australia, and New Zealand were common knowledge to American progressives, many of whom had studied abroad or traveled to see them firsthand. At home they pointed to these precedents as a way of framing American reforms. Jane Addams, an active social reformer and world traveler, noted in her speech seconding Theodore Roosevelt's presidential nomination at the Progressive Party's 1912 convention, "The United States lagged behind other great nations" in achieving social justice.[14]

The campaign for female suffrage in the United States became part of the international reform movement. Carrie Chapman Catt, who became president of the National American Woman Suffrage Association in 1900, spearheaded the creation of an international suffrage alliance in 1902. The 1908 meeting hosted delegates from twenty-one countries. Catt and her American colleagues subsequently reported on the progress of women's rights around the world, noting that nine countries had granted women the right to vote by 1919. Although Catt favored a more conventional state-by-state strategy to advance female suffrage, the militancy of British suffragettes influenced the confrontational tactics of Alice Paul and her colleagues.[15]

An additional spur to progressivism arose from downturns in the economy, especially the depression of the 1890s. The numerous strikes during this tumultuous decade, particularly the Pullman strike (1894), unnerved many and ignited fears of a revolution. The Populist Party, largely agrarian in composition and situated primarily in the South and West, briefly challenged established politics. Populists and others blamed corporate arrogance for the economic debacle, and they criticized self-interested political bosses' ineffective governance. Tax revolts forced retrenchment of public accounts around the country and sparked efforts to increase taxes on business. Historian David Thelen argues that the stresses of the depression provoked a "new civic consciousness" (at least in Wisconsin), weakening older laissez-faire attitudes. The economic crisis was apparently a wake-up call for civic-minded individuals.[16]

Less appreciated in the historical literature is how later economic difficulties triggered similar misgivings about governance. The Panic of 1907 provoked a sharp depression in 1908; the economy had partially recovered by 1909, only to dip again in 1910–1911, followed by another recession in 1914–1915. This sequence of economic fluctuations kept wages flat while prices rose, twin maladies that stressed the budgets of urban households, especially those headed by blue-collar workers. City governments, the states, and the United States all experienced budget deficits during these recession years. Businesses, especially new and smaller firms, were forced to scramble to stay solvent, and many did not succeed.

The political significance of the stagflation (a business slowdown coupled with rising prices) that occurred between 1907 and 1915 is tied to the emergence of a consumer society. Millions of people left the farm for the city during the Gilded Age and Progressive Era; incomes trended away from rural-based activities to industrial and service employment. By the early twentieth century half the nation's households were dependent on consumer purchases for everyday life, with food being the primary item. A chorus of complaints about the rising cost of living was heard between 1910 and 1914, challenging political leaders to identify its causes and provide remedies. A collection of policy innovations followed in the wake of this economic squeeze. Depression, wage stagnation, and rising prices were not the sole causes of these responses. But the sequence of economic irritants helped create opportunities for policymakers to enact solutions.[17]

The adoption of income taxes illustrates the political fallout from the recession and stagflation. Proposals to tax the income of individuals predated the 1910s. Congress levied an income tax during the Civil War and again in 1894, although the Supreme Court declared the latter law unconstitutional. Theodore Roosevelt put the income tax back on the national agenda in his 1906 annual presidential message. The fiscal crisis of 1907 sidetracked the proposal but also put many governmental accounts in deficit. The idea of budgeting, wherein systematic accounting would provide an efficient solution to overspending, arose in this context.[18]

Democrats seized the opportunity presented by the economic squeeze. They blamed the Republican Party for supporting high tariff rates, contending that excessive customs duties allowed big business to charge monopoly prices. The tactic worked in 1910, contributing to major Democratic victories in races for northern state legislatures and Congress, gains that were expanded two years later. In fact, 1912 was the only year that Democrats held a majority of gubernatorial seats in the North and enjoyed unified party control of the national government between 1896 and 1933. Republican defections to the Progressive Party, with its national ticket headed by Theodore Roosevelt, aided the election of a Democratic president in 1912. The enlarged Democratic presence in state legislatures and cross-party coalitions with Progressives and progressive-oriented Republicans were critical in ratifying the Sixteenth Amendment to the Constitution, authorizing a federal income tax. Economic stagnation had upset conventional politics and opened the door to passage of the Income Tax Act of 1913, as well as other measures enacted during the first Wilson administration.[19]

PROGRESSIVISM IN THE STATES AND CITIES

Historian Richard P. McCormick has observed, "Progressivism brought major innovations to almost every facet of public and private life in the United States."[20] His assessment succinctly sums up the extraordinary breadth of governmental actions adopted in the early twentieth century. Cities and states continued to be the civic workhorses in America, contributing the largest output of such policies. Most segments of society were affected, though not necessarily in ways that everyone approved of, such as the segregation and disfranchisement of African Americans in the South and the prohibition of alcoholic beverages. Regardless of the nature of these actions, subnational governments, especially the states, broadened and deepened statebuilding.

The outpouring of new state laws peaked between 1911 and 1913, largely at the hands of Democratic lawmakers, with occasional assistance from progressive Republicans. The plethora of statutes can be sorted into four broad categories: the political process (e.g., election laws), public finance, the economy, and moral regulations and assistance for specific groups.[21] The timing and appeal of issues varied among the states, depending on the subject matter. Some ideas caught fire among policymakers and were adopted by most states within a short time span. These popular policies included direct primaries, workers' compensation, health regulations for milk, and the registration of automobiles (adopted in forty-eight states between 1901 and 1914). A classic case of the contagion effect was the enactment of gasoline taxes, which swept through the states in the 1920s.[22]

Other matters proved more contentious, leading to a slower pace of enactment and fewer state adoptions. This pattern characterized the acceptance of civil service requirements for government employees, the coordination of state highway networks, personal income taxes, and executive budgets, although some states took halfway steps toward this last reform. Other issues, such as compulsory education, protection of children and women working in factories, and antimonopoly statutes, all of which first appeared in the late nineteenth century, won passage in some laggard states after 1900. The nature of the issue affected the rate and scope of policy diffusion across jurisdictions.

Opponents of change became adept at using federalism to block or weaken disfavored proposals, especially those concerning the regulation of business, the recognition of workers' rights, and taxation. Critics argued that such actions would weaken the economy by driving businesses out of their states.[23]

The success of reform was partially a consequence of a state's socioeconomic makeup. Urban, industrial states in the Northeast and the Midwest, the most affluent regions of the country, led the nation in enacting progressive reforms, especially concerning labor and workplace standards, the regulation of utilities, and financial support of education and institutions caring for special populations. States in the South, plains, and mountains lagged behind the leaders; the Pacific coast states had a mixed record. These regional tendencies were not rigid, suggesting that reform impulses were also linked to political and historical conditions. New York, Massachusetts, Illinois, and, to a lesser degree, Ohio and California took the lead in labor and regulatory matters, setting policy models for lawmakers in other states. New York, for example, was a leader in regulating utilities through a nonpartisan commission, establishing a program of workers' compensation for on-the-job injuries, requiring the registration of motor vehicles and the licensing of nurses, and limiting work hours for women and children. Reforms adopted in New York and other major industrial states frequently diffused horizontally across the federal system.[24]

Large cities radiated a similar influence, providing policy models for smaller municipalities and channeling reform cues to their state capitals. Such a pathway occurred with the use of budgets to improve the management of public finances. Several trends gave birth to the budgeting movement. First, municipalities increased their expenditures during the Gilded Age and Progressive Era (see chapter 10), as greater outlays followed expanding civic agendas. Revenue to pay for these higher municipal costs derived primarily from a levy on real estate, which fell disproportionately on urban homeowners, many of them in the middle class. Second, city councils had traditionally voted on appropriations with little control from mayors. Reform-oriented citizens charged that city bosses spent these monies capriciously, padding city payrolls to reward supporters and pocketing bribes for the awarding of utility franchises. Critics believed their rising tax bills were a consequence of machine politics. Third, the economic slump that followed the Panic of 1907 saddled many public treasuries with deficits. To citizens who habitually interpreted overspending and indebtedness as cardinal sins, deficits fed a call for fiscal retrenchment and better money management.[25]

The path to budgeting began with accounting, a process developed by railroads and corporations after the Civil War. Close, systematic tracking of costs and revenue became a staple of corporate management by the turn of the century.[26] A key step in this direction was the classification of finances by a uniform accounting system, a proposal pushed by the Committee on Uniform Municipal Accounts and Statistics (established in 1901) of the National Municipal League (created in 1894). The proposal caught on in several cities, especially New York, where a citizens' group sponsored the formation of the Bureau of Municipal Research in 1907. Run by nonpartisan experts, the bureau pushed to put city finances under the direction of the mayor, a reform adopted in 1908.[27]

Budgeting spread to other cities, including Boston, one of the numerous Massachusetts municipalities that had experienced financial deficits. Following a mandate from the state to review tax procedures, Boston created a finance commission in 1907. The city's report blamed fiscal difficulties on the "city council dominated by spoilsmen" and recommended that the mayor control the budget process. The state legislature followed up in 1909 by voting for a new city charter that gave the mayor the power to create a finance commission to draft a budget. Other cities around the nation also adopted "businesslike" management of their finances; Chicago's budgetary reform (1910) utilized a bureau of public efficiency.[28]

The appeal of budget reform percolated up to the states. Additional pressure came from the Taft administration in Washington, which formed the National Commission on Economy and Efficiency in 1910. That body was headed by accounting experts hired to find a more efficient manner of managing national finances. Numerous states formed their own efficiency commissions, which went on to recommend state budgets. By 1917 nearly half the states had instituted budget systems; by 1921 virtually all the states had signed on. Congress was among the last holdouts, delaying the adoption of an executive budget (housed in the Treasury Department) until 1921. Political complaints about the traditional partisan management of government, the rise of professional accountants and academic researchers, and alarm over recession-induced deficits had transformed the way governments approached financial policy.[29]

As a rule, budget reform was not a highly partisan issue in the state legislatures. An exception was Democratic opposition in 1909 to Boston's new city charter, which a unified Republican delegation passed. The Connecticut senate recorded sharp partisan division in 1911 over electing members of the public utility commission, abolishing property qualifications for voting in local elections, and strengthening the power of the governor. Measures to allow citizen policy initiatives and referenda, establish workers' compensation, and prohibit child labor in dangerous places—all classic progressive reforms—did not generate sharp partisan conflict, largely due to division among Republicans. Many prominent progressive reforms, such as workers' compensation, limited hours for female factory workers, and improved railroad and mine safety, produced little conflict. Less partisan than members of Congress, state lawmakers responded to most of the progressive agenda with minimal disagreement along party lines.[30]

Party was, however, the key to some policy outcomes. Election victories in 1910 and 1912 gave Democrats a majority or a sizable minority in many northern state legislatures. This Democratic resurgence proved to be a critical factor in ratification of the Sixteenth Amendment (federal income tax) in New York and Massachusetts. Northern Democrats displayed less unity, however, on social regulations, such as limiting the sale of alcoholic beverages, licensing dance halls, gambling, and restricting Sunday activities. On these issues, urban-rural and ethnic divisions underlay much of the disagreement.

ADMINISTRATIVE REFORM IN THE STATES

Effective administration to implement legislative goals became increasingly common during the Progressive Era. Policymakers created units staffed with experts to oversee the technical dimensions of policy, such as tax and public utility commissions and highway and agricultural departments. These reforms underscored the growing consensus that nonpartisan experts made better policy administrators than patronage appointees. A second strand of administrative reform increased state supervision of local governments. These steps were visible in the certification of teachers (most schools were run locally) and the regulation of financial activities, such as the assessment of property taxes, the use of standardized accounting methods, and the imposition of limits on taxation and indebtedness.[31]

A consensus also crystallized around the notion that better administration required greater authority for executives. This sentiment was visible in the extension of new powers to mayors and later by efforts to give governors managerial responsibility for state administration. Influenced by a model proposed by the New York Bureau of Municipal Research, the New York Constitutional Convention of 1915 recommended a state reorganization plan that gave the governor greater authority; voters rejected it in a popular referendum. But Illinois legislators enacted a similar reform by a bipartisan vote in 1917. The Illinois Reorganization Act consolidated half of Illinois' one hundred state boards, agencies, and commissions into nine executive departments, each with a director appointed by the governor. The Department of Finance was charged with preparing a state budget for the governor, who submitted it to the legislature. Similar state reorganizations continued in the 1920s after World War I.[32]

Administrative reform was partially a response to an enlarged public workforce. Piecemeal data suggest that the number of state government workers grew as much as 100 percent between 1900 and 1915. This rate far exceeded the increase in the general population. City employees followed a similar growth trajectory; Milwaukee doubled its workforce during this period, while New York City's workforce increased by 80 percent, giving it more employees than any single state government.[33]

The hiring of additional public workers increased state and local expenditures, which rose about 50 percent between 1900 and 1916 (in per capita, inflation-adjusted dollars), with city spending still outpacing state outlays. Rising public costs placed a greater burden on property tax revenue, which accentuated criticisms about methods of assessing property values and the tax's inelastic response to economic ups and downs. Consequently, lawmakers looked for alternative revenue sources, such as the taxation of corporations and public utilities (e.g., gas and electric companies), the adoption of or increase in inheritance taxes, and the imposition of fees, such as for motor vehicle registration. Some reformers saw personal income taxes as a logical fiscal accompaniment to a workforce that was increasingly paid in wages and salaries and wealth that was generated from the ownership of stocks and bonds. Wisconsin enacted the first modern income tax in 1911, with Massachusetts and Virginia following in 1916 and New York in 1919.[34]

The expansion of civic programs, the reform of public administration, and the adoption of new revenue sources substantially enhanced the capacity of cities and states to govern. Numerous scholars have characterized these trends as the beginning of bureaucratic government in the United States, yet the reach of improved administration was still limited. Labor reformers lamented faulty factory inspections. Industrial accidents among miners and railroaders—very dangerous occupations—occurred at substantially higher rates in the United States than in Europe. Cotton dust and open machinery made work in textile mills hazardous to workers' health. Consumers continued to battle public utilities. Child labor laws in the South were ignored. Determined opposition stymied many progressive proposals, especially those concerning the regulation of business, the rights of labor unions, and social justice issues. Progressive reform developed incrementally; improvements came gradually, not by revolution.[35]

FEDERAL POLICY INNOVATIONS

Progressivism's pattern of enlarging the role of government also expanded the national agenda. Washington lawmakers enacted new business regulations (e.g., railroad rates, antimonopoly restrictions, practices of national banks), offered new services and assistance (e.g., aid to states for highways, loan assistance to farmers for irrigation, subsidized agricultural research and education, expanded rural mail delivery), and tapped new revenue sources (e.g., adoption of the Sixteenth Amendment, authorizing a personal income tax). Congress joined the states in enacting new social controls, such as prohibiting interstate traffic in prostitution and banning illiterate immigrants. The US Supreme Court had upheld racial segregation by the states in its 1896 ruling (*Plessy v. Ferguson*) and added to this legal permissiveness in subsequent rulings.

Federal lawmakers acted on issues concerning consumers and workers, especially if public opinion had been aroused over an issue. Congress passed the 1906 Pure Food and Drug Act, the 1916 Railroad Labor Act (mandating eight-hour days for railroad workers), and the 1914 Anti-Narcotics Act. Congress approved a statute in 1916 that limited child labor, which the Supreme Court subsequently declared unconstitutional. Progressive Era presidents expanded national forest reserves, and Congress created the National Park Service in 1916. Sentiment for political reform was visible in congressional approval of the Seventeenth Amendment, whose ratification mandated the popular election of US senators in every state.

Similarities between reforms at the national and subnational levels occurred in part because municipal and state actions provided policy models, and sometimes lobbying pressure, for federal lawmaking. Limits on workers' hours, child labor restrictions, antimonopoly actions, and budgeting practices illustrate the flow of policy ideas up the federal ladder. The Pure Food and Drug Act (1906) and the Federal Highway Act (1916), areas pioneered by the states, provide further examples.[36] State politics influenced congressional action through constituent pressure and referenda on controversial issues.[37] Influence worked in the opposite direction too, such as the federal mandate (1916) that states create highway departments in order to qualify for national highway funds. President Taft's Commission on Economy and Efficiency was widely replicated in the states. Headed by the former director of New York's Bureau of Municipal Research, the national commission recommended that states institute executive-based budgeting. Increasingly, the federal system had become a two-way conduit for policy development.

The economic disturbances of 1907–1912 created conditions that advanced fiscal reform in Washington. The stagnation of commerce produced deficits in the US Treasury in 1908, 1909, and 1910, shortfalls that were unacceptable to fiscal conservatives. President Taft acknowledged the impact of the recession in his inaugural address of 1909, when he predicted that the search for tariff reform would require "new kinds of taxation." The president cautioned against a major cut in expenditures because "the scope of a modern government . . . has been widened far beyond the principles laid down by the old 'laissez faire' school." He supported an excise tax on corporations to raise additional revenue, which Congress enacted in 1909, and he urged lawmakers to approve an income tax amendment to the Constitution, which lawmakers also accepted.[38]

Growing unemployment and rising consumer prices between 1909 and 1913 provoked wide discussions of the causes and cures. The Democrats pointed to the tariff as the source of inflation. The party endeavored to convince voters that high customs duties drove up prices by fostering corporate monopolies. Because the tariff was the federal government's main tool for fine-tuning the economy, the Democratic indictment provided a rationale to levy income taxes. Democratic victories in 1910 were instrumental in ratification of the Sixteenth Amendment by the state legislatures. The Democrats' successes continued in 1912 when they captured the presidency and a congressional majority. Democrats fulfilled their pledges by passing the Underwood Tariff Act on straight party-line votes in both the House and the Senate. The law included a tax on personal income that was designed to cover the shortfall from the reduction in the tariff.[39]

Levying federal income taxes on individuals and businesses was the most significant legislative reform in the Progressive Era. The income tax not only gave the national government a potent fiscal instrument that tapped the growing affluence of the American economy; it also provided a tool to achieve other policy objectives, such as allowing individuals to purchase homes and donate to charity (via deductions from taxable income). Along with the creation of the Federal Reserve System (another policy related partially to stagflation), the federal government was authorized to implement fiscal and monetary policy. The Democratic majority in Congress also pushed through the Clayton Act, which prohibited interwoven corporate directories (an amendment to the Sherman Antitrust Act) and created the Federal Trade Commission. Both these 1914 measures reflected the widespread animus toward big business, an issue that had festered during the early twentieth century and was accentuated after 1907 by stagflation. At the state level, regulation of banking and public utilities, the creation of tax commissions and workers' compensation plans, laws limiting the work hours of women and children, and increased state oversight of local finance also had links to the economic climate (see table A.3 in the appendix).

Although it was significant and historic, the new federal involvement in the economy should not be overstated. Federal management of commercial activity occurred in incremental steps, not revolutionary shifts. This was especially true for the enforcement of business regulations; gradual policy adjustments were a political necessity for such legislation to gain approval. The Federal Reserve Banking Act suggests this trend. Banking regulations had been on the agenda of state legislatures and Congress long before the Progressive Era. The 1913 act did not create a single national bank under the supervision of federal appointees, as some had wanted; instead, it provided for a dozen regional banks, with two-thirds of their boards of governors appointed by private member banks in the region. Banks with national charters were required to join the system, but state banks were not. The fragmented and decentralized history of the American polity had a potent influence on the design of national banking policy. Incrementalism also characterized the first personal income tax, which applied to only 1 percent of workers, set very low rates on incomes that qualified for taxation (most did not), and relied on employee compliance to pay the tax in the year after the income was received.[40]

The limits on federal penetration into business are visible in the Pure Food and Drug Act of 1906, which prohibited adulteration and misbranding of food and drugs and regulated the manufacture and sale of poisonous commodities. The law applied only to interstate commerce (as opposed to business confined wholly within one state). The act neither required a drug to be safe nor set standards for adulteration. Lawmakers failed to create an agency dedicated to enforcing the statute, nor did they adequately fund the Bureau of Chemistry, which was given oversight responsibilities. A 1912 amendment made a drug illegal if its label was both "false and fraudulent," wording that impeded legal convictions for bogus advertising.[41]

Washington's regulation of business corporations was similarly cautious and restrained. The Clayton Act made price discrimination, certain kinds of contracts, and acquisition of a rival firm illegal if the action lessened competition. But the law cited no specific practices as unlawful, putting that determination in the hands of the courts, where antitrust prosecutions were already routed. The Federal Trade Commission, drawing on state models of regulatory boards, was instructed to identify unfair methods of competition. Essentially a fact-finding body, the commission lacked enforcement powers; it could issue "cease and desist" orders to a firm, but it had to refer ongoing violations to the Justice Department for prosecution. The new antitrust laws were as much symbolic as they were an effective oversight of commercial practices. Americans disliked corporate monopolies, but their admiration for free enterprise and limited government tempered their legal rectitude about businesses. The Supreme Court shared this view. Although it broke up Rockefeller's Standard Oil Corporation into small units because of predatory practices in 1911, the justices held that "reasonable monopolies" were legal. Nine years later the high court ruled in a suit against US Steel that the size of a firm alone was not a violation of the Sherman Antitrust Act. A partial exception to this regulatory posture were laws passed in 1906 and 1910 that allowed the Interstate Commerce Commission to set certain railroad rates.[42]

Despite this mixed record of regulation, federal administrative capacity expanded in the Progressive Era. The Washington establishment gained twenty-seven new departments, bureaus, and agencies between 1901 and 1916, reflecting increased administrative differentiation. New units were created for agricultural research, forestry, roads, children's welfare, banking and business, police investigation (a forerunner of the FBI), shipping, and national parks.[43] More agencies required more employees. The federal government's workforce increased from 208,000 in 1899 to 480,000 in 1916, a rate of growth significantly exceeding that of the general population. By the end of the period a majority of the federal workforce was covered by civil service rules. The US Department of Agriculture (USDA) grew from about 2,000 employees in 1895 to nearly 19,000 in 1916. The Office of Public Roads (originally the Office of Road Inquiry) hired 53 people in 1907 and 450 in 1915, the year prior to the enactment of federal grants to states for highways. The US Post Office, the largest federal department, grew from 136,000 employees in 1901 to 212,000 in 1916, during which time rural free delivery, postal savings, and parcel post service began.[44]

More federal functions and more employees meant greater costs. Federal expenditures rose 42 percent between 1900 and 1916.[45] The army and navy accounted for the largest share of these appropriations, and military pensions accounted for the largest single domestic outlay of funds. By 1915 virtually all surviving veterans of the Union army were enrolled as pensioners. Veterans' benefits, much like Social Security at a later date, represented income support payments for citizens, not government workers. Expenditures for running a department offer a better gauge of administrative activity. The USDA, which had blossomed into a client agency serving farmers and agribusinesses and performed a variety of research activities, received less than $4 million in 1900, compared with $28 million in 1916. Construction of the Panama Canal consumed substantial funds. Spending to run Congress and support the presidency grew as well, reflecting new perks and staff for lawmakers and expanded Secret Service protection for the president. Despite ongoing resistance to bureaucracy and federal expansion, incremental growth in federal agencies, personnel, and expenditures is clearly visible between 1901 and 1917.[46]

The crystallization of a national administrative regime had its roots in the Gilded Age. Some federal departments had hired experts to direct technical tasks before 1900. The USDA, which led the national government in scientific work, illustrates this trend. Among its professional cadre was Harvey Wiley, head of the USDA's Division of Chemistry, who became a tireless advocate for the regulation of food and drugs. He guided the Association of Official Agricultural Chemists (whose members worked for the states) in this crusade and invited other professional and interest groups, such as the General Federation of Women's Clubs, to join this lobbying network.[47]

Other federal administrators replicated Wiley's policy advocacy. Gifford Pinchot, chief forester in the USDA and a favorite of Theodore Roosevelt, actively recruited private organizations to implement his ideas about public lands. Roy Stone of the Office of Road Inquiry and his successors in the Office of Public Roads advocated federal highway aid for the states. Logan Page, appointed director in 1905, encouraged the states to create highway departments and orchestrated lobbying support for the 1916 Federal Highway Aid Act, which he helped write. Post office officials, whose inauguration of rural mail delivery sparked interest in road improvement, were active in expanding the department's mission. The Interstate Commerce Commission, whose work made it intimately familiar with railroad economics, pushed for new legislation. One of the most conspicuous examples of a federal professional who proposed policy reforms was Frederick A. Cleveland, formerly of the New York Bureau of Municipal Research and chair of President Taft's Commission on Economy and Efficiency. He became one of the nation's leading spokesmen for the creation of a financial budget under executive supervision. These stories underscore how professionals in federal service acted as promoters of national statebuilding.[48]

PROGRESSIVISM AND STATEBUILDING

The Progressive Era, recognized as the first broad period of reform in the twentieth century, substantially advanced American statebuilding. Three key trends highlight this development. First, the scope of public authority over existing functions was expanded, as in the case of regulating business and providing assistance for economic development, agricultural research, and education. State governments continued the tradition of imposing moral restrictions, such as on liquor, gambling, boxing, cigarettes, and prostitution. Progressive actions ranged from racial segregation to female suffrage to new forms of taxation and the supervision of elections.

While most of these enactments were incremental adjustments to older civic concerns, some actions represented bolder policy innovations. The federal income tax and Federal Reserve banks gave the national government substantial new authority over the economy. In time, income taxes became Washington's chief revenue source. The Federal Reserve Board evolved into a tool of macroeconomic stabilization, a role only dimly foreseen in 1913. Both enactments represented practical responses to specific problems of the period, yet over time, these two mechanisms became critical levers in building a more powerful national state.

Second, progressivism forged greater centralization of government. This tendency was visible in the expansion of state oversight of local activities, such as setting standards for teachers, public health, taxation and indebtedness, and financial aid for schools and transportation. State governments copied several administrative innovations initially begun at the municipal level. The national government assumed a larger role in promoting and regulating the economy, such as its oversight of railroads, investigation of business practices, forestry preservation, and promotion of irrigation for western farms. Using its authority under the commerce clause of the Constitution, Congress restricted the interstate transportation of liquor and prostitutes ("white slavery") and mandated an eight-hour day for railroad workers. Congress voted grants-in-aid to states for agricultural research (beginning in 1887 and later expanded), demonstration farms (1914), rural highways (1916), and vocational education (1917). In 1911 Congress mandated that states match "categoric" grants with their own contributions and required states to observe certain administrative standards as a requirement for receiving federal funds. Federal grants not only forged new cooperative linkages between Washington and the states but also created a mechanism by which Congress could circumvent traditional political impediments to legislating domestic affairs.[49]

Congress moved gingerly at first with its grant program, which left the framework of dual federalism intact. The ratio of federal to state and local expenditures changed little through 1916; local and state governments continued to spend the most public funds, especially for domestic functions. Yet observers sounded an alarm about cracks in the foundation of federalism. Some worried that an inevitable march toward national control was under way. They could point to a list of statutes in which Congress had blocked (preempted) state interference with national policy. Progressives such as Theodore Roosevelt, as well as business leaders involved with national markets, emphasized the limitations of traditional federalism, which had nurtured a complex matrix of state law and competitive fear of economic harm from new regulations. Prodded by attorneys and others, state lawmakers tried to counter this unevenness by adopting standardized policies in certain areas. A few "uniform state laws" were enacted, but the broader effort at legislative cooperation failed. By 1916 some constitutional experts were predicting the continued erosion of traditional federalism.[50]

Third, elected executives at all levels of government gained new power in the early twentieth century. Some of this additional authority was conveyed by statute: revised city charters assigned greater powers to mayors, and governors were permitted to veto specific appropriations. Beginning with Illinois' Reorganization Act of 1917, states allowed governors to create cabinet-style departments similar to the national arrangement. But the enhanced authority of mayors, governors, and the president entailed more than just specific authorizations. The public came to expect executives to assert political leadership. Theodore Roosevelt became the model for the new executive. Always a whirlwind of activity and an instinctive politician, Roosevelt maximized the potential of the governor's office and then the presidency. He used his national position as a "bully pulpit," reaching out to the public on behalf of numerous causes. His 1905 State of the Union message totaled fifty pages, touching subjects from *A* to *Z*. His 1907 and 1908 messages were even bolder in staking out new directions for federal power. He skillfully courted the press in advocacy of his lengthy agendas. The press, in turn, portrayed the president as the human face of government.[51]

President Taft lacked Roosevelt's political skill, but his advocacy of an executive budget and a personal income tax were major policy innovations. He sent drafts of legislation to Congress. President Wilson was an astute political practitioner and a dynamic orator. He used these abilities to cajole Democrats to support ambitious domestic reforms during his first term. All three Progressive Era presidents concurred that social and economic conditions in the United States necessitated a more activist national government, one less bound by older restrictive ideologies. While they all remained committed partisans, they also governed pragmatically. None among this presidential triad dwelled on the older ideological homilies that had impeded national governance in the past. Roosevelt had little tolerance for the observance of states' rights.[52]

These three civic trends significantly enhanced the governing capacity of the national state. Some policy innovations evoked fierce opposition and modified or stalled particular reforms, yet the flow of opinion drifted away from laissez-faire toward greater tolerance for the pragmatic exercise of civic authority. Aside from some naval officers and their civilian cheerleaders, such as Roosevelt, who urged the United States to assume a greater role in world affairs, most policy proposals flowed from specific efforts to address problems at home. No grand scheme of statebuilding directed municipal, state, or national policymakers. Yet the multitude of policies adopted during the Progressive Era added block after block to an institutional base that accumulated greater governmental power over a wider scope of operation. Incremental growth within the traditional structure of republican government helps explain the paradox of American statebuilding.

12

The Wartime State

On September 26, 1918, 300,000 young Americans climbed out of their trenches and dashed through fog, mud, and exploding artillery shells into no-man's-land and toward German entrenchments in the Argonne forest, ninety miles east of Paris. The opening days of the drive did not go well. German artillery and hidden machine gun nests wiped out entire companies. Roads became virtually impassable because of mud, shell craters, and traffic. Horses were critical to carting supplies to the front and transporting wounded to the rear. The few light tanks under the command of Lieutenant Colonel George S. Patton were picked off one by one as they lost the support of ground troops. After four days, the Americans had been stopped in their tracks. French commanders, contemptuous of the inexperienced Americans whose early actions often resulted in disorganized chaos, said, "We told you so."

There were some bright spots for the doughboys in the opening days of the Meuse-Argonne offensive. Private Alvin York, a former conscientious objector, single-handedly killed 28 Germans, took 132 prisoners, and captured 35 machines guns. Despite the "slackers" who took refuge in the rear, most Americans demonstrated an aggressive will to fight, hurling themselves straight at German positions. Directing the American effort was General John J. Pershing, fifty-seven years old and looking every bit the man in charge, standing ramrod straight in a crisply pressed uniform that matched his steely personality. As supreme commander of the American Expeditionary Force in Europe, Pershing resisted French and British appeals to integrate American troops with battle-tested Allied divisions. He was adamant that Americans fight as a self-contained unit operating under its own commanders. This plan, he believed, would give his troops the motivation to win.

President Woodrow Wilson stood by his commander, despite appeals from French and British leaders to integrate Americans with Allied forces. Wilson and Pershing realized that the doughboys, sometimes thrust into combat with minimal training, would have to learn on the job. Despite very high casualties in the campaign, Pershing demanded that his men keep attacking. To prepare for the offensive, he had peppered Secretary of War Newton Baker with requests for more men, more supplies, and especially more horses. The lack of American ships created a bedeviling bottleneck. A deal with Britain for transport vessels helped immensely, shipping 300,000 Yanks a month to France by the summer of 1918.

German contempt for the American military turned to disbelief as advancing Yanks drove the enemy from their bunkers and trenches. Outnumbered and dispirited, German commanders decided to push for a truce rather than see French, British, Canadian, and American troops march into the fatherland. Pershing wanted an unconditional surrender but settled for the armistice signed November 11, 1918, which amounted to the same thing. American intervention had turned the tide of the war, changing a stalemated impasse that had lasted more than four years into victory. Pershing deserves some credit for the outcome, but many hands contributed to the Allies' success. Regardless of who gets the credit for the German defeat, World War I was a critical moment in American statebuilding.[1]

AMERICA ENTERS THE WORLD STAGE

The path to the American intervention into World War I began in the late nineteenth century, when a global outreach commenced. Influenced by European imperialism and the buildup of national navies, the United States modernized its fleet and defeated Spain in 1898, which put the Philippines, Puerto Rico, and Guam under American control. Hawaii was annexed the same year, bolstering America's Pacific presence, which already included Alaska and the Midway Islands (1867). Wake and Eastern Samoa were added in 1899.

With US possessions in the Caribbean and the Pacific, and with expanding commercial aspirations, the construction of an interocean canal in Central America gained support. President Theodore Roosevelt used the navy and diplomacy to assist Panama's break from Colombia in 1903 and persuaded Congress to fund the Panama Canal, which opened in 1914. Bases in Cuba's Guantanamo Bay and in Puerto Rico protected the investment; the purchase of the Virgin Islands from Denmark in 1916 added other safe harbors. In the years just prior to World War I, the US Navy landed troops in Cuba, the Dominican Republic, Haiti, Honduras, Nicaragua, and Mexico. John Pershing gained combat experience in the campaign to suppress Filipino revolutionaries (1899–1902) and notoriety by leading the expedition to catch Pancho Villa (1916–1917) in Mexico during its revolution. For all intents and purposes, the Caribbean had become an American lake, policed through "gunboat diplomacy."

American outreach in the Pacific also expanded. The United States sent troops to China during the Boxer Rebellion (1900) and displayed its naval prowess in Tokyo when sixteen American battleships toured the world

(1907–1909). President Roosevelt encouraged the "white fleet's" visit to Japan, whose navy had defeated Russia in 1905. American naval planners formulated Plan Orange to block the Japanese should they advance on the Philippines.[2]

By and large, Americans accepted these military-diplomatic developments as consistent with the country's continental dominance. Yet most people in the United States were surprised when Britain, France, and Russia (the Allies) went to war against Germany and Austria-Hungary in August 1914. President Wilson announced American neutrality, the nation's traditional posture concerning conflicts in Europe. No diplomatic pact tied the United States to any of the belligerents, although American sympathies, especially among those of English heritage, leaned toward Britain. The president's efforts to steer clear of entanglements, however, faced impediments from geography, economics, ethnic culture, and the flow of military events.[3]

The Atlantic Ocean had long served as a great moat that guarded the United States from an overseas invasion, as well as a highway for American commerce. The Great War was good for American businesses, farmers, and financiers, as European purchases lifted the country out of a sharp recession (1914–1915) at the war's outset.[4] To the displeasure of Germany, most American goods flowed to England, assisted by US loans. Most trans-Atlantic shipments traveled on British ships under the protection of the British navy, which had bottled up Germany's vessels in port and blockaded the continent. The German command fought back with new technology: the submarine. To be useful, submarines needed stealth, attacking without warning while submerged; otherwise, these fragile craft could be destroyed by ramming or by rounds fired from deck guns. Although Germany had warned travelers to avoid the "war zone" around Great Britain, the *Lusitania*, a British ship sailing from New York, was torpedoed off the coast of Ireland in May 1915, claiming 1,198 lives, including Americans. This was denounced as an outrageous attack on civilians, and some Americans urged military retaliation.

The *Lusitania* tragedy forced Wilson to make midcourse corrections. He informed German leaders he would hold them to "strict accountability" if they continued to use their *Underseebooten* in surprise attacks on ships carrying nonbelligerents. After an intensification of the British blockage enticed more aggressive submarine strikes, Wilson threatened to sever diplomatic relations with Germany unless its navy inspected belligerent vessels prior to attacks. Germany agreed.

The attack on the *Lusitania* also prodded Wilson to support "preparedness" at home. With a small army and a navy inferior to those of the European powers, America lacked the military capacity to confront Germany. Congress approved the Defense Act of 1916, which increased the size of the US Army to 175,000 over five years and allowed the National Guard to be folded into the national armed forces when called on, a provision that circumvented restrictions on its deployment outside the United States. The Naval Act of 1916 provided for a substantial expansion of naval vessels, including battleships, although their completion was years away. Both statutes looked toward the future security of the nation and were not predicated on an imminent intervention in the European war. Demands for preparedness were nonetheless politically compelling, leading Wilson to pay lip service to a program of quasi-military training. In late 1916 the War Department initiated planning for universal military training, the first step toward a draft. More effective in readying the military for war was the expedition into Mexico under General Pershing in quest of Pancho Villa, who had led a murderous raid into New Mexico.[5]

Aided by legislation that pleased labor and rural residents and by his acceptance of military preparation, which pleased conservatives, Wilson won reelection by a razor-slim margin in 1916. Critical to Wilson's victory was the Democratic Party's boast that the president had "kept us out of war," an appeal aimed at German Americans and Irish Americans who opposed assistance for Great Britain. Wilson's lectures to Germany about the rights of neutrals, however, could not change the military calculus in Europe. The western front had settled into stalemated trench warfare, which cost tens of thousands of lives without budging the battle lines and eroded the combatants' capacity to continue the struggle. Faced with this crisis, German militarists overruled their civilian counterparts, arguing that resumption of unrestricted submarine attacks could knock Britain and France out of the war by cutting off critical supplies before the Americans could enter the conflict.

It was a daring gamble that failed. German submarines attacked ships around Great Britain in 1917, sinking some American merchant vessels. Wilson polled his cabinet, which was united behind a decision for war. Wilson delivered the war message to Congress in person on April 2, 1917, outlining three primary reasons for going to war. First, Germany had violated American neutrality rights by "ruthless" submarine attacks, and he condemned the Germans as "outlaws." Second, German military conduct was unethical, constituting "a war against mankind." Third, Germany's aggression was an extension of its "autocratic government," referring to the monarchy (the kaiser) that controlled military policy. America would fight "for the ultimate peace of the world," the president said, so that it would "be made safe for democracy" and "the rights of mankind." This ideological justification became the hallmark of Wilsonian diplomacy. The House voted 373–50 and the Senate 82–6 in favor of the war resolution.

Historians have speculated about Wilson's motivations. The president was clearly pro-British by background and intellectual inclination. He was aware that a German victory could jeopardize American wartime loans to Britain. The Russian Revolution had broken out in March, pointing to Russia's withdrawal from the war; this would remove an "autocracy" from the Allied coalition and free the German armies to fight on the western front. The president apparently agreed with Secretary of State Robert Lansing that the "military oligarchy" in Germany threatened American national security because it sought "to become the overlord of the world."[6] The so-called Zimmerman telegram in which Germany offered to help Mexico recover territory in the United States gave creditability to charges of German aggression. Important, too, was Wilson's aspiration to establish a world forum to prevent future wars. His League of Nations proposal would have a better chance of acceptance if the United States were a full partner in the peace negotiations.

In whatever way these factors combined to edge Wilson toward war, his public justification for intervention is a matter of public record. He wanted to gain popular consent for his decision, and his war message was filled with imagery that resonated with Progressive Era thinking. The clenched-fist agenda of the German autocrats was reminiscent of the power of political bosses and industrial barons in America. Denouncing submarine warfare as immoral carried a reproach analogous to the wickedness of white slave traffickers (of prostitutes) and the saloon power the prohibitionists battled. Portraying German behavior as a threat to democracy resonated with progressives who had struggled to cleanse the polity of corruption. Germany had become a problem. American military power was the solution. The great crusade against Germany was consistent with the intellectual and popular sentiments that animated progressives' reliance on the state to remedy problems.[7]

MOBILIZATION FOR WAR

Congress voted overwhelmingly for war against Germany, yet the country was woefully unprepared for it. The regular army numbered fewer than 133,000; its arsenal of weapons was gravely deficient. The War Department had a staff of eighteen in Washington to remedy these deficiencies. The navy had fighting ships but little capacity to transport troops across the Atlantic or protect them from submarine attacks. Given these weaknesses, many Americans, including members of Congress, were surprised when the president announced his decision to draft Americans into military service and send them to Europe. Wilson's selective service bill passed the House with a solid majority: 313 for and 109 against. The opposition included Claude Kitchen, the majority leader of the president's party and part of the southern resistance to conscription. The initial law required men between the ages of twenty-one and thirty to register for the draft; a later revision stretched the age range to between eighteen and forty-five. The selection of draftees was assigned to 4,600 Selective Service Boards across the United States, an arrangement that reflected the influence of localism in politics. Twenty-four million men eventually registered for the draft, and 4.8 million were put into uniform, two-thirds by conscription. Perhaps two million others evaded military service by failing to register, failing to appear when called, or fleeing once they were inducted into service. Enforcing the draft became a major preoccupation of officials charged with administering "Mr. Wilson's war."[8]

The challenge for the United States was to enroll, train, and equip a military force of nearly four million virtually from scratch. Training raw recruits was a formidable task in itself, but furnishing them with weapons and equipment and transporting them to France were equally challenging. Most items of warfare, from uniforms and helmets to modern weaponry, were in short supply or, in the case of tanks, planes, and artillery, virtually nonexistent. The Allies supplied most of the latter weapons, as well as a model for the US Army's first metal helmet. Britain transported half the expeditionary force sent to France and much of its supplies. Reinforced with fifty new destroyers and 400 wooden subchasers to escort troop transports, the US Navy did not lose a single American vessel to German attacks en route to Europe.[9] Through trial and error, negotiation and compromise, and a shared dedication to winning the war, two million doughboys got to Europe.

A token unit of American troops reached France in July 1917. The large body of doughboys did not arrive until 1918 and did not fight in a major battle until the summer, more than a year after Congress had declared war. After their arrival, the Americans had to travel to the front, some 400 miles to the east from the coast of France. Pershing was unwilling to commit the Americans to combat unless they formed a complete, fully equipped fighting unit. He resisted most entreaties from French and British commanders to integrate Americans with Allied troops but acceded to an exception in the spring of 1918, when Germany massed forces for a major offensive. Pershing consented to the temporary loan of American troops in exchange for a British commitment to provide more transports.

The German attack was halted, but circumstances forced Pershing to accelerate his combat schedule, as the French supreme commander ordered a massive fall offensive. Despite incomplete training for newly arrived divisions and a lack of experienced officers, Pershing accepted the challenge, committing 600,000 Americans to the Meuse-Argonne phase of the campaign. After forty-seven days of fighting, during which Pershing continually ordered his commanders forward, Germany consented to the armistice.

Supplying the American Expeditionary Force presented the government with a formidable challenge. Some groundwork had been laid in 1916 with an appropriations act that allowed the president to operate the railroads during a crisis. Wilson used this authority to place the carriers under federal management when rail transportation became badly snarled in late 1917. Congress approved the arrangement, making sure that railroad owners and their workers were generously compensated. The Shipping Board, formed in September 1916 to encourage ship production, commandeered hulls under construction as well as large ships operated by American owners. A subsidiary, the Emergency Fleet Corporation, constructed 480 ships, a program aided by government loans to house shipyard workers. Wilson created a War Industries Board by executive order in July 1917 that brought together representatives from government, the military, private industry, and labor to coordinate the allocation of resources and set priorities for war orders, for which the military contracted with private suppliers. The government usually bought supplies by cost-plus contracts, which pleased producers.[10]

Congress expanded the president's authority to manage mobilization with the Lever Act (August 1917). The law stated that, "by reason of the existence of the state of war, it is essential to . . . the successful prosecution of the war . . . to assure an adequate supply and equitable distribution . . . of food, fuel . . . and equipment . . . and . . . to prevent . . . monopolization, hoarding, injurious speculation . . . affecting such supply." The act gave the president the power to fix the price of wheat and coal and prohibited the manufacture and importation of distilled spirits. In an "extreme" emergency he could regulate any industry.

A blizzard of agreements between public officials and private companies strained Washington's capacity to coordinate the wartime economy. To help manage this task, Congress passed the Overman Act (April 1918), which granted the president greater authority to reorganize the executive branch of the federal government for the duration of the war. Utilizing this power, Wilson delegated wide discretion to Bernard Baruch, a financier who headed the War Industries Board. Baruch's style meshed with the board's practices; it operated collaboratively with business, especially large corporations, which received the lion's share of contracts. Separate administrative boards were created to manage food production, fuel, labor relations, railroads, shipping, and war financing. Farmers benefited substantially from federal purchases, while labor fared less well, despite a Labor Board that attempted to settle disputes over wages and hours.

The Great War revamped federal finances. Congress relaxed its tightfist-

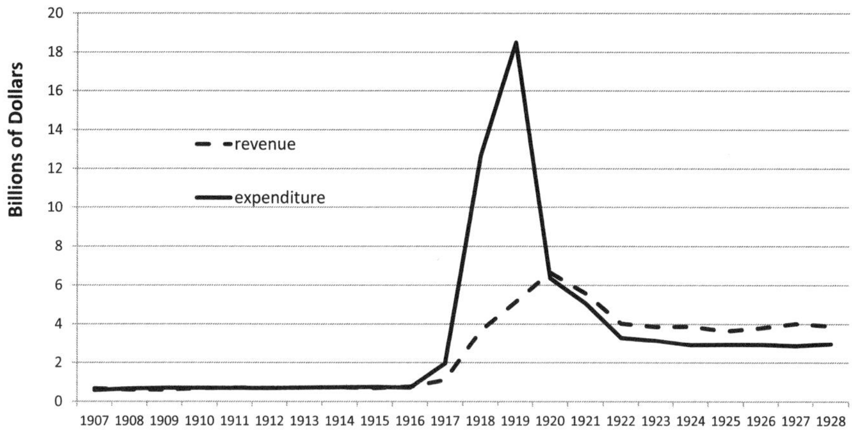

Figure 12.1. Federal expenditures and revenue, 1907–1928. *Source:* Susan B. Carter et al., *Historical Statistics of the United States* (New York: Cambridge University Press, 2006), tables Ea584–585.

edness and approved expenditures that increased twenty-five-fold between 1916 and 1919 (see figure 12.1). The federal government's contribution to the gross national product (a dollar measure of economic activity) grew from 1 percent in 1915 to 23 percent in 1918. The extraordinary spike in spending led to important questions about how to pay for it. Wilson left the issue largely to his son-in-law, Secretary of the Treasury William McAdoo, who devised a mixture of taxation and borrowing. The amount of annual earnings that triggered federal income tax liability was lowered, expanding the proportion of the workforce that had to pay. Wartime legislation also raised the tax rate in steps, based on the amount of income received. The 1918 income tax (enacted in early 1919) had a maximum rate of 77 percent (including a surtax) for those with very high incomes, which some denounced as confiscatory. The other major source of war funds came from borrowing. Liberty loans were purchased primarily by banks and wealthy investors, who were rewarded by tax-exempt interest on the loans. Liberty bonds were sold directly to the public in small denominations, with purchases payable in installments. Celebrities helped promote the sale of these bonds. Borrowing paid for two-thirds of the war and left the federal government with a debt that was twenty times higher in 1920 than in 1916.[11]

Paying for the war had a significant impact on postwar finances. Federal expenditures contracted sharply with peace but did not return to prewar levels (see figure 12.1). Federal revenue followed a similar course, as Treasury receipts were five times greater in the 1920s than during the Progressive Era. This upward trajectory in Treasury operations constituted a "ratchet effect," whereby a crisis (e.g., war) permanently raised the level of federal accounts.[12] The explosion of fiscal activity during the war breathed new life into the proposal for an executive budget, which Congress had previously rejected. Taking cues from how the US Army's Quartermaster Corps and federal agencies managed their accounts, the House of Representatives passed an executive budget bill in 1919, with the Senate agreeing in 1920. Wilson vetoed the legislation on a technicality, delaying its approval until 1921.[13]

Wilson sensed correctly that the administration's mobilization policies would draw criticism. Socialists and sympathetic labor groups charged that the war would fatten the coffers of American capitalists. To head off damaging criticism, the president created the Committee on Public Information, which became synonymous with its director, George Creel. His job was to promote support for the war effort, which the committee did by publishing a blizzard of materials, issuing thousands of press releases, and engaging "four-minute men," who donated their time to urge patriotic contributions to the war effort. Broadcasting the government's message that the war was a struggle between American democracy and German militarism, the committee became a handmaiden to industry, which delighted in blocking labor radicalism, and to zealous champions of Americanism, who urged the coerced assimilation of immigrants.

Other federal agencies acted to ensure compliance with wartime objectives. The postmaster general used his authority under the Espionage Act (June 1917) to ban left-wing and antiwar publications from the mail. The attorney general pushed hard to censure protesters who purportedly obstructed the war effort, including critics of the draft, and urged stricter controls on speech related to the war. Herbert Hoover, head of the Food Administration, oversaw a network of half a million persons, recruited from fraternal and women's groups, who went door to door urging housewives to conserve food. The War Department and other agencies relied heavily on the cooperation of private groups, such as the Red Cross and Boy Scouts, to help provide services for the troops and sell war bonds.[14] In various ways, the federal government's shift to a wartime footing unleashed pressures to stifle criticism of the war, tame if not eradicate labor radicalism, and cajole citizens to embrace 100 percent Americanism.

REPERCUSSIONS OF WAR

The impact of World War I extended well beyond the goal of defeating Germany. The war opened up opportunities for groups to advance their agendas on several long-standing issues. Opponents of saloons and the "liquor interests" were among the most successful. Efforts to limit the manufacture and sale of alcoholic beverages had a long history in the United States. The antiliquor movement spread in the late nineteenth century when the Women's Christian Temperance Union battled the "demon rum." But the distilling and brewing industries had expanded and become intensely competitive, leading to tie-ins with saloons between the late 1800s and the Progressive Era. Their nemesis appeared in 1893 with the formation of the Anti-Saloon League. Dominated by men, the organization had a centralized administration with a paid staff and branches in most states. The Anti-Saloon League emerged as a model pressure group, targeting state lawmakers who opposed its objectives. League advocates focused their attack on saloons, which were depicted as dens of drugs, prostitution, and political corruption, not to mention the consumption of alcohol. By 1917 seventeen states had gone dry.

Each state that accepted prohibition exerted pressure on its congressional delegation to support antisaloon legislation. World War I opened a window of opportunity for the Anti-Saloon League to achieve its goal on a national level. The Lever Act had already restricted the brewing of beer and the distilling of spirits to conserve grains. Amid rising antagonism toward anything German, such as beer gardens, Congress passed the Eighteenth Amendment to the Constitution (Prohibition) in December 1917. Following its ratification by state legislatures in 1919, Congress adopted the Volstead Act, which criminalized the sale of beverages with an alcohol content of one-half percent or higher but allowed the possession of spirits for personal consumption. By the end of the year the Treasury Department employed 1,500 prohibition agents, who worked in collaboration with law enforcement agencies in cooperating states, many of which enacted "search and seizure" laws. The intergovernmental campaign substantially reduced the flow of beer and liquor during the 1920s.[15]

The campaign for female suffrage exhibited similarities to the quest for national Prohibition, especially in the use of state victories to leverage the passage of a constitutional amendment. Like Prohibition, the campaign for women's voting rights predated the Civil War but had made only minimal progress before 1910. Four states had granted women the right to vote by 1896, but no new states joined that list through 1909. Voters turned down referenda on female suffrage in four northeastern states in 1915. The opposition of (some) men, Democrats, liquor interests, and recent immigrants was slowing a change that some observers considered a logical progressive reform.

The war helped women break through these barriers, with Carrie Chapman Catt leading the way. A former schoolteacher from Iowa and president of the National American Woman Suffrage Association (1900–1904 and 1915–1920), Catt saw state adoption as the key. The more states that accepted women's suffrage, she reasoned, the greater the pressure on congressional representatives to support a suffrage amendment to the Constitution. Knowing that success in an influential eastern state was critical, Catt targeted New York, where she launched the Woman's Suffrage Party. New Yorkers turned down a suffrage referendum in 1915, only to return a positive vote in 1917. With the war on, Catt moved to the nation's capital to lobby the president, telling him that the United States should reward women for their dedication to the war effort by supporting a suffrage amendment. To overcome male skepticism, she argued that women's suffrage would suppress the "ignorant vote," meaning blacks and immigrants, and would reduce immoral activities such as prostitution. Moral persuasion coupled with political leverage did the trick. The House passed the Nineteenth Amendment in 1918, on the strength of Republican and northern Democratic votes, but the amendment failed to win the required two-thirds majority in the Senate until 1919. It took more than a year to overcome last-ditch efforts in the states to reject the amendment during the ratification process.[16]

Suffragettes boosted their campaign by demonstrating their allegiance to the United States, but other groups criticized American intervention in the war. Radical laborites such as members of the Industrial Workers of the World (Wobblies) and supporters of the Socialist Party denounced the war as a capitalist ploy and governmental collaboration with large corporations. Other groups resented antiwar pacifists who were conscientious objectors. Federal officials and local police sought to dampen criticism of the war. Worried about the loyalty of German Americans, President Wilson urged Congress to pass the Espionage Act (June 1917), which prohibited making false reports to help the enemy, inciting rebellion among the armed forces, or obstructing the draft. Conviction carried a sentence of up to twenty years in prison. The law allowed the postmaster general to censor the mail for materials that advocated resistance to the war effort. Unwilling to tolerate dissent to his foreign policy, Wilson encouraged activities that energized demonstrations of patriotism. Aided by officials in his administration and in state and local governments, the president bore much of the responsibility for igniting a vindictive campaign toward individuals who did not conform to "100 percent Americanism."[17]

Enforcement of the Espionage Act fell to Attorney General Thomas Gregory, who in turned assigned the job to the Justice Department's Bureau of Investigation. Federal officials solicited local police to keep tabs on known pacifists and German sympathizers. Gregory used his mandate to silence militant labor unionists and left-wing critics of the Wilson administration. Wilson, Gregory, and like-minded conservatives saw a link between aliens (immigrants who were not yet citizens) and hostility to American institutions, especially big corporations. The Immigration Act of 1917 allowed the deportation of newcomers affiliated with "anarchist" organizations. More than 6,000 German aliens were placed in internment camps.

When Gregory wanted broader authority to clamp down on war resisters, labor radicals, and communists, Congress complied by passing the Sedition Act (May 1918), which criminalized speech and writing that were disloyal to and abusive of the federal government, the Constitution, or the armed services. The law made it a crime to advocate, teach, or favor the cause of the German Empire or oppose "the cause of the United States" and its institutions. The Sedition Act, along with supporting statutes, gave federal officials broad authority to track and arrest individuals because of their political beliefs. The most famous person arrested for criticizing the war was Eugene Debs, the Socialist Party candidate for president in 1912. The Justice Department put him under surveillance and transcribed his speeches. Even though his address in Canton, Ohio, that provoked his arrest attacked American capitalism as much as the war, Debs was sentenced to ten years in the federal penitentiary for violating the Espionage Act. Wilson denied requests for his pardon, even after Debs commended the president's advocacy of a League of Nations. The Supreme Court brushed aside challenges to Debs's arrest as an unconstitutional limitation on free speech.[18]

The wartime loyalty statutes and their energetic application against labor radicals and left-wing groups were unusual for their restriction of political expression, yet they were not without precedent. Both the states and the national government had previously placed limits on acceptable political speech. The New York Anarchy Act (1902), adopted in the wake of the McKinley assassination, made it illegal to advocate the forceful overthrow of the government. The 1903 immigration law, urged by President Roosevelt, banned political radicals from immigrating to the United States. New York enacted a 1917 statute that allowed the removal of teachers convicted of making treasonous or seditious utterances. Idaho in 1917 and Montana in 1918 passed criminal syndicalist laws, which made it illegal to express contempt for the US government, the Constitution, the flag, or the armed services. By the end of 1919 all nonsouthern states had passed one or more laws that criminalized "radical" political activity. Even the US Army got into the act, raiding Wobbly offices and breaking up strikes in lumbering and mining districts of the Northwest. The war had whipped up a frenzy of anxiety about suspected disloyalty and supposed threats to national security from labor radicals. The large inflow of immigrants from central and eastern Europe—including Russia, where Bolsheviks overthrew the tsar in 1917—fanned these fears. Attorney General Gregory, the US Army Military Intelligence Section, the postmaster general, and many local officials in the West operated on the assumption that an uprising of alien-backed communists was possible. As one historian asserted, the war and international events had created a "surveillance state."[19]

The congressional elections of 1918 offered a verdict on Wilsonian war policies. The voting took place just days before the armistice was officially announced, although it was clear by then that the Allies had beaten Germany. This good news should have advantaged the Democrats; Wilson urged voters to keep his party in power, which would facilitate the adoption of his Fourteen Points plan for the postwar settlement. A majority of voters, however, turned against the president and the Democrats, who lost control of both the House and the Senate, even though the Democratic slippage in the overall vote was minimal. Democrats lost at the state level too; they held eighteen governorships in the North in 1913 but were reduced to just three in 1919.

Several grievances underlay the backlash against the administration. This was the first election since the declaration of war in 1917. Two large ethnic groups that typically leaned Democratic, German Americans and Irish Americans, were unhappy with Wilson's collaboration with Britain. Many Germans in the United States retained sentimental attachments to their homeland, and Ireland was on the brink of revolt from British control. Moreover, the Wilson administration's heavy-handed approach to war mobilization, conscription, and forced loyalty did not sit well with many Americans. The government's hunt for draft "slackers," abetted by private groups, alienated some voters. In addition, Wilson vetoed a measure that would have maintained price supports for wheat, which angered midwestern farmers, who thought the administration showed favoritism toward southern cotton producers. Consumer prices and rents had nearly doubled since 1916, which negated wage and salary increases, while big business continued to reap large profits. Wartime shortages of food and fuel were an irritant for families. Plainly, numerous voters had legitimate complaints about the consequences of wartime governance.[20]

The Democrats' troubles continued into 1919. Wilson went to France after New Year's Day to head the American delegation to the peace conference at Versailles. Except for one brief trip back to the States, he remained in France until July. A rousing welcome greeted his arrival in Paris, reflecting French appreciation for the Americans' contribution to victory. Allied leaders, however, were less enthusiastic about Wilson's performance at the peace conference, where the president was preoccupied with his League of Nations proposal. The league was the centerpiece of the president's vision for peace, which he had set forth in his Fourteen Points. But the leaders of France, Italy, and England had minimal interest in Wilson's international forum and an enormous desire to punish Germany. French premier Clemenceau pushed relentlessly to saddle the Germans with responsibility for the war, pressing for heavy financial reparations and demanding that Germany be stripped of its territory and colonies. Obsessed with securing his league, Wilson bartered away his opposition to a harsh settlement, despite his belief that a vindictive treaty would leave Germany vulnerable to bolshevism. Fear stalked the land that a communist revolution was poised to upend the Western world.[21]

Republicans back home were even less enthusiastic about a League of Nations, which some saw as Wilson's attempt to build a case for his reelection. The president had hardly helped his cause by failing to select any prominent Republicans to join him at the peace conference. Now he faced a Republican majority in the US Senate, where a two-thirds majority was needed to ratify the Treaty of Versailles. The key stumbling block was Article X, which required league members to recommend ways to counter international aggression. Senator Henry Cabot Lodge, who, like Wilson, was a scholar in politics but harbored a deep dislike of the president, led the bloc of Republican senators opposed to Article X, which they argued could obligate US military action. Despite widespread pleas that he compromise, Wilson refused to change a word in the document. Instead, he embarked on a speaking tour in the western states to lobby for the League of Nations, which was embedded in the peace treaty. Illness forced the president to suspend the tour in September 1919, and shortly thereafter he suffered a major stroke that left him partially paralyzed and unable to resume a full schedule. Yet he regained sufficient cognizance to refuse any modification to the treaty. Its rejection in the Senate was a bitter disappointment to idealistic individuals who viewed America's participation in the war as a way to advance political self-determination.

Americans experienced a tumultuous year while Wilson was in France and then recuperating at home after his stroke. The year 1919 recorded 3,000 strikes involving three million workers, who saw prices spiral as their wages lagged. A strike of longshoremen in Seattle escalated into a citywide general strike that was broken with the assistance of the US Army. Federal troops intervened in a steel strike that involved a quarter million workers; Gary, Indiana, was put under martial law. Steel company executives called striking workers communists. A strike of 300,000 in the coalfields stretching from Pennsylvania into the Midwest was cut short by a federal court injunction against the United Mine Workers Union. The US Fuel Administration, which continued to operate under wartime emergency rules, had urged that decision. Boston police walked off the job over wages and a demand for unionization. President Wilson called the walkout "a crime against civilization." Trouble brewed in cities and towns in the heat of summer, when racial clashes erupted. The Chicago race riot in July left twenty-three blacks and fifteen whites dead in thirteen days of fighting. It took 6,000 National Guardsmen to restore order to the city's South Side.

Bombs mailed to political officials underscored the explosiveness of 1919. One detonation destroyed the front porch of the home of US Attorney General A. Mitchell Palmer. Palmer swung into action, enlisting the help of J. Edgar Hoover, a young lawyer in the Justice Department's Bureau of Investigation, which had kept tabs on suspected German spies and saboteurs during the war. Believing that communists and anarchists were responsible for the terrorism, Hoover was put in charge of the bureau's Radical Division, and his instructions were to round up the culprits.

The twenty-four-year-old Hoover leaped at the opportunity to channel his enormous energy and zealous commitment to suppress bolshevism. He read everything he could find about international communism. He mined innumerable sources of information, including US military intelligence, for names of suspects, and he prepared crib sheets for Palmer, who testified before Congress on the purported communist uprising. As the finale to the campaign, Hoover arranged a raid on meetings of alien radicals in thirty-three cities on January 2, 1920. With only 579 agents, the Bureau of Investigation required assistance from local law enforcement agencies and help from civilian groups to pull off the nighttime arrests. The so-called Palmer raids detained upward of 6,000 supposed radicals, whom Hoover sought to deport, but few individuals were expelled. Protests over the arrests, which lacked evidence of illegal acts, and resistance from the Department of Labor, which had jurisdiction over immigrant deportations, blocked most expulsions. As 1920 unfolded, widespread fears of a communist uprising faded. But the administrative base of the Bureau of Investigation had expanded, in part due to the enforcement of Prohibition.[22]

Uncertainty over whether Wilson would run again handicapped the Democratic search for a presidential candidate in 1920. The party eventually nominated James Cox, governor of Ohio, after a long convention fight. Cox's campaign had to contend with voters angered by the criminalization of buying beer, wine, and liquor. His equivocation on Prohibition and on Wilson's League of Nations reflected the political hurdles of 1920, when the Democratic Party's nominal leader remained an invalid in the White House. Republicans nominated Warren G. Harding, Ohio's junior senator, who continued the GOP's opposition to the League of Nations and promised to return the nation to "normalcy." Voting results gave Republicans an overwhelming victory, as Democrats suffered major setbacks around the country in congressional and state races, even in the South and in the bigger cities.

Events of 1920 are usually interpreted as a repudiation of idealist Wilsonian diplomacy and the nation's turn toward conservatism. While these factors were clearly present, other dynamics were also at work. The sweeping rejection of Democrats was linked to the rapid spike in government power and its uneven application. The federal government's increased intervention in the economy, abetted by state cooperation, generated annoying regulations. When the fighting in Europe ended abruptly, so did the federal stimulus to the economy—the government yanked defense contracts, terminated most price supports, ended protection for labor unions, and allowed coal price hikes that caused fuel shortages. Both consumer prices and unemployment jumped higher in late 1920. By the end of the year stagflation had enveloped the country, and many voters held the incumbent Democrats culpable for the economic malaise.[23]

Voters harbored other grievances as well. The Wilson administration had sponsored numerous political restrictions that irritated Democrats especially. The administration had gone after immigrants and labor unions (under the guise of political radicalism) and encouraged a nationwide campaign to elevate patriotism. Wilson was a prominent cheerleader for the latter movement, which targeted German Americans. As a result, German American support for Democrats dropped noticeably in 1920, as did the Irish vote. Rather than stem the intolerance toward draft shirkers and war critics or try to cap rising prices, the president appeared to be tone deaf to problems at home while he pursued his obsession for a League of Nations abroad. Then he fell out of sight due to illness. The majority of Americans turned toward the Republicans and Harding, who blamed the administration for excess taxation and a high cost of living, thanks to an "autocratic" chief executive. The abrupt expansion of the state during the Great War had created a massive political backlash.[24]

CONTROL, COERCION, AND THE DOCUMENTARY STATE

The United States' participation in World War I fostered a remarkable expansion of governmental power. The national government drafted 2.7 million individuals into the military and sent more than 2 million soldiers to fight in France. Washington officials spent $32 billion to pay for the war, implemented controls over the private economy, and imposed new restrictions on the political activity of individuals. National policymakers designed this agenda, with states and localities playing a compliant role by implementing national policy and adding provisions of their own. By thrusting its military muscle into Europe, the United States demonstrated that it was a major world power. World War I proved that the United States could act like a state.

This new assertiveness took numerous forms. New taxes were levied on individuals. Restrictions were placed on permissible speech and personal consumption. Temporary regulations were imposed on private enterprise. Increased cooperation between national and local officials occurred. In various ways during the war and in its immediate aftermath, the government broadened the controls and coercion that had characterized the Progressive Era. Wartime governance, in fact, can be seen as an extension of the crusading and moralizing features that made progressivism distinctive.

J. Edgar Hoover, the boyish attorney who ran the Justice Department's Radical Division, was a caricature of progressive organization. To prepare for his dragnet, Hoover ransacked publications and data collections to build a file of 60,000 "radically inclined individuals." He continued to add to his files after the Palmer raids. In 1921 he was promoted to assistant director of the Bureau of Investigation; three years later he became its head, directing searches for criminal activity related to passports, stolen vehicles, prostitution rings, and alien radicals. He had already become the custodian of the fingerprint archive created by the Association of Police Chiefs. By 1930 the Bureau of Investigation (which became the Federal Bureau of Investigation [FBI] in 1935) had a collection of two million fingerprints and an archive of five million criminal records.[25] The enormous power Hoover wielded over his long career as director of the FBI derived in good measure from his ability to master the Progressive Era's penchant for organization and data collection.

Hoover's files on individuals represented a major step toward the creation of a documentary state. His data collections reflected the mission of his agency, combined with his personal distaste for political radicals and suspected criminals. The process of gathering information about individuals, however, had a long history in the United States (see table A.6 in the appendix). Recording and archiving the names of military enlistees enabled the United States to provide benefits to veterans, beginning with those who served during the American Revolution. The national government maintained records of individuals who obtained land in the public domain. The post office began home mail delivery in 1863 to individuals who had specific urban addresses. The US Constitution mandated that the federal government count the country's population every ten years. The 1790 census attempted to list the name of the head of every free household and, by 1850, the name of every resident at each address. Tabulating these and other data constituted statistics, a term from the Greek meaning the study of information about state affairs.[26]

Local governments collected the greatest volume of personal information in the nineteenth century. All communities kept records of property owners and tax payments. As the century unfolded, subnational governments received reports on births and deaths, school attendance, and criminal activity. The licensing of health and other professionals generated additional lists; toward the end of the century, municipalities began inspecting places of business and commercial dwellings. A few states, such as New York and Iowa, conducted their own population censuses.

The long Progressive Era (1890s–1910s) witnessed an acceleration of systemic data collection about individuals, with state governments playing an increasing role. Motor vehicles stimulated a growth in personal documentation, as states required vehicle registrations starting in 1901, followed shortly thereafter by driver's licenses, which still constitute a nationally recognized form of identification. Early in the twentieth century states enacted laws requiring marriage licenses; eventually, a medical examination was required prior to their issuance. States also set up their own criminal bureaus that functioned in cooperation with the state police. Voter registration, which expanded after 1890, was a quintessential progressive reform and represented how statebuilding had advanced.

The appeal of collecting data about various activities attracted administrators in many federal positions. The Treasury Department relieved the states of the task of examining immigrants in 1891, a process that required the retention of inspection reports. The post office started delivering mail to rural families in 1896. In 1913 the national government initiated the personal income tax, which mandated that individuals report their earnings to revenue officials. Much larger bodies of data about individuals came from the national government's compilation of birth and death data collected in the states, which were instructed to observe specific reporting protocols. Registration for the draft in 1917 and 1918 generated twenty-four million individual data cards. With the advent of World War I, foreign travelers and immigrants desiring entry into the United States were required to obtain passports and visas.[27] J. Edgar Hoover's project to profile radicals in America built on a pattern of counting, categorizing, and analyzing information about individual behavior that became characteristic of the expanding state.[28] That tendency complemented industrializing societies' need to enumerate, record, and quantitatively calibrate human activity. World War I provided a rationale for officials to broaden governmental control over individuals.

13

The End of the Long Nineteenth Century

In his inaugural address in 1925 President Calvin Coolidge referenced American aid to Europe and the country's intervention in the Caribbean, commenting that these actions sprang from "our vast powers" and "the place we hold in the world." The Vermont native was known for his opposition to greater federal activism, but he was conscious of the national government's expanded capacity, enlarged budget, and elevated global status. Coolidge's agenda was to slow this expansion of federal power. A similar mind-set was observed at the local level of the political system. Writing about "Middletown," one of most researched small cities in the United States, sociologists Robert and Helen Lynd reported that, between the 1890s and the mid-1920s, the city created more agencies, hired more officials, spent considerably more money, and oversaw more regulations. Middletown residents were apparently satisfied with these new services but, like Coolidge, clung to traditional political values.[1]

Scholars voiced agreement in the 1920s that the American polity had entered a new era. The growth of government, wrote political scientist Charles Beard, "is a fact, not a theory." He observed that "the very concept of government . . . has undergone marked changes during the past fifty years," noting that even the "activities of the Federal Government are reaching deeply into the affairs of the people." Other scholars echoed this assessment and noted that the drift of power toward Washington was eroding the role of the states. Washington, DC, took on greater importance in the 1920s, as organizations set up shop in the city as a base to lobby Congress. This heightened status was underscored by a doubling of federal employees in Washington between 1910 and 1930. But all governments, not just the national establishment, had assumed additional functions, broadened old ones, and altered traditional relationships over the past several decades. The scale and scope of public life in the 1920s vastly overshadowed the civic footprint of the Gilded Age.[2]

World War I certified that the United States had become a major world power. Although the size of its army shrank after the armistice, the navy remained among the largest in the world. The United States never joined the League of Nations, yet it did not withdraw from international affairs or world trade. American military forces occupied several Caribbean countries in the 1920s. Spending on defense decreased after the war but remained competitive with European outlays. America's military stature in the 1920s rested as much on its potential as on its force in place. The United States ranked second behind Russia in population among the major powers. Its national wealth ranked first in the world, both in total economic output and in average income per person. American manufacturers produced more in 1920 than the countries of Europe combined. Viewing the national, state, and local governments as a single polity in terms of their fiscal and coercive capacity, scope of civic functions, and global presence, the United States had joined the fraternity of national superpowers by 1920.

THE DYNAMICS OF GROWTH

The transformation of the national state between Reconstruction and World War I was the product of interactions between long-term factors and shorter-term intrusions. The complexity of these pathways impedes the identification of the precise cause of political development; however, one can identify broad currents that framed the background for decisionmakers. Geography and socioeconomic development played instrumental roles in this process. By the early twentieth century America's huge landmass supplied the economy with a bounty of resources and homes for millions. The great distances between points on this landscape spurred transportation innovations, such as national railroad networks, steel-hulled ships, mass-produced motor vehicles, and aircraft that could fly from coast to coast. The vastness of this space and the new connections between points on the map probably reinforced the commitment to a federal system and to a sense of nationhood. Folding western territories into the union had a major effect on the structure of governance. Montana was as large as Japan and twice the size of New England. All of Spain could fit inside Texas. California had more land than Germany. Collectively, these "little republics" added new synergies to political development.

The nation's population grew two and a half times larger between 1870 and 1920. This human expansion fueled economic growth, which increased per capita wealth by 150 percent during this half century. America's population growth occurred primarily through a natural process whereby births exceeded deaths. By global standards, America had a youthful population; Americans' median age was twenty in 1870 and twenty-five in 1920. That year there were more white males in their twenties than men older than fifty—the age of senior political leaders. Presidents Roosevelt, Taft, and Wilson were all born before the Civil War.

The incorporation of each new generation into the population has the potential to induce political change. The young differ from their elders not only in physical and psychological characteristics but also in their maturation during different socioeconomic eras. The twenty-something generation born around 1895 became adults during World War I.[3] Those raised in an urban middle-class family probably had electricity, indoor plumbing, and a telephone; they probably held or looked for salaried or wage-paying jobs in a city or small town. Going to a movie or a dancehall or riding the trolley to a park was an option, perhaps with an unchaperoned date. Young women likely scanned the advertisements in the woman's section of the city newspaper. Both girls and boys from the city likely attended high school.[4] For those living on farms, rural free delivery brought the Sears Roebuck catalog loaded with merchandise that could be delivered to their homes by the US Post Office. Youngsters from industrial areas might have witnessed or perhaps even participated in the labor strikes of 1910–1912. They probably heard about the sinking of the *Titanic*, the German torpedoing of the *Lusitania*, and the Bolshevik Revolution in Russia. Most young men registered for the draft, perhaps riding to the draft board in a Model T Ford.

Generational succession probably contributed to Progressive Era reform. Richard Hofstadter is one of numerous scholars who have pointed to the importance of mood cycles in American politics, and he cites generational change as a source of progressivism in his classic *The Age of Reform*. He notes that Progressive Era leaders such as Roosevelt, Bryan, La Follette, and Wilson, who were in their thirties during the 1890s, had lived through the "searing experience" of that decade's devastating depression and had witnessed how the antiestablishment outbursts of the Populist Party "frightened the middle classes."[5] Unanticipated intrusions—catastrophes and crises—tend to leave lasting impressions on formative minds.[6] It is possible, perhaps even likely, that individuals who reached adulthood around World War I were more acclimated to governmental intervention than generations that came of age before the 1890s.

War, depression, and horrendous disasters undoubtedly contributed to the formation of worldviews among the young, and policymakers were challenged to cope with each crisis. As noted in earlier chapters, the depressions of the 1870s and 1890s and the stagflation of 1910–1912 influenced electoral and policy changes. World War I significantly intensified the scope of civic power and generated pressure from all levels of government to encourage and coerce "100 percent Americanism." Catastrophes such as the Triangle Shirtwaist fire and the sinking of the *Titanic* motivated policymakers to formulate strategies to mitigate future disasters. Unanticipated events, ranging from presidential assassinations and terrorist bombings to prolonged economic stagnation and military engagement, can send shock waves through society.[7]

Longer-term trends exerted a more gradual but perhaps just as significant influence on attitudes. The shift of population from rural to urban settings, the emergence of women as a distinct consumer group and as activists, and the widespread attainment of a high school education were key trends that challenged traditional outlooks. Communications underwent several technological revolutions between the invention of the telephone and the advent of the radio and "talkie" movies. Millions of immigrants flowing into American society during the Gilded Age and Progressive Era had numerous ramifications for government and politics. Historian Robert Wiebe famously attributes these transformations to the "breakdown" of "island communities" that were rooted in the "local autonomy" of the nineteenth century. "The needs of urban-industrial life" eroded these older, "personal, informal ways" in the face of a growing aspiration for "continuity and predictability in a world of change."[8]

The formal constitutional footing of the national state did not change appreciably between Reconstruction and World War I. Only four amendments—the Fourteenth through Seventeenth—were added to the Constitution between 1868 and 1913, although the Fourteenth and Sixteenth Amendments conveyed significant new authorities. The Eighteenth Amendment (Prohibition; repealed in 1933) and the Nineteenth Amendment (female suffrage) were ratified in 1919 and 1920, respectively. But the national charter held latent powers that were activated through legislative actions, court rulings, and executive decisions. Reliance on this implied repository of authority accelerated during the Gilded Age, the Progressive Era, and World War I.[9] The new states added to the union broadened patterns of competition and emulation, fueling the diffusion of policy innovations around the nation, some of which filtered into Congress.[10]

The electoral system was a vector for tapping the Constitution's latent power. The elections of 1874, 1894, 1910–1912, and 1918–1920 produced major shifts in party alignments among officeholders, facilitating policy shifts at both the national and state levels. The Democratic upsurgence in 1910 and 1912, for example, enabled an outpouring of progressive reforms; the restoration of Republican control of Congress following the 1918 election doomed Woodrow Wilson's quest for America to join the League of Nations. Party played a smaller role in governance at the state and local levels, where cross-party legislative coalitions were prevalent. At all levels of government, however, leadership could be a decisive factor in advancing new programs. Theodore Roosevelt and Woodrow Wilson blazed a trail for modern presidential activism, a hallmark of elected executives in the twentieth century.[11]

Numerous influences, in short, reinforced the trend toward greater reliance on government after the Civil War. No national leader publicly advanced a master blueprint to reframe the American state. Dreamers who envisioned an expanded state, such as novelist Edward Bellamy and socialist Eugene Debs, made little political headway.[12] America's traditional reluctance to enlarge the national government remained resilient; support for the fragmented, decentralized federal system held firm after the Civil War. The judicial embrace of laissez-faire, which blocked commercial regulation and assistance for workers, reinforced these axioms. American resistance to centralized power, deeply embedded in the nation's ideological psyche, survived into the twenty-first century.

The history of the American national state thus presents a paradox. In spite of America's antistatist tradition, which remained vibrant after the Civil War, government grew in functional scope and financial commitment; its capacity and power expanded. A key to this transformation was broad public acceptance of civic intervention to remedy problems. These issues ran the gamut from removing wastewater and maintaining roads to authorizing a national currency and combating German militarism. The unintended consequence of these decisions was the expansion of a more powerful civic regime, reinforced by broadening popular support for America, the nation.[13]

THE 1920S

Americans continued their pragmatic tradition of governance in the 1920s. That decade is commonly remembered as a time of conservatism and governmental stasis, if not civic contraction. Much of the political rhetoric embraced these themes, especially regarding taxation and limitations on the federal government. The wartime fever for 100 percent Americanism lingered.[14] But the broader picture shows a public sector that did not return to prewar levels. Government spending was higher in the 1920s than in the Progressive Era. The National Industrial Conference Board calculated that total public spending (in inflation-controlled dollars) in 1927 was twice as high as in 1913. The "ratchet" effect of World War I was clearly present in the federal government's outlays (see figure 12.1). State and local expenditures also increased markedly; local governments continued the nineteenth-century pattern of outspending the US and state governments combined.[15]

Few major governmental programs were terminated during the 1920s. Although federal income tax rates were scaled back from wartime levels, the levy itself remained. The army returned to peacetime status, although its manpower exceeded prewar numbers. The navy retained much of its wartime capability, some of which was used for interventions in the Caribbean.

No major commerce and business statutes were overturned, although federal regulators had no vendetta against private enterprise. The Federal Reserve System remained in place. The Justice Department's Bureau of Investigation (later FBI) expanded its operations. The Department of Agriculture offered new services and undertook additional scientific investigations. World War I created a new class of military veterans, a million of whom received disability benefits in 1927. Congress increased federal aid to the states for road construction. The post office expanded rural deliveries. The United States continued to administer and preserve public lands and added several national parks, national monuments, and battlefield sites. Mount Rushmore, where the visages of George Washington, Thomas Jefferson, Abraham Lincoln, and Theodore Roosevelt were carved into a granite wall in South Dakota, became a national memorial in 1925.

Most federal policies initiated after the Civil War were institutionalized, not terminated, in subsequent years. A similar development occurred at the state and local levels through the 1920s. Several dynamics supported these continuities. Once it was created, each program tended to spawn a set of interested constituencies, including administrators who oversaw the policy and nongovernmental organizations that benefited from the program or supported its goals. Some programs, especially those providing services and benefits, gained broad popularity among the electorate. Legislators, who increasingly sought reelection, understood this constituent interest and catered to it. Supporting programs got more votes than killing them.[16]

While preserving most of their prior commitments, governments also took on new responsibilities in the 1920s. The most dramatic federal interventions concerned restrictions on the manufacture and sale of alcoholic beverages and the regulation of immigration. Congress imposed a temporary limit on immigration in 1921, fixed numerical quotas for European countries in 1924, and retained bans on Asian immigration. Enforcing national Prohibition and immigration restrictions required bigger federal agencies. The Bureau of Immigration doubled in size between 1915 and 1932. The massive scope of Prohibition required the cooperation of 200,000 state and local law enforcement officials. The number of federal prisoners, some held in state facilities, increased more than sixfold between 1915 and 1930; most were incarcerated for liquor, drug, and auto theft offenses.[17]

State and local governments broadened their initiatives as well, investing their greatest energy in education and roads. Local communities provided kindergartens and grade schools; most jurisdictions established high schools as well. The construction of hard roads became an extremely popular undertaking as more and more Americans drove motor vehicles. By the late 1920s paved highways traversed most states. This development owed much to the discovery of a nearly painless way to pay for these roads: a tax on the sale of gasoline, with private vendors, not government agents, collecting the levy. More cars on the road led to the creation of state police forces, whose troopers patrolled the highways and also took on anticrime duties, including the enforcement of Prohibition. Incarceration in state and local facilities doubled between the Progressive Era and the Great Depression. State law entered new fields, such as the regulation of trucking companies, and expanded older activities, such as providing assistance to special-needs populations and adopting standards for agricultural commodities. These functions and higher costs generated support for the creation of budget departments and the reorganization of state offices into cabinet-style administrations under the supervision of the governor.[18] If Google's eye in the sky had scanned the Eastern Seaboard in the late 1920s, it would have photographed US Route 1, a highway paved with state and federal funds that connected Maine to Florida.

This willingness to put government to work on societal problems confirms the observation of French statesman Alexis de Tocqueville in the 1830s: "Americans are more addicted to the practical than theoretical science."[19] This pragmatic tradition, in which crisis commonly trumps ideology and innovative civic initiatives coexist with antistatist sentiments, spanned America's long nineteenth century. The acceleration of civic capacity during the Great Depression of the 1930s, World War II, and the decades afterward reinforced rather than invented America's long history of statebuilding.

APPENDIX

Methodology for Data Selection

The data set for state and city policy actions includes state statutes, court decisions, and city ordinances that reflected important policy decisions. Many of these policies were innovative, whereby a city or state embarked on a new (or relatively new) civic activity. Although legislative statutes are emphasized, the entries also reference constitutional provisions—either amendments to an existing charter or a whole new constitution. To the extent state statutes enabled or instructed local government to do certain things, they empowered local action. But in some cases, I included municipal ordinances directly. I selected six states (and each one's major city) for the 1783–1870 data set and eight states for 1870–1917. States were selected based on their geographic diversity and influence on American governance.

My sampling technique loosely follows the research design in David R. Mayhew, *Divided We Govern: Party Control, Lawmaking and Investigations, 1946–2000* (New Haven, CT: Yale University Press, 2005). Mayhew wanted to ascertain the important legislative accomplishments of the post–World War II Congresses. To achieve this objective, he reviewed accounts of journalists who assessed the activities of each Congress, as well as authors who published studies of specific policy areas. Mayhew used a similar methodology, based on secondary literature, for *America's Congress: Actions in the Public Sphere, James Madison through Newt Gingrich* (New Haven, CT: Yale University Press, 2000), ch. 2.

My goal was to identify important policy actions at the state and municipal levels. I relied principally on secondary works concerning a particular state or city as my source for relevant information. The most useful publications are listed in the sources below. In some cases I identified pertinent policy actions from comparative studies of state governance, such as Carter Goodrich, *Government Promotion of American Canals and Railroads, 1880–1890* (New York: Columbia University Press, 1960), and Theda Skocpol, *Protecting Soldiers and Mothers: The Political Origins of Social Policy in the United States* (Cambridge, MA: Harvard University Press, 1992). Most of these works are cited in the endnotes.

Regarding the dating of actions, I generally used the year a new law was enacted, rather than the date it became operational. Thus, I record the date the Erie Canal was authorized by New York (1817) rather than the year it opened to traffic from Buffalo to Albany (1825). Some municipal actions complicated this protocol, in that both state and city decisions were involved, as illustrated by authorization for the Boston Public Library. Massachusetts permitted cities and towns to appropriate funds for public libraries in 1851; Boston approved trustees for a library in 1852 and opened the facility in a temporary home in 1853. That year, the state passed special legislation that allowed Boston to commit funds for construction of the library; the

Boylston Street facility was built in 1855–1857. For table A.1 on Massachusetts, I used 1851 as the date for the Boston Public Library; for table 5.1 (Boston Governance, 1821–1863), I used 1852. In some cases, the sources do not note whether an action was a state enabling act or a municipal decision. But these gaps and discrepancies in dating do not alter the broader policy patterns contained in the data.

The data set includes approximately 1,850 entries for the years 1783–1929. Sources for state policy actions are divided into two parts: six states for 1783–1870, and eight states for 1870–1917 and the 1920s. I included a few dates that lay outside the chronological boundaries to complete certain policy stories.

Sources for Tables A.1 and A.2 (1783–1870)

CALIFORNIA

Delmatier, Royce D., et al. *The Rumble of California Politics, 1848–1970*. New York: John Wiley & Sons, 1970.

Fankhauer, William G. *A Financial History of California: Public Revenues, Debt, and Expenditures*. Berkeley: University of California, 1913.

McDonald, Terrence J. *The Parameters of Urban Fiscal Policy: Socioeconomic Change and Political Culture in San Francisco, 1860–1906*. Berkeley: University of California Press, 1986.

Nash, Gerald D. *State Government and Economic Development: A History of Administrative Policies in California, 1849–1933*, Berkeley: University of California Press, 1964.

Pierce, John M. "420 State Activities: California Government Continues to Expand." *Tax Digest* (August 1936): 261, 281–286.

Pisani, Donald J. *To Reclaim a Divided West: Water, Law, and Public Policy, 1848–1902*. Albuquerque: University of New Mexico Press, 1992.

ILLINOIS

Cole, Arthur C. *The Era of the Civil War, 1848–1870*. Springfield: Illinois Centennial Commission, 1919.

Howard, Robert P. *Illinois: A History of the Prairie State*. Grand Rapids, MI: William B. Eerdmans, 1972.

Labovita, I. M. "The Illinois Revenue System, 1818–1936." *Illinois Tax Commission Special Report* 4 (1936).

Monkkonen, Eric H. *The Local State: Public Money and American Cities*. Stanford, CA: Stanford University Press, 1995.

Pease, Theodore C. *The Frontier State, 1818–1848*. Springfield: Illinois Centennial Commission, 1918.

Pierce, Bessie Louise. *A History of Chicago*. Vols. 1–3. Chicago: University of Chicago Press, 1937, 1940, 1957.

Tingley, Donald F., ed. *Essays on Illinois History*. Carbondale: Southern Illinois University Press, 1968.

MASSACHUSETTS

Abbott, Richard H. "Massachusetts. Maintaining Hegemony." In *Radical Republicans in the North: State Politics during Reconstruction*, ed. James C. Mohr. Baltimore: Johns Hopkins University Press, 1976.

Baum, Dale. *The Civil War Party System: The Case of Massachusetts, 1848–1876*. Chapel Hill: University of North Carolina Press, 1984.

Bullock, Charles J. *Historical Sketch of the Finances and Financial Policy of Mass., from 1780 to 1905*. 3rd ser., vol. 8:2. New York: Publications of the American Economic Association, 1907.

Formisano, Ronald. *Transformation of Political Culture: Massachusetts Parties, 1790s–1840s*. New York: Oxford University Press, 1983.

Handlin, Oscar. *Commonwealth: A Study of the Role of Government in the American Economy: Massachusetts, 1774–1861*. 2nd ed. Cambridge, MA: Harvard University Press, 1969.

Hart, Albert B., ed. *Commonwealth History of Massachusetts*, vol. 4, *1820–1889*. New York: States History Co., 1930.

Huse, Charles P. *The Financial History of Boston, 1822–1909*. Cambridge, MA: Harvard University Press, 1916.

Koren, John. *Boston, 1822 to 1922: The Story of Its Government*. Boston: City of Boston Printing Department, 1922.

Lane, Roger. *Policing the City: Boston, 1822–1905*. Cambridge, MA: Harvard University Press, 1967.

Whitten, Robert H. *Public Administration in Massachusetts: The Relation of Central to Local Authority*. New York: Columbia University, 1898; reprint, New York: AMS Press, 1969.

NEW YORK

Benson, Lee. *The Concept of Jacksonian Democracy: New York as a Test Case*. Princeton, NJ: Princeton University Press, 1961.

Bidwell, Frederick D. *Taxation in New York State*. Albany, NY: J. B. Lyon, 1918.

Ellis, David M., et al. *A History of New York State*. Ithaca, NY: Cornell University Press, 1967.

Galie, Peter J. *Ordered Liberty: A Constitutional History of New York State*. New York: Fordham University Press, 1996.

Gunn, L. Ray. *The Decline of Authority: Public Economic Policy and Political Development in New York, 1800–1860*. Ithaca, NY: Cornell University Press, 1988.

Hartog, Hendrik. Public *Property and Private Power: The Corporation of the City of New York in American Law, 1730–1870*. Chapel Hill: University of North Carolina Press, 1983.

Henretta, James A. "The Rise and Decline of 'Democratic-Republicanism': Political Rights in New York and the Several States, 1800–1905." In *Toward a Usable Past*, ed. Paul Finkelman and Stephen E. Gottlieb. Athens: University of Georgia Press, 1991.

Mohr, James C. *The Radical Republicans and Reform in New York during Reconstruction.* Ithaca, NY: Cornell University Press, 1973.

New York State Constitutional Convention Committee. *Problems Relating to Taxation and Finance*, vol. 4, *State and Local Government in New York.* 1938.

Schneider, David M. *History of Public Welfare in New York State*, vol. 1, *1609–1866.* Chicago: University of Chicago Press, 1938.

Sowers, Don C. *The Financial History of New York State: From 1789 to 1912.* New York: Columbia University Press, 1914.

OHIO

Aumann, Francis R., and Harvey Walker. *The Government and Administration of Ohio.* New York: Thomas Y. Crowell, 1956.

Bogart, Ernest L. *Financial History of Ohio.* Urbana: University of Illinois Press, 1912.

Orth, Samuel P. *The Centralization of Administration in Ohio.* New York: Columbia University Press, 1903.

Roseboom, Eugene H. *The Civil War Era, 1850–1873*, vol. 4 of *The History of the State of Ohio.* Columbus: Ohio State Archaeological and Historical Society, 1944.

Roseboom, Eugene H., and Francis P. Weisenburger. *A History of Ohio.* Columbus: Ohio State Archaeological and Historical Society, 1953.

Scheiber, Harry N. *Ohio Canal Era: A Case Study of Government and the Economy, 1820–1861.* Athens: Ohio University Press, 1969.

Weisenburger, Francis P. *The Passing of the Frontier, 1825–1850*, vol. 3 of *The History of the State of Ohio.* Columbus: Ohio State Archaeological and Historical Society, 1941.

VIRGINIA

Goodrich, Carter. "The Virginia System of Mixed Enterprise: A Study of State Planning of Internal Improvements." *Political Science Quarterly* 64 (1949): 355–387.

Heineman, Richard, J. Kolp, A. Parent, and Wm. G. Shade. *Old Dominion, New Commonwealth: A History of Virginia, 1607–2007.* Charlottesville: University Press of Virginia, 2007.

Hodges, Wiley E. "Pro-Governmentalism in Virginia, 1789–1836: A Pragmatic Liberal Pattern in the Political Heritage." *Journal of Politics* 25 (May 1963): 333–360.

Nelson, Margaret V. *A Study of Judicial Review in Virginia, 1789–1928.* New York: Columbia University Press, 1947.

Risjord, Norman K., and Gordon DenBoer. "The Evolution of Political Parties in Virginia, 1782–1800." *Journal of American History* 60 (1974): 961–984.

Shade, William G. *Democratizing the Old Dominion: Virginia and the Second Party System, 1824–1861.* Charlottesville: University Press of Virginia, 1997.

Shafer, Alan. "Virginia's 'Critical Period.'" In *The Old Dominion: Essays for Thomas Perkins Abernethy*, ed. Darrett B. Rutman. Charlottesville: University Press of Virginia, 1964.

Sydenstricker, Edgar. *A Brief History of Taxation in Virginia.* Richmond: Superintendent of Public Printing, 1915.

Sources for Tables A.3 (1870–1917) and A.7 (1918–1929)

CALIFORNIA

Blackford, Mansel G. *The Politics of Business in California, 1890–1920.* Columbus: Ohio State University Press, 1977.

Issel, William, and Robert W. Cherny. *San Francisco, 1865–1932: Politics, Power, and Urban Development.* Berkeley: University of California Press, 1986.

Mowry, George. *The California Progressives.* Berkeley: University of California Press, 1951.

Starr, Kevin. *Americans and the California Dream, 1850–1915.* New York: Oxford University Press, 1973.

Swisher, Carl B. *Motivation and Political Technique in the California Constitutional Convention, 1878–79.* Claremont, CA: Pomona College, 1930.

Williams, Hal. *The Democratic Party and California Politics, 1880–1896.* Stanford, CA: Stanford University Press, 1973.

Wollenberg, Charles M. *All Deliberate Speed: Segregation and Exclusion in California Schools, 1855–1975.* Berkeley: University of California Press, 1976.

FLORIDA

Brookings Institution. *The Florida Fiscal Situation: A Preliminary Study.* Tallahassee: Tax Inquiry Council of Florida, 1941.

Colburn, David R., and Richard K. Scher. *Florida's Gubernatorial Politics in the Twentieth Century.* Gainesville: University Presses of Florida, 1981.

Dauer, Manning J., and William C. Harvard. "The Florida Constitution of 1885—A Critique." *University of Florida Law Review* 8 (1955).

Doyle, Wilson K., A. Laird, and S. Weiss. *The Government and Administration of Florida.* New York: Thomas Crowell, 1954.

Flynt, Wayne. *Duncan Upshaw Fletcher: Dixie's Reluctant Progressive.* Tallahassee: Florida State University Press, 1971.

Kendrick, Bayard H. *Florida Trails to Turnpikes, 1914–1964.* Gainesville: University of Florida Press, 1964.

McDonell, Victoria H. "The Businessman's Politician: A Study of the Administration of John Wellborn Martin, 1925–1929." MA thesis, University of Florida, 1968.

Price, Hugh Douglas. *The Negro and Southern Politics: A Chapter in Florida History.* New York: New York University Press, 1957.

Proctor, Samuel. *Napoleon Bonaparte Broward: Florida's Fighting Democrat.* Gainesville: University of Florida Press, 1950.

Tebeau, Charlton W. *A History of Florida.* Coral Gables: University of Miami Press, 1971.

University of Florida, Bureau of Economic and Business Research. Economic leaflets, 1941–1960.

Williamson, Edward C. *Florida Politics in the Gilded Age, 1877–1893*. Gainesville: University of Florida Press, 1976.

ILLINOIS

Bogart, Ernest L., and John M. Mathews. *The Modern Commonwealth, 1893–1918*. Springfield: Illinois Centennial Commission, 1920.

Bogart, Ernest L., and Charles M. Thompson. *The Industrial States, 1870–1893*. Springfield: Illinois Centennial Commission, 1920.

Buenker, John D. "Urban Immigrant Lawmakers and Progressive Reform in Illinois." In *Essays in Illinois History*, ed. Donald F. Tingley. Carbondale: South Illinois University Press, 1968.

Campbell, Ballard C. *Representative Democracy: Public Policy and Midwestern Legislatures in the Late Nineteenth Century.* Cambridge, MA: Harvard University Press, 1980.

Garvey, Neil F. *The Government and Administration of Illinois.* New York: Thomas Crowell, 1958.

Ginger, Ray. *Altgeld's America, 1890–1905*. Chicago: Quadrangle, 1965.

Keisser, John H. *Building for the Centuries: Illinois, 1865–1898*. Urbana: University of Illinois Press, 1977.

Kirschner, Don S. *City and Country: Rural Responses to Urbanization in the 1920s.* Westport, CT: Greenwood, 1970.

Pegram, Thomas R. *Partisans and Progressives: Private Interests and Public Policy in Illinois.* Urbana: University of Illinois Press, 1992.

Tingley, Donald F. *The Structuring of a State: The History of Illinois, 1899–1928.* Urbana: University of Illinois Press, 1980.

MASSACHUSETTS

Abrams, Richard. *Conservatism in a Progressive Era: Massachusetts Politics, 1900–1912*. Cambridge, MA: Harvard University Press, 1964.

Blodgett, Geoffrey. *The Gentle Reformers: Massachusetts Democrats in the Cleveland Era.* Cambridge, MA: Harvard University Press, 1996.

Campbell, Ballard C. "Public Policy and State Government." In *The Gilded Age: Perspectives on the Origins of Modern America*, ed. Charles W. Calhoun. 2nd ed. Lanham, MD: Rowman & Littlefield, 2007.

Cheape, Charles W. *Moving the Masses: Urban Public Transit in New York, Boston, and Philadelphia, 1880–1912*. Cambridge, MA: Harvard University Press, 1980.

Connolly, James J. *The Triumph of Ethnic Progressivism: Urban Political Culture in Boston, 1900–1925*. Cambridge, MA: Harvard University Press, 1998.

Dodd, E. Merrick. *The First Half-Century of Statutory Regulation of Business Corporations in Massachusetts.* Cambridge, MA: Harvard University Press, 1934.

Frisch, Michael H. *Town into City: Springfield, Massachusetts, and the Meaning of Community, 1840–1880*. Cambridge, MA: Harvard University Press, 1972.

Hart, Albert B., ed. *Commonwealth History of Massachusetts*, vol. 5, *1889–1930*. New York: Russell & Russell, 1930.

Huthmacher, J. Joseph. *Massachusetts People and Politics: The Transition from Republican to Democratic Dominance, 1919–1933*. Cambridge, MA: Harvard University Press, 1959.

Keyssar, Alexander. *Out of Work: The First Century of Unemployment in Massachusetts*. New York: Cambridge University Press, 1986.

Kirkland, Edward C. *Men, Cities, and Transportation: A Study in New England History, 1820–1900*. Cambridge, MA: Harvard University Press, 1948.

Lazerson, Marvin. *Origins of the Urban School: Public Education in Massachusetts, 1870–1915*. Cambridge, MA: Harvard University Press, 1971.

Leiby, James. *Carroll Wright and Labor Reform: The Origins of Labor Statistics*. Cambridge, MA: Harvard University Press, 1960.

Rosenkrantz, Barbara G. *Public Health and the State: Changing Views in Massachusetts, 1842–1936*. Cambridge, MA: Harvard University Press, 1972.

Tager, Jack, ed. *Massachusetts in the Gilded Age*. Amherst: University of Massachusetts Press, 1985.

Van de Woestyne, Royal S. *State Control of Local Finance in Massachusetts*. Cambridge, MA: Harvard University Press, 1935.

NEW YORK

Baker, Paula. *Moral Frameworks of Public Life: Gender, Politics, and the Sate in Rural New York, 1870–1930*. New York: Oxford University Press, 1991.

Caldwell, Lynton. *The Government and Administration of New York*. New York: Thomas Crowell, 1954.

Ingalls, Robert P. *Herbert H. Lehman and New York's Little New Deal*. New York: New York University Press, 1975.

McCormick, Richard L. *From Realignment to Reform: Political Change in New York State, 1893–1910*. Ithaca, NY: Cornell University Press, 1981.

Prescott, Frank W., and Joseph F. Zimmerman. *The Politics of the Veto of Legislation in New York State*. 2 vols. Washington, DC: University Press of America, 1980.

Schick, Thomas. *The New York State Constitutional Convention of 1915 and the Modern State Governor*. N.p.: National Municipal League, 1978.

Schneider, David M. *Public Welfare in New York State*, vol. 2. Chicago: University of Chicago Press, 1938.

Wesser, Robert F. *Charles Evans Hughes: Politics and Reform in New York, 1905–1910*. Ithaca, NY: Cornell University Press, 1967.

OHIO

Warner, Hoyt L. *Progressivism in Ohio, 1897–1917*. Columbus: Ohio State University Press, 1964.

OREGON

Burton, E. *Democrats of Oregon: The Pattern of Minority Politics, 1900–1956*. Eugene: University of Oregon Press, 1970.

Burton, E. "The New Deal in Oregon." In *The New Deal*, vol. 2, *The State and Local Levels*, ed. John Braeman et al. Columbus: Ohio State University Press, 1975.

Dodds, Gordon B. *Oregon: A Bicentennial History.* New York: Norton, 1977.

Higgens-Evenson, Rudy. "Parties, Patronage, Professionals, and the State: A History of Oregon Institutions, 1859–1900." MA thesis, University of Oregon, 1995.

Isseks, Morris S. *History of State Administrative Agencies in Oregon, 1843–1937*. Salem: Oregon State Planning Board, 1939.

MacColl, E. Kimbark. *The Growth of a City: Power and Politics in Portland, Oregon, 1915–1950*. Portland, OR: Georgian Press, 1979.

Swarthout, John M., and Kenneth R. Gervais. "Oregon: Political Experiment Station." In *Politics in the American West*, ed. Frank H. Jonas. Salt Lake City: University of Utah Press, 1969.

VIRGINIA

Heinemann, Ronald L. *Depression and New Deal in Virginia.* Charlottesville: University of Virginia Press, 1983.

Magruder, F. A. *Recent Administration in Virginia.* Baltimore: Johns Hopkins University Press, 1912.

Moger, Allen W. *Virginia: Bourbonism to Byrd, 1870–1925*. Charlottesville: University of Virginia Press, 1968.

Pate, James E. "State Supervision over Local Fiscal Officers in Virginia." *American Political Science Review* 25 (1931): 1004–1008.

Pulley, Raymond H. *Old Virginia Restored: An Interpretation of the Progressive Impulse, 1870–1930*. Charlottesville: University of Virginia Press, 1968.

Renda, Lex. "The Advent of Agricultural Progressivism in Virginia." *Virginia Magazine of History and Biography* 96 (1988): 55–82.

Silver, Christopher. *Twentieth-Century Richmond: Planning, Politics, and Race.* Knoxville: University of Tennessee Press, 1984.

Tables

In the following tables, cities are abbreviated as follows: Bos = Boston; Chic = Chicago; Cinc = Cincinnati; Clev = Cleveland; Jack = Jacksonville (FL); NYC = New York City; Rich = Richmond; San Fr = San Francisco. USDA = US Department of Agriculture.

Table A.1. Massachusetts Policy Innovations in the Antebellum Era

Social policy:	
Education	• Authorized district system, 1789 • Free schools (towns enabled), 1827 • State Board of Education (powers over local aid), 1837 • Normal schools, 1839 (Lexington, later Framingham State College; W. Barre, later Westfield State College) • Libraries: city and town support, 1851 • Compulsory education, 1852, 1858
Children	• Ten-hour workday for children in industries, 1842 • Adoption of children, 1851
Indigent persons, immigrants, and dependents	• Aid to towns, 1794 • Boston almshouse (House of Industry), 1821 • Feebleminded (insane): 1833 (Worcester Street Hospital), 1848 (school) • Immigrants: bonding required of shipping companies (head tax), 1837; Board of Alien Passengers, 1851 • State almshouse, 1854 • Committee on Public Charitable Institutions, 1859 • Town authority to deny residency to paupers, 1860
Community values	• Restrict lotteries, 1801, 1817, 1837 • Liquor: o License, 1838 o Prohibition, 1852 • Race: o Personal liberty law, 1843 o Prohibit school segregation, 1855 • Women: o Property rights, 1845 o Prohibit contraceptive information, 1847
Criminal justice and public order	• Militia Act, Riot Act, Sedition Act, 1786 • Prison (Charleston), 1802; adopt Auburn model, 1829 • Reform schools (Boston), 1826 (boys), 1855 (girls) • Abolition of imprisonment for debt (partial), 1834 • Uniformed police, 1859
Commercial assistance	• Savings banks, 1816; general incorporation, 1834 • Agriculture: o Geographic survey, 1830 o Board, 1852 o Census, 1845 • Railroads: o State investment, 1835–1841 o Charters, 1852 o Hoosac Tunnel, 1854 o Street railways, 1854 • Manufacturing, 1851 • “Free” banks, 1851; general incorporation, 1852

(continued on the next page)

Table A.1. (*continued*)

Commercial assistance	• Gas companies, 1855
	• Physicians: elimination of most licensing restrictions, 1859
	• Physicians: elimination of most licensing restrictions, 1859
Commercial regulation	• Licensing:
	○ Ferries, 1796
	○ Liquor, 1838
	○ Pilots, 1855
	• State system of weight standards, 1835
	• Bank commissioners, 1838
	○ Commission, 1852
	○ Specie minimum, 1858
	• Workers: hours, exemption from criminal conspiracy, 1842
	• Railroads: regulate charters, 1852
	• Cities: regulation of street railways, 1854
	• Insurance board, 1855; general regulations, 1856
Health and safety	• Cochituate water system for Boston, 1836
	• Towns required to establish board of health, 1849
	• Compulsory vaccination, 1850
	• Prohibition of milk adulteration, 1856, 1858
Government	• Executive veto:
	○ Governor, 1780 (first used 1827)
	○ Boston mayor, 1854
	• Suffrage:
	○ Small property qualification, 1780 constitution
	○ Taxpayers, 1821 (constitutional amendment)
	○ English literacy required, 1857
	○ Citizenship required, 1859–1863
	• Creation of cities authorized, 1820 (constitutional provision)
	• Legislature:
	○ Legislator compensation, 1825
	○ Property qualification abolished, 1840
	○ House set at 240 members, 1857
	• Authorization of state census, 1840
	• "Police power" recognized, 1851 (*Commonwealth v. Alger*)
Finance	• State property, circa 1780
	• Tax on banks, 1812
	• Immigrant head tax, 1848

Table A.2. State Actions, 1783–1870: California, Illinois, Massachusetts, New York, Ohio, Virginia

Governmental Structure and Process	
Suffrage: property qualifications abolished	OH: 1802 IL: 1818 MA, NY: 1821

	MA: 1840 (legislature)
	VA: 1851
Popular election of governors	NY: 1777
	MA: 1780
	IL: 1818
	CA: 1849
	VA: 1851
Governor veto	NY: 1821
	MA: 1827 (first use)
	IL: 1848
	CA: 1849
	VA: 1870
	OH: 1903
Election of officials	NY: 1839 (mayors)
	CA: 1849
	MA: 1855 (department heads)
Election of judges	NY: 1846
	IL: 1848
	CA: 1849
	VA, OH: 1851
Biennial legislative sessions	VA, OH: 1851
	IL: 1855
	CA: 1862
Incorporation of cities	Cinc: 1810
	MA: 1820 (general)
	Clev: 1836
	Chic: 1837
	NY: 1837 (general)
	San Fr: 1850
	OH: 1852 (general)
	IL: 1872 (general)
State police powers	NY: 1827 (*Vanderbilt v. Adams*)
	MA: 1851 (*Commonwealth v. Alger*)
	VA: 1865
	IL: 1871 (*Munn v. Illinois*)
Social Policy	
Education:	
Public schools established	MA: 1789, 1827
	NY: 1812, 1867
	CA: 1849
	OH: 1853
	IL: 1855
	VA: 1870
Free high schools	OH: 1849
	NY: 1856
Compulsory education	MA: 1852, 1858

(continued on the next page)

Table A.2. (*continued*)

Social Policy	
Education:	
State board of education	MA: 1837 CA: 1852 NY, OH: 1853 IL: 1857
State financial aid	MA: 1834 CA, NY: 1851 IL: 1855 VA: 1882
Normal schools	MA: 1839 NY: 1844 IL: 1857 CA: 1862
State university	OH: 1804 VA: 1819 MA: 1863 NY: 1865 IL: 1867 CA: 1868
Care of indigent and dependents:	
Almshouses	Bos: 1821 NY: 1824 (county), 1848 MA: 1854 (institution for paupers) IL: 1856 (soldiers, orphans) OH: 1858 (boys)
Blind	NY: 1834 OH: 1837, 1850 VA: 1839 IL: 1848
Insane	VA: 1828 MA: 1833 OH: 1834, 1858 (boys) NY: 1836 IL: 1847 CA: 1853
Feebleminded	MA: 1853, 1851 OH: 1857
Board of charities	MA: 1863 NY, OH: 1867 IL: 1869
Immigration control	MA: 1837, 1851 NY: 1847, 1855
Community values:	
Liquor: license	MA: 1838 NY: 1845 OH: 1851 (no license) IL: 1853

Liquor: prohibition	MA: 1852
	NY: 1855 (unconstitutional)
Sunday closing of saloons	IL: 1827, 1841
Restriction of lotteries	MA: 1801, 1837
	OH: 1830
Abolition and racial exclusion	IL: 1820s (antiblack laws)
	VA: 1836 (suppress abolitionist mail)
	CA: 1851 (schools)
	MA: 1855 (schools)
Personal liberty law	NY: 1840
	MA: 1843
	OH: 1857
Marital property rights for women	MA: 1845
	NY: 1848
	OH: 1861
	IL: 1867
Restriction of personal behavior	NY: 1845 (antiabortion)
	MA: 1866 (begging)
Parks	Bos: 1824
	NYC: 1857
	San Fr: 1870
Public Health and Safety	
Fresh water systems	Rich: 1830 (James River)
	NYC: 1834
	Cinc: 1839 (Ohio River)
	Bos: 1846
	Clev: 1854 (Lake Erie)
	Chic: 1854 (Lake Michigan)
Sewer systems	NYC: 1849
	Chic: 1855
Food adulteration	MA: 1856 (milk), 1872 (meat)
	NY: 1862 (milk)
Compulsory vaccination	MA: 1850
Board of health	NY: 1866 (metro)
	Chic: 1867
	MA: 1869
	CA: 1870
	Bos: 1873
Criminal Justice	
Capital punishment reform	NY: 1796, 1835, 1841
	OH: 1824
	MA: 1839
	VA: 1844
Prisons	NY: 1796 (Newgate), 1816 (Auburn)
	VA: 1796 (Richmond)

(continued on the next page)

Table A.2. (*continued*)

Criminal Justice	
Prison boards	NY: 1846 CA: 1855 IL: 1867
Police: uniformed	NYC: 1856 San Fr: 1857 Chic: 1858 Bos, Cinc: 1859
Reform schools	NYC: 1824, 1848 Bos: 1826 MA: 1846 OH: 1856 IL: 1861
Reform schools for girls	MA: 1855 OH: 1869
Commercial Assistance	
Promotion of transportation	VA: 1816 (internal improvement fund), 1817 (turnpikes) NY: 1817 (Erie Canal), 1836 (expanded) OH: 1825 (canal system), 1836–1845 IL: 1829–1836 (canal acts); 1835, 1837 (loans); 1849 (county investment) MA: 1835–1841 (railroad investment), 1854–1868 (Hoosac Tunnel) CA: 1859 (for cities and counties), 1863–1873 (rail subsidy) San Fr: 1863 (harbor)
Incorporation of private enterprise:	NY: 1811 (selected industries), 1827 (limited liability)
Manufacturing: general law	NY: 1848 CA: 1850 MA: 1851 VA, OH: 1852
Banks: "free banking"	NY: 1838 IL, OH, VA: 1851 MA: 1852 CA: 1864
Railroads	MA: 1852 (charters), 1854 (street railways)
Stay laws for debtors	OH: 1820, 1841 NY: 1820, 1842 IL: 1821, 1841 (unconstitutional) VA: 1837, 1842
Agriculture:	
Board of agriculture	NY: 1841 OH: 1846 MA: 1852 CA: 1854

Geological survey	MA: 1830 IL: 1851 CA: 1854 OH: 1869
Water regulations	CA: 1854
Workers:	
Hours	MA: 1842, 1866 (children), 1874 (women) IL: 1867 (8-hour day) NY: 1870 (state workers)
Exemption from criminal conspiracy	MA: 1842 (*Commonwealth v. Hunt*) NY: 1870
Commercial Regulations	
Banking	MA: 1799 (note redemption, 1810), 1838 NY: 1829–1866 (safety fund), 1851, 1871 (savings) OH: 1839, 1845 (state bank) IL: 1851, 1871 (savings)
Insurance	NY: 1850 MA: 1855, 1866 CA: 1868 IL: 1869
Railroads	OH: 1849 (rates), 1867 (commission) MA: 1852 (via charters), 1854 (street railroads), 1869 (commission) IL: 1869 (commission)
Usury	OH: 1803, 1869 NY: 1837 IL: 1849, 1857
Abolition of imprisonment for debt	NY: 1817, 1831 MA: 1834, 1855 OH: 1838
Public Finance	
Business taxes:	
On banks	MA: 1812, 1862 (excise) OH: 1815, 1846 VA: 1838
On corporations	OH: 1831, 1846 VA: 1842, 1856 (railroads) CA: 1862 MA: 1864
Business and vendor license fees	VA: 1807 (peddlers), 1838 (graduated licenses) OH: 1825 (merchants) CA: 1851 (express companies), 1882 (insurers)
State property tax	MA, VA, OH: 1780s OH: 1825 IL: 1841 NY: 1842

(continued on the next page)

Table A.2. (*continued*)

	Public Finance
Board of equalization	NY: 1859 IL: 1867
Fiscal controls:	
Debt limit on state	NY: 1846 IL: 1848, 1870 CA: 1849 OH: 1851
Prohibition of investment in corporations and internal improvements:	
Debt limitations on cities	San Fr: 1856
Tax limitations	IL: 1845 (cities) San Fr: 1856

Table A.3. State Actions, 1870–1917: California, Florida, Illinois, Massachusetts, New York, Ohio, Oregon, Virginia

	Gilded Age (1870–1900)	*Progressive Era (1901–1917)*
	Governmental Structure and Process	
Legislature:		
Legislative Reference Bureau	NY: 1890	CA: 1904 MA, OH: 1910 IL, OR: 1913 VA: 1914
Apportionment: county system	NY: 1894	OH: 1903
Elections:		
Female suffrage	School elections: MA: 1879 NY: 1880 OR: 1882 IL: 1891 OH: 1894	General elections: CA: 1911 OR: 1912 IL: 1913 NY: 1917
Secret ballot	MA: 1888 CA, IL, OH, OR: 1891 NY, VA: 1894 FL: 1895	
Voter registration	MA: 1884 VA: 1884, 1894 IL: 1885 (Chic) NY: 1890	VA: 1902
Regulation of campaign finances/parties	CA: 1886 OH: 1889	VA: 1902 FL: 1905

	NY: 1890 MA: 1892, 1894	OR: 1908 OH: 1911
Direct primary		OR: 1904 IL: 1910 MA, CA: 1911 VA: 1912 FL, NY, OH: 1913
Initiative and referendum		OR: 1903 CA: 1911 OH: 1913 MA: 1918
Executives and administration:		
Civil service	NY: 1883 MA: 1884	OH: 1903 IL: 1905, 1911 CA, OH: 1913 FL: 1938 VA: 1942
Governor's veto	VA: 1870 NY: 1876 (item veto) IL: 1884	VA: 1902 OH: 1903 CA: 1908 MA: 1918
Municipal:		
Strengthening of mayor	IL: 1875 NY: 1884 Bos: 1885 (item veto) Clev: 1891 San Fr: 1898	OH: 1902 NYC: 1908 (budget) Bos: 1909 (charter reform)
Home rule		Chic: 1903 OR: 1906 CA: 1911 (commission government) OH: 1912 NY: 1915
Zoning authority		VA: 1908 MA: 1911 IL: 1913 NY: 1914 OR: 1919
Judicial review	NY: 1885 (*In Re Jacobs*) IL: 1895 (*Ritchie v. People*)	OR: 1908 (recall of judges) OH: 1912 (restriction of court)
	Public Finance	
Tax commission (permanent)	MA: 1864 IL: 1887 NY: 1896	OR: 1909 OH: 1910 FL: 1913 IL: 1919 VA: 1923

(continued on the next page)

Table A.3. (*continued*)

	Gilded Age (1870–1900)	*Progressive Era (1901–1917)*
	Public Finance	
Taxation:		
Corporations	NY: 1880 VA: 1880 OH: 1898 (franchise)	CA: 1905, 1910 (constitutional amendment) VA: 1915 (income)
Utilities	MA: 1882 OH: 1894 NY: 1899	NY: 1901, 1905 (stock), 1917 (income) OR: 1906, 1913 (valuation) CA: 1910, 1913
Inheritance	NY: 1885 MA: 1891 OH: 1893 IL: 1895	OR: 1903 CA: 1905 MA: 1908 IL: 1908 (increase; progressive) NY: 1910 (stronger) VA: 1916
Auto registration		NY: 1901, 1910 MA: 1903 CA, FL, OR: 1905 OH: 1906 IL: 1907 VA: 1910
Personal income tax		MA, VA: 1916 NY: 1919
Financial controls:		
State supervision of local government	NY: 1872 IL: 1876 MA: 1879 (county) CA: 1895	MA: 1906 (local reports)
Local accounting standards		NY: 1905, 1907 MA: 1912
Municipal debt limit	IL: 1870 Cinc: 1877 CA: 1879 MA: 1879 (county), 1885 NY: 1884	OH: 1911 MA: 1913
Municipal tax limit	IL: 1879 MA: 1885	IL: 1901, 1915 (classification) OH: 1910
State budget systems		CA: 1911 OH, OR: 1913 IL: 1917

		MA, VA: 1918 FL, NY: 1921
	Social Policy	
Civil rights:		
Racial discrimination	FL: 1885 (schools), 1889 (poll tax) CA: 1885 (Asians, Indians in schools)	VA: 1902 (segregation, disenfranchisement) 1912 (residential) CA: 1913, 1920 (anti-Japanese)
Racial nondiscrimination	NY: 1895 (open accommodations) OH: 1887 (schools)	
Education:		
Compulsory education	CA, NY, OH: 1874 IL: 1883 OR: 1889	VA: 1908 (local option) FL: 1915
Free textbooks	MA: 1884	CA: 1911 FL: 1925
Teachers' retirement	Chic, NYC: 1895 MA: 1900	MA, VA: 1908 NY: 1911 CA: 1913 IL: 1915 OH: 1919 FL: 1939
Care of indigent and dependents:		
Insane	NY: 1890 CA: 1897 MA: 1898	VA: 1902 (board) MA: 1904 (state)
Blind	CA, FL: 1885	IL: 1903 MA: 1906
Mothers' pensions		IL: 1911 MA, CA, OH: 1913 NY, OR: 1915 VA: 1918 FL: 1919
Veterans' home	IL: 1885 OH: 1886 FL: 1891 VA: 1892 CA: 1897	
Mores:		
Female suffrage	IL: 1891 (school) OH: 1894 (school)	CA: 1911 OR: 1912 IL: 1913 NY: 1917 OH: 1923 MA: 1924
Liquor: local option	MA: 1881 CA, IL: 1883	OR: 1904

(continued on the next page)

Table A.3. (*continued*)

	Gilded Age (1870–1900)	*Progressive Era (1901–1917)*
	Social Policy	
Mores:		
Liquor: local option	FL: 1885	OH, VA: 1886 NY: 1896
Liquor: state prohibition		OR, VA: 1914 OH: 1916 FL: 1918
Gambling (horse races)		NY: 1908 FL: 1931
Parks and reserves	NY: 1883 (Adirondack) MA: 1893 (metro district), 1896 (Revere Beach), 1898 (Bos playgrounds), 1898 (Mt. Greylock State Forest)	FL: 1935
	Public Health	
State board	VA: 1872 IL: 1877 CA: 1879 NY: 1880 OH: 1886 FL: 1889	OR: 1903
Department		VA: 1908 NY: 1909 MA: 1914 IL, OH: 1917
Water standards	MA: 1878, 1886 VA: 1892	OH: 1908
Metropolitan sewers	NY: 1849 Bos: 1876 MA: 1998 IL: 1889 OH: 1898 San Fr: 1899	MA: 1919 (metro district commission)
Food and drug adulteration	NY: 1881 IL: 1881, 1899 MA: 1882 OH: 1886 VA: 1899	OH: 1904 CA, FL: 1907 VA: 1908
Sanitary code/tenement regulation	IL: 1881 MA: 1888 (schools) OH: 1893	NY: 1901 (tenements), 1909 OH: 1908 (tenements VA: 1910 MA: 1912

Tuberculosis sanatoriums	MA: 1898	OH: 1908 (county option) VA: 1910 IL: 1915 (Chic)
Licensing:		
Physicians	CA: 1875 IL: 1877 VA: 1884 FL, NY, OR: 1889 MA: 1894 OH: 1896	
Pharmacists	IL: 1881 OH: 1884 MA: 1885 VA: 1886 FL, NY: 1889 CA, OR: 1891	
Dentists	IL: 1881 VA: 1886 FL, MA, OR: 1887 NY: 1895	
Nurses		NY, VA: 1903 CA: 1905 IL: 1907 MA: 1910 OR: 1911 FL: 1913 OH: 1915
Undertakers (embalmers)	VA: 1894	OH: 1902 MA: 1904 CA: 1915 FL: 1917 OR: 1921
	Public Safety	
Vagrancy law strengthened	IL: 1874, 1877 MA: 1875, 1880 NY: 1880 MA: 1896, 1898	
Militia reorganization	IL: 1879 NY: 1883 OR: 1887 MA: 1888	
Antiriot/conspiracy	IL: 1887	NY: 1902 (Anarchy Act) IL: 1905
Parole	OH: 1884 MA: 1891 CA: 1893 IL: 1895	MA: 1913 OH: 1913 FL: 1940 VA: 1942

(continued on the next page)

Table A.3. (*continued*)

	Gilded Age (1870–1900)	*Progressive Era (1901–1917)*
	Social Policy	
Prohibition of the leasing of convicts		OH: 1906 FL: 1923
State prison farm	VA: 1894 FL: 1911	OH: 1913
Juvenile court	Chic: 1899 NYC: 1900	Clev: 1902 Bos: 1906 OH: 1913 FL: 1951
State police	MA: 1865	CA: 1905, 1917 NY: 1917
	Workers	
Bureau of labor statistics	MA: 1869 OH: 1877 IL: 1879 NY, CA: 1883 VA: 1898	OR: 1903
Labor arbitration	MA, NY, OH: 1886 CA: 1891 IL: 1895	NY: 1901
Limited hours: women and children	NY: 1886, 1892 OR, VA: 1890 (women) MA: 1892 (10 hours) IL: 1893 (women)	MA: 1900, 1911 (54-hour week) IL: 1903 (children), 1909 (women) NY: 1903 (children), 1913 (women) OH: 1905 (children), 1911 FL: 1907 VA: 1908 CA: 1911 OR: 1913
Eight-hour day, state workers		MA: 1911 OH: 1912
Factory conditions, standards	Chic: 1879 MA, NY: 1887 CA: 1889	IL: 1905 OH: 1912
Factory inspectors	OH: 1885 IL: 1893	OR: 1903 IL: 1907 NY: 1913 OH: 1913 (industrial commission)
Anti-sweatshop	MA: 1891 NY: 1892, 1900 IL: 1893	

Mine regulations	IL: 1872, 1883 (board) OH: 1873 CA: 1880 NY: 1890	IL: 1905 OR: 1911 OH: 1914
Compulsory payment of money wages	OH: 1878 MA: 1886 NY: 1889 IL: 1891	OR: 1913 (semimonthly)
Minimum wage		MA: 1912 (women) CA, OR: 1913
Employment offices	OH: 1890 IL: 1899	MA: 1906 NY: 1914 CA: 1915
Employer liability defined	MA: 1887	NY: 1902
Anti-injunction law	IL: 1898 (unconstitutional)	CA: 1906 MA: 1914
Workers' compensation		OH: 1913 FL: 1935
	Commercial Assistance	
General incorporation	MA: 1882 NY: 1892 (holding companies) IL: 1887 (general banking)	MA: 1903 (rules relaxed)
Licensing of accountants	NY: 1896	CA: 1901 OR: 1913 MA: 1923 FL: 1927
Agriculture:		
Experiment stations	IL: 1876 CA: 1877 NY: 1880 MA, OH: 1882 VA: 1886 OR: 1888	
Dairy commission/bureau	IL: 1872 NY: 1884 FL: 1885 OH: 1886 MA: 1892 OR: 1893 CA: 1895	CA: 1907 (quality standards) VA: 1908
Cattle commission	MA: 1860 OH: 1884 IL: 1885 NY: 1893 VA: 1898 CA: 1899 OR: 1913	

(continued on the next page)

Table A.3. (*continued*)

	Gilded Age (1870–1900)	*Progressive Era (1901–1917)*
	Commercial Assistance	
Anti-oleo	NY: 1877, 1884 FL: 1881 VA: 1892 CA, OR: 1895 IL: 1897	
Commodity standards	IL: 1872 (board of trade) CA: 1880 (viticulture) VA: 1890 (fertilizer)	CA: 1909 (dairy certification) IL: 1911 (grain) FL: 1911 (citrus)
Department of agriculture	IL: 1884 FL: 1885 NY: 1893	OH: 1913 IL: 1917 CA: 1919
Transportation:		
Highways: state aid	MA: 1892 NY: 1898	OH: 1904 IL: 1905 VA: 1906 CA: 1909 OR: 1911 FL: 1915
Highway commission	MA: 1893 CA: 1895	OH: 1904 IL: 1905 VA: 1906 NY: 1908 OR: 1913 FL: 1915
Registration of motor vehicles (annual)		MA, NY: 1901 CA, FL: 1905 OH: 1906 IL: 1907 VA: 1910 OR: 1911
Subway	Bos: 1893	NYC: 1904
Waterways	MA: 1879 (Bos harbor) OH: 1888 (canal commission) OR: 1891 (Portland harbor commission) NY: 1895 (Erie Canal enlargements)	NY: 1903 (barge canal) CA: 1910 MA: 1911 (Bos harbor) FL: 1912 (Jack harbor commission)
Resources:		
Fish/fishing	NY: 1868 IL: 1875 OR: 1878, 1893	

	CA: 1885 MA: 1886	
Forestry	CA, FL, OH: 1885 (boards) NY: 1885 (department)	MA: 1904, 1914 CA: 1905 NY: 1909 OR: 1911 OH: 1914 FL: 1927
Reclamation	FL: 1881 (drainage) OR: 1895	FL: 1905 (Everglades drainage) VA: 1910 (drainage) OH: 1913 (flood)
	Commercial Regulation	
Banking	CA: 1878, 1895 (strengthened NY: 1884, 1892 IL: 1887 OH: 1891 (building and loan)	NY: 1905 MA: 1906) OR: 1907 OH: 1908 MA: 1908 (commissioner) CA: 1909 VA: 1910
Insurance	OH, NY: 1886 (fire) OR: 1887 CA: 1891 IL: 1893	NY, VA: 1906 OR: 1909 (commissioner)
Railroad commission	OH: 1867 MA: 1869 IL: 1870 VA: 1877 OR: 1877–1898 CA: 1880 NY: 1883 FL: 1897	OH: 1906 (passengers) NY: 1911 (expanded jurisdiction)
Gas	MA: 1885	NY: 1905, 1907 (commission)
Electricity	MA: 1887	NY: 1905
Telephones		FL: 1909 NY: 1910 MA: 1913
Public utility commission (including railroads)		VA: 1902 NY: 1905 OR: 1907 CA, FL, OH: 1911 IL, MA: 1913
Small loans	MA: 1888 IL: 1891	OR: 1913 NY: 1915 IL: 1917 FL: 1925

(continued on the next page)

Table A.3. (*continued*)

	Gilded Age (1870–1900)	Progressive Era (1901–1917)
	Commercial Regulation	
Antimonopoly	CA: 1889 IL: 1891 OH: 1898	CA: 1907 MA: 1911 (prices) VA: 1919
Futures ("bucket shops")	IL: 1887	NY: 1908
Securities ("blue sky" laws)		NY: 1907 (utilities) OH: 1908, 1913 CA: 1913 IL: 1917

Table A.4. Presidential Administrations and Policy Actions, 1869–1901

Administration	*Year*	*Policy Actions*
Ulysses S. Grant (1869–1877)	1870	• Fifteenth Amendment (ratified) • Justice Department • National Weather Service (from US Army to USDA)
	1871	• Coast and Geodetic Survey
	1872	• Yellowstone National Park
	1873	• Silver coinage stopped
	1875	• Resumption of coin-for-greenback swap
Rutherford B. Hayes (1877–1881)	1877	• Federal troops used in great railroad strike • Desert Land Act (assistance for irrigation)
	1878	• Bland-Allison Silver Purchase Act
	1879	• US Geological Survey • National Board of Health
James A. Garfield (1881)/ Chester A. Arthur (1881–1885)	1881	• Forest Agency (in USDA)
	1882	• Chinese Exclusion Act
	1883	• Civil Service Act • First appropriations act for construction of steel naval ships
	1884	• Bureau of Labor Statistics
Grover Cleveland (1885–1889)	1886	• Appropriations to build a "modern" navy
	1887	• Interstate Commerce Act • Indian Reorganization Act (Dawes Severalty Act)

		• Agricultural experiment stations (grants to states)
	1889	• Agriculture elevated to department status
Benjamin Harrison (1889–1893)	1890	• Sherman Antitrust Act
		• McKinley tariff
		• Sherman Silver Purchase Act
		• Appropriations to build three battleships
		• Dependents Pension Act
	1891	• General Land Act: national forest system established
		• Federal appeals courts established
		• Immigration regulations (Immigration and Naturalization Service)
		• "Billion-dollar Congress" (51st)
	1893	• Good roads appropriations—Office of Road Inquiry (1894)
		• Railway Safety Appliance Act
Grover Cleveland (1893–1897)	1893–1896	• Appropriations for five battleships
	1893	• Sherman Silver Purchase Act repealed
	1894	• Federal troops used to break Pullman strike
		• Wilson tariff, with income tax provision
		• Treasury purchases gold; additional
		• purchases in 1895
	1896	• Rural free delivery of mail
		• Veto of immigration law requiring literacy
William McKinley (1897–1901)	1897	• Dingley tariff
		• Registration of copyrights
	1898	• Hawaii annexed
		• Spanish-American War
	1899	• Puerto Rico and Philippines acquired
	1900	• Gold Standard Act

Table A.5. Federal Agencies, 1867–1921

Year	*Agency*
1867	• Office of Education (Interior Department)
1870	• National Weather Service (from US Army to USDA)
	• Army Signal Corps
	• Justice Department
1871	• Coast and Geodetic Survey
	• Office of Commissioner of Fish and Fisheries

(continued on the next page)

Table A.5. (*continued*)

Year	*Agency*
1879	• US Geological Survey
	• National Board of Health
1881	• Forest Agency (USDA)
1883	• Civil Service Commission
1884	• Bureau of Labor Statistics (independent department as of 1888)
1887	• Interstate Commerce Commission
1888	• Office of Experiment Stations (USDA)
1889	• USDA given cabinet status
1890	• Weather Bureau transferred from US Army to USDA
1891	• Immigration and Naturalization Service
	• National forest system
1894	• Office of Road Inquiry (Office of Public Roads, 1905)
1897	• Register of Copyrights (Library of Congress)
1901	• Bureau of Plant Industry (USDA)
	• Bureau of Chemistry and Soils (USDA)
	• Bureau of Forestry (USDA)
1902	• Reclamation Service (Bureau of Reclamation, 1922)
	• Bureau of the Census
1903	• Bureau of Corporations
	• Department of Commerce and Labor (until 1913)
	• Antitrust Division, Justice Department
1904	• Bureau of Entomology (USDA)
1905	• Forest Service
1907	• Bureau of Plant Industry (USDA)
1908	• Bureau of Investigation, Justice Department (FBI, 1935)
1910	• Bureau of Mines
1912	• Children's Bureau
	• US Public Health Service
1913	• Department of Labor
	• Department of Commerce
1914	• Agricultural Extension Service (USDA)
	• Federal Reserve Board (per 1913 act)
	• Federal Trade Commission
1915	• Bureau of Efficiency
	• Naval Consulting Board
	• Bureau of Public Roads
1916	• Grain Standards Act (USDA)
	• Tariff Commission (investigatory authority)
	• US Shipping Board
	• National Park Service
	• Federal Farm Loan Board
1917	• War Industries Board
	• US Employment Service
	• US Housing Corporation
	• Federal Board for Vocational Education
1918	• Women's Bureau

1919	• Bureau of Public Roads
1920	• Federal Power Commission
1921	• Bureau of the Budget
	• Grain Futures Administration
	• General Accounting Office

Table A.6. The Documentary State: Information about Individuals, 1789–1920

Period Beginning	*Information Collected From*
1789	• Military records: US and state
1790	• US census
	• State censuses
	• Land entries in public domain (US territories)
	• Local property and tax records
1850	• State birth records
	• State death records
	• Municipal health inspections
1862	• Distillers' licenses and inspections (US excise tax)
1863	• US postal addresses: urban delivery
1870s	• Municipal criminal records
	• School records
	• Professional and occupational licenses: dentists, pharmacists, physicians, engineers, veterinarians, vessel pilots, undertakers
1890	• Voter registration
1891	• Immigration control
1896	• US postal addresses: rural delivery
1901	• Auto registrations
	• National death registrations
1903	• State police
1905	• State criminal bureaus
1906	• Driver's licenses
1907	• Marriage licenses (some required medical certification)
1908	• US Bureau of Investigation
1909	• Local fingerprint files
1913	• US income tax
1914	• US narcotics control (e.g., Harrison Act)
1915	• National birth registrations
1917–1918	• World War I draft registrations
	• US passports (e.g., Travel Control Act)

Table A.7. State Actions, 1918–1929: California, Florida, Illinois, Massachusetts, New York, Ohio, Oregon, Virginia

Governmental Structure and Process	
State budget	CA: 1911 (1921), 1922
	OH, OR: 1913, 1927
	NY: 1916
	IL: 1917, 1927
	MA: 1918
	FL: 1921
State administrative reorganization	IL: 1917
	MA: 1919
	CA, OH: 1921
	NY: 1925 (partial)
	VA: 1927
Public employee pensions	MA: 1911
	NY: 1920
	FL: 1927
Voter literacy	NY: 1922
	FL, OR: 1926
Social Policy	
Civil rights	CA: 1921 (Alien Land Act: anti-Japanese)
	VA: 1925 (racial segregation of private accommodations)
Education:	
School aid increased	MA: 1919
	CA: 1920
	FL: 1924
	NY: 1925
School consolidation	VA: 1923
Care of indigent and dependents:	
Deaf, blind	NY: 1922
	MA: 1923
	CA: 1929 (aid to blind)
Veterans	CA, OH: 1921
Old-age pensions	CA: 1929
Welfare department	MA: 1919
	CA: 1925
	FL: 1927 (board)
Housing: slum clearance	NY: 1926
Prohibition enforcement	NY: 1926
Public Health and Safty	
Children's health	CA: 1919
Housing regulation	NY: 1920
Mental health	MA: 1922
Automobile insurance required	MA: 1925

State police	NY: 1917 IL: 1921 (highway) MA: 1921 FL: 1939 (highway)
Sedition/antiradicalism	CA, IL, MA, NY, OH, OR: 1919
Bureau of criminal investigation, anticrime	CA: 1917, 1927 OH: 1921 NY: 1926
	Workers
Anti-injunction provisions	IL: 1925
Hours	NY: 1927 (maximum of 48 for women)
Industrial safety	OH: 1919 OR: 1920
	Commercial Assistance
Licenses:	
Accountants	MA: 1923
Fishing	CA: 1919
Transportation:	
Dedicated highway funds	OR: 1919 MA: 1925
State highway system; county road aid	VA: 1918 NY: 1920 OH: 1927
Port	NY: 1921 (authority)
Corporations	IL: 1919 (revised incorporation)
Agriculture:	
Marketing cooperatives	CA: 1915 VA: 1922 FL: 1929
Commodity standards	FL: 1925, 1929 (citrus, milk) CA: 1927 (fruit)
Resources	MA: 1920 (forest purchases) CA: 1920 (license offshore drilling), 1929 (oil, gas controls) NY: 1921 (water power commission) IL: 1925 (department of conservation) FL: 1927 (forests), 1929 (Okeechobee flood control)
	Commercial Regulation
Trucking	CA: 1917, 1919 IL, NY, OH, OR: 1921, 1924 VA: 1923 FL: 1929
Securities	IL: 1919 OH: 1929

(continued on the next page)

Table A.7. (*continued*)

	Commercial Regulation
Airports	CA: 1927
Small businesses	CA: 1927 (dry cleaners), 1929 (gas production)
Loans	FL: 1925
	Finance
Motor vehicle fuel tax	IL: 1924 (unconstitional), 1927
	OH: 1925
	MA, NY: 1929
Corporations	IL: 1919 (franchise)
	MA: 1919 (income)
	FL: 1925 (license), 1927 (insurance)
	NY: 1926 (financial institutions)
	CA, OR: 1929 (income)
Personal income tax	NY: 1919
	OR: 1924 (repealed 1930)
	FL: 1924 (prohibited)
Financial controls:	
Borrowing	MA: 1918 (two-thirds vote of legislature)
Supervision of local finance	OH: 1925
	MA: 1926
	VA: 1927
	CA: 1929
Property classification permitted	OH: 1929

NOTES

1. *The Dynamics of American Statebuilding*

1. Recent reassessments include Gary Gerstle, *Liberty and Coercion: The Paradox of American Government from the Founding to the Present* (Princeton, NJ: Princeton University Press, 2015); Brian Balough, *A Government out of Sight: The Mystery of National Authority in Nineteenth Century America* (New York: Cambridge University Press, 2009); Desmond King and Robert C. Liberman, "Ironies of State Building: A Comparative Perspective on the American State," *World Politics* 61 (July 2009): 547; William J. Novak, "The Myth of the 'Weak' American State," *American Historical Review* 113, 3 (June 2008): 752–772, esp. note 8, which cites recent social scientists who contend that the United States was stateless in the nineteenth century; Richard R. John, ed., *Ruling Passions: Political Economy in Nineteenth Century America* (University Park: Pennsylvania State University Press, 2006); Ira Katznelson, "Flexible Capacity: The Military and Early American Statebuilding," in *Shaped by War and Trade: Influences on American Political Development*, ed. Ira Katznelson and Martin Shefter (Princeton, NJ: Princeton University Press, 2002).

Also see Sheldon D. Pollack, *War, Revenue, and State Building: Financing and the Development of the American State* (Ithaca, NY: Cornell University Press, 2009); Jack P. Greene, "Colonial History and National History: Reflections on a Continuing Problem," *William and Mary Quarterly* 54 (April 2007): 235–250; Stephen J. Rockwell, *Indian Affairs and the Administrative State in the Nineteenth Century* (New York: Cambridge University Press, 2010), esp. chs. 1, 10; William E. Leuchtenburg, "The Pertinence of Political History: Reflections on the Significance of the State in America," *Journal of American History* 73, 3 (December 1986): 585–600; Hugh Davis Graham, "The Stunted Career of Policy History: A Critique and an Agenda," *Public Historian* 15, 2 (Spring 1993): 15–37.

2. On situational policymaking and the dynamics of governmental action, see Ballard C. Campbell, *The Growth of American Government: Governance from the Cleveland Era to the Present*, rev. and expanded ed. (Bloomington: Indiana University Press, 2015), ch. 2, esp. 51–52.

3. James Bryce, *The American Commonwealth*, 3rd ed., vol. 1 (New York: Macmillan, 1893), 15, 17–18. Bryce first published his classic study in 1889.

4. S. E. Finer, *The History of Government*, 3 vols. (New York: Oxford University Press, 1997), 1:1–34, 3:1261–1306; Raymond Grew, "The Nineteenth-Century European State," in *Statemaking and Social Movements*, ed. Charles Bright and Susan Harding (Ann Arbor: University of Michigan Press, 1984); Michael Mann, "The Autonomous Power of the State: Its Origins, Mechanisms and Results," in *States, War, Capitalism: Studies in Political Sociology* (New York: Blackwell, 1988); Michael Mann, *The Sources of Social Power*, vol. 2, *The Rise of Classes and Nation-States,*

1760–1914 (New York: Cambridge University Press, 1993), esp. ch. 3; Gianfranco Poggi, *The State: Its Nature, Development and Prospects* (Stanford, CA: Stanford University Press, 1990), esp. ch. 2; Charles Tilly, ed., *The Formation of National States in Western Europe* (Princeton, NJ: Princeton University Press, 1975), esp. chs. 1 (Charles Tilly) and 2 (Samuel E. Finer); Charles Tilly, ed., *Coercion, Capital, and European States, A.D. 900–1990* (Cambridge: Blackwell, 1990). This and the next several paragraphs emphasize European states, which were the most important referents for Americans.

5. S. E. Finer has criticized the overuse of the term "nation-state," which he reserves for states where sovereignty is democratically exercised. He prefers the term "national state" for entities where a common national identity has emerged in the context of statebuilding, such as France after the French Revolution. Finer, *History of Government*, 1:3–4.

6. Philip Bobbitt, *The Shield of Achilles: War, Peace, and the Course of History* (New York: Anchor Books, 2002), 333; see Bobbitt's chapter 7, "From Kingly States to Territorial States: 1648–1766," for an insightful synthesis of this history and its literature. On war and statebuilding in European history, see Carlo M. Cipolla, *Guns, Sails and Empires: Technological Innovation and the Early Phases of European Expansion, 1400–1700* (New York: Pantheon Books, 1966); Paul Kennedy, *The Rise and Fall of the Great Powers: Economic Change and Military Conflict from 1500 to 2000* (New York: Random House, 1987); Andrew Lambert, *War at Sea in the Age of Sail, 1650–1850* (Washington, DC: Smithsonian Institution, 2005); William H. McNeill, *The Pursuit of Power: Technology, Armed Force, and Society since A.D. 1000* (Chicago: University of Chicago Press, 1982); Geoffrey Parker, *The Military Revolution, Military Innovation and the Rise of the West, 1500–1800* (New York: Cambridge University Press, 1990); Bruce Porter, *War and the Rise of the State* (New York: Free Press, 1994); John Brewer, *The Sinews of Power: War, Money and the English State, 1688–1783* (New York: Knopf, 1989); Pollack, *War, Revenue, and State Building.*

In *The Rise of the West: A History of the Human Community* (Chicago: University of Chicago Press, 1991), 576, William H. McNeill argues that the history of Western civilization displayed "a deeply rooted pugnacity" and "European warlikeness," contrasting it with Chinese, Muslim, and Hindu society.

On the global outbreak of wars and major violent encounters from 1840 to 1880 (numbering 177, according to the Global Wars Project) and their impact on state alignments, see Michael Geyer and Charles Bright, "Global Violence and Nationalizing Wars in Eurasia and America: The Geopolitics of War in the Mid-Nineteenth Century," *Comparative Studies in Society and History* 38 (1996): 619–657.

7. Tilly, *Coercion, Capital, and European States*, 26. Mann, *Sources of Social Power*, 2:87, concurs. On the dynamics of statebuilding, also see Bobbitt, *Shield of Achilles*, chs. 5–9; Brewer, *Sinews of Power*; Poggi, *The State*, 33, ch. 6.

8. Finer, *History of Government*, 3:13–14.

9. The application of these conceptual references is integrated with a factual historical narrative in this book. Paul Kleppner, *The Cross of Culture: A Social Analysis of Midwestern Politics, 1850–1900* (New York: Free Press, 1970), 4, explains this

order of analysis: "We can't ask *why* until we first have systematically identified *what* happened and *who* caused it to happen."

10. Robert E. Lipsey, "U.S. Foreign Trade and the Balance of Payments, 1800–1913," in *The Cambridge Economic History of the United States*, vol. 2, ed. Stanley L. Engerman and Robert E. Gallman (Cambridge: Cambridge University Press, 2000); Bernard DeVoto, *The Course of Empire* (Boston: Houghton Mifflin, 1952), ch. 10, esp. 404; David Potter, *People of Plenty: Economic Abundance and the American Character* (Chicago: University of Chicago Press, 1954); Carl N. Degler, *Out of Our Past: The Forces that Shaped Modern America* (New York: Harper & Row, 1970), 109, 129–134; Gavin Wright, "The Origins of America's Industrial Success," *American Economic Review* 80 (1990): 651–668.

Thomas C. Cochran, *Challenges to American Values: Society, Business and Religion* (New York: Oxford University Press, 1985), 8–9, argues that the opportunities offered by the "geographical environment . . . were dominant in shaping the traditional American values and social practices."

11. D. W. Meinig, "The Continuous Shaping of America: A Prospectus for Geographers and Historians," *American Historical Review* 83 (December 1978): 1205. Meinig executed his plan in *The Shaping of America: A Geographical Perspective on 500 Years of History*, 4 vols. (New Haven, CT: Yale University Press, 1986–2004). William Cronon provides a model for tracing the spatial diffusion of social and economic relationships in *Nature's Metropolis: Chicago and the Great West* (New York: Norton, 1991). Also see Susan Schulten, *Mapping the Nation: History and Cartography in Nineteenth-Century America* (Chicago: University of Chicago Press, 2012).

12. On the influence of weather (meteorological conditions) on economies, see John D. Post, *The Last Great Subsistence Crisis in the Western World* (Baltimore: Johns Hopkins University Press, 1977); John D. Post, "Climate Change and Historical Explanation," *Journal of Interdisciplinary History* 10 (1979): 291–301; John D. Post, "The Mortality Crises of the Early 1770s and European Demographic Trends," *Journal of Interdisciplinary History* 21 (Summer 1990): 29–62; Ted Steinberg, *Acts of God: The Unnatural History of Natural Disaster in America* (New York: Oxford University Press, 2000).

13. James R. Akerman, "The Structuring of Political Territory in Early Printed Atlases," *Imago Mundi* 47 (1995): 138–154; Michael Biggs, "Putting the State on the Map: Cartography, Territory and European State Formation," *Comparative Studies in Society and History* 41, 2 (1999): 374–405; Jeremy Black, *Maps and Politics* (Chicago: University of Chicago Press, 1997), esp. 76–77, 112; J. B. Hartley, "Power and Legitimization in the English Geographic Atlases of the Eighteenth Century," in *Images of the World: The Atlas through History*, ed. John A. Wolter and Ronald Grim (Washington, DC: Library of Congress, 1997), esp. 181–192; Matthew H. Edney, *Mapping an Empire: The Geographic Construction of British India, 1765–1843* (Chicago: Chicago University Press, 1997), esp. ch. 1; John Rennie Short, *Representing the Republic: Mapping the United States, 1600–1900* (London: Reaktion, 2001), esp. 19; William H. Goetzmann, *Exploration and Empire: The Explorer and the Scientist in the Winning of the American West* (New York: Norton, 1966), a

prize-winning study that tracks the routes of explorers and scientists with numerous detailed maps.

14. For an overview of America's military tradition, see Allan R. Millett and Peter Maslowski, *For the Common Defense* (1994; reprint, New York: Free Press, 2012). Also see Fred Anderson and Andrew Cayton, *The Dominion of War: Empire and Liberty in North America, 1500–2000* (New York: Viking, 2005); John K. Mahon, *History of the Militia and the National Guard* (New York: Macmillan, 1983); Russell F. Weigley, *History of the United States Army*, enlarged ed. (Bloomington: Indiana University Press, 1984). Despite its age, Walter Millis's *Arms and Men: A Study in American Military History* (New York: G. P. Putnam's Sons, 1956) remains insightful. Thomas Patterson et al., *American Foreign Relations*, 5th ed. (Belmont, CA: Wadsworth, 2009), reviews the geopolitical context of military activity and cites the relevant literature. Subsequent chapters cite historical studies of American policing.

15. Theda Skocpol et al., "Patriotic Partnerships: Why Great Wars Nourished American Civil Voluntarism," in Katznelson and Shefter, *Shaped by War and Trade*, 141. On war and American statebuilding, see Marc Allen Eisner, *From Warfare State to Welfare State: World War I, Compensatory State Building, and the Limits of the Modern Order* (University Park: Pennsylvania State University Press, 2000); Robert Higgs, *Crisis and Leviathan: Critical Episodes in the Growth of American Government* (New York: Oxford University Press, 1987).

16. Hugh Rockoff, *America's Economic Way of War* (Cambridge: Cambridge University Press, 2012), esp. ch. 2.

17. See, for example, Kevin H. O'Rourke, "The Worldwide Economic Impact of the Revolutionary and Napoleonic Wars," *Journal of Global History* 1 (2006): 123–149; Eisner, *From Warfare State to Welfare State.*

18. Patrick O'Brien, "Central Government and the Economy, 1688–1815," in *The Economic History of Britain since 1700*, vol. 1, ed. Roderick Floud and Deirdre McCloskey (Cambridge: Cambridge University Press, 1994), 205–241; Jan DeVries, *Economy of Europe in an Age of Crisis, 1600–1750* (Cambridge: Cambridge University Press, 1976), ch. 8; Kennedy, *Rise and Fall of Great Powers*, xxii, 17, 197, 439; Mann, *Sources of Social Power*, 2:723; Hans Pohl, "Economic Powers and Political Powers in Early Modern Europe: Theory and History," *Journal of European Economic History* 28, 1 (Spring 1999): 139–168; Porter, *War and Rise of the State,* ch. 2; Tilly, *Coercion, Capital, and European States*, ch. 2.

Overviews of American economic development and its linkage to long nineteenth-century governance include Engerman and Gallman, *Cambridge Economic History of the United States*, vols. 1 and 2; Jonathan Hughes, *The Governmental Habit: Economic Controls from Colonial Times to the Present* (Princeton, NJ: Princeton University Press, 1991); Paul A. C. Koistinen, *Beating Plowshares into Swords: The Political Economy of American Warfare, 1606–1865* (Lawrence: University Press of Kansas, 1996); Paul A. C. Koistinen, *Mobilizing for Modern War: Political Economy of American Warfare, 1865–1919* (Lawrence: University Press of Kansas, 1997).

On the stages of economic development, see Harry N. Scheiber, "Government and the American Economy: Three Stages of Historical Change, 1790–1941," in *Essays from the Lowell Conference on Industrial History*, ed. Robert Weible (Lowell, MA: Lowell Conference, 1981), 128–144.

19. On economic fluctuations during the colonial and early national periods, see John J. McCusker and Russell R. Menard, *The Economy of British America, 1607–1789* (Chapel Hill: University of North Carolina Press, 1985), table 3.4; Post, *Last Great Subsistence Crisis*. For later years, see Joseph H. Davis, "An Improved Annual Chronology of U.S. Business Cycles since the 1790s," Working Paper 11157 (National Bureau of Economic Research, 2005); Peter Temin, "The Causes of American Business Cycles: An Essay in Economic Historiography," Working Paper 6692 (National Bureau of Economic Research, 1998). Also see David Hackett Fischer, *The Great Wave: Price Revolutions and the Rhythm of History* (New York: Oxford University Press, 1996).

20. There is an extensive literature on crisis and change. Here is a sampling: Jack A. Goldstone, *Revolution and Rebellion in the Early Modern World* (Berkeley: University of California Press, 1991); Peter Gourevitch, *Politics of Hard Times: Comparative Responses to Industrial Economic Crisis* (Ithaca, NY: Cornell University Press, 1986); Eric Jones, *The European Miracle: Environments, Economies and Geopolitics in the History of Europe and Asia*, 3rd ed. (New York: Cambridge University Press, 2003), esp. 22–23; Emmanuel LeRoy Ladurie, *Territory of the Historian* (Chicago: University of Chicago Press, 1973), 111–131; Mann, *Sources of Social Power*, 2:221–226; Randolph Starn, "Historians and 'Crisis,'" *Past and Present* 52 (1971): 3–22; Sidney Verba, "Sequences and Development," in *Crises and Sequences in Political Development*, ed. Leonard Binder et al. (Princeton, NJ: Princeton University Press, 1971); Charles P. Kindleberger, *Manias, Panics, and Crashes: A History of Financial Crises* (1978; reprint, New York: Basic Books, 2000). "A crisis is a break, a discontinuity, a moment in time," according to Fernard Braudel and F. Spooner, "Prices in Europe from 1450 to 1750," in *The Cambridge Economic History of Europe*, vol. 4 (London: Cambridge University Press, 1967), 430.

For a model of how depression impacts American government, see Ballard C. Campbell, "Tax Revolts and Political Change," *Journal of Policy History* 10 (1998): 153–178, reprinted in David Brian Robertson, *Loss of Confidence: Politics and Policy in the 1970s* (University Park: Pennsylvania State University Press, 1998); Campbell, *Growth of American Government*, 51–52, 295–300. Also see Larry Neal, "A Shocking View of Economic History," *Journal of Economic History* 60 (2000): 317–334; Robert Sobel, *Panic on Wall Street: A History of America's Financial Disasters* (New York: Macmillan, 1968); Douglas Hibbs, "Political Parties and Macro-Economic Policy," *American Political Science Review* 71 (1977): 1467–1487.

21. For long-term economic cycles and their impact, see Fischer, *Great Wave*; Andrew Tylecote, *The Long Wave in the World Economy: The Current Crisis in Historical Perspective* (New York: Routledge, 1991).

22. Ian Tyrell argues: "It can be said that the United States exhibited strong evidence of a nation in sentiment and ideology before it developed a strong state apparatus." Ian Tyrell, "Making Nations/Making States: American Historians in the Context of Empire," *Journal of American History* 86, 3 (December 1999): 1023. On nationalism in the United States, see Hans Kohn, *American Nationalism: An*

Interpretive Essay (New York: Collier Books, 1957); Wilbur Zelinsky, *Nation into State: The Shifting Symbolic Foundations of American Nationalism* (Chapel Hill: University of North Carolina Press, 1988).

23. D. W. Meinig, *Continental America, 1800–1867* (New Haven, CT: Yale University Press, 1993), 400; see in general 399–417. Also see D. W. Meinig, *Atlantic America, 1492–1800* (New Haven, CT: Yale University Press, 1986), 447, 45–53. The classic statement of regional influences on American history is Frederick Jackson Turner, *The Significance of Section in American History* (New York: Henry Holt, 1932). Also see Michael Conzen, "American Homelands: A Dissenting View," in *Homelands: A Geography of Culture and Place across America*, ed. Richard L. Nostrand and Lawrence E. Estaville (Baltimore: Johns Hopkins University Press, 2002), 238–271. An interesting essay on how regional cultures persist over time and influence political attitudes is Colin Woodard's *American Nations: A History of the Eleven Rival Regional Cultures of North America* (New York: Viking, 2011).

24. Helpful in defining these issues are Benedict Anderson, *Imagined Communities: Reflections on the Origins and Spread of Nationalism* (London: Verso, 1983); Joan Hoff, *Law, Gender and Injustice: A Legal History of Women* (New York: New York University Press, 1991); Alexander Keysaar, *The Right to Vote* (New York: Basic Books, 2000); James H. Kettner, *The Development of American Citizenship, 1608–1870* (Chapel Hill: University of North Carolina Press, 1978); Rogers M. Smith, *Civic Ideals: Conflicting Visions of Citizenship in United States History* (New Haven, CT: Yale University Press, 1997).

25. In addition to the socioeconomic development of the United States, the primary attributes of statebuilding traced in this book are territorial expansion, including the creation of governmental entities (local, state, and congressional representation); ideology, both popular and legal-constitutional; statutory actions at all levels of government; public finance (expenditures, revenue, debt, budgeting); administrative capacity, including the size and authority of the "bureaucracy"; and coercive actions, a domain that encompasses wars and military actions, policing, and criminal justice, including capital punishment and incarceration. The appendix to this book contains tables of policy enactments for selected states and cities.

Howard H. Lenter, "The Concept of the State," *Comparative Politics* 16 (April 1984): 368, lists ten components of a "complex political organization."

26. A useful overview of federalism and its literature is David Brian Robertson, *Federalism and the Making of America* (New York: Routledge, 2012). Classic overviews are W. Brooke Graves, *American Intergovernmental Relations: Their Origins, Historical Development, and Current Status* (New York: Charles Scribner's Sons, 1964), and Harry N. Scheiber, "The Condition of American Federalism: A Historian's View," in *The New Federalism*, ed. Frank Smallwood (Hanover, NH: Public Affairs Center, Dartmouth College, 1967).

2. *Rise of the Little Republics*

1. D. W. Meinig, *Atlantic America, 1492–1800* (New Haven, CT: Yale University Press, 1986), esp. 23–154; Richard Hofstadter, *America at 1750: A Social Portrait*

(New York: Knopf, 1971), ch. 1; Charles O. Paullin, *Atlas of the Historical Geography of the United States* (Washington, DC: Carnegie Institute, 1932), plates 22–25; Seymour I. Schwartz and Ralph E. Ehrenberg, *The Mapping of America* (New York: H. N. Abrams, 1980). A lyrical geographic portrait on North America appears in Bernard DeVoto, *The Course of Empire* (Boston: Houghton Mifflin, 1952), 403–410.

2. By the mid-seventeenth century many North Americans probably had pocket-sized atlases such as John Gibson's *Atlas Minimus or, a New Set of Pocket Maps of the Several Empires, Kingdoms, and States of the Known World* (London, 1758). See Martin Bruckner, *The Geographic Revolution in Early America: Maps, Literacy and National Identity* (Chapel Hill: University of North Carolina Press, 2006); Niall Ferguson, *Empire: The Rise and Demise of the British World Order and the Lessons for Global Power* (New York: Basic Books, 2002), 6, 38, 79; Andrew Lambert, *War at Sea in the Age of Sail, 1650–1850* (Washington, DC: Smithsonian Books, 2005).

3. Paul Kennedy, *The Rise and Fall of the Great Powers* (New York: Random House, 1987), 76–86; John Brewer, *Sinews of Empire: War, Money, and the English State, 1688–1783* (Cambridge, MA: Harvard University Press, 1988); Peter Mathias, *First Industrial Nation: An Economic History of Britain* (New York: Charles Scribner's Sons, 1969), table 12; P. J. Marshall, ed., *The Oxford History of the British Empire*, vol. 2, *The Eighteenth Century* (New York: Oxford University Press, 1998), 100, 337.

4. Robert E. Lipsey, "U.S. Trade and Balance of Payments," in *Cambridge Economic History of the United States*, ed. Stanley L. Engerman (New York: Cambridge University Press, 2008), 2:722–723.

5. Paul Studenski and Herman E. Krooss, *Financial History of the United States* (New York: McGraw-Hill, 1963), 17.

6. On population growth as the primary source of economic growth, see Engerman, *Cambridge Economic History of the United States*, 1:226–227.

7. Henry Nash Smith, *Virgin Land: The American West as Symbol and Myth* (New York: Vintage, 1950), ch. 11; Charles Sellers, *The Market Revolution: Jacksonian America, 1815–1846* (New York: Oxford University Press, 1991), ch. 1; Ray Allen Billington, *Westward Expansion: A History of the American Frontier* (New York: Macmillan, 1960), 134–136.

8. Ron Chernow, *George Washington: A Life* (New York: Penguin, 2010), 43–45, 153, 197–210, 244, 643–658, chs. 13, 45; Fred Anderson and Andrew Cayton, *The Dominion of War* (New York: Viking, 2005), chs. 3, 4; Lawrence Martin, ed., *The George Washington Atlas* (Washington, DC: US George Washington Bicentennial Commission, 1932), plate 48.

9. Bruckner, *Geographic Revolution in Early America*, 56–57, 95.

10. Barnet Schester, *George Washington's America: A Biography through His Maps* (New York: Walker, 2010), 10, 275–280 (reproduction of his "Yale" atlas); H. W. Brands, *The First American: The Life and Times of Benjamin Franklin* (New York: Doubleday, 2000), 244, 296–297, 306, 323, 336–337; John Rennie Short, *Representing the Republic: Mapping the United States, 1600–1900* (London: Reaktion Books, 2001), 56, 92, 93; Thomas Jefferson, *Notes on Virginia* [1781] (original English edition published 1785; reprint, New York: Harper & Row, 1964); Douglas

L. Wilson, "Thomas Jefferson's Library and the French Connection," *Eighteenth-Century Studies* 26 (1993): 681–682; David McCullough, *John Adams* (New York: Simon & Schuster, 2001), 149; Lucille Griffith, *The Virginia House of Burgesses, 1750–1774* (University: University of Alabama Press, 1968), 131; Bruckner, *Geographic Revolution in Early America*, ch. 2.

11. Henry Popple's *America Septentrionalis, a Map of the British Empire in America* (1733) was "the first large-scale printed map of North America," according to Short, *Representing the Republic*, 59. Popple, clerk to the Board of Trade, was assigned the task of producing a British cartographic version of North America; the Board of Trade sent a copy to each governor of the American colonies.

12. Short, *Representing the Republic*, 93; McCullough, *John Adams*, 148; Brands, *First American*, 335, 348; Dumas Malone, *Jefferson the Virginian* (Boston: Little Brown, 1948), 218, 334–335; Gordon S. Wood, *Empire of Liberty: A History of the Early Republic, 1789–1815* (New York: Oxford University Press, 2009), 357, 773; Smith, *Virgin Land*, 146.

13. Richard Hofstadter, *America at 1750: A Social Portrait* (New York: Knopf, 1970), chs. 1, 5; Meinig, *Atlantic America*, 245–250, 426; Engerman, *Cambridge Economic History of the United States*, 1:249–250; Daniel J. Boorstin, *The Americans: The Colonial Experience* (New York: Vintage Books, 1958), books 1 and 2.

14. Meinig, *Atlantic America*, 303–306; Jack P. Greene, "Empire and Identity from the Glorious Revolution to the American Revolution," in Marshall, *Oxford History of the British Empire*, 2:212–222; Eliga H. Gould, "A Virtual Nation: Greater Britain and the Imperial Legacy of the American Revolution," *American Historical Review* 104 (1999): 481, 484; Timothy H. Breen, "Ideology and Nationalism on the Eve of the American Revolution: Revisions Once More in Need of Revising," *Journal of American History* 84 (1997): 19–31.

15. Bernard Bailyn, *The Origins of American Politics* (New York: Vintage, 1968), 57, 136, 160.

16. Milton Klein, "Leadership in Colonial and Revolutionary America," in *Law as Culture and Culture as Law*, ed. Hendrick Hartog and William E. Nelson (Madison, WI: Madison House Publishers, 2000), 58–80; Griffith, *Virginia House of Burgesses*, ch. 7. A classic portrait of political leadership in colonial Virginia is Charles S. Sydnor, *Gentlemen Freeholders: Political Practices in Washington's Virginia* (Chapel Hill: University of North Carolina Press, 1952).

17. Jack P. Greene, "Colonial Assemblies," in *Encyclopedia of the American Legislative System*, vol. 1, ed. Joel H. Silby (New York: Charles Scribner's Sons, 1994), 23–37. Greene's bibliography includes many of his own publications on colonial legislatures.

18. Robin L. Einhorn, *American Taxation, American Slavery* (Chicago: University of Chicago Press, 2006), 24–109; H. James Henderson, "Taxation and Political Culture: Massachusetts and Virginia, 1760–1800," *William and Mary Quarterly* 47, 1 (1990): 90–144; Nicolas R. Parrillo, *Against the Profit Motive: The Salary Revolution in American Government, 1780–1940* (New Haven, CT: Yale University Press, 2013), 58–66; Griffith, *Virginia House of Burgesses*, 134, 138–139; John L. Brooke, *The Heart of the Commonwealth: Society and Political Culture in Worces-*

ter County, Massachusetts, 1713–1861 (New York: Cambridge University Press, 1989), ch. 1.

19. Fred Anderson, *A People's Army: Massachusetts Soldiers and Society in the Seven Years War* (New York: Norton, 1974), 41–61; Allan R. Millett and Peter Maslowski, *For the Common Defense: The Military History of the United States of America* (New York: Free Press, 1994), 1–12; Stuart Banner, *The Death Penalty: An American History* (Cambridge, MA: Harvard University Press, 2002), 6–22.

20. James H. Kettner, *The Development of American Citizenship, 1608–1870* (Chapel Hill: University of North Carolina Press, 1978), chs. 4, 5; Rogers M. Smith, *Civic Ideals: Conflicting Visions of Citizenship in United States History* (New Haven, CT: Yale University Press, 1997), ch. 2.

21. Henderson, "Taxation and Political Culture," 94–95, 98; Barry Levy, *Town Born: The Political Economy of New England from Its Founding to the Revolution* (Philadelphia: University of Pennsylvania Press, 2009), chs. 3, 8.

22. DeVoto, *Course of Empire*, 224.

23. Thomas Bender, *A Nation among Nations: America's Place in World History* (New York: Hill & Wang, 2006), 61.

24. Jack P. Greene, *Peripheries and Center: Constitutional Development in the Extended Polities of the British Empire and the United States, 1607–1788* (Athens: University of Georgia Press, 1986).

25. Greene, *Peripheries and Center*, 89, 108, 133.

26. Robert Middlekauff, *The Glorious Cause: The American Revolution, 1763–1789* (New York: Oxford University Press, 1982), chs. 1–11; Jack N. Rakove, *The Beginnings of National Politics: An Interpretative History of the Continental Congress* (Baltimore: Johns Hopkins University Press, 1979), chs. 2, 3.

27. Jack P. Greene, "Colonial History and National History: Reflections on a Continuing Problem," *William and Mary Quarterly* 64 (April 2007): 241.

28. For speculations on British intransigence, see Greene, *Peripheries and Center*, 143; David Hawk, *The Colonial Experience* (Indianapolis: Bobbs-Merrill, 1966), 568. Also see Brewer, *Sinews of Power.*

29. Bailyn, *Origins of American Politics*, 153–158.

30. Peter G. Thomas, *Lord North* (New York: St. Martin's Press, 1976), 71–91; Eliga H. Gould, *The Persistence of Empire: British Political Culture in the Age of the American Revolution* (Chapel Hill: University of North Carolina Press, 2000), ch. 4, 190–193; Anderson, *People's Army*, 61; James K. Martin and Mark E. Lender, *A Respectable Army: The Military Origins of the Republic 1763–1789* (Wheeling, IL: Harlan Davidson, 2006), 19, 26; Millett and Maslowski, *For the Common Defense*, 9, 56, 58.

3. *Forging a National State*

1. Robert A. Gross, *The Minutemen and Their World* (New York: Hill & Wang, 1976); Robert Middlekauff, *The Glorious Cause* (New York: Oxford University Press, 1982), chs. 11–13; Eric Nellis, *The Long Road to Change: America's Revolution, 1750–1820* (Peterborough, ON: Broadview Press, 2007), ch. 3.

2. David McCullough, *1776* (New York: Simon & Schuster, 2005), chs. 1–3.

3. Middlekauff, *Glorious Cause*, 322–323; David McCullough, *John Adams* (New York: Simon & Schuster, 2001), 92; Jack N. Rakove, *The Beginnings of National Politics: An Interpretive History of the Continental Congress* (Baltimore: Johns Hopkins University Press, 1979), 97, 312.

4. Morton Borden and Penn Borden, *The American Tory* (New York: Prentice Hall, 1972), 23; Catherine S. Crary, ed., *The Price of Loyalty: Tory Writings from the Revolutionary Era* (New York: McGraw-Hill, 1973).

5. Rakove, *Beginnings of National Politics*, ch. 5.

6. McCullough, *1776*, 134–148.

7. Pauline Maier, *American Scripture: Making the Declaration of Independence* (New York: Knopf, 1997).

8. In addition to coastal locations, the war spread west of the Appalachian Mountains. Patrick Griffin, *American Leviathan: Empire, Nation, and Revolutionary Frontier* (New York: Hill & Wang, 2007).

9. McCullough, *1776*, 293. Ron Chernow, *George Washington: A Life* (New York: Penguin, 2010), skillfully describes Washington's personal qualities. See also Don Higginbotham, "Military Leadership in the American Revolution," in *War and Society in Revolutionary America: The Wider Dimensions of Conflict* (Columbia: University of South Carolina Press, 1988), 84–105; James K. Martin and Mark Edward Lender, *A Respectable Army: The Military Origins of the Republic, 1763–1789* (Wheeling, IL: Harlan Davidson, 2006).

10. Ron Chernow, *Alexander Hamilton* (New York: Penguin, 2004), 139.

11. Piers Mackesy, *The War for America, 1775–1783* (Cambridge, MA: Harvard University Press, 1965), 130–133; Middlekauff, *Glorious Cause*, 376, 406, 462, 576–578; Allan R. Millet and Peter Maslowski, *For the Common Defense* (New York: Free Press, 1994), 51; Russell F. Weigley, *History of the United States Army* (Bloomington: Indiana University Press, 1984), 19–21, 29–43.

12. John Richard Alden, *The American Revolution, 1775–1783* (New York: Harper & Row, 1954), 241–245.

13. Paul Koistinen, *Beating Plowshares into Swords: The Political Economy of American Warfare, 1606–1865* (Lawrence: University Press of Kansas, 1996), ch. 2; Curtis P. Nettles, *The Emergence of a National Economy, 1775–1815* (New York: Harper & Row, 1962), chs. 1, 2; Walter Nugent, *Structures of American History* (Bloomington: Indiana University Press, 1981), 24–28. According to Nettles, *Emergence of a National Economy*, 11–12, Massachusetts issued 1,554 commissions for privateering, and Congress issued 550.

14. John W. Shy, *A People Numerous and Armed: Reflections on the Military Struggle for American Independence* (Lansing: University of Michigan Press, 1990), 177; see also 173–177, 237–242; Koistinen, *Beating Plowshares into Swords*, 20–21; John K. Mahon, *History of the Militia and the National Guard* (New York: Macmillan, 1983), ch. 3; Walter Millis, *Arms and Men: A Study in American Military History* (New York: G. P. Putnam's Sons, 1956), 23, 35–37.

15. Francois Furstenberg, "The Significance of the Trans-Appalachian Frontier in Atlantic History," *American Historical Review* 113 (June 2008): 655; Richard W.

Van Alstyne, *Empire and Independence: The International History of the American Revolution* (New York: John Wiley & Sons, 1967), 1, 8, ch. 8; H. W. Brands, *The First American: The Life and Times of Benjamin Franklin* (New York: Doubleday, 2000), 335, 348; Henry Nash Smith, *Virgin Land: The American West as Symbol and Myth* (New York: Vintage, 1950), 139–149.

16. D. W. Meinig, *Atlantic America, 1492–1800* (New Haven, CT: Yale University Press, 1986), 311–323; James H. Kettner, *The Development of American Citizenship, 1608–1870* (Chapel Hill: University of North Carolina Press, 1978), chs. 7, 8; Nettles, *Emergence of a National Economy*, 140; Chernow, *George Washington*, 538, 594–595. For a fine portrait of the trials of a loyalist, see James S. Leamon, *The Reverend Jacob Bailey, Maine Loyalist: For God, King, and for Self* (Amherst: University of Massachusetts Press, 2012), chs. 5, 6. Also see James W. Ely Jr., *The Guardian of Every Other Right: A Constitutional History of Property Rights* (New York: Oxford University Press, 1998), 32–38.

17. Marc Kruman, *Beyond Authority and Liberty: State Constitution Making in Revolutionary America* (Chapel Hill: University of North Carolina Press, 1997); Gordon S. Wood, *The Creation of the American Republic, 1776–1787* (Chapel Hill: University of North Carolina Press, 1969); Roscoe L. Ashley, *The American Federal State* (New York: Macmillan, 1902), appendixes E and G.

An ongoing debate is whether the states preceded the formation of a national government. My reading of this question is twofold. First, there is no simple answer because the choice between options (states or Congress) requires assumptions about the identification of a viable government. The political situation was fluid in 1775 and 1776, as colonists sought effective organizations to resist an invading army. A reciprocal interaction occurred between local (state, town, county) and national (congressional) bodies—all elected in some fashion—during this crisis period. Second, the issue is largely irrelevant because the American national state has always contained state and national components, with a history of continuous negotiation between parts of the polity.

18. Peter S. Onuf, "The Origins and Early Development of State Legislatures," in *Encyclopedia of the American Legislative System*, ed. Joel H. Silbey (New York: Scribner, 1994), 1:175–194; Kruman, *Beyond Authority and Liberty*, chs. 3–7.

19. Roger H. Brown, *Redeeming the Republic: Federalists, Taxation, and the Origins of the Constitution* (Baltimore: Johns Hopkins University Press, 1993), 12–13; Koistinen, *Beating Plowshares into Swords*, ch. 2; Allan Nevins, *American States during and after the Revolution, 1775–1789* (New York: Macmillan, 1924), ch. 9; Paul Studenski and Herman E. Krooss, *Financial History of the United States* (New York: McGraw-Hill, 1963), ch. 3.

Generalizations about state and municipal actions face several constraints. The large number of subnational governments (eventually fifty states and several thousand municipalities) and the widening scope of their policy activity, coupled with gaps in the archival records and scholarship on the subject, impede a comprehensive reconstruction of past governance. Readers must understand that some statements about subnational governments are informed approximations. The state and municipal actions listed in the appendix suggest patterns of subnational statutory enactments and judicial rulings.

20. Gordon S. Wood, *Empire of Liberty: A History of the Early Republic, 1789–1815* (New York: Oxford University Press, 2009), 39–48; Richard D. Brown, *Modernization: The Transformation of American Life, 1600–1865* (New York: Hill & Wang, 1976), ch. 4.

21. Marcus Cunliffe, *George Washington: Man and Monument* (Boston: Little Brown, 1958), ch. 1; Nevins, *American States*, 555; Chernow, *George Washington*, ch. 38, 627; Barry Schwartz, *George Washington: The Making of an American Symbol* (New York: Free Press, 1987), chs. 2, 3; Andrew Robertson, "Look on This Picture . . . and on This! Nationalism, Localism, and Partisan Images in the United States, 1787–1820," *American Historical Review* 106 (October 2001): 1268.

22. Wood, *Creation of the American Republic*, 393–394.

23. Charles T. Bullock, *Historical Sketch of the Finances and Financial Policy of Massachusetts from 1780 to 1905* (New York: American Economic Association, 1907), 9–20; Cathy D. Matson and Peter S. Onuf, *A Union of Interests: Political and Economic Thought in Revolutionary America* (Lawrence: University Press of Kansas, 1990), 37–47; Nevins, *American States*, ch. 9; Brown, *Redeeming the Republic*, ch. 3, 83–84, 123–135; Van Beck Hall, *Politics without Parties: Massachusetts, 1780–1791* (Pittsburgh: University of Pittsburgh Press, 1972), ch. 4; James Madison to Thomas Jefferson, January 22, 1786, in *The Papers of James Madison*, ed. Robert A. Rutland and William M. E. Rachal (Chicago: University of Chicago Press, 1973), 8:479. Madison referred to "the pestilent effects of paper money" in Federalist 44 and pushed tirelessly for restrictions on state legislatures that enacted such "evils."

24. Alexander Hamilton, Federalist 6, in *The Federalist*, ed. Jacob E. Cooke (Cleveland, OH: Meridian Books, 1961), 35; James Madison to Thomas Jefferson, March 18, 1786, in Rutland and Rachal, *Papers of James Madison*, 8:502; Samuel McKee, ed., *Alexander Hamilton's Papers on Public Credit, Commerce and Finance* (New York: Liberal Arts Press, 1957), 9.

25. John J. McCusker and Russell R. Menard, *The Economy of British America, 1607–1789* (Chapel Hill: University of North Carolina Press, 1985), 63 (table 3.4), 367–375; Cathy Matson, "The Revolution, the Constitution, and the New Nation," in *The Cambridge Economic History of the United States*, ed. Stanley L. Engerman and Robert E. Gallman (New York: Cambridge University Press, 1996), 1:375–381; Nettles, *Emergence of a National Economy*, ch. 3; Richard B. Morris, *The Forging of the Union* (New York: Harper & Row, 1987), ch. 6, 259–265; Gordon C. Bjork, "The Waning of the American Economy: Independence, Market Changes, and Economic Development," *Journal of Economic History* 24 (1964): 541–560; Oscar Handlin and Mary Flug Handlin, *Commonwealth: A Study of the Role of Government in the American Economy: Massachusetts, 1774–1861* (Cambridge, MA: Harvard University Press, 1969), 35–42; David P. Szatmary, *Shays' Rebellion: The Making of an Agrarian Insurrection* (Amherst: University of Massachusetts Press, 1980), esp. ch. 2; Alan Schaffer, "Virginia's 'Critical Period,'" in *Old Dominion: Essays for Thomas Perkins Abernathy*, ed. Darrett Bruce Rutman (Charlottesville: University of Virginia Press, 1964); John H. Flannagan Jr., "Trying Times: Economic Depression in New Hampshire, 1781–1789" (Ph.D. diss., Georgetown University, 1972), 5–81.

26. David M. Ludlum, *Early American Winters*, vol. 1, *1604–1820* (Boston:

American Meteorological Society, 1966), 151–154; David Hackett Fischer, *The Great Wave: Price Revolutions and the Rhythm of History* (New York: Oxford University Press, 1996), 142; Rutland and Rachal, *Papers of James Madison*, 8:11, 16, 346, 514; Chernow, *George Washington*, 624, 648–649, 658, 665, 702, 723, 737. Washington noted, "A great Hoar frost and ice at least ⅛ of an inch thick" on April 16, 1785, in *The Diaries of George Washington*, ed. Donald Jackson and Dorothy Twohig (Charlottesville: University of Virginia Press, 1978), 4:121. H. H. Lamb, *Climate: Present, Past and Future*, vol. 2, *Climate History and the Future* (New York: Barnes & Noble, 1978), 835, cites the winters of 1783–1784 and 1784–1785 as the coldest on record since 1738 in the eastern United States.

27. On the historical recurrence of depressions and tax revolts, see Ballard C. Campbell, "Tax Revolts and Political Change," *Journal of Policy History* 10 (1998): 153–178; Ballard C. Campbell, "Depressions and Politics in American History," *Long Term View: A Journal of Informed Opinion* 4 (1999): 13–21.

28. Brown, *Redeeming the Republic*, 41–49, 94–96, 110–122, 126; Flannagan, "Trying Times," esp. 177–180; Merrill Jensen, *The New Nation: A History of the United States during the Confederation, 1781–1789* (New York: Vintage, 1950), 238–240; Nettles, *Emergence of a National Economy*, 83–88; Szatmary, *Shays' Rebellion*, 57, 83, 124–126; Norman K. Risjord, *Chesapeake Politics, 1781–1800* (New York: Columbia University Press, 1978), ch. 6; Morris, *Forging of the Union*, 157–158 (on New York). Also see Cathy Matson, "Liberty, Jealousy, and Union: The New York Economy in the 1780s," in *New York in the Age of the Constitution, 1775–1800*, ed. Paul A. Gilje and William Pencak (Rutherford, NJ: Fairleigh Dickinson University Press, 1992). State tax efforts in the late 1780s are reported in Max M. Edling, *A Revolution in Favor of Government: Origins of the United States Constitution and the Making of the American State* (New York: Oxford University Press, 2003), tables 1–4.

29. Szatmary, *Shays' Rebellion*, 128.

30. Chernow, *George Washington*, 695; Morris, *Forging of the Union*, 266; James T. Flexner, *George Washington and the New Nation* (Boston: Little Brown, 1969), 98–105.

31. On the depression and tax revolts as accelerators of the movement to hold a constitutional convention, see Fred Anderson and Andrew Cayton, *The Dominion of War* (New York: Viking, 2005), 185–186; Brown, *Redeeming the Republic*, esp. 160–167, 85–90; Matson and Onuf, *Union of Interests*, chs. 3, 4; Morris, *Forging of the Union*, 265; Nettles, *Emergence of a National Economy*, 60, 89–92; Nevins, *American States*, 570; Schaffer, "Virginia's 'Critical Period,'" 159; Szatmary, *Shays' Rebellion*, 120–128. Wood, *Creation of the American Republic*, chs. 10, 11, esp. 404, 465, expressed an alternative view. Also see Woody Holton, *Unruly Americans and the Origins of the Constitution* (New York: Hill & Wang, 2007), chs. 9–11.

32. Brown, *Redeeming the Republic*, 179–180.

33. For overviews of the Constitutional Convention, see Middlekauff, *Glorious Cause*, ch. 25; Merrill Jensen, *The Making of the Constitution* (Princeton, NJ: Van Nostrand, 1964); Don Higginbotham, "George Washington's Contribution to American Constitutionalism," in *War and Society in Revolutionary America*; Don

Higginbotham, "War and State Formation in Revolutionary America," in *Empire and Nation: The American Revolution in the Atlantic World*, ed. Eliga H. Gould and Peter Onuf (Baltimore: Johns Hopkins University Press, 2005). Papers of the key figures of the period are available online at http://founders.archives.

34. Brown, *Redeeming the Republic*, sees conservatives' desire to counteract the states' refusal to pay war debts with specie as the central dynamic behind the writing of the Constitution (3–41, 49, 179–180); Federalists, he argues, inserted the term "justice" in the preamble of the Constitution as a rebuke to laws that paid creditors in deflated paper money (227).

35. See James Madison to Thomas Jefferson, May 8, 1784, October 3, 1785, January 22 and March 18, 1786, and James Madison to George Washington, December 9, 1785, in Rutland and Rachal, *Papers of James Madison*, vol. 8. In the parlance of eighteenth-century political theory, "faction" meant a conspiratorial group that used corrupt means to gain power and install a despotism. Today, the term refers to an interest group or a group within a political party.

36. Chernow, *Alexander Hamilton*, ch. 13. Hamilton wrote fifty-one of the Federalist essays, Madison wrote twenty-nine, and John Jay wrote five.

37. Richard Henry Lee, "Letters from the Federal Farmer," October 8, 1787, in *The Complete Anti-Federalist*, ed. Herbert J. Storing (Chicago: University of Chicago Press, 1981), 2:227.

38. Charles A. Beard, *An Economic Interpretation of the Constitution of the United States* (New York: Macmillan, 1913), esp. 188. My assessment of Beard's contention about the writers of the Constitution rests on several theorems. First, among any group of legislators, there are likely to be several motivations influencing policy decisions; seldom, if ever, do individuals within a large body think exactly alike. Moreover, individual lawmakers may be motivated by several factors related to a specific issue. Second, there is no way to prove that the economic motives of decisionmakers predominated in their policy deliberations. Simply put, overt behavior does not disclose motivation, which originates in the psychological recesses of the human mind. Third, logic suggests that most individuals do not consciously act contrary to their *personal* economic interests, assuming that decisionmakers clearly recognize that how they vote will have a significant impact on their interests. These axioms apply to the debate in the states over ratification of the Constitution in 1787 and 1788. Fourth, legislators (and delegates) tend to explain their decisions publicly with reasoning designed to influence political outcomes, which may or may not overlap with their private feelings. It is well known among students of Congress that speeches on the chamber floor are often framed to please the speaker's constituents.

39. Jackson Turner Main, *The Anti-Federalists: Critics of the Constitution, 1781–1788* (Chapel Hill: University of North Carolina Press, 1961); Forrest McDonald, *The Formation of the American Republic, 1776–1790* (Baltimore: Penguin Books, 1965); Brown, *Redeeming the Republic*; Edling, *Revolution in Favor of Government*; Wood, *Creation of the American Republic*, chs. 10–13.

40. Jack P. Greene, *Peripheries and Center: Constitutional Development in the Extended Polities of the British Empire and the United States, 1607–1788* (Athens:

University of Georgia Press, 1986), ch. 9; Daniel J. Boorstin, *The Americans: The National Experience* (New York: Vintage, 1965), 394–395.

41. Henry Steele Commager, "Leadership," in *American History and the Social Sciences*, ed. Edward N. Saveth (New York: Free Press, 1964), 258–273; Chernow, *Alexander Hamilton*, 52–53.

42. James Huston, "The American Revolutionaries, the Political Economy of Aristocracy, and the American Concept of the Distribution of Wealth, 1765–1900," *American Historical Review* 98 (October 1993): 1079–1105, offers an instructive explanation of the link among aristocracy, wealth, and republican political theory in the Revolutionary era. He argues that a government controlled by wealthy aristocrats was bound to turn a republic into a tyrannous oligarchy. Aristocrats gained their wealth by governmental favoritism and special privileges, and they used their wealth to corrupt politics, leading down the path to despotism.

43. S. E. Morison, *Sources and Documents Illustrating the American Revolution and the Formation of the Federal Constitution* (New York: Oxford University Press, 1929), 313.

44. Jensen, *Making of the Constitution*, chs. 11–13; Brown, *Redeeming the Republic*, ch. 14; McDonald, *Formation of the American Republic*, 7, 8; Main, *Anti-Federalists*; Hall, *Politics without Parties*, ch. 9; Flannagan, "Trying Times," ch. 6; Greene, *Peripheries and Center*, ch. 9; Storing, *Complete Anti-Federalist*, esp. vol. 1; Chernow, *Alexander Hamilton*, 260–269.

45. Brutus argued in the *New York Journal* (October 1787) that the new government was a complete government, not a confederation. Storing, *Complete Anti-Federalist*, 1:365, 391.

4. *Geographic and Economic Expansion*

1. On Jefferson's empire of liberty, see Gordon S. Wood, *Empire of Liberty: A History of the Early Republic, 1789–1815* (New York: Oxford University Press, 2009), 357, 376; Peter Gay, "The Enlightenment," in *Comparative Approach to American History*, ed. C. Vann Woodward (1968; reprint, New York: Oxford University Press, 1997), 44; Bernard DeVoto, *The Course of Empire* (Boston: Houghton Mifflin, 1952), 396.

2. Thomas G. Patterson, J. Garry Clifford, and Kenneth J. Hagan, *American Foreign Relations* (Boston: Houghton Mifflin, 2000), 1:100; Frank Freidel and Norman Pollack, eds., *Builders of American Institutions: Readings in United States History* (Chicago: Rand McNally, 1963), 184, 186 ("Annexation of Texas"); James D. Richardson, comp., *Messages and Papers of the Presidents* (Washington, DC: Bureau of National Literature and Art, 1910), 5:3336, 3339.

3. S. E. Finer, *The History of Government* (New York: Oxford University Press, 1997), 1:8; Merle E. Curti, *The Roots of American Loyalty* (New York: Columbia University Press, 1946), 40–41; William H. Goetzmann, *When the Eagle Screamed: The Romantic Horizon in American Diplomacy, 1800–1860* (New York: John Wiley & Sons, 1966), xiv–xv, 104–105. In *Cohen v. Virginia* (1821), Chief Justice John Marshall referred to the American states as "members of one great empire." Stanley

I. Kutler, ed., *The Supreme Court and the Constitution: Readings in American Constitutional History*, 2nd ed. (New York: Norton, 1977), 48.

4. Richardson, *Messages and Papers of the Presidents*, 3:2231.

5. I use the term "antebellum era" to refer to the years between 1790 and 1860.

6. D. W. Meinig, *Continental America, 1800–1867* (New Haven, CT: Yale University Press, 1993), 18–23, pt. I, ch. 9.

7. B. R. Mitchell, *International Historical Statistics* (New York: Palgrave Macmillan, 2003), volumes for *Europe, Asia and Africa*, and *Americas*; David Landes, *Wealth and Poverty of Nations: Why Some Are so Rich and Some so Poor* (New York: Norton, 1998), 232; Angus Maddison, *The World Economy: A Millennial Perspective* (Paris: OECD, 2001), tables A1-c, A2-c, A3-c.

8. A useful review of these themes is Meinig, *Continental America*, 3, 197–211.

9. Daniel J. Boorstin, *The Americans: The National Experience* (New York: Random House, 1965), ch. 32; Reginald Horsman, "The Dimensions of an 'Empire for Liberty': Expansion and Republicanism, 1775–1825," *Journal of the Early Republic* 9, 1 (September 1989): 1–20; Meinig, *Continental America*, 214–217; Robert H. Wiebe, *The Opening of American Society* (New York: Knopf, 1984), 133–138; Paul Frymer, *Building an American Empire: The Era of Territorial and Political Expansion* (Princeton, NJ: Princeton University Press, 2017).

10. Ron Chernow, *George Washington: A Life* (New York: Penguin, 2010), 672.

11. Wood, *Empire of Liberty*, 286, ch. 10; DeVoto, *Course of Empire*, ch. 10, esp. 411, 430. Robert Lee, "Accounting for Conquest: The Price of the Louisiana Purchase of Indian Country," *Journal of American History* 103, 4 (March 2017): 924, estimates that the purchase of 222 land cessions from Native Americans cost $2.6 billion in nominal terms.

12. DeVoto, *Course of Empire*, chs. 10, 11, esp. 397, 424, 527; Wood, *Empire of Liberty*, 374–382.

13. The story of American penetration of the Far West is traced in Goetzmann, *When the Eagle Screamed*; William H. Goetzmann, *Exploration and Empire: The Explorer and the Scientist in the Winning of the American West* (New York: Norton, 1966), chs. 1–9; Meinig, *Continental America*; John Rennie Short, *Representing the Republic: Mapping the United States 1600–1900* (London: Reaktion Books, 2001), chs. 5–7.

14. On the popularity of geography textbooks, see Short, *Representing the Republic*, 14–17.

15. On the idea of "natural" boundaries of the United States, see Meinig, *Continental America*, 211–212. Transcontinental railroad predictions are from George H. Douglas, *All Aboard: The Railroad in American Life* (New York: Paragon House, 1992), 97–98; James A. Ward, *Railroads and the Character of America, 1820–1887* (Knoxville: University of Tennessee Press, 1986), 46, 48, 96; Goetzmann, *Exploration and Empire*, 265.

16. Meinig, *Continental America*, 128–158.

17. Daniel Walker Howe, *What Hath God Wrought: The Transformation of America, 1815–1848* (New York: Oxford University Press, 2007), 686–688. The

"reannexation" of Texas derives from the region's cession to Mexico in the treaty of 1819.

18. Ray Allen Billington, *The Far Western Frontier, 1830–1860* (New York: Harper & Row, 1956), ch. 7.

19. Polk left little information that explains his interest in expanding the United States. He died in 1849. On his motivations concerning Oregon, Texas, and the West, see Charles Sellers, *James K. Polk: Continentalist, 1843–1846* (Princeton, NJ: Princeton University Press, 1966), ch. 6, esp. 232; Goetzmann, *When the Eagle Screamed*, chs. 3, 4, esp. 239; Meinig, *Continental America*, 145; Kenneth J. Hagan, *The People's Navy: The Making of American Sea Power* (New York: Free Press, 1991), 132–137; Howe, *What Hath God Wrought*, 766–767. Generally, see Frederick Merk, *Manifest Destiny and Mission in American History* (New York: Knopf, 1963).

20. Frederick Merk, "Dissent in the Mexican War," in *Dissent in Three American Wars*, ed. S. E. Morison et al. (Cambridge, MA: Harvard University Press, 1970), 44.

21. Michael F. Holt, *The Rise and Fall of the Whig Party: Jacksonian Politics and the Onset of the Civil War* (New York: Oxford University Press, 1999), 247–255; Merk, *Manifest Destiny*, chs. 4, 5.

22. Meinig, *Continental America*, 458.

23. Stephen J. Rockwell, *Indian Affairs and the Administrative State in the Nineteenth Century* (New York: Cambridge University Press, 2010), 11–12, gives a range of between 600,000 and 1.8 million Amerindians.

24. Meinig, *Continental America*, pt. I, ch. 5; Francis Prucha, *The Great Father: The United States Government and the American Indians* (Lincoln: University of Nebraska Press, 1984); Malcom J. Rohrbough, *Trans-Appalachian Frontier: People, Societies and Institutions, 1775–1850* (Bloomington: Indiana University Press, 2008); Richard White, *The Middle Ground: Indians, Empires, and Republics in the Great Lakes Region, 1650–1815* (Cambridge: Cambridge University Press, 1991); Paul VanDevelder, *Savages and Scoundrels: The Untold Story of America's Road to Empire through Indian Territory* (New Haven, CT: Yale University Press, 2009), esp. ch. 6; Andrew Cayton, "Separate Interests and the Nation-State: The Washington Administration and the Origins of Regionalism in the Trans-Appalachian West," *Journal of American History* 79 (June 1992): 39–67.

25. Joel Dorman Steele and Esther Baker Steele, *A Brief History of the United States* (1871; reprint, New York: American Book Co., 1912), 12–15.

26. Frymer, *Building an American Empire*, 36–40.

27. In addition to the original thirteen states, Vermont, Kentucky, Tennessee, Maine (originally part of Massachusetts), Texas, West Virginia (originally part of Virginia), Alaska, and Hawaii did not possess a public domain.

28. James C. Scott, *Seeing Like a State: How Certain Schemes to Improve the Human Condition Have Failed* (New Haven, CT: Yale University Press, 1998), ch. 1, discusses the motives and implications of state-imposed schemes of systematic measurement and data archiving.

29. A readable account of federal land policy is Everett Dick, *The Lure of the Land: A Social History of the Public Land from the Articles of Confederation to the New Deal* (Lincoln: University of Nebraska Press, 1970). Roughly a quarter of

the public domain disposed of in the fifty states by 1960 occurred via the homestead law. Patricia Nelson Limerick, *Legacy of Conquest: The Unbroken Past of the American West* (New York: Norton, 1987), ch. 2, esp. 58, 67–68, captures Americans' passion to own property, how US policy helped them get it, and the significance of land distribution to American history.

30. On settlement, see Billington, *Far Western Frontier*; Rohrbough, *Trans-Appalachian Frontier*, 158; Meinig, *Continental America*, 457–458, esp. figs. 27 and 28, which display the paths of migration.

31. The states form the institutional building blocks of representation in the national legislature (House and Senate) and are the units for the selection of presidential electors.

32. Meinig, *Continental America*, pt. II, esp. figs. 68 and 71.

33. William Cronon, *Nature's Metropolis: Chicago and the Great West* (New York: Norton, 1991), offers a superb portrait of how Chicago integrated agricultural and resource industries and their marketing and transportation dimensions. Oscar Handlin, *Boston's Immigrants* (1941; reprint, New York: Atheneum, 1968), 73–82, provides a classic view of Boston and identifies manufacturing and other new enterprises.

34. Harold Underwood Faulkner, *American Economic History*, 8th ed. (New York: Harper & Brothers, 1960), 28.

35. For profiles of the land, see Paul Gates, *The Farmer's Age: Agriculture, 1815–1860* (New York: Harper & Row, 1960); Meinig, *Continental America*, pt. II, chs. 3–6. Diana Muir, *Reflections on Bullough's Pond: Economy and Ecosystem in New England* (Hanover, NH: University Press of New England, 2000), is informative about New England's natural endowment.

On the importance of land to American economic development, see Robert E. Gallman, "Economic Growth and Structural Change in the Long Nineteenth Century," in *Cambridge Economic History of the United States*, vol. 2, ed. Stanley L. Engerman and Robert E. Gallman (New York: Cambridge University Press, 2008), 1–56; Robert E. Lipsey, "U.S. Foreign Trade and the Balance of Payments, 1800–1913," in Engerman and Gallman, *Cambridge Economic History*, 2:685–732; Stanley Lebergott, "The Demand for Land: The United States, 1820–1860," *Journal of Economic History* 45 (June 1985): 181–212; Peter Temin, "Free Land and Federalism," *Journal of Interdisciplinary History* 21, 3 (Winter 1991): 371–390; Gavin Wright, *The Political Economy of the Cotton South* (New York: Norton, 1978), esp. 45–47, 72; John Agnew, *The United States in the World Economy: A Regional Geography* (New York: Cambridge University Press, 1987), 11–12.

36. Ballard C. Campbell, *American Wars* (New York: Facts on File, 2012), 244–245.

37. The discussion of the spread of agriculture and the growth of industries related to natural resources in this and the next several paragraphs is based largely on Gates, *Farmer's Age*; Meinig, *Continental America*; Faulkner, *American Economic History*; Engerman and Gallman, *Cambridge Economic History of the United States*, vol. 2, esp. chs. 1, 8; Cronon, *Nature's Metropolis*; Muir, *Reflections on Bullough's Pond*. See also James Norris, *Frontier Iron* (Madison: State Historical Society of Wisconsin, 1964).

38. For an incisive portrait of agriculture in the antebellum period, see Gates, *Farmer's Age*; Wright, *Political Economy of the Cotton South*, esp. 55–62, 90–91.

39. Evan Cornog, *The Birth of Empire: DeWitt Clinton and the American Experience, 1769–1828* (New York: Oxford University Press, 1998), 107–169; Carter Goodrich, *Government Promotion of American Canals and Railroads, 1800–1890* (New York: Columbia University Press, 1960), esp. chs. 1–4; Julius Rubin, "An Imitative Public Improvement: The Pennsylvania Mainline," in *Canals and American Economic Development*, ed. Carter Goodrich (New York: Columbia University Press, 1960), 67–106; Harry N. Scheiber, *Ohio Canal Era: A Case Study of Government and the Economy* (Athens: Ohio University Press, 1969).

40. George Rogers Taylor, *The Transportation Revolution, 1815–1860* (New York: Harper & Row, 1951); Albert Fishlow, "Transportation in the Nineteenth and Early Twentieth Centuries," in Engerman and Gallman, *Cambridge Economic History of the United States*, 2:542–543; Meinig, *Continental America*, pt. II, chs. 8, 9; T. J. Stiles, *The First Tycoon: The Epic Life of Cornelius Vanderbilt* (New York: Knopf, 2009), chs. 3–6, 11; John L. Brooke, *The Heart of the Commonwealth: Society and Political Culture in Worcester County, Massachusetts* (New York: Cambridge University Press, 1989), ch. 9.

41. Winifred B. Rotherberg, "The Invention of American Capitalism," in *Engines of Enterprise: An Economic History of New England*, ed. Peter Temin (Cambridge, MA: Harvard University Press, 2000), esp. 93; Mansel G. Blackford and K. Austin Kerr, *Business Enterprise in American History* (Boston: Houghton Mifflin, 1994), ch. 3.

42. Thomas C. Cochran, "The Business Revolution," *American Historical Review* 79 (1974): 1449–1466, emphasizes the importance of "social structure and culture values" in promoting economic growth. Also see Walter Licht, *Industrializing America: The Nineteenth Century* (Baltimore: Johns Hopkins University Press, 1995), esp. 90; Wiebe, *Opening of American Society*, 151–152, 219–221, on banking and personalized credit.

43. Meinig, *Continental America*, pt. II, chs. 8–12. Also see Licht, *Industrializing America*, chs. 1–3; Muir, *Reflections on Bullough's Pond*, esp. ch. 10; Jonathan Prude, *The Coming of Industrial Order: Town and Factory Life in Rural Massachusetts, 1810–1860* (New York: Cambridge University Press, 1983); Mansel Blackford, *A History of Small Business in America* (New York: Twayne, 1991), ch. 1.

44. I agree with Wiebe, *Opening of American Society*, ch. 13, on this point concerning the industrial transformation.

45. Gallman, "Economic Growth and Structural Change in the Long Nineteenth Century," esp. table 1.6. The sparseness of data about the macrodimensions of the antebellum economy cautions against a literal acceptance of quantitative indicators of national income; a more prudent approach is to read the data as a basis for reasoned conjecture.

5. *Nationalism and Public Policy*

1. Ron Chernow, *George Washington: A Life* (New York: Penguin, 2010), 45–58.

2. Hans Kohn, *Nationalism: Its Meaning and History* (New York: Collier, 1955), 9–10.

3. Benedict Anderson, *Imagined Communities: Reflections on the Origins and Spread of Nationalism* (London: Verso, 1983); Eric J. Hobsbawm, *Nations and Nationalism since 1780: Programme, Myth, Reality* (Cambridge: Cambridge University Press, 1990); David Potter, "Historian's Use of Nationalism," *American Historical Review* 67 (July 1962): 936. Also instructive on modern nationalism is S. E. Finer, *The History of Government*, vol. 3, *Empires, Monarchies and the Modern State* (New York: Oxford University Press, 1997), 1447, 1547–1553, 1649; Robert H. Wiebe, *Who We Are: A History of Popular Nationalism* (Princeton, NJ: Princeton University Press, 2001).

4. David Waldstreicher, *In the Midst of Perpetual Fetes: The Making of American Nationalism, 1776–1820* (Chapel Hill: University of North Carolina Press, 1997); Susan-Mary Grant, *North over South: Northern Nationalism and American Identity in the Antebellum Era* (Lawrence: University Press of Kansas, 2000).

5. Mary P. Ryan, *Civic Wars: Democracy and Public Life in the American City during the Nineteenth Century* (Berkley: University of California Press, 1997), ch. 2.

6. Quoted in Wilbur Zelinsky, *Nation into State: The Shifting Symbolic Foundations of American Nationalism* (Chapel Hill: University of North Carolina Press, 1988), 15.

7. Michael Kraus and David D. Joyce, *The Writing of American History* (Norman: University of Oklahoma Press, 1985), 92–97; Barbara J. Mitnick, ed., *George Washington: American Symbol* (New York: Hudson Hills Press, 1999), 9–108; Zelinsky, *Nation into State*, 186, 215–220.

8. Howard H. Martin, "The Fourth of July Oration," *Quarterly Journal of Speech* 44 (December 1958): 393–401. My comments on the development of nationalism in antebellum America rely heavily on Daniel J. Boorstin, *The Americans: The National Experience* (New York: Random House, 1965), pt. 7, esp. 308–323 on oratory; Martin Bruckner, *The Geographic Revolution in Early America: Maps, Literacy and National Identity* (Chapel Hill: University of North Carolina Press, 2006); Henry Steele Commager, "The Search for a Usable Past," *American Heritage* 16 (February 1965): 4–9, 90–96; Merle E. Curti, *The Roots of American Loyalty* (New York: Columbia University Press, 1946), ch. 16; D. W. Meinig, *Continental America, 1800–1867* (New Haven, CT: Yale University Press, 1993); Paul C. Nagel, *One Nation Indivisible: The Union in American Thought, 1776–1861* (New York: Oxford University Press, 1964); Zelinsky, *Nation into State*; in addition to the works cited in notes 10–13 below.

9. Meinig, *Continental America*, 413.

10. On schools and schooling, literacy, and publications, see Lawrence A. Cremin, *American Education: The National Experience, 1783–1876* (New York: Harper & Row, 1980), esp. chs. 5, 9, 11, 14; Daniel Walker Howe, *What Hath God Wrought: The Transformation of America, 1815–1848* (New York: Oxford University Press, 2007), 226–229, chs. 12, 16; Louis B. Wright, *Culture on the Moving Frontier* (New York: Harper & Bros., 1955); Meinig, *Continental America*, 415–416.

The Massachusetts Historical Society was founded in 1791, the New York Historical Society in 1804, the Boston Athenaeum in 1807, the Boston Public Library in 1852, and the New York Public Library in 1854.

11. Richard R. John, *Spreading the News: The American Postal System from Franklin to Morse* (Cambridge, MA: Harvard University Press, 1995); Brian Balogh, *A Government out of Sight: The Mystery of National Authority in Nineteenth-Century America* (New York: Cambridge University Press, 2009), 220–231.

12. Curti, *Roots of American Loyalty*, ch. 2; Ray Allen Billington, ed., *Frontier and Section: Selected Essays of Frederick Jackson Turner* (Englewood Cliffs, NJ: Prentice-Hall, 1961), 51, 56, 86–138.

13. John Rennie Short, *Representing the Republic: Mapping the United States, 1600–1900* (London: Reaktion, 2001), 17–18, 121–157; David Bjelajac, *American Art: A Cultural History* (London: Laurence King, 2000), 192–197; James H. Merrell et al., *American Conversations* (Boston: Pearson, 2013), ch. 12. Barbara Novak, *Nature and Culture: American Landscape Painting, 1825–1875* (1980; reprint, New York: Oxford University Press, 2007), 13, claims that nature worship was more strongly nationalistic in America than anywhere else.

14. Howe, *What Hath God Wrought*, 698; James A. Ward, *Railroads and the Character of America, 1820–1887* (Knoxville: University of Tennessee Press, 1986), chs. 1, 2; Frank Friedel and Norman Pollack, eds., *Builders of American Institutions: Readings in United States History* (Chicago: Rand McNally, 1963), 187–188; D. W. Meinig, *Transcontinental America, 1850–1915* (New Haven, CT: Yale University Press, 1998), 4–8.

15. For the suggestion that socioeconomic conditions impact politics, see Robert H. Wiebe, *The Opening of American Society: From the Adoption of the Constitution to the Eve of Disunion* (New York: Knopf, 1984); Robert H. Wiebe, *Self Rule: A Cultural History of American Democracy* (Chicago: University of Chicago Press, 1995), chs. 1–3. Charles Sellers, *The Market Revolution: Jacksonian America, 1815–1846* (New York: Oxford University Press, 1991), ch. 1, emphasizes the influence of religious evangelicalism and the rise of democratic politics. See also Alexander Keyssar, *The Right to Vote: The Contested History of Democracy in the United States* (New York: Basic Books, 2000), chs. 1–3.

Key statements on the development of political parties are William N. Chambers and Walter Dean Burnham, eds., *The American Party Systems: Stages of Political Development* (New York: Oxford University Press, 1967); the essays by Ronald P. Formisano and William G. Shade in Paul Kleppner, ed., *The Evolution of American Electoral Systems* (Westport, CT: Greenwood, 1981); Joel H. Silbey, *American Political Nation, 1838–1893* (Stanford, CA: Stanford University Press, 1991); and the essays by Ronald Formisano, David Waldstreicher, Joel Silbey, and Michael Holt in Byron E. Shafer and Anthony J. Badger, eds., *Contesting Democracy: Substance and Structure in American Political History, 1775–2000* (Lawrence: University Press of Kansas, 2001).

16. Wiebe, *Self Rule*, 83; William N. Chambers, "Parties and Nation-Building in America," in *Political Parties and Political Development*, ed. J. LaPalombaa and M. Weiner (Princeton, NJ: Princeton University Press, 1966). On the connection among citizenship, politics, and nationalism through the War of 1812, see Waldstreicher, *In the Midst of Perpetual Fetes*; Andrew Robertson, "Look on This Picture . . . and on This: Nationalism, Localism, and Partisan Images of Otherness in the United States,

1787–1820," *American Historical Review* 106 (October 2001): 1263–1280; Nicole Eustace et al., "Interchange: The War of 1812," *Journal of American History* 99 (September 2012): 520–555.

17. Rogers M. Smith, *Civic Ideals: Conflicting Visions of Citizenship in U.S. History* (New Haven, CT: Yale University Press, 1997), chs. 4–8. On the conflict over national ideals, see Curti, *Roots of American Loyalty*, ch. 6.

18. Western New York and northern New England (Vermont, New Hampshire, and Maine) is an example of a regional cluster of states.

19. Frederick Jackson Turner, "Sections and Nation," *Yale Review* (1922), in Billington, *Frontier and Section*, 136–153. A recent Turnerian approach to American politics is Colin Woodard, *American Nations: A History of the Eleven Rival Regional Cultures of North America* (New York: Viking, 2011). On regionalism, see D. W. Meinig, *Atlantic America, 1492–1800* (New Haven, CT: Yale University Press, 1986), 400–405, 444–453; Meinig, *Continental America*, pt. II. In the latter (ch. 3), Meinig identifies four regions in the early nineteenth century: New England; Virginia, Kentucky, and the southern Midwest; the midlands of central Ohio, Indiana, and Illinois; and South Carolina and its extension into the Gulf coast. Waldstreicher, *In the Midst of Perpetual Fetes*, ch. 5, sees distinct versions of nationalism in New England, the South, and the West.

20. William H. Goetzmann and William N. Goetzmann, *The West of the Imagination* (New York: Norton, 1986), esp. pt. 2, ch. 13; William H. Truettner, "Ideology and Image: Justifying Westward Expansion," in *The West as America: Reinterpreting Images of the Frontier, 1820–1920*, ed. William H. Truettner (Washington, DC: Smithsonian Institution Press, 1991), 27–53; Patricia Hills, "Picturing Progress in the Era of Westward Expansion," in Truettner, *West as America*, 97–147.

21. Bryan F. LeBeau, *Currier and Ives: America Imagined* (Washington, DC: Smithsonian Institution Press, 2001).

22. US Census Office, *Seventh Census of the United States*, vol. 4, *Compendium* (Washington, DC: Robert Armstrong, 1853), 152. Illiteracy among whites aged twenty years and older was 1.88 percent in New England and 9.22 in the South.

23. Joseph A. Conforti, *Imagining New England: Explorations of Regional Identity from the Pilgrims to the Mid-Twentieth Century* (Chapel Hill: University of North Carolina Press, 2001), 202.

24. Gordon S. Wood, *Empire of Liberty: A History of the Early Republic, 1789–1815* (New York: Oxford University Press, 2009), 732–738; Grant, *North over South*, 50. Richard D. Brown, *Modernization: The Transformation of American Life, 1600–1865* (Prospect Heights, IL: Waveland Press, 1976), ch. 6, describes the South as the region least in step with trends of modernization.

25. Boorstin, *Americans*, 170, ch. 22; Gavin Wright, *The Political Economy of the Cotton South* (New York: Norton, 1978), chs. 2–4; William R. Taylor, *Cavalier and Yankee: The Old South and American National Character* (New York: Doubleday, 1961); Grant, *North over South;* Waldstreicher, *In the Midst of Perpetual Fetes*; John L. Brooke, "Cultures of Nationalism, Movements of Reform, and the Composite-Federal Polity: From Revolutionary Settlement to Antebellum Crisis," *Journal of the Early Republic* 29 (Spring 2009): 1–33.

Excellent comparative analyses of interstate and intrastate variations are James H. Broussard, *The Southern Federalists, 1800–1816* (Baton Rouge: Louisiana State University Press, 1978), on Virginia, North Carolina, and South Carolina; Norman K. Risjord, *Chesapeake Politics, 1781–1800* (New York: Columbia University Press, 1978), on Virginia, Maryland, and North Carolina. The intensifying conflict between sectionalism and nationalism is explored in chapter 7.

26. Meinig, *Continental America*, ch. 13. Liam Riordan, *Many Identities, One Nation: The Revolution and Its Legacy in the Mid-Atlantic* (Philadelphia: University of Pennsylvania Press, 2007), closely examines the connection of religion, race, and localism to personal identities and politics in the Delaware River region (1770s–1830s). On local identities in the Midwest, see James H. Madison, *Heart Land: Comparative Histories of the Midwestern States* (Bloomington: Indiana University Press, 1988).

27. Turner, "Sections and Nation," 152.

28. Report no. 107, House of Representatives, 22nd Congress, 2nd session (February 25, 1833), 3.

29. On the origin and development of federalism, see Boorstin, *Americans*, pt. 8, 395, who cites the diffusion of power in colonial America and its collective relation to the British government as the origin of American federalism; David Brian Robertson, *Federalism and the Making of America* (New York: Routledge, 2012); Ballard C. Campbell, *The Growth of American Government*, rev. ed. (Bloomington: Indiana University Press, 2015), esp. citations beginning on 349. On the fragility of a consensus about the union during the early republic, see Nagel, *One Nation Indivisible*, ch. 1; Michael Kammen, *A Machine that Would Go of Itself: The Constitution in American Culture* (New York: Vintage, 1986), 51–67, chs. 3, 4; William G. Shade, *Democratizing the Old Dominion: Virginia and the Second Party System, 1824–1861* (Charlottesville: University Press of Virginia, 1996), chs. 2, 3, 320, 241.

30. William Anderson, *The Units of Government in the United States: An Enumeration and Analysis* (Chicago: Public Administration Service, 1934), fig. 1; US Bureau of the Census, *Historical Statistics of the United States: Colonial Times to 1970* (Washington, DC: Government Printing Office, 1975), series A43–52. I estimated the number of town and township governments by multiplying the number of counties in the fifteen states that had towns or townships in 1850 by a factor of fifteen subcounty governments per county. My estimate of subcounty governments per county was based on the number of towns in all Wisconsin counties in 1900. In 1900 Wisconsin had 70 counties, 1,045 towns, 115 cities, and 146 villages. Wisconsin Legislative Reference Bureau, *The Wisconsin Bluebook 1968* (Madison: Wisconsin Legislative Reference Bureau, 1968), 89.

31. A very long list of scholars has made this point since the classic portrayal of American federalism by James Bryce, *The American Commonwealth* (London: Macmillan, 1888), esp. chs. 26–28. A fine illustration is Donald U. Pisani, "Promotion and Regulation: Constitutionalism and the American Economy," *Journal of American History* 74 (December 1987): 740–768.

32. Regarding federalism and spatial diversity, Boorstin, *Americans*, 402, observes that "American politics was primarily a by-product of geography."

33. Stephen Skowronek argues that the noncentralized governmental structure of federalism was "most clearly responsible for the distinctive sense of statelessness in our political culture." Stephen Skowronek, *Building a New American State: The Expansion of National Administrative Capacities, 1877–1920* (New York: Cambridge University Press, 1982), 23. Bryce, *American Commonwealth*, 18, observes that America's "double organization" government was "puzzling" to Europeans.

34. Jon C. Teaford, *The Unheralded Triumph: City Government in America, 1870–1900* (Baltimore: Johns Hopkins University Press, 1984), 85–95, 143; Hendrik Hartog, *Public Property and Private Power: The Corporation of the City of New York in American Law, 1730–1870* (Chapel Hill: University of North Carolina Press, 1983), 97–99; Robin L. Einhorn, *Property Rules: Political Economy in Chicago, 1833–1872* (Chicago: University of Chicago Press, 1991); Harold L. Platt, *City Building in the New South: The Growth of Public Services in Houston, Texas, 1830–1915* (Philadelphia: Temple University Press, 1983), 86. Hartog, *Public Property and Private Power*, 97n50, reports that New York State adopted 38 acts affecting New York City between 1786 and 1795, 199 between 1826 and 1835, and 412 between 1846 and 1855.

35. Clay McShane, "Gilded Age Boston," *New England Quarterly* 74 (June 2001): 274–302; sources listed for Massachusetts in the appendix.

36. Charles P. Huse, *The Financial History of Boston* (Cambridge, MA: Harvard University Press, 1916), 366. When considering this and later observations about fiscal activities as indicators of governance, it is important to recognize two critical points. First, the impact of civic action does not reduce solely to fiscal activity, as governmental power touches numerous elements of society. Second, financial data for the nineteenth century, especially related to local governments, are incomplete.

37. Joel Tarr, "The Evolution of Urban Infrastructure in the Nineteenth and Twentieth Centuries," in *Perspectives on Urban Infrastructure*, ed. Royce Hanson (Washington, DC: National Academy Press, 1984), 13–18; Martin Melosi, *The Sanitary City: Urban Infrastructure from Colonial Times to the Present* (Baltimore: Johns Hopkins University Press, 2000), ch. 4, esp. table 4.3; Eric H. Monkkonen, *America Becomes Urban* (Berkeley: University of California Press, 1988), ch. 4; Eric H. Monkkonen, *Police in Urban America, 1860 to 1920* (New York: Cambridge University Press, 1981), esp. appendix, table A.1, on police uniform adoption dates; Sam Bass Warner, *The Private City: Philadelphia in Three Periods of Its Growth* (Philadelphia: University of Pennsylvania Press, 1968), ch. 6.

38. Boorstin, *Americans*, pt. 3; Meinig, *Continental America*, 363–371; Richard C. Wade, *The Urban Frontier* (Chicago: University of Chicago Press, 1959), 314–319, 322–323; Tarr, "Evolution of Urban Infrastructure," 8, 13; William Cronon, *Nature's Metropolis: Chicago and the Great West* (New York: Norton, 1991), 31–41, 295–303, on the great competition between Chicago and St. Louis. On New York constitutional and legal action as a model for other states, see Joseph A. Ranney, *Wisconsin and the Shaping of American Law* (Madison: University of Wisconsin Press, 2017), esp. ch. 3.

39. Important studies of the mercantile and egalitarian phases of state economic policy are L. Ray Gunn, *The Decline of Authority: Public Economic Policy and*

Political Development in New York, 1800–1860 (Ithaca, NY: Cornell University Press, 1988); Oscar Handlin and Mary Handlin, *Commonwealth: A Study of the Role of Government in the American Economy: Massachusetts, 1774–1861* (New York: New York University Press, 1947); Louis Hartz, *Economic Policy and Democratic Thought: Pennsylvania, 1776–1860* (Cambridge, MA: Harvard University Press, 1948); Harry N. Scheiber, "Federalism and the American Economic Order, 1789–1910," *Law and Society Review* 10 (Fall 1975): 58–118; Theodore C. Pease, *The Frontier State, 1818–1848* (Springfield: Illinois Centennial Commission, 1918), 221–232, 317; Colleen A. Dunlavy, *Politics and Industrialization: Early Railroads in the United States and Prussia* (Princeton, NJ: Princeton University Press, 1994); Edward C. Kirkland, *Men, Cities, and Transportation: A Study in New England History 1820–1900*, vol. 1 (Cambridge, MA: Harvard University Press, 1948), 132–137; William G. Shade, "Louis Hartz and the Myth of Laissez Faire," *Pennsylvania History* 59 (July 1992): 256–273. Pisani, "Promotion and Regulation," assesses much of this literature. Also see the citations in chapter 4 concerning internal improvements. The appendix lists sources for the state actions in tables A.2 and A.3. The depression of 1837–1844 is examined in chapter 6.

40. The concept of law as an instrument that releases entrepreneurial energy is from James William Hurst, *Law and Conditions of Freedom in the Nineteenth-Century United States* (Madison: University of Wisconsin Press, 1956). State action, courts, and legal instrumentalism are assessed in William Novak, *The People's Welfare: Law and Regulation in Nineteenth-Century America* (Chapel Hill: University of North Carolina Press, 1996).

41. David B. Davis, "Movement to Abolish Capital Punishment in America, 1787–1861," *American Historical Review* 63 (October 1957): 23–46; Stuart Banner, *The Death Penalty* (Cambridge, MA: Harvard University Press, 2002), chs. 4, 5; David Rothman, *The Discovery of the Asylum* (Boston: Little Brown, 1971), 48–81, 238–254; Carole Shammas, *A History of Household Government in America* (Charlottesville: University of Virginia Press, 2002), ch. 5. The national government did not authorize federal penitentiaries until the 1890s.

42. The militia was also called into New York City for riots in 1806 and 1834. James F. Richardson, *The New York Police: Colonial Times to 1901* (New York: Oxford University Press, 1970), chs. 1–4; Monkkonen, *America Becomes Urban*, ch. 4; Monkkonen, *Police in Urban America*; Charles S. Syndor, *The Development of Southern Sectionalism, 1819–1848* (Baton Rouge: Louisiana State University Press, 1948), 36–37; Allen Steinberg, *The Transformation of Criminal Justice in Philadelphia, 1800–1880* (Chapel Hill: University of North Carolina Press, 1989), 141–142.

43. Cremin, *American Education*, esp. ch. 5; John S. Gilkeson Jr., *Middle-Class Providence, 1820–1940* (Princeton, NJ: Princeton University Press, 1986), 32–35.

44. Gilkeson, *Middle-Class Providence*, 32–35; Richard F. Hamm, *Shaping the Eighteenth Amendment: Temperance Reform, Legal Culture, and the Polity, 1800–1920* (Chapel Hill: University of North Carolina Press, 1995), 19–21, 49; Shammas, *History of Household Government*, 116–120. For state and municipal actions, see tables A.1 (on Massachusetts) and A.2 (sample states) in the appendix.

45. Leonard D. White, *The Federalists: A Study in Administrative History* (New

York: Macmillan, 1948), appendix II; Paul Studenski and Herman E. Krooss, *Financial History of the United States*, 2nd ed. (New York: McGraw-Hill, 1963), chs. 5–11.

46. Ron Chernow, *Alexander Hamilton* (New York: Penguin, 2004), chs. 15–18.

47. Paul A. C. Koistinen, *Beating Plowshares into Swords: The Political Economy of American Warfare, 1606–1865* (Lawrence: University Press of Kansas, 1960), chs. 3, 4; Allan R. Millett and Peter Maslowski, *For the Common Defense: A Military History of the United States* (New York: Free Press, 1994), 99, 124–139; Carter Goodrich, *Government Promotion of American Canals and Railroads, 1800–1890* (New York: Columbia University Press, 1960), chs. 1, 2, 5; Todd Shallat, *Structures in the Stream: Water, Science, and the Rise of the U.S. Army Corps of Engineers* (Austin: University of Texas Press, 1994), chs. 4, 5; Louis C. Hunter, *Steamboats on the Western Rivers: An Economic and Technological History* (Cambridge, MA: Harvard University Press, 1949), 189–192; John G. Burke, "Bursting Boilers and the Federal Power," *Technology and Culture* 7 (Winter 1966): 1–23; Dunlavy, *Politics and Industrialization*, ch. 2; Leonard D. White, *The Jacksonians: A Study in Administrative History, 1829–1861* (New York: Macmillan, 1954), esp. ch. 23.

48. A. Hunter Depree, *Science in the Federal Government: A History of Policies and Activities to 1940* (Cambridge, MA: Harvard University Press, 1957), 36–37, 91–114; William H. Goetzmann, *Exploration and Empire: The Explorer and the Scientist in the Winning of the American West* (New York: Norton, 1966), chs. 7–9; John, *Spreading the News*; Wood, *Empire of Liberty*, 478–479.

49. Margo J. Anderson, *The American Census: A Social History* (New Haven, CT: Yale University Press, 1988), 15, 56, notes that the census at midcentury was "probably" the largest centralized clerical operation of the federal government; John, *Spreading the News*.

50. Balogh, *Government out of Sight*. The governing activities reviewed here and in chapters 9 and 10 render Skowronek's characterization of the nineteenth century as a polity of "courts and parties" a misleading oversimplification. See Skowronek, *Building a New American State*, ch. 2.

6. *The Dynamics of Antebellum Governance*

1. Gordon S. Wood, *Empire of Liberty: A History of the Early Republic, 1789–1815* (New York: Oxford University Press, 2009), ch. 27; Leonard D. White, *The Jeffersonians: A Study in Administrative History, 1801–1829* (New York: Macmillan, 1951), 139, 153, 157, chs. 29, 30.

2. US Census Bureau, *Historical Statistics of the United States: Colonial Times to 1970* (Washington, DC: Government Printing Office, 1975), series R163; Richard R. John, *Spreading the News: The American Postal System from Franklin to Morse* (Cambridge, MA: Harvard University Press, 1995), esp. table 2.1, 104; White, *Jeffersonians*, 328–329.

3. Leonard D. White, *The Jacksonians: A Study in Administrative History, 1829–1861* (New York: Macmillan, 1954), 170; White, *Jeffersonians*, 329.

4. Allan R. Millet and Peter Maslowski, *For the Common Defense: A Military

History of the United States of America (New York: Free Press, 1994), chs. 4, 5; Russell F. Weigley, *History of the United States Army* (Bloomington: Indiana University Press, 1984), chs. 6–9.

5. Matthew A. Crenson, *The Federal Machine: Beginnings of Bureaucracy in Jacksonian America* (Baltimore: Johns Hopkins University Press, 1975), argues that the Jacksonians emphasized the character of administrators over the efficiency of administrative bureaus. White, *Jacksonians*, is the classic study, esp. chs. 20–22, 27. Also see Nicholas R. Parrilo, *Against the Profit Motive: The Salary Revolution in American Government, 1789–1940* (New Haven, CT: Yale University Press, 2013); L. Ray Gunn, *The Decline of Authority: Public Economic Policy and Political Development in New York, 1800–1860* (Ithaca, NY: Cornell University Press, 1988), 89–98.

6. Joseph Cooper, *The Origins of the Standing Committees and the Development of the Modern House* (Houston, TX: Rice University Studies, 1970); Norman K. Risjord, "Congress in the Federalist-Republican Era, 1789–1828," Allan G. Bogue, "The U.S. Congress: The Era of Party Patronage and Sectional Stress, 1829–1881," and William G. Shade, "State Legislatures in the Nineteenth Century," all in *Encyclopedia of the American Legislative System*, vol. 1, ed. Joel H. Silbey (New York: Charles Scribner's Sons, 1994); Ronald P. Formisano, *The Transformation of Political Culture: Massachusetts Parties, 1790s–1840s* (New York: Oxford University Press, 1983), 35–37; Jonathan Prude, *The Coming of Industrial Order: Town and Factory Life in Rural Massachusetts, 1810–1860* (Cambridge: Cambridge University Press, 1983), 161. This discussion is also based on my research into the legislative journals and manuals of all the states.

7. James R. Beniger, *The Control Revolution: Technology and Economic Origins of the Information Society* (Cambridge, MA: Harvard University Press, 1986), chs. 6, 7; Robert J. Gordon, *The Rise and Fall of American Growth: The United States Standard of Living since the Civil War* (Princeton, NJ: Princeton University Press, 2016), ch. 2, esp. 57–59. The outbreak of yellow fever in Philadelphia in 1793 caused many federal workers to abandon the city for several months. The availability of mass-produced pencils was also a post–Civil War development.

8. Police force size is based on Alan Anderson, *The Origins and Resolution of an Urban Crisis: Baltimore, 1890–1930* (Baltimore: Johns Hopkins University Press, 1977), 38; Roger Lane, *Policing the City: Boston, 1822–1905* (Cambridge, MA: Harvard University Press, 1967), 126; James F. Richardson, *The New York Police: Colonial Times to 1901* (New York: Oxford University Press, 1970), 51; Allen Steinberg, *The Transformation of Criminal Justice: Philadelphia, 1800–1880* (Chapel Hill: University of North Carolina Press, 1989), 149; US Census Office, *Seventh Census of the United States*, vol. 4, *Compendium* (Washington, DC: Robert Armstrong, 1853), 142, 147. Data on incarceration facilities (jails and prisons) are not available, but it is a good bet that virtually every county and all but the smallest municipalities had a lockup. Federal employee data are from US Census Bureau, *Historical Statistics of the United States: Colonial Times to 1970* (Washington, DC: Government Printing Office, 1975), series R163, Y308, Y309.

9. Graham H. Stuart, *The Department of State: A History of Its Organization, Procedure and Personnel* (New York: Macmillan, 1949), 22, 36, 69, chs. 7, 8, 11;

James S. Young, *The Washington Community, 1800–1828* (New York: Harcourt, Brace & World, 1966), 29.

10. Ronald L. Hatzenbuehler and Robert L. Ivie, *Congress Declares War: Rhetoric, Leadership, and Partisanship in the Early Republic* (Kent, OH: Kent State University Press, 1983), 21–22; E. B. Smith, *The Presidency of James Buchanan* (Lawrence: University Press of Kansas, 1975), 68–76.

11. Arthur M. Schlesinger Jr., *The Imperial Presidency* (Boston: Houghton Mifflin, 1973), 51; Kenneth J. Hagan, *This People's Navy: The Making of American Sea Power* (New York: Free Press, 1991), chs. 3–5.

12. Patrick Griffin, *American Leviathan: Empire, Nation, and Revolutionary Frontier* (New York: Hill & Wang, 2007), ch. 9; Richard White, *The Middle Ground: Indians, Empires and Republics in the Great Lakes Region, 1650–1815* (Cambridge: Cambridge University Press, 1991), ch. 11; Stephen J. Rockwell, *Indian Affairs and the Administrative States in the Nineteenth Century* (New York: Cambridge University Press, 2010), chs. 1–3.

13. Steinberg, *Transformation of Criminal Justice*, esp. ch. 1; Richardson, *New York Police*, 74.

14. William J. Novak, *The People's Welfare: Law and Regulation in Nineteenth-Century America* (Chapel Hill: University of North Carolina Press, 1996), 12–17, 60, 74, ch. 2, 274n46; Harold M. Hyman and William M. Wiecek, *Equal Justice under Law: Constitutional Development, 1835–1875* (New York: Harper & Row, 1982), chs. 2, 3; Stanley K. Schultz, *Constructing Urban Culture: American Cities and City Planning, 1800–1920* (Philadelphia: Temple University Press, 1989), 53–57. The classic legal treatise on the police power is Thomas M. Cooley, *Constitutional Limitations* (1868; reprint, Boston: Little Brown, 1871), esp. 573–596.

15. Hyman and Wiecek, *Equal Justice under Law*, ch. 2; Melvin I. Urofsky and Paul Finkelman, *A March of Liberty: A Constitutional History of the United States* (New York: Oxford University Press, 2011), ch. 13.

16. Edward S. Corwin, "The Extension of Judicial Review in New York, 1783–1905," *Michigan Law Review* 15 (February 1917): 281–313; Peter J. Galie, *Ordered Liberty: A Constitutional History of New York* (New York: Fordham University Press, 1996), 79–80; James A. Henretta, "The Rise and Decline of 'Democratic-Republicanism': Political Rights in New York and the Several States, 1800–1905," in *Toward a Usable Past: Liberty under State Constitutions*, ed. Paul A. Finkelman and Stephen E. Gottlieb (Athens: University of Georgia Press, 1991), 50–90; Morton Keller, *Affairs of State: Public Life in Late Nineteenth Century America* (Cambridge, MA: Harvard University Press, 1977), 36; Margaret V. Nelson, *A Study of Judicial Review in Virginia, 1789–1928* (New York: Columbia University Press, 1947), 32–35, 202, 205; Hendrik Hartog, *Public Property and Private Power: The Corporation of the City of New York in American Law, 1730–1870* (Chapel Hill: University of North Carolina Press, 1983), 222–229.

17. On the Supreme Court in the antebellum era, see Urofsky and Finkelman, *March of Liberty*; Alfred H. Kelly, Winfred A. Harbison, and Herman Belz, *The American Constitution: Its Origins and Development* (New York: Norton, 1991). Also see Wood, *Empire of Liberty*, 438–455.

18. Herbert Kaufman, *Are Government Organizations Immortal?* (Washington, DC: Brookings Institution, 1976), 48–49.

19. Richard McCormick's contention in "The Party Period and Public Policy: An Exploratory Hypothesis," *Journal of American History* 66 (September 1979): 279–298, that public policy during most of the nineteenth century was largely "distributive" in nature, and Stephen Skowronek's claim in *Building a New American State: The Expansion of National Administrative Capacities* (New York: Cambridge University Press, 1982), ch. 2, esp. 24, that "courts and parties" characterized the antebellum polity, distort the reality of the period. Regulation, taxation, the provision of services, and the use of coercive force were major lines of civic action.

20. Age data are from US Census Bureau, *Historical Statistics of the United States* (1975), series A119–134. Here, the original states include the first thirteen plus Vermont and Maine. Also see Walter Nugent, *Structures of American Social History* (Bloomington: Indiana University Press, 1981), ch. 3.

21. Charles Sellers, *The Market Revolution: Jacksonian America, 1815–1846* (New York: Oxford University Press, 1991), chs. 4, 5, 12; Robert H. Wiebe, *The Opening of American Society: From the Adoption of the Constitution to the Eve of Disunion* (New York: Knopf, 1984), chs. 7, 8, 14, 15. Also see John L. Brooke, *Columbia Rising: Civil Life on the Upper Hudson from the Revolution to the Age of Jackson* (Chapel Hill: University of North Carolina Press, 2010), esp. ch. 2; Carole Shammas, *A History of Household Government in America* (Charlottesville: University of Virginia Press, 2002), chs. 4, 5; Wood, *Empire of Liberty*, ch. 19; Daniel Walker Howe, *What Hath God Wrought: The Transformation of America, 1815–1848* (New York: Oxford University Press, 2007).

22. On panics and depressions in the antebellum era, see B. U. Ratchford, *American State Debts* (Durham, NC: Duke University Press, 1941); Samuel Rezneck, *Business Depressions and Financial Panics: Essays in American Business and Economic History* (New York: Greenwood, 1969); George Rogers Taylor, *The Transportation Revolution, 1815–1860* (New York: Harper & Row, 1951), 372–378, 334–351; Charles Warren, *Bankruptcy in the United States* (Cambridge, MA: Harvard University Press, 1935); and the works cited below in notes 23 and 24.

23. Howe, *What Hath God Wrought*, 146–147, 396; John D. Post, *The Last Great Subsistence Crisis in the Western World* (Baltimore: Johns Hopkins University Press, 1977); Murray N. Rothbard, *The Panic of 1819: Reactions and Policies* (New York: Columbia University Press, 1957); Sellers, *Market Revolution*, chs. 4, 5; Richard C. Wade, *The Urban Frontier* (Chicago: University of Chicago Press, 1959), ch. 6.

24. Carter Goodrich, "The Revulsion against Internal Improvements," *Journal of Economic History* 10 (November 1950): 145–169; Gunn, *Decline of Authority*, esp. chs. 5, 6; Kermit Hall, "Mostly Anchor and Little Sail: The Evolution of American State Constitutions," in Finkelman and Gottlieb, *Toward a Usable Past*; Galie, *Ordered Liberty*, ch. 6; Sellers, *Market Revolution*, 149, 164–171.

25. Carter Goodrich, *Government Promotion of American Canals and Railroads, 1800–1890* (New York: Columbia University Press, 1960), chs. 3, 4. Eugene H. Roseboom, *The Civil War Era, 1850–1873* (Columbus: Ohio State Archaeological

and Historical Society, 1944), 44–45; Harvey H. Segal, "Cycles of Canal Construction," in *Canals and Economic Growth*, ed. Carter Goodrich (New York: Columbia University Press, 1961), 169–215. According to Ray Allan Billington, *The Far Western Frontier* (New York: Harper & Row, 1956), 135, the population of Texas grew from 36,000 in 1836 to 143,000 in 1846.

26. On the rise of the second party system, see Michael F. Holt, *The Political Crisis of the 1850s* (New York: Wiley, 1968), 17–22; Richard P. McCormick, "Political Development and the Second Party System," in *The American Party Systems: Stages of Political Development*, ed. William N. Chambers and Walter D. Burnham (New York: Oxford University Press, 1967), 90–116; Ronald P. Formisano, "Federalists and Republicans: Parties, Yes–System, No," in *The Evolution of American Electoral Systems*, ed. Paul Kleppner (Westport, CT: Greenwood, 1981), 33–76; William G. Shade, "Political Pluralism and Party Development: The Creation of the Modern Party System, 1815–1852," in Kleppner, *Evolution of American Electoral Systems*, 77–112; Joel H. Silbey, *American Political Nation, 1838–1893* (Stanford, CA: Stanford University Press, 1991). For citations to the literature, see Byron E. Shafer and Anthony J. Badger, eds., *Contesting Democracy: Substance and Structure in American Political History, 1775–2000* (Lawrence: University Press of Kansas, 2001). Howe, *What Hath God Wrought*, offers a superb survey of these events.

27. Michael F. Holt, *The Rise and Fall of the American Whig Party: Jacksonian Politics and the Onset of the Civil War* (New York: Oxford University Press, 1999), esp. 154, tables on 72, 1042, 1050, 1108; Michael F. Holt, "The Election of 1840, Voter Mobilization, and the Emergence of the Second American Party System: A Reappraisal of Jacksonian Voting Behavior," in *A Master's Due*, ed. William J. Cooper et al. (Baton Rouge: Louisiana State University Press, 1985), 16–58.

28. Thomas B. Alexander, *Sectional Stress and Party Strength: A Study of Roll-Call Voting Patterns in the United States House of Representatives, 1836–1860* (Nashville, TN: Vanderbilt University Press, 1967); Joel H. Silbey, *The Shrine of Party: Congressional Voting Behavior, 1841–1852* (Pittsburgh: University of Pittsburgh Press, 1967).

Excellent state studies include Lee Benson, *The Concept of Jacksonian Democracy: New York as a Test Case* (Princeton, NJ: Princeton University Press, 1961); Formisano, *Transformation of Political Culture*; Mark W. Kruman, *Parties and Politics in North Carolina, 1836–1865* (Baton Rouge: Louisiana State University Press, 1983); Lex Renda, *Running on the Record: Civil War Era Politics in New Hampshire* (Charlottesville: University Press of Virginia, 1997); William G. Shade, *The Democratization of the Old Dominion: Virginia and the Second Party System, 1824–1861* (Charlottesville: University Press of Virginia, 1996); William G. Shade, *Banks or No Banks: The Money Issue in Western Politics, 1832–1865* (Detroit: Wayne State University Press, 1972).

29. James L. Huston, *The Panic of 1857 and the Coming of the Civil War* (Baton Rouge: Louisiana State University Press, 1987); Eric Foner, *Free Soil, Free Labor, Free Men: The Ideology of the Republican Party before the Civil War* (New York: Oxford University Press, 1970), 24–28, 173, 202–203; Shade, *Banks or No Banks*, 200–223.

The impact of economic depression on parties and politics requires a cautionary note. First, like other aspects of the economy, depression was usually not the sole influence on political behavior. Second, the impact of economic stress on politics varied geographically—among regions and states and even within states—during the nineteenth century. The formation of a broadly nationalized economy was a development of the twentieth century. The economic localism of the antebellum era was a primary reason, but not the sole reason, that economic shocks played out differently in different locations and sometimes at different times. The connection between local economies and depression remains greatly understudied.

30. William N. Chambers, "Party Development and the American Mainstream," in Chambers and Burnham, *American Party Systems*, 3–32; Wiebe, *Opening of American Society*, ch. 16.

31. Suggestive on these points is Daniel W. Howe, "The Evangelical Movement and Political Culture in the North during the Second Party System," *Journal of American History* 77 (March 1991): 1216–1239; Michael Kammen, *A Machine that Would Go of Itself: The Constitution in American Culture* (New York: Vintage, 1987); William G. Shade, "The Myth of Laissez Faire," *Pennsylvania History* 59 (July 1992): 256–273.

32. Brian Balogh, *A Government out of Sight: The Mystery of National Authority in Nineteenth-Century America* (New York: Cambridge University Press, 2009). Several historians have argued that sectional conflict linked to the South's defense of slavery and its fierce states' rights sentiment constrained the exercise of federal powers. See Ronald P. Formisano, "State Development in the Early Republic, 1775–1840," in Shafer and Badger, *Contesting Democracy*, 7–35; Colleen A. Dunlavy, *Politics and Industrialization: Early Railroads in the United States and Prussia* (Princeton, NJ: Princeton University Press, 1994), ch. 3.

33. In addition to the citations in chapters 4 and 5 on the connections among federalism, civic competition, and economic promotion, see D. W. Meinig, *The Shaping of America*, vol. 2, *Continental America, 1800–1867* (New Haven, CT: Yale University Press, 1991), ch. 8; Harry N. Scheiber, "Urban Rivalry and Internal Improvements in the Old Northwest, 1820–1860," *Ohio History* 71 (October 1962): 227–239, 290–292.

34. The use of coercive force alone calls into question the contention that no state existed before the Civil War. To paraphrase Shakespeare, a rose by any other name is still a rose.

7. *The Civil War Builds New States*

1. Michael E. Woods, "What Twenty-First-Century Historians Have Said about the Causes of Disunion: A Civil War Sesquicentennial Review of the Recent Literature," *Journal of American History* 99 (September 2012): 415–439.

2. My selection of factors closely resembles the four "central issues" in Arthur Bestor, "The American Civil War as a Constitutional Issue," *American Historical Review* 69 (1964): 327–352, a classic interpretation of the breakdown of the union. Roy F. Nichols, *Blueprints for Leviathan: American Style* (New York: Atheneum,

1963), suggests that overlapping regional cultures could not overcome territorial and socioeconomic stresses.

3. James D. Richardson, comp., *Messages and Papers of the Presidents* (Washington, DC: National Bureau of Literature and Art, 1910), 208, 1512–1513. This philosophical motif was repeated by presidents in the late nineteenth century. See Ballard C. Campbell, *The Growth of American Government* (Bloomington: Indiana University Press, 2015), 15–16.

4. Les L. Benedict, "Abraham Lincoln and Federalism," *Journal of the Abraham Lincoln Association* 10 (1988–1989): 1–45. Different perspectives on the nature of the federal union were reflected in the use of terms such as "confederate republic" and "compact." For example, in the election of 1852, the three major parties—Democratic, Whig, and Free-Soil—acknowledged that the federal government had limited powers. Arthur M. Schlesinger Jr., *History of American Presidential Elections*, vol. 3 (New York: Chelsea House, 1971), 951, 954, 956.

5. Richard D. Brown, *Modernization: The Transformation of American Life, 1600–1865* (New York: Hill & Wang, 1976).

6. Susan-Mary Grant, *North over South: Northern Nationalism and American Identity in the Antebellum Era* (Lawrence: University Press of Kansas, 2000), chs. 3, 6.

7. Roy Franklin Nichols, *The Disruption of American Democracy* (New York: Macmillan, 1948), is a famous charge against parties. E. E. Schattschneider, *The Semisovereign People: A Realist's View of Democracy in America* (New York: Holt, Rinehart & Winston, 1960), esp. chs. 1, 2, suggests how an expansion of the scope of political conflict changes the calculus for outcomes.

8. The drama and significance of the Civil War have understandably attracted many scholars, and they have crafted some of the finest historical literature. James M. McPherson, *Ordeal by Fire* (New York: McGraw-Hill, 2001), and David H. Donald, Jean Baker, and Michael F. Holt, *The Civil War and Reconstruction* (New York: Norton, 2001), are excellent overviews. My personal favorites on events leading up to the Civil War are Eric Foner, *Free Soil, Free Labor, Free Men: The Ideology of the Republican Party before the Civil War* (New York: Oxford University Press, 1970); Harold M. Hyman and William M. Wiecek, *Equal Justice under Law: Constitutional Development* (New York: Harper & Row, 1982); Michael F. Holt, *The Political Crisis of the 1850s* (New York: Wiley, 1978); James McPherson, *Battle Cry of Freedom: The Civil War Era* (New York: Oxford University Press, 1988); David H. Donald, *Lincoln* (New York: Simon & Schuster, 1995); David M. Potter, *The Impending Crisis, 1848–1861* (New York: Harper & Row, 1976). The volume of scholarship reviewed by Woods, "What Twenty-First-Century Historians Have Said about the Causes of Disunion," demonstrates this continuing interest.

9. Robert W. Fogel, "Toward a New Synthesis on the Role of Economic Issues in the Political Realignment of the 1850s," in *American Economic Development in Historical Perspective*, ed. Thomas Weiss and Donald Schaefer (Stanford, CA: Stanford University Press, 1994), esp. 181–187.

10. Prior to southerners' withdrawal from Congress, the Republicans had 29 Sen-

ate seats and their opponents 37; in the House, Republicans controlled 108 seats and their opponents 129.

11. A provisional constitution was adopted on February 7 and was replaced by a second document on March 11, 1861. Virginia, Arkansas, North Carolina, and Tennessee joined the Confederacy between April 17 and June 8, 1861.

12. Peter B. Knupfer, *The Union as It Is: Constitutional Unionism and Sectional Compromise* (Chapel Hill: University of North Carolina Press, 1991).

13. A conspiracy is a covert plot among two or more schemers to achieve an objective. Conspiratorial plots are often viewed as corrupt, in the sense that individuals use secretive, illegal, or immoral means to gain their ends. Conspiratorial ideas may have apparent links to reality, but as nobody can predict the future with total accuracy, many far-fetched outcomes may seem possible. Potter, *Impending Crisis*, 252; Foner, *Free Soil*, 87–102; William E. Gienapp, *Origins of the Republican Party* (New York: Oxford University Press, 1987), 360–365.

14. Holt, *Political Crisis of the 1850s*, chs.7, 8, esp. 236–242, 258–259; Hyman and Wiecek, *Equal Justice under Law*, 195; William H. Seward, "Irrepressible Conflict," in *The Works of William H. Seward*, vol. 4, ed. George E. Baker (Boston: Houghton, Mifflin, 1884), 299; Foner, *Free Soil*, esp. 87–90, 97–102, chs. 4, 9; Gienapp, *Origins of the Republican Party*, 360–365; Jean H. Baker, *Affairs of Party: The Political Culture of Northern Democrats in the Mid-Nineteenth Century* (Ithaca, NY: Cornell University Press, 1983), 147.

15. David Brion Davis, *The Fear of Conspiracy: Images of Un-American Subversion from the Revolution to the Present* (Ithaca, NY: Cornell University Press, 1971), 105; McPherson, *Battle Cry of Freedom*, 131–132, 241–245; Hyman and Wiecek, *Equal Justice under Law*, 125–139; Potter, *Impending Crisis*, ch. 17, esp. 454.

16. Robert H. Wiebe, *The Opening of American Society* (New York: Knopf, 1984), 356–370; Grant, *North over South*, ch. 6; William R. Taylor, *Cavalier and Yankee: The Old South and American National Character* (Garden City, NY: Anchor Books, 1961), 311–313. It is important to note that opinion was hardly unanimous in the North or the South; the literature that traces the coming of the Civil War demonstrates this diversity.

17. Richardson, *Messages and Papers of the Presidents*, 3336–3339. On European nationalism and its possible influence on Lincoln's conception of nation, see Hans Kohn, *American Nationalism: An Interpretive Essay* (New York: Collier Books, 1957), ch. 3; Carl Degler, "One among Many: The U.S. and National Unification," in *Lincoln: The War President*, ed. Gabor S. Boritt (New York: Oxford University Press, 1992), ch. 4. Michael Geyer and Charles Bright, "Global Violence and Nationalizing Wars in Eurasia and America: The Geopolitics of War in the Mid-Nineteenth Century," *Comparative Studies in Society and History* 38 (1996): 619–657, discuss the political ramifications of 177 wars and armed conflicts that occurred between 1840 and 1880.

18. Richardson, *Messages and Papers of the Presidents*, 3334. An insightful analysis of how circumstances prodded Lincoln and the Republicans toward war is David Potter, "Why Republicans Rejected Both Compromise and Secession," in *The Best American History Essays on Lincoln*, ed. Sean Wilentz (New York: Palgrave Macmil-

lan, 2009), 175–188. Also see Thomas Bender, *A Nation among Nations: America's Place in World History* (New York: Hill & Wang, 2006), 125–138, 156–160.

19. General Joseph Johnston surrendered to General William T. Sherman on April 26, 1865, in North Carolina.

20. White males in uniform represented roughly half the white male population aged fifteen to forty-nine.

21. Russell F. Weigley, *History of the United States Army*, enlarged ed. (Bloomington: Indiana University Press, 1984), ch. 10.

22. Mark R. Wilson, *The Business of the Civil War: Mobilization and the State, 1861–1865* (Baltimore: Johns Hopkins University Press, 2006); Weigley, *History of the United States Army*, 216–232; Paul A. C. Koistinen, *Beating Plowshares into Swords: The Political Economy of American Warfare, 1606–1865* (Lawrence: University Press of Kansas, 1996), ch. 6. Union war mobilization was conducted according to prevailing capitalist and republican norms: the national government purchased goods and services from private enterprises at negotiated prices (as opposed to confiscation and forced labor); Congress and state legislatures imposed taxes via conventional political processes (i.e., elected representatives, votes on fiscal legislation). See Richard Franklin Bensel, *Yankee Leviathan: The Origins of Central State Authority in America, 1859–1877* (New York: Cambridge University Press, 1990), ch. 3, esp. 188, 192.

23. McPherson, *Ordeal by Fire*, 2:26–248; Weigley, *History of the United States Army*, 220–224; Donald, *Lincoln*, 458.

24. Heather Cox Richardson, *The Greatest Nation on the Earth: Republican Economic Policies during the Civil War* (Cambridge, MA: Harvard University Press, 1997), ch. 3; Paul Studenski and Herman E. Krooss, *Financial History of the United States* (New York: McGraw-Hill, 1963), chs. 13, 14; Bensel, *Yankee Leviathan*, ch. 3.

25. Richardson, *Greatest Nation on the Earth*, ch. 4. See Bensel, *Yankee Leviathan*, ch. 4, for a detailed analysis of federal finance during the Civil War and early Reconstruction.

26. Richardson, *Greatest Nation on the Earth*. On party responses to legislative issues during the Civil War and Reconstruction, see Allan G. Bogue, *The Earnest Men: Republicans of the Civil War Senate* (Ithaca, NY: Cornell University Press, 1981); Allan G. Bogue, *The Congressman's Civil War* (New York: Cambridge University Press, 1989); Glenn M. Linden, "'Radical' Political and Economic Policies: The Senate, 1873–1877," *Civil War History* 14 (September 1968): 240–249; John L. McCarthy, "Reconstruction Legislation and Voting Alignments in the House of Representatives, 1863–1869" (Ph.D. diss., Yale University, 1970). Ariel Ron, "Summoning the States: Northern Farmers and the Transformation of American Politics in the Mid-Nineteenth Century," *Journal of American History* 103 (September 2016): 347–374, notes the influence of constituent pressure on passage of the Agricultural College Act (1862).

27. Koistinen, *Beating Plowshares into Swords*, ch. 5; Charles J. Bullock, *Historical Sketch of the Finances and Financial Policy of Mass. from 1780 to 1905*, 3rd ser., vol. 8:2 (New York: Publications of the American Economic Association, 1907), 59–69, 130; Charles P. Huse, *The Financial History of Boston* (Cambridge, MA: Har-

vard University Press, 1916), 143–149, 161–171; Robin L. Einhorn, *Property Rules: Political Economy in Chicago, 1833–1872* (Chicago: University of Chicago Press, 1991), 196–202; Eugene H. Roseboom, *The Civil War Era, 1850–1873* (Columbus: Ohio State Archaeological and Historical Society, 1944), 145, 380, 426–427; Arthur C. Cole, *The Era of the Civil War, 1848–1870* (Springfield: Illinois Centennial Commission, 1919), 274–284.

28. James McPherson, "Lincoln and the Strategy of Unconditional Surrender," in Wilentz, *Best American History Essays*, 175–188.

29. McPherson, *Battle Cry of Freedom*, is a splendid review of Civil War military operations; the major turning points of the war are reviewed on 858. Also see John Keegan, *The American Civil War* (New York: Vintage, 2009). A handy synopsis of major battles and accompanying maps is Aaron Sheehan-Dean, *Concise Historical Atlas of the Civil War* (New York: Oxford University Press, 2009).

30. Keegan, *American Civil War*, 121–122, 142, speculates that McClellan chose an amphibious route to Richmond during his Peninsula Campaign because of the numerous rivers that obstructed a land march south from Washington, DC. The undulating Mississippi River, with its many bayous and swamps, greatly complicated Grant's attack on Vicksburg in 1863.

31. Walter Millis, *Arms and Men: A Study in American Military History* (New York: G. P. Putnam's Sons, 1956), ch. 2.

32. Weigley, *History of the United States Army*, 233–255; T. Harry Williams, *Lincoln and His Generals* (New York: Random House, 1952).

33. There is a huge literature on Lincoln as a war leader. See, for example, McPherson, *Battle Cry of Freedom*; Donald, *Lincoln*; Wilentz, *Best American History Essays*. Mark E. Neely Jr., *The Union Divided: Party Conflict in the Civil War North* (Cambridge, MA: Harvard University Press, 2002), ch. 7, argues that customary partisanship devolved during the war into Republicans' denunciation of northern Democrats for treasonous conspiracy.

34. Eric Foner, *Reconstruction: America's Unfinished Revolution* (New York: Harper & Row, 1988); Richard White, *The Republic for Which It Stands: The United States during Reconstruction and the Gilded Age, 1865–1896* (New York: Oxford University Press, 2017), chs. 1–3; Michael Les Benedict, *The Impeachment and Trial of Andrew Johnson* (New York: Norton, 1974). Hyman and Wiecek, *Equal Justice under Law*, chs. 9–12, track changes in southern state constitutions.

35. Brooks Simpson, "1868," in *American Presidential Campaigns and Elections*, vol. 2, ed. William G. Shade and Ballard C. Campbell (Armonk, NY: M. E. Sharpe, 2003), 438–439; Joel H. Silbey, *A Respectable Minority: The Democratic Party in the Civil War Era, 1860–1868* (New York: Norton, 1877), 190, 191.

36. Charles W. Calhoun, *The Presidency of Ulysses S. Grant* (Lawrence: University Press of Kansas, 2017).

37. On southern terrorism and northern intervention, see Foner, *Reconstruction*, chs. 9–12.

38. The adoption of the Civil Rights Act of 1875, which declared that all persons were entitled to use private accommodations, was an exception; the Supreme Court declared the law unconstitutional in 1883.

39. For further discussion of the political repercussions of the 1870s depression, see chapters 9 and 10. Also see Foner, *Reconstruction*, ch. 11; Ballard C. Campbell, "1873: Financial Panic and Depression," in *American Disasters* (New York: Checkmark Books, 2008).

40. Foner, *Reconstruction*, 523. Republicans lost twenty-four House seats in the Northeast, twenty-three in the Midwest, eight in the West, and thirty-nine in the South. House election results are based on my analysis of data in Michael J. Dubin, *United States Congressional Elections, 1788–1997* (Jefferson, NC: McFarland, 1998); Stanley B. Parsons, *United States Congressional Districts and Data, 1843–1881* (New York: Greenwood, 1986); Kenneth C. Martis, *The Historical Atlas of Political Parties in the United States Congress, 1789–1989* (New York: Macmillan, 1989). Dale Baum, *The Civil War Party System: The Case of Massachusetts, 1848–1876* (Chapel Hill: University of North Carolina Press, 1984), 190–201, and Paul Kleppner, *The Third Electoral System, 1853–1892: Parties, Voters, and Political Cultures* (Chapel Hill: University of North Carolina Press, 1979), 121–142, found that antitemperance (liquor policy) sentiments contributed to Democratic gains in some states.

41. Michael F. Holt, "From Center to Periphery: The Market Revolution and Major-Party Conflict, 1835–1880," in *The Market Revolution in America*, ed. Melvyn Stokes and Stephen Conway (Charlottesville: University Press of Virginia, 1996), 224–256; Emma Lou Thornbrough, *Indiana in the Civil War Era, 1850–1880* (1965; reprint, Indianapolis: Indiana Historical Society, 1992), ch. 7; Walter T. K. Nugent, *Money and American Society, 1865–1880* (New York: Free Press, 1968), chs. 15, 16, 268–269.

42. Morton Keller, *Affairs of State: Public Life in Late Nineteenth Century America* (Cambridge, MA: Harvard University Press, 1977), 1–2; Harold M. Hyman, *A More Perfect Union: The Impact of the Civil War and Reconstruction on the Constitution* (Boston: Houghton Mifflin, 1973), 545ff; Bensel, *Yankee Leviathan*, ch. 6. Bensel argues that the failure of Reconstruction was linked to "the stalemated American state of the late nineteenth century" (413).

43. Texas v. White, 7 Wall 700 (1869); Collector v. Day, 11 Wall 178 (1871).

44. Bensel, *Yankee Leviathan*, chs. 4, 5, esp. 268–292.

45. Susan Carter et al., *Historical Statistics of the United States: Millennial Edition* (New York: Cambridge University Press, 2006), table Ea636.

46. For city and state finances, see the sources listed for table 5.2 in chapter 5 and for tables A.2 and A.3 in the appendix. Foner, *Reconstruction*, 486.

47. US Bureau of the Census, *Historical Statistical of the United States to 1970* (Washington, DC: Government Printing Office, 1975), series Y308, Y309. Also see Bensel, *Yankee Leviathan*, tables 6.4 and 6.5 for 1877. Brown, *Modernization*, ch. 7, called the expansion of the federal bureaucracy during the Civil War an expression of modernization. Also see Lawrence A. Cremin, *American Education: The National Experience, 1783–1876* (New York: Harper & Row, 1980), 515–516.

48. James C. Mohr, *The Radical Republicans and Reform in New York during Reconstruction* (Ithaca, NY: Cornell University Press, 1973); Lex Renda, *Running on the Record: Civil War–Era Politics in New Hampshire* (Charlottesville: University

Press of Virginia, 1997), 147–151, 159–160, 173–176, 218–219. See tables A.2 and A.3 in the appendix.

49. Michael Kammen, *Mystic Chords of Memory: The Transformation of Tradition in American Culture* (New York: Knopf, 1991), 88–90; Grant, *North over South*, 153–172; Wilbur Zelinsky, *Nation into State: The Shifting Symbolic Foundations of American Nationalism* (Chapel Hill: University of North Carolina Press, 1988), 203; Degler, "One among Many"; David M. Potter, "Civil War," in *The Comparative Approach to American History*, ed. C. Vann Woodward (1968; reprint, New York: Oxford University Press, 1997), 135–145.

8. *Social and Economic Transformations*

1. Theodore Roosevelt, *Hunting Trips of a Ranchman: Sketches of Sport on the Northern Cattle Plains* (1885; reprint, New York: Modern Library, 1996), 9–10.

2. Carleton Putnam, *Theodore Roosevelt*, vol. 1, *The Formative Years, 1858–1886* (New York: Charles Scribner's Sons, 1958), 313–346.

3. Edmund Morris, *The Rise of Theodore Roosevelt* (New York: Ballantine Books, 1979), 325 (map), 198–201, 216–220, 363–366, 372–373; Rodman W. Paul, *The Far West and the Great Plains in Transition, 1859–1900* (1988; reprint, Norman: University of Oklahoma Press, 1998), ch. 9.

4. James Bryce, *The American Commonwealth*, 2nd ed., vol. 2 (New York: Macmillan, 1893), 829.

5. Robert Wooster, *The American Military Frontiers: The U.S. Army in the West, 1783–1900* (Chapel Hill: University of North Carolina Press, 2009), chs. 10–12; Russell F. Weigley, *History of the United States Army* (Bloomington: Indiana University Press, 1984), 267–270; D. W. Meinig, *Transcontinental America, 1850–1915* (New Haven, CT: Yale University Press, 1995), 159–161.

6. Charles W. Calhoun, *The Presidency of Ulysses S. Grant* (Lawrence: University Press of Kansas, 2017), 265–275, 247–248.

7. Calhoun, *Presidency of Grant*, 274.

8. Meinig, *Transcontinental America*, prologue, pt. 2, chs. 1–8, pt. 3, chs. 2, 3; Richard White, *Railroaded: The Transcontinentals and the Making of Modern America* (New York: Norton, 2011); Albro Martin, *Railroads Triumphant* (New York: Oxford University Press, 1992); John F. Stover, *The Routledge Historical Atlas of the American Railroads* (New York: Routledge, 1999), esp. 40–41, 48–49, 52–53. The early transcontinental railroads required the transfer of people and goods between lines at key junctures; not until the advent of standardized rail gauges, coordinated time zones, and the construction of union stations in the 1880s could a passenger ride a single train from coast to coast.

9. Carl Abbott, *How Cities Won the West: Four Centuries of Urban Change in Western North America* (Albuquerque: University of New Mexico Press, 2008), ch. 8; Donald J. Pisani, *To Reclaim a Divided West: Water, Law, and Public Policy, 1848–1902* (Albuquerque: University of New Mexico Press, 1992), 99–103, 170–177; Kevin Starr, *Material Dreams: Southern California through the 1920s* (New York: Oxford University Press, 1990), ch. 3; Robert Cherny and William Issel, *San Fran-*

cisco, 1865–1932: Politics, Power and Urban Development (Berkeley: University of California Press, 1986), 162, 175–176, 182–184. On efforts to attract eastern capital to develop western economies, see Noam Maggor, "To Coddle and Caress These Great Capitalists: Eastern Money, Frontier Populism, and the Politics of Market-Making in the American West," *American Historical Review* 122 (February 2017): 55–84.

10. Meinig, *Transcontinental America*, pt. 2, pt. 3, ch. 5; Abbott, *How Cities Won the West*, chs. 4–7; Philip R. VanderMeer, *Desert Visions and the Making of Phoenix, 1860–2009* (Albuquerque: University of New Mexico Press, 2010).

11. David Ward, *Cities and Immigrants: A Geography of Change in Nineteenth Century America* (New York: Oxford University Press, 1971), tables 1-3, 1-4; Don H. Doyle, *New Men, New Cities, New South: Atlanta, Nashville, Charleston, Mobile, 1860–1910* (Chapel Hill: University of North Carolina Press, 1990), esp. ch. 1.

12. Maggor, "To Coddle and Caress These Great Capitalists."

13. Ernst G. Timme, ed., *The Blue Book of the State of Wisconsin* (Madison, WI: Democratic Printing Co., 1885), 402–407; Walter F. Dodd, *State Government* (New York: Century Co., 1923), ch. 15; Charles A. Beard, *American Government and Politics* (New York: Macmillan, 1928), 768–775. Specific county offices (and county functions) varied both between and within states. New York had 932 towns in 1918; a report to the Illinois legislature in 1935 counted 12,000 local governments in the state, including 1,463 townships and 1,123 incorporated municipalities.

14. There is no comprehensive census of the number of governments in the nineteenth century. James Bryce reported that Ohio possessed 1,284 subcounty governments in 1888, divided among 38 cities, 429 villages, 32 hamlets, and 785 unincorporated places or towns. Bryce, *American Commonwealth*, 610n1, ch. 48 generally. In 1900 Pennsylvania had 2,382 minor civil divisions, Tennessee had 1,551, and New York had 974. US Bureau of the Census, *A Century of Population Growth, 1790–1900* (Washington, DC: Government Printing Office, 1909), 77. See chapter 4 for my estimate of towns and townships in the antebellum era.

15. William H. Goetzmann, *Exploration and Empire: The Explorer and the Scientist in the Winning of the American West* (1966; reprint, New York: Knopf, 2006), chs. 9–15.

16. Carter Goodrich, *Government Promotion of American Canals and Railroads, 1800–1890* (New York: Columbia University Press, 1960), 237–258; White, *Railroaded.* On state and local subsidies, see Edward C. Kirkland, *Men, Cities, and Transportation: A Study in New England History, 1820–1900*, vol. 2 (Cambridge, MA: Harvard University Press, 1948), 309–316, 431–432; Emma Lou Thornbrough, *Indiana in the Civil War Era, 1850–1880* (Indianapolis: Indiana Historical Society, 1992), 340–345. On the restriction of local rail subsidies, see Carter Goodrich, "The Revulsion against Internal Improvements," *Journal of Economic History* 10 (November 1950): 156–159; Horace Scrist, *An Economic Analysis of the Constitutional Restriction upon Public Indebtedness in the United States* (Madison: University of Wisconsin, 1914), 54–60, appendix II; Jon C. Teaford, *The Unheralded Triumph: City Government in America, 1870–1900* (Baltimore: Johns Hopkins University Press, 1984), 286–288.

17. Paul W. Gates, *History of Public Land Law Development* (Washington, DC: Government Printing Office, 1968); Alfred Runte, *National Parks: The American Experience* (Lincoln: University of Nebraska Press, 1987), chs. 1–4.

18. Albert J. Churella, *The Pennsylvania Railroad*, vol. 1, *1846–1914* (Philadelphia: University of Pennsylvania Press, 2012), 448–451.

19. Stover, *Routledge Historical Atlas of American Railroads*, 21, 38–39, 48–49, 52–53; Meining, *Transcontinental America*, pt. 3, ch. 3, 255 (map of Iowa); Thornbrough, *Indiana*, 351 (map); Stephen J. Hornsby and Richard Judd, *Historical Atlas of Maine* (Orono: University of Maine Press, 2015), plate 44; John F. Stover, *American Railroads* (Chicago: University of Chicago Press, 1961), 143–144, 149–150.

20. Charles W. Cheape, *Moving the Masses: Urban Public Transit in New York, Boston, and Philadelphia* (Cambridge, MA: Harvard University Press, 1980); Teaford, *Unheralded Triumph*, 234–240; William B. Munro, *Municipal Administration* (New York: Macmillan, 1934), ch. 44; Hornsby and Judd, *Historical Atlas of Maine*, plate 44; Sam Bass Warner, *Streetcar Suburbs: The Process of Growth in Boston, 1870–1920* (Cambridge, MA: Harvard University Press, 1962), 64.

21. David B. Tyler, *Steam Conquers the Atlantic* (New York: Appleton-Century, 1939), 353–380.

22. David A. Hounshell, *From the American System to Mass Production, 1800–1932* (Baltimore: Johns Hopkins University Press, 1984), chs. 6, 7; Bernard A. Weisberger, *The Dream Maker: William C. Durant, Founder of General Motors* (Boston: Little, Brown, 1979), chs. 5–7; Stanley Lebergott, *The American Economy: Income, Wealth, and Want* (Princeton, NJ: Princeton University Press, 1976), 290.

23. James R. Beniger, *The Control Revolution: Technological and Economic Origins of the Information Society* (Cambridge, MA: Harvard University Press, 1986), ch. 6; William Cronon, *Nature's Metropolis: Chicago and the Great West* (New York: Norton, 1991), 333; Robert J. Gordon, *The Rise and Fall of American Growth: The U.S. Standard of Living since the Civil War* (Princeton, NJ: Princeton University Press, 2016), ch. 6.

24. Alfred D. Chandler Jr., *The Visible Hand: The Managerial Revolution in American Business* (Cambridge, MA: Harvard University Press, 1972), 109–117; Alfred D. Chandler Jr., *Scale and Scope: The Dynamics of Industrial Capitalism* (Cambridge, MA: Harvard University Press, 1990), 53–58, 419; Kirkland, *Men, Cities, and Transportation*, 2:318–334, 435–442. An excellent case study is Richard C. Overton, *Burlington Route: A History of the Burlington Lines* (New York: Knopf, 1965), esp. chs. 9–14. On the role of investment banking and railroads, see Vincent P. Carosso, *Investment Banking in America: A History* (Cambridge, MA: Harvard University Press, 1970), chs. 2–4, 7; White, *Railroaded*, ch. 1.

25. Hounshell, *From the American System*, chs. 6, 7.

26. Thomas K. McCraw, *American Business since 1920: How It Worked* (Wheeling, IL: Harlan Davidson, 2009), ch. 2; Cronon, *Nature's Metropolis*, ch. 7; Gordon, *Rise and Fall of American Growth*, ch. 3.

27. Robert E. Gallman, ed., *Cambridge Economic History of the United States*, vol. 2 (Cambridge: Cambridge University Press, 2000), ch. 1, esp. 3–6, 23, 56; Meinig, *Transcontinental America*, 240. Gordon, *Rise and Fall of American Growth*,

pt. I, argues that per capita measures of national income significantly understate the advance in the standard of living between 1870 and 1940.

28. Peter Temin, "Free Land and Federalism: A Synoptic View of American Economic History," *Journal of Interdisciplinary History* 21 (Winter 1991): 371–389; Michael R. Haines, "The Population of the United States, 1790–1920," in Gallman, *Cambridge Economic History*, 2:143–206; Robert E. Lipset, "U.S. Foreign Trade and the Balance of Payments, 1800–1913," in Gallman, *Cambridge Economic History*, 2:685–732; Gavin Wright, "The Origins of American Industrial Success," *American Economic Review* 80 (1990): 651–668; Edward C. Kirkland, *Industry Comes of Age: Business, Labor, and Public Policy, 1860–1897* (Chicago: Quadrangle Books, 1961), ch. 7. For a portrait of economic development in the West, see Paul, *Far West*. Gordon, *Rise and Fall of American Growth*, contends that individuals' greater longevity, largely due to health improvements, led to increased growth in the gross domestic product after 1900. The bulk of American exports in the nineteenth century were agricultural commodities and refined minerals.

29. Claudia Goldin, "America's Graduation from High School: The Evolution and Spread of Secondary Schooling in the Twentieth Century," *Journal of Economic History* 58 (June 1998): 345–374; Claudia Goldin and Lawrence F. Katz, "Education and Income in the Early Twentieth Century: Evidence from the Prairies," *Journal of Economic History* 60 (September 2000): 782–818.

30. Allan G. Bogue, "Changes in Mechanical and Plant Technology: The Corn Belt, 1910–1940," *Journal of Economic History* 43 (March 1983): 1–25. Increases in yields and outputs suggest the impact of science and technology on agriculture.

31. "Greatest Engineering Achievements of the Twentieth Century," National Academy of Engineering, 2000, http://www.greatachievements.org/.

32. Joel Mohr, *The Lever of Riches: Technological Creativity and Economic Progress* (New York: Oxford University Press, 1990); Chandler, *Visible Hand*, chs. 8, 9; Charles K. Hyde, "Iron and Steel Technologies Moving between Europe and the United States before 1914," in *International Technology Transfer: Europe, Japan, and the USA*, ed. David J. Jeremy (Brookfield, VT: Elgar, 1991), 51–73. Gordon, *Rise and Fall of American Growth*, pt. I, stresses the role of technology in improving the standard of living.

33. On corporate organization and expansion, see Chandler, *Visible Hand*; Glenn Porter, *The Rise of Big Business, 1860–1920*, 3rd ed. (Arlington Heights, IL: Harlan Davidson, 2006); Tony Freyer, *Regulating Big Business: Anti-Trust in Great Britain and America, 1880 to 1980* (New York: Cambridge University Press, 1992); Naomi R. Lamoreaux, *The Great Merger Movement in American Business, 1895–1904* (Cambridge: Cambridge University Press, 1985).

34. On the panics and depressions between 1873 and 1915, see Ballard C. Campbell, *American Disasters: 201 Calamities that Shook the Nation* (New York: Checkmark Books, 2008), 134–138, 168–171, 202–206; Ballard C. Campbell, "Depressions and Taxes in the United States, 1873–1915," in *Taxation, State, and Civil Society in Germany and the United States in the 18th to the 20th Century*, ed. Christoph Strupp and Alexander Nutzenadel (Baden-Baden, Germany: Nomos Verlag, 2007), 67–81; Ballard C. Campbell, "Economic Causes of Progressivism," *Journal*

of the Gilded Age and Progressive Era 4 (January 2005): 7–22. For 1920–1922, see George Soule, *Prosperity Decade: From War to Depression, 1917–1929* (New York: Holt, Rinehart & Winston, 1964), chs. 5, 9; Derek H. Aldcroft, *From Versailles to Wall Street, 1919–1929* (Berkeley: University of California Press, 1981), chs. 2–4. A suggestive timeline of depression severity is provided in Harold U. Faulkner, *American Economic History*, 8th ed. (New York: Harper & Bros., 1960), 641. For an overview of economic fluctuations during the Gilded Age, see Kirkland, *Industry Comes of Age*, ch. 1.

A word of caution is in order concerning generalizations about economic depressions between 1873 and 1922. First, modern data series used to track economic fluctuations are scarce before 1900, especially with regard to local conditions. Second, depressions during the Gilded Age and Progressive Era are understudied, particularly the links between economic fluctuations and sociopolitical reactions. Important exceptions are Alexander Keyssar, *Out of Work: The First Century of Unemployment in Massachusetts* (New York: Cambridge University Press, 1986); Sven Beckert, *The Monied Metropolis: New York City and the Consolidation of the American Bourgeoisie, 1850–1896* (New York: Cambridge University Press, 2001); Jonathan Levy, *Freaks of Fortune: The Emerging World of Capitalism and Risk in America* (Cambridge, MA: Harvard University Press, 2012); Cronon, *Nature's Metropolis*, ch. 6.

35. Charles Z. Lincoln, ed., *Messages of the Governors: State of New York* (Albany, NY: J. B. Lyons, 1909), 7:5. The political repercussions of depressions are discussed in chapters 10 and 11.

36. Kerry A. Odell and Marc D. Weidenmier, "Real Shock, Monetary Aftershock: The 1906 San Francisco Earthquake and the Panic of 1907," *Journal of Economic History* 64 (December 2004): 1002–1027; Ron Chernow, *House of Morgan: An American Banking Dynasty and the Rise of Modern Finance* (New York: Atlantic Monthly Press, 1990), ch. 7; Levy, *Freaks of Fortune*, ch. 8; Robert F. Bruner and Sean D. Carr, *The Panic of 1907: Lessons Learned from the Market's Perfect Storm* (Hoboken, NJ: John Wiley & Sons, 2007). See also the works cited in note 34.

37. The literature that describes economic regionalism in the Gilded Age and Progressive Era is huge. My favorites include Meinig, *Transcontinental America*; John Brinckerhoff Jackson, *American Space: The Centennial Years, 1865–1876* (New York: Norton, 1972); Peter Temin, ed., *Engines of Enterprise: An Economic History of New England* (Cambridge, MA: Harvard University Press, 2000); Diana Muir, *Reflections in Bullough's Pond: Economy and Ecosystem in New England* (Hanover, NH: University Press of New England, 2000); Cronon, *Nature's Metropolis*; Hal S. Barron, *Mixed Harvest: The Second Great Transformation of the Rural North, 1870–1930* (Chapel Hill: University of North Carolina Press, 1997); Howard W. Odum, *Southern Regions of the United States* (Chapel Hill: University of North Carolina Press, 1936); Edward L. Ayers, *The Promise of the New South: Life after Reconstruction* (New York: Oxford University Press, 1992); Paul, *Far West*. The complexity of localized and regional economics complicates the tracking of the effects of depression. This subject deserves more study.

38. Gordon, *Rise and Fall of American Growth*, ch. 8; David B. Robertson, *Capital, Labor, and State: The Battle for Labor Markets from the Civil War to the*

New Deal (New York: Rowman & Littlefield, 2000), chs. 1–4; Alice Kessler Harris, *Out to Work: A History of Wage-Earning Women in the United States* (New York: Oxford University Press, 1982), ch. 6; Keyssar, *Out of Work*; David Montgomery, "Strikes in Nineteenth-Century America," *Social Science History* 4 (February 1980): 81–104; Gerald N. Grob, *The Deadly Truth: A History of Disease in America* (Cambridge, MA: Harvard University Press, 2002), 164–165; David Rosner and Gerald Markowitz, eds., *Dying for Work: Workers' Safety and Health in Twentieth Century America* (Bloomington: Indiana University Press, 1987).

39. Gallman, *Cambridge Economic History*, 2:21–26; Gordon, *Rise and Fall of American Growth*, 29–30, pt. I generally.

40. Gallman, *Cambridge Economic History*, chs. 3, 17; John McClymer, "Late Nineteenth-Century Working Class Living Standards," *Journal of Interdisciplinary History* 17 (Autumn 1986): 379–398; Harold U. Faulkner, *The Decline of Laissez Faire, 1897–1917* (New York: Holt, Rinehart & Winston, 1951), 415 (table); Gordon, *Rise and Fall of American Growth*, 60–67, 271.

41. Robert G. Barrows, "Beyond the Tenement: Patterns of American Urban Housing, 1870–1930," *Journal of Urban History* 9 (August 1983): 395–420; Stephan Thernstrom, *The Other Bostonians: Poverty and Progress in the American Metropolis* (Cambridge, MA: Harvard University Press, 1973), 299; Oliver Zunz, *Changing Face of Inequality: Urbanization, Industrial Development, and Immigrants in Detroit, 1880–1920* (Chicago: University of Chicago Press, 1982), ch. 6; Lebergott, *American Economy*, 251–281; Gordon, *Rise and Fall of American Growth*, chs. 2, 4, 8. In the Gilded Age, many workers built their own homes.

42. Julie A. Golia, "Courting Women, Courting Advertisers: The Woman's Page and the Transformation of American Newspapers, 1895–1935," *Journal of American History* 103 (December 2016): 606–628; Goldin, "America's Graduation from High School"; Barron, *Mixed Harvest*, ch. 5.

43. Gordon, *Rise and Fall of American Growth*, 304.

9. *Nationalism, Parties, and the Coercive State, 1870–1917*

1. Edmund S. Ions, *James Bryce and American Democracy* (New York: Humanities Press, 1970), chs. 4, 5, 7, 8.

2. James Bryce, *The American Commonwealth*, 2nd ed. (New York: Macmillan, 1893), 15, 404; D. W. Meinig, *Transcontinental America, 1850–1915* (New Haven, CT: Yale University Press, 1995), 293.

3. Raymond H. Robinson, "The Making of an Icon," in *George Washington: American Symbol*, ed. Barbara J. Mitnick (New York: Hudson Hills Press, 1999), 109–121; Barry Schwartz, "George Washington: A New Man for a New Century," in Mitnick, *George Washington*, 123–139; Bryan F. LeBeau, *Currier and Ives: America Imagined* (Washington, DC: Smithsonian Institution Press, 2001), 36–47; Joseph A. Conforti, *Imagining New England: Explorations of Regional Identity from the Pilgrims to the Mid-Twentieth Century* (Chapel Hill: University of North Carolina Press, 2000), ch. 5.

4. Merle E. Curti, *The Roots of American Loyalty* (New York: Columbia Univer-

sity Press, 1946), ch. 7; John Pettigrew, "'The Soldier's Faith': Turn of the Century Memory of the Civil War and the Emergence of Modern American Nationalism," *Journal of Contemporary History* 31 (January 1996): 49–73; Mary R. Dearing, *Veterans in Politics: The Story of the G.A.R.* (Baton Rouge: Louisiana State University Press, 1952), ch. 12; Richard J. Ellis, *To the Flag: The Unlikely History of the Pledge of Allegiance* (Lawrence: University Press of Kansas, 2005), chs. 1–3; David Tyack, Thomas James, and Aaron Benavot, *Law and the Shaping of Public Education, 1785–1954* (Madison: University of Wisconsin Press, 1987), table 6.3; Cecilla E. O'Leary, *To Die For: The Paradox of American Patriotism* (Princeton, NJ: Princeton University Press, 1999), chs. 9, 10.

5. William M. Landes and Lewis C. Solomon, "Compulsory Schooling Legislation: An Economic Analysis of Law and Social Change in the Nineteenth Century," *Journal of Economic History* 32 (1972): 54–89; Tyack, James, and Benavot, *Law and the Shaping of Public Education*, table 6.3; Jean H. Baker, *Affairs of Party: The Political Culture of North Democrats in the Mid-Nineteenth Century* (Ithaca, NY: Cornell University Press, 1983), 80–86; Joel Dorman Steele and Esther Baker Steele, *A Brief History of the United States* (1871; reprint, New York: American Book Co., 1912), 1–2; Michael Krause and Davis D. Joyce, *The Writing of American History* (Norman: University of Oklahoma Press 1985), ch. 10; John Higham, *History: Professional Scholarship in America* (Baltimore: Johns Hopkins University Press, 1983), 9–16, 20, 148–157, 158–159; Merle Curti, "The Democratic Theme in American Historical Literature," *Mississippi Valley Historical Review* 39 (June 1952): 4–14; Hazel Whitman Hertzberg, "The Teaching of History," in *The Past before Us*, ed. Michael Kammen (Ithaca, NY: Cornell University Press, 1980), 474–504; Thomas Cochran, "The 'Presidential Synthesis' in American History," *American Historical Review* 53 (July 1948): 748–759. Cochran emphasizes the "enormous burden on the historian" to synthesize the record of the states and the elitist bent of nineteenth-century historians.

Even Frederick Jackson Turner, the historian who popularized the study of sections in America around the turn of the century, wrote from a nationalist perspective; his "frontier thesis" epitomized the viewpoint that differences between the United States and Europe made the former "exceptional." See Allan G. Bogue, *Frederick Jackson Turner: Strange Roads Going Down* (Norman: University of Oklahoma Press, 1998), 113, 352, 380. On the connection between exceptionalism and nationalism, see Ian Tyrell, "American Exceptionalism in an Age of International History," *American Historical Review* 96, 4 (1991): 1031–1050; Michael Mann, *The Sources of Social Power*, vol. 2, *The Rise of Classes and Nation-States, 1760–1914* (Cambridge: Cambridge University Press, 1993), 636–658. Rogers M. Smith, *Civic Ideals: Conflicting Visions of Citizenship in U.S. History* (New Haven, CT: Yale University Press, 1997), 497, notes the capacity of history to nurture distinctive features of American national identity.

6. Susan Schulten, *The Geographic Imagination in America, 1880–1950* (Chicago: University of Chicago Press, 2001), chs. 1–3, 5; Ballard C. Campbell, *Representative Democracy: Public Policy and Midwestern Legislatures in the Late Nineteenth Century* (Cambridge, MA: Harvard University Press, 1980), 28, 92, 114–116. For

a sample of midwestern opinion supporting a patriotic agenda in public schools, see *Chicago Tribune*, April 13, 1893; *Milwaukee Journal*, March 24, 1893; *Iowa State Register*, January 5, 1888; John W. Meyer et al., "Public Education as Nation-Building in America: Enrollments and Bureaucracy in the American States, 1870–1930," *American Journal of Sociology* 85 (November 1979): 591–613.

7. Thomas J. Schlereth, *Victorian America: Transformations in Everyday Life, 1876–1915* (New York: HarperCollins, 1991), 19, 216–217; Hugh DeSantis, "The Democratization of Travel: The Agent in History," *Journal of American Culture* 1 (April 1978): 1–19; Anne Farrar Hyde, *An American Vision: Far Western Landscape and National Culture, 1820–1920* (New York: New York University Press, 1990), chs. 3–6; Hal Rothman, *Devil's Bargain: Tourism in the Twentieth-Century West* (Lawrence: University Press of Kansas, 1998), 45, 51–62; Albert J. Churella, *The Pennsylvania Railroad*, vol. 1 (Philadelphia: University of Pennsylvania Press, 2012), 448–450.

8. Marguerite S. Shaffer, *See America First: Tourism and National Identity, 1880–1940* (Washington, DC: Smithsonian Institution Press, 2001), 4–5; John Sears, *Sacred Places: American Tourist Attractions in the Nineteenth Century* (New York: Oxford University Press, 1989), 172–177; Hyde, *American Vision*, 301, 304; William H. Goetzmann and William N. Goetzmann, *The West of the Imagination* (New York: Norton, 1986), 190; Alfred Runte, *National Parks: The American Experience* (Lincoln: University of Nebraska Press, 1997), ch. 1.

9. See, for example, *New Unrivaled Atlas of the World* (Boston: De Wolfe, Fiske, 1898), esp. 4–5; William R. Shepherd, *Historical Atlas* (New York: Henry Holt, 1911), esp. 179–182; Schulten, *Geographic Imagination in America*, ch. 3.

10. E. J. Hobsbawm, *Nations and Nationalism since 1780* (Cambridge: Cambridge University Press, 1990); E. J. Hobsbawm, *Age of Empire,1875–1914* (New York: Pantheon Books, 1987), ch. 3; Paul Kennedy, *The Rise and Fall of the Great Powers: Economic Change and Military Conflict from 1500 to 2000* (New York: Random House, 1987), ch. 5; Niall Ferguson, *Empire: The Rise and Demise of the British World Order and the Lessons for Global Power* (New York: Basic Books, 2003), 240–264; Gail Bederman, *Manliness and Civilization: A Cultural History of the United States, 1880–1917* (Chicago: University of Chicago Press, 1995), 187; Roosevelt's 1905 inaugural address, in James D. Richardson, comp., *Messages and Papers of the Presidents*, vol. 10 (Washington, DC: Bureau of the National Literature and Art, 1910), 7060.

11. Nina Silber, "Reunion and Reconciliation, Reviewed and Reconsidered," *Journal of American History* 103 (June 2016): 59–83; Bryce, *American Commonwealth*, 2:844.

12. O'Leary, *To Die For*, chs. 3, 4, 8–10; Patricia Nelson Limerick, *The Legacy of Conquest: The Unbroken Past of the American West* (New York: Norton, 1987), chs. 6–8.

13. O'Leary, *To Die For*, chs. 5–6; Philip N. Cohen, "Nationalism and Suffrage: Gender Struggles in Nation-Building America," *Signs* 21 (Spring 1996): 707–727; Rebecca Edwards, *Angels in the Machinery: Gender in American Party Politics from the Civil War to the Progressive Era* (New York: Oxford University Press, 1997),

esp. ch. 4; Barbara Finkelstein, "Dollars and Dreams: Classrooms as Fictitious Message Systems, 1790–1930," *History of Education Quarterly* 34 (Winter 1991): 472–473, 480–481. In some localities, women gained the vote in school and municipal elections prior to the adoption of statewide female suffrage and the Nineteenth Amendment to the Constitution (1919). Kathryn Kish Sklar, *Florence Kelley and the Nation's Work* (New Haven, CT: Yale University Press, 1995), xv–xvi, maintains that women's political identity was less a function of gender than of their "social, political, and economic structures and values." Walter L. Williams, "United States Indian Policy and the Debate over Philippine Annexation: Implications for the Origins of American Imperialism," *Journal of American History* 66 (March 1980): 810–831, contends that designating Native Americans as "subject peoples" in the nineteenth century set a precedent for the treatment of Puerto Ricans and Philippine residents after the Spanish-American War. Also see chapter 10.

14. John Higham, *Strangers in the Land: Patterns of American Nativism, 1860–1925* (New York: Atheneum, 1963), esp. chs. 4, 7. Ethnic conflict was a staple of political life in the Midwest during the Gilded Age. See Harman J. Deutsch, "Yankee-Teuton Rivalry in Wisconsin Politics of the Seventies," *Wisconsin Magazine of History* 14 (March and June 1931): 262–282, 403–318; Campbell, *Representative Democracy*, ch. 2. National identity among ethnic groups is reviewed in Philip Gleason, "American Identity and Americanization," in *Harvard Encyclopedia of American Ethnic Groups*, ed. Stephan Thernstrom (Cambridge, MA: Harvard University Press, 1980), 31–58; Mona Harrington, "Loyalties: Dual and Divided," in Thernstrom, *Harvard Encyclopedia*, 676–686; Read Ueda, "Naturalization and Citizenship," in Thernstrom, *Harvard Encyclopedia*, 734–748.

15. James R. Barrett, "Americanization from the Bottom Up: Immigration and the Remaking of the Working Class in the United States, 1800–1930," *Journal of American History* 79 (December 1992): 996–1020. On the American "core" culture, see Milton Gordon, *Assimilation in American Life: The Role of Race, Religion, and National Origins* (New York: Oxford University Press, 1964), esp. 72–74.

16. Mark Lawrence Kornbluh, *Why America Stopped Voting: The Decline of Participatory Democracy and the Emergence of Modern American Politics* (New York: New York University Press, 2000), ch. 5; Marion T. Bennett, *American Immigration Policies: A History* (Washington, DC: Public Affairs Press, 1963), 21–22, 127–134, 326–327; Ueda, "Naturalization and Citizenship"; Edward G. Hartmann, "The Movement to Americanize the Immigrant" (Ph.D. thesis, Columbia University, 1948), chs. 1–3. Also see Alexander Keyssar, *The Right to Vote: The Contested History of Democracy in the United States* (New York: Basic Books, 2000), chs. 5, 6; Smith, *Civic Ideals*, ch. 11, 441–442.

17. Bryce, *American Commonwealth*, 2:844, thought that children of immigrants were eager to become Americans. Marcus Lee Hansen expanded this observation into the third-generation hypothesis: "what the son wishes to forget the grandson wishes to remember." Marcus Lee Hansen, *The Problem of the Third Generation Immigrant* (Rock Island, IL: Augustana Historical Society Publications, 1938), 9. On the model of middle-class norms, see Alexander B. Callow Jr., *The Tweed Ring* (New York: Oxford University Press, 1965), 62; Marcus Lee Hansen, *The Immigrant in*

American Society (Cambridge, MA: Harvard University Press, 1940), ch. 4; Stephan Thernstrom, *Poverty and Progress: Social Mobility in a Nineteenth Century City* (Cambridge, MA: Harvard University Press, 1964), ch. 3; Barrett, "Americanization from the Bottom Up." Herbert G. Gutman, "Work, Culture, and Society in Industrializing America, 1815–1919," *American Historical Review* 78 (1973): 531–588, indicates that little was known about the "consciousness" of workers in various ethnic subcultures (565, 585) but implies that worker protests grew out of traditional responses to "injustice" rather than antagonistic attitudes toward the American state (567–583). One assumes that most immigrants went along with American norms to get along (i.e., to gain employment and social acceptance), yet there is reason to believe that some ethnic groups, such as conservative German Catholics, saw Americanization as a threat to their religious culture. See Philip Gleason, *The Conservative Reformers: German-American Catholics and the Social Order* (Notre Dame, IN: University of Notre Dame Press, 1968), ch. 2.

18. David Brian Robertson, *Capital, Labor, and State: The Battle for American Labor Markets from the Civil War to the New Deal* (Lanham, MD: Rowman & Littlefield, 2000); Howard L. Hurwitz, *Theodore Roosevelt and Labor in New York State, 1880–1900* (New York: Columbia University Studies in Social Science, 1943); David Montgomery, "Strikes in Nineteenth-Century America," *Social Science History* 4 (February 1980): 81–104. On Republicans and nativism in the 1890s, see editorials in the *Chicago Tribune*, May 30, 1891; Usher to E. C. Wall, September 11, 1893, Letterbook 11, Ellis B. Usher Papers, Wisconsin State Historical Society. Usher cites the GAR and the Sons of Veterans in Wisconsin as instigators of anti-Catholicism. Also see Higham, *Strangers in the Land*, 165–175.

19. Kornbluh, *Why America Stopped Voting*, esp. chs. 1–3; Michael Perman, *Struggle for Mastery: Disfranchisement in the South, 1888–1908* (Chapel Hill: University of North Carolina Press, 2001). Robert H. Wiebe, *The Segmented Society: An Introduction to the Meaning of America* (New York: Oxford University Press, 1975), 139–140, among other authors, sees political parties as cultural conduits in American society. Voter fraud was commonplace during the Gilded Age, which may have inflated some election returns. See Peter H. Argersinger, "New Perspectives on Election Fraud in the Gilded Age," *Political Science Quarterly* 100 (Winter 1985–1986): 669–687; Richard Franklin Bensel, *The Political Economy of American Industrialization, 1877–1900* (New York: Cambridge University Press, 2000), ch. 3 (Bensel's position on election issue orientation is based on a review of state political party platforms between 1877 and 1900); Charles W. Calhoun, ed., *The Gilded Age: Perspectives on the Origins of Modern America* (Lanham, MD: Rowman & Littlefield, 2007).

20. Jerry M. Cooper, *The Army and Civil Disorder: The Federal Military Intervention in Labor Disputes, 1877–1900* (Westport, CT: Greenwood, 1980), ch. 5; Jerry M. Cooper, *The Rise of the National Guard: The Evolution of the American Militia, 1865–1920* (Lincoln: University of Nebraska Press, 1997), ch. 3. See Ballard C. Campbell, *American Disasters: 201 Calamities that Shook the Nation* (New York: Checkmark Books, 2008), for an overview of the Pullman strike.

21. Hurwitz, *Theodore Roosevelt and Labor*, 247–253; John K. Mahon, *History*

of the Militia and the National Guard (New York: Macmillan, 1983), 110–123; Daniel R. Fusfield, "Government and the Suppression of Radical Labor, 1877–1918," in *Statemaking and Social Movements*, ed. Charles Bright and Susan Harding (Ann Arbor: University of Michigan Press, 1984), 346–352; James Edward Wright, *The Politics of Populism: Dissent in Colorado* (New Haven, CT: Yale University Press, 1974), 236–239; Sven Beckert, *The Monied Metropolis: New York City and the Consolidation of the American Bourgeoisie, 1850–1896* (New York: Cambridge University Press, 2001), 293–295. Robert Wiebe titled his widely read book on the industrial transition period *The Search for Order, 1877–1920* (New York: Hill & Wang, 1967).

22. Herbert G. Gutman, "The Tompkins Square 'Riot' in New York City on January 13, 1874: A Re-examination of Its Causes and Its Aftermath," *Labor History* 6 (Winter 1965): 44–70; Campbell, *American Disasters*, 151–153; Eric H. Monkkonen, *The Dangerous Class: Crime and Poverty in Columbus, Ohio, 1860–1885* (Cambridge, MA: Harvard University Press, 1975); Mark H. Haller, "Historical Roots of Police Behavior, Chicago, 1890–1925," *Law and Society Review* 10, 2 (1976): 303–324; Howard N. Rabinowitz, "The Conflict between Blacks and the Police in the Urban South, 1865–1900," *Historian* 39 (November 1976): 62–76. See David Montgomery, *Citizen Worker: The Experience of Workers in the United States with Democracy and the Free Market during the Nineteenth Century* (New York: Cambridge University Press, 1995), esp. ch. 2, for a review of the expansion of "the coercive capacity of government," which was forged largely to "discipline" workers (114).

23. Blake McKelvey, *American Prisons: A History of Good Intentions* (1936; reprint, Montclair, NJ: Patterson Smith, 1974), ch. 7, esp. 178, 179–180, 192–194. Census data recorded 32,901 inmates in state prisons in 1870 and 57,070 in 1904; by 1923 the figure had risen to 76,000 in ninety-nine state facilities. In 1910 at least 40,000 persons were held in county and municipal jails and 25,000 in juvenile facilities. See Margaret Werner Cahalan, *Historical Corrections Statistics in the United States, 1850–1984* (Washington, DC: US Department of Justice, 1987), tables 3-1, 8-2, 8-6, 8-8; Howard Gill, "State Prisons in America: 1787–1937," in US Department of Justice, *The Attorney General's Survey of Release Procedures*, vol. 5 (Washington, DC: Government Printing Office, 1939–1940), 1–39.

24. Edward L. Ayers, *The Promise of the New South: Life after Reconstruction* (New York: Oxford University Press, 1992), 154–158; Albert Bushnell Hart, *The Southern South* (New York: Appleton, 1910), chs. 14, 15, esp. 184, 197; Christopher Waldrep, *The Many Faces of Judge Lynch: Extralegal Violence and Punishment in America* (New York: Palgrave Macmillan, 2002); Limerick, *Legacy of Conquest*, 242, 262–269; Stuart Banner, *The Death Penalty: An American History* (Cambridge, MA: Harvard University Press, 2002), 208–220, 313 (for reference to a data set that recorded 19,248 executions before 1930, the year the Justice Department began its tabulation). Michael A. Trotti, "What Counts: Trends in Racial Violence in the Postbellum South," *Journal of American History* 100 (September 2013): 375–400, argues that lynchings of blacks in the South have been undercounted.

25. Thomas R. Pegram, *Battling Demon Rum: The Struggle for a Dry America,*

1800–1933 (Chicago: Ivan Dee, 1998); Richard F. Hamm, *Shaping the Eighteenth Amendment: Temperance Reform, Legal Culture, and the Polity, 1880–1920* (Chapel Hill: University of North Carolina Press, 1995); Harry Barnard, *Eagle Forgotten: The Life of John Peter Altgeld* (Indianapolis: Bobbs Merrill, 1938), 161; Amy Dru Stanley, "Beggars Can't Be Choosers: Compulsion and Contract in Postbellum America," *Journal of American History* 78 (March 1992): 1265–1293; Carl V. Harris, *Political Power in Birmingham, 1871–1921* (Knoxville: University of Tennessee Press, 1977), 200–211; Higham, *Strangers in the Land*, ch. 4; Walter Thompson, *Federal Centralization: A Study and Criticism of the Expanding Scope of Congressional Legislation* (New York: Harcourt Brace, 1923), 106–121.

26. Smith, *Civic Ideals*, chs. 11, 12; Leonard D. White, *The Republican Era, 1869–1901: A Study in Administrative History* (New York: Macmillan, 1958), 116–117; Bryce, *American Commonwealth*, 2:852.

27. Good overviews of Gilded Age politics are Robert W. Cherny, *American Politics in the Gilded Age, 1868–1900* (Wheeling, IL: Harlan Davidson, 1997); Charles W. Calhoun, *From Bloody Shirt to Full Dinner Pail: The Transformation of Politics and Governance in the Gilded Age* (New York: Hill & Wang, 2010).

28. In the 1874 House elections, Democrats took seats from Republicans in big-city, small-town, and rural districts. My analysis of House election returns is based on US census data and Michael J. Dubin, *United States Congressional Elections, 1788–1997* (Jefferson, NC: McFarland, 1998); Kenneth C. Martis, *The Historical Atlas of Congressional Districts* (New York: Macmillan, 1982); Stanley B. Parsons et al., *United States Congressional Districts and Data, 1843–1881* (New York: Greenwood, 1986).

29. My comparison of Republican seats in Congress and GOP victories in state assemblies is based on my file of election returns, taken from state legislative manuals ("bluebooks"), legislative directories, and "Partisan Division of American State Governments, 1834–1985" (ICPSR data set 16 [Walter D. Burnham state data set], University of Michigan). On the Illinois system of minority representation, see Campbell, *Representative Democracy*, 9–10, 19–24.

30. Paula Baker, "The Culture of Politics in the Late Nineteenth Century: Community and Political Behavior in Rural New York," *Journal of Social History* 18 (Winter 1984): 167–193, illustrates the influence of local conditions on voting behavior. For partisan outcomes in state elections, see Jerome M. Clubb, William H. Flanigan, and Nancy H. Zingale, *Partisan Realignment: Voters, Parties and Government in American History* (Beverly Hills, CA: Sage Publications, 1980), esp. ch. 6. No comprehensive analysis of partisan outcomes in American cities during the Gilded Age exists. For suggestions of urban partisanship, see Terrence J. McDonald, *The Parameters of Urban Fiscal Policy: Socioeconomic Change and Political Culture in San Francisco, 1860–1906* (Berkeley: University of California Press, 1986), 242–243; Edmund Morris, *The Rise of Theodore Roosevelt* (New York: Ballantine Books, 1979), esp. chs. 6–8, 14; and histories of specific cities during the Gilded Age, some of which are cited in the appendix.

31. Cherny, *American Politics*; Paul Kleppner, *The Third Electoral System, 1853–1892: Parties, Voters, and Political Cultures* (Chapel Hill: University of North

Carolina Press, 1979); Paul Kleppner, *Continuity and Change in Electoral Politics, 1893–1928* (Westport, CT: Greenwood, 1987). On independent Republicans, see Richard L. McCormick, *From Realignment to Reform: Political Change in New York State, 1893–1910* (Ithaca, NY: Cornell University Press, 1981), chs. 2–4.

32. Walter Dean Burnham, "The System of 1896: An Analysis," in *The Evolution of American Electoral Systems*, ed. Paul Kleppner et al. (Westport, CT: Greenwood, 1981), 147–202; Kleppner, *Continuity and Change*, table 2; Kornbluh, *Why America Stopped Voting*, chs. 4, 5; McCormick, *From Realignment to Reform*.

33. Ballard C. Campbell, "Economic Causes of Progressivism," *Journal of the Gilded Age and Progressive Era* 4, 1 (January 2005): 7–17; Paolo E. Coletta, "Election of 1908," in *History of Presidential Elections*, vol. 3, ed. Arthur M. Schlesinger (New York: Chelsea House, 1971), 2089; Lewis L. Gould, *Four Hats in the Ring: The 1912 Election and the Birth of Modern American Politics* (Lawrence: University Press of Kansas, 2008), ch. 1; David Sarasohn, *The Party of Reform: Democrats in the Progressive Era* (Jackson: University of Mississippi Press, 1989), ch. 4.

10. *The Federal State during the Gilded Age*

1. Carleton Putnam, *Theodore Roosevelt*, vol. 1, *The Formative Years, 1858–1886* (New York: Charles Scribner's Sons, 1958), ch. 15, esp. 254.

2. Ballard C. Campbell, *Representative Democracy: Public Policy and Midwestern Legislatures in the Late Nineteenth Century* (Cambridge, MA: Harvard University Press, 1980), 31–32, 44–45, 228; Philip R. VanderMeer, *The Hoosier Politician: Officeholding and Political Culture in Indiana, 1896–1920* (Urbana: University of Illinois Press, 1985), table 36; Joseph F. Mahoney, "The Impact of Industrialization on the New Jersey Legislature, 1870–1900," in *New Jersey since 1860*, ed. William C. Wright (Trenton: New Jersey Historical Commission, 1972), 69; David Henry Ray, "Membership Stability in Nine State Legislatures, 1891–1970" (Ph.D. diss., Stanford University, 1979), tables I.1, I.2. L. Ray Gunn, "Political Recruitment and Career Patterns in the New York State Legislature, 1850–1890" (paper presented at the Organization of American Historians annual meeting, April 1985), reported that 80 percent of legislators were first-term members in 1850, 60 percent in 1875, and 48 percent in 1890. Belle Zeller, *Pressure Politics in New York: A Study of Group Representation before the Legislature* (New York: Prentice-Hall, 1937), 292, indicated that 59 percent of representatives and senators in the 1882 session had no previous legislative experience, which averaged 1.1 years for all members.

3. On Roosevelt's assembly career, see Putnam, *Theodore Roosevelt*, chs. 15, 16, 19, 21; Edmund Morris, *The Rise of Theodore Roosevelt* (New York: Ballantine Books, 1979), chs. 6, 7, 9.

4. James Bryce, *The American Commonwealth*, vol. 1, 3rd ed. (New York: Macmillan, 1893), ch. 44; Roosevelt's "Phases of State Legislation," *Century* (January 1885), is quoted on 540–541. Bryce also quoted Roosevelt's "Machine Politics in New York City," *Century* (November 1886), in chs. 63 and 68. Also see C. Deming, "The Blight on Legislatures," *Nation* 54 (June 23, 1892): 460–461; James Eckels, "The Menace of Legislation," *North American Review* 165 (August 1897): 241–244.

For a sampling of the indictment thesis, see Matthew Josephson, *The Politicos, 1865–1896* (New York: Harcourt, Brace, World, 1938), 102, 344–345, 409; Richard Hofstadter, *The American Political Tradition and the Men Who Made It* (New York: Knopf, 1948), ch. 7; Ray Ginger, *Age of Excess: The United States from 1877 to 1914* (1965; reprint, New York: Macmillan, 1975), esp. ch. 6. The indictment literature of the Gilded Age identified one feature of politics that has persisted: corporate money.

5. On the New York legislature, see "Report of the Commission to Recommend Changes in Methods of Legislation" (November 30, 1895), in *New York Assembly Documents* (Albany, NY, 1896), document 20; Robert Luce, *Legislative Assemblies* (Boston: Houghton-Mifflin, 1924), 423–431, 461 (on improvements); Allan Nevins, *Grover Cleveland: A Study in Courage* (New York: Dodd, Mead, 1932), 110–111; Richard L. McCormick, *From Realignment to Reform: Political Change in New York State, 1893–1910* (Ithaca, NY: Cornell University Press, 1981), chs. 1–3.

6. Theodore Roosevelt, "Phases of State Legislation," *Century* (January 1885), reprinted in *The Works of Theodore Roosevelt* (New York: Charles Scribner's Sons, 1923–1926), 15:81. Roosevelt also wrote that the New York legislature, "taken as a whole, is by no means as bad a body as we would be led to believe" by the metropolitan newspapers (84).

7. See the appendix for the sources of state action in New York.

8. Editorial, *Chicago Tribune*, May 19, 1889. For a sketch of the unhealthiness of urban environments, see Lawrence H. Larsen, "Urban Services in Gilded Age Wisconsin," *Wisconsin Magazine of History* 71 (Winter 1987): 83–117; Don H. Doyle, *New Men, New Cities, New South: Atlanta, Nashville, Charleston, Mobile, 1860–1910* (Chapel Hill: University of North Carolina Press, 1990), ch. 10; Robert J. Gordon, *The Rise and Fall of American Growth: The U.S. Standard of Living since the Civil War* (Princeton, NJ: Princeton University Press, 2016), ch. 6. On major city fires, see Ballard C. Campbell, *American Disasters: 201 Calamities that Shook the Nation* (New York: Checkmark Books, 2008), including Chicago (1871), Boston (1872), Iroquois Theater (1903), San Francisco (1906), and Triangle Shirtwaist Factory (1911).

9. Barbara G. Rosenkrantz, *Public Health and the State: Changing Views in Massachusetts, 1842–1936* (Cambridge, MA: Harvard University Press, 1972); Charles P. Huse, *The Financial History of Boston, 1822–1909* (Cambridge, MA: Harvard University Press, 1916); Martha H. Bowers and Jane Carola, *The Water Supply System of Metropolitan Boston, 1845–1947* (Boston: Metropolitan District Commission, 1985), esp. appendix C.

10. Ira Cohen and Ann Elder, "Major Cities and Disease: A Comparative Perspective," *Social Science History* 13 (Spring 1989): 25–63; John Duffy, *The Sanitarians: A History of American Public Health* (Urbana: University of Illinois Press, 1990), ch. 10: Stanley K. Schultz, *Constructing Urban Culture: American Cities and City Planning, 1800–1920* (Philadelphia: Temple University Press, 1989), chs. 7, 8; Martin V. Melosi, *The Sanitary City: Urban Infrastructure in America from Colonial Times to the Present* (Baltimore: Johns Hopkins University Press, 2000), esp. ch. 9; Joel A. Tarr, "The Evolution of Urban Infrastructure in the Nineteenth and Twentieth

Centuries," in *Perspectives on Urban Infrastructure*, ed. Royce Hansen (Washington, DC: National Academy Press, 1984), 22–23.

11. Melosi, *Sanitary City*, 175–197; Stanley K. Schultz and Clay McShane, "To Engineer the Metropolis: Sewers, Sanitation, and City Planning in Nineteenth Century America," *Journal of American History* 65 (September 1978): 389–411; Jon C. Teaford, *Unheralded Triumph: City Government in America, 1870–1900* (Baltimore: Johns Hopkins University Press, 1984), 210–213, 246–250; Gordon, *Rise and Fall of American Growth*, chs. 2, 7; Judith W. Leavitt, "Politics and Public Heath: Smallpox in Milwaukee, 1894–95," *Bulletin of the History of Medicine* 50 (Winter 1976): 553–568.

12. Eric H. Monkkonen, *Police in Urban America, 1860–1920* (New York: Cambridge University Press, 1981), ch. 7; Teaford, *Unheralded Triumph*, 166–171, 275–279, 199–204, 240–245.

13. Carter Goodrich, "The Revulsion against Internal Improvements," *Journal of Economic History* 10 (November 1950): 145–169; Eric H. Monkkonen, *The Local State: Public Money and American Cities* (Stanford, CA: Stanford University Press, 1995), 9; Horace Secrist, *An Economic Analysis of the Constitutional Restrictions upon Pubic Indebtedness in the United States* (Madison: University of Wisconsin Press, 1914), 54–60; Peter J. Galie, *Ordered Liberty: A Constitutional History of New York* (New York: Fordham University Press, 1996), 145–146, 148–152; Teaford, *Unheralded Triumph*, ch. 10; Clifton K. Yearley, *The Money Machines: The Breakdown and Reform of Governmental and Party Finance in the North, 1860–1920* (Albany: State University of New York Press, 1970), ch. 1, 179–182, on academic and intellectual reformers who were "keenly aware of the expansion of government." Also see Sven Beckert, *The Monied Metropolis: New York City and the Consolidation of the American Bourgeoisie, 1850–1896* (New York: Cambridge University Press, 2001), ch. 7.

14. Teaford, *Unheralded Triumph*, esp. chs. 8, 9.

15. The remaining ten state legislatures, six located in the South, convened biennially; there was no time limit on sessions, and lawmakers were paid by the day. The classification of state legislatures is based on my review of state manuals and legislative documents; Roscoe L. Ashley, *The American Federal State: A Text-Book in Civics for High Schools and Academics* (New York: Macmillan, 1902), table II, 585; William G. Shade, "State Legislatures in the Nineteenth Century," in *Encyclopedia of the American Legislative System*, ed. Joel H. Silbey (New York: Charles Scribner's Sons, 1994), 1:195–214; Philip R. VanderMeer, "Congress and Other Legislatures," in Silbey, *Encyclopedia of the American Legislative System*, 3:1547–1567. Numerous grievances, including the fiscal consequences of economic depressions, fed support for restricting state legislative meetings. See Ballard C. Campbell, "Tax Revolts and Political Change," *Journal of Policy History* 10 (1998): 153–178.

16. VanderMeer, "Congress and Other Legislatures," 1549–1550; James Q. Dealey, *Growth of American State Constitutions* (Boston: Ginn, 1915), ch. 16; Campbell, *Representative Democracy*, 9–10; John D. Buenker, *Urban Liberalism and Progressive Reform* (New York: Norton, 1973), 13–16; Peter H. Argersinger, "The Value of the Vote: Political Representation in the Gilded Age," *Journal of American*

History 76 (June 1989): 59–90. Argersinger cites various inequalities in legislative representation (e.g., gerrymandered districts) that inhibit effective policymaking. With regard to the broader political system, he argues that "institutional inequities," "fraud and corruption," and narrow partisanship "constrained" effective governance, especially the regulation of private business, during the Gilded Age. Peter H. Argersinger, "The Transformation of the American Politics: Political Institutions and Public Policies, 1856–1910," in *Contesting Democracy: Substance and Structure in American Political History, 1775–2000*, ed. Bryan E. Shafer and Anthony J. Badger (Lawrence: University Press of Kansas, 2001), 117–147.

17. See Campbell, *Representative Democracy*, esp. chs. 5, 10; Peter H. Argersinger, "Populists in Power: Public Policy and Legislative Behavior," *Journal of Interdisciplinary History* 18 (Summer 1987): 81–105; A. Lawrence Lowell, "The Influence of Party upon Legislation in England and America," in *Annual Report of the American Historical Association for the Year 1901*, vol. 1 (Washington, DC, 1902), 321–542; Allen W. Trelease, "The Fusion Legislatures of 1895 and 1897: A Roll-Call Analysis of the North Carolina House of Representatives," *North Carolina Historical Review* 57 (July 1980): 280–309; James E. Wright, *The Politics of Populism: Dissent in Colorado* (New Haven, CT: Yale University Press, 1974); James E. Wright, *The Progressive Yankees: Republican Reformers in New Hampshire, 1906–1916* (Hanover, NH: University Press of New England, 1987).

The evidence I reviewed suggests that the large majority of legislators in most states, especially in the Northeast and Midwest, did not engage in illegal activities, such as accepting payments for a vote. However, there is no question that some lawmakers accepted bribes on certain issues, especially concerning private businesses, most notably urban transit and utility franchises. It was well known that railroads provided free passes to state lawmakers until the practice was prohibited in the early twentieth century. Corruption is discussed in the section on administration in this chapter.

On the significance of states and state legislatures in the expansion of governance in the Gilded Age, see Jonathan R. T. Hughes, *The Governmental Habit Redux: Economic Controls from Colonial Times to the Present* (Princeton, NJ: Princeton University Press, 1991), 199; Sidney Fine, *Laissez Faire and the General Welfare State: A Study of Conflict in American Thought* (Ann Arbor: University of Michigan Press, 1956), 141, 353–354.

18. The survey of state policy actions in the next several paragraphs is based on secondary literature and a database of "important" statutes enacted by eight sample states (see table A.3 in the appendix). On Massachusetts, see Ballard C. Campbell, "Public Policy and State Governments," in *Origins of Modern America: Essays on the Late Nineteenth Century*, 2nd ed., ed. Charles W. Calhoun (Lanham, MD: Rowman & Littlefield, 2007), 353–371.

Some readers may question whether a tabulation of session laws indicates much about governance without an examination of the statutes' content and administration. I agree, up to a point, with Daniel P. Carpenter, *The Forging of Bureaucratic Autonomy: Networks and Policy Innovation in Executive Agencies, 1862–1928* (Princeton, NJ: Princeton University Press, 2001), 11, that "legislation cannot hardwire administrative outcomes." Nonetheless, the adoption of a statute is an expression of governmental authority; collectively, a survey of laws (including city ordinances and court decisions) identifies subjects garnering policy attention. But it is also true that the design of a statute bears on its implementation.

19. On the linkages between tensions over labor activities and an enhanced police presence, see Sam Mitrani, *The Rise of the Chicago Police Department: Class and Conflict, 1850–1894* (Urbana: University of Illinois Press, 2013). See also data on incarceration facilities and inmates in chapter 9.

20. Richard L. McCormick, *The Party Period and Public Policy* (New York: Oxford University Press, 1986), has popularized the idea of "distributive policy," which I think has greater veracity for Congress than for states and cities.

21. Allan G. Bogue et al., "Members of the House of Representatives and the Process of Modernization, 1789–1960," *Journal of American History* 58 (September 1976): 284, 289; Nelson W. Polsby, "The Institutionalization of the U.S. House of Representatives," *American Political Science Review* 57 (March 1968): 144. Also see Margaret Susan Thompson, *The "Spider's Web": Congress and Lobbying in the Age of Grant* (Ithaca, NY: Cornell University Press, 1985); David J. Rothman, *Politics and Power: The United States Senate, 1869–1901* (Cambridge, MA: Harvard University Press, 1969); *Congressional Quarterly Guide to Congress*, 3rd ed. (Washington, DC: Congressional Quarterly, 1982), 404, 477, 580–581. The Legislative Reference Service, a unit of the Library of Congress, provided research and compilations of laws for congressional committees. A Legislative Drafting Service was created in 1918.

22. Nelson W. Polsby, "The Growth of the Seniority System in the U.S. House of Representatives," *American Political Science Review* 57 (September 1969): 787–807.

23. Garrison Nelson, "The Modernizing Congress, 1870–1930," in Silbey, *Encyclopedia of the American Legislative System*, 1:131–156; Carl V. Harris, "Right Fork or Left Fork? The Section-Party Alignment of Southern Democrats in Congress, 1873–1897," *Journal of Southern History* 42 (November 1976): 471–506; David W. Brady, *Congressional Voting in a Partisan Era* (Lawrence: University Press of Kansas, 1973); William G. Shade et al., "Partisanship in the United States Senate, 1869–1901," *Journal of Interdisciplinary History* 4 (Autumn 1973): 185–206.

24. Annexation of the Philippines was not on the national agenda until after the US Navy defeated the Spanish in the Pacific. Richard Hofstadter expertly tells this story in "Cuba, the Philippines and Manifest Destiny," in *The Paranoid Style in American Politics and Other Essays* (New York: Vintage, 1967), ch. 5.

25. US Bureau of the Census, *Historical Statistics of the United States, Colonial Times to 1970* (Washington, DC: Government Printing Office, 1975), series H526; Michael Mann, *The Sources of Social Power*, vol. 2, *The Rise of Classes and Nation-States, 1760–1914* (New York: Cambridge University Press, 1993), ch. 11, esp. 391; David Tyack et al., *Law and the Shaping of Public Education, 1785–1954* (Madison: University of Wisconsin Press, 1987), 59. By 1900 twenty-eight states had boards of education, seventeen had qualifications for teacher certification, and thirty-seven had compulsory education laws. Jim B. Pearson and Edgar Fuller, eds., *Education in the States*, vol. 2 (Washington, DC: National Education Association, 1969), 29, 391–392.

26. Roger Lane, *Policing the City: Boston, 1822–1885* (Cambridge, MA: Harvard University Press, 1967), 192–198, 202; James F. Richardson, *The New York Police: Colonial Times to 1901* (New York: Oxford University Press, 1970), 152, 173–175; Bryce, *American Commonwealth*, 1:616; Mitrani, *Rise of the Chicago Police Department*; Kermit L. Hall and Peter Karsten, *The Magic Mirror: Law in American History*, 2nd ed. (New York: Oxford University Press, 2009), ch. 9. The decline in arrest rates during the Gilded Age suggests that policing in the bigger cities improved. See Monkkonen, *Police in Urban America*, ch. 2, 144, 147. Larsen, "Urban Services in Gilded Age Wisconsin," found that small cities lagged in the modernization of police and other functions, while Mark H. Haller, "Historical Roots of Police Behavior, Chicago, 1890–1925," *Law and Society Review* 10 (1976): 303–324, reported that policing changed only minimally in the Windy City before World War I.

27. On city and rural public employment, see Solomon Fabricant, *The Trend of Governmental Activity in the United States since 1900* (New York: National Bureau of Economic Research, 1952), 29, tables B1, B9, B13; Steven P. Erie, "Politics, the Public Sector, and Irish Social Mobility: San Francisco, 1870–1900," *Western Political Quarterly* 31 (June 1978): tables 2, 6; Bryce, *American Commonwealth*, 1:637, 526; Rebecca Menes, "Limiting the Reach of the Grabbing Hand," in *Corruption and Reform: Lessons from American Economic History*, ed. Edward L. Glaeser and Claudia Goldin (Chicago: University of Chicago Press, 2006), ch. 2; Charles A. Glaab and A. Theodore Brown, *A History of Urban America*, 2nd ed. (New York: Macmillan, 1976), ch. 10. Also see notes 28–31.

28. Teaford, *Unheralded Triumph*, 62, reported that New York City's Law Department employed more lawyers than the US Justice Department. Also see David B. Tyack, *The One Best System: A History of American Urban Education* (Cambridge, MA: Harvard University Press), 90, 96; Marvin Lazerson, *Origins of the Urban School: Public Education in Massachusetts, 1870–1915* (Cambridge, MA: Harvard University Press, 1971), 24–25; Schultz, *Constructing Urban Culture*, 187–191. Teaford, *Unheralded Triumph*; Theda Skocpol, *Protecting Soldiers and Mothers: The Political Origins of Social Policy in the United States* (Cambridge, MA: Harvard University Press, 1992),145; and Edward L. Glaeser and Claudia Goldin, "Corruption and Reform: An Introduction," NBER Working Paper 10775 (September 2004), are some of the recent scholars who have disputed the traditional charge of rampant political corruption in public affairs during the late nineteenth century.

29. A key work on state administration in the Gilded Age is William R. Brock, *Investigation and Responsibility: Public Responsibility in the United States, 1865–1900* (Cambridge: Cambridge University Press, 1984). Also see Albert Bushnell Hart, *Actual Government* (New York: Longmans, Green, 1903); Leonard D. White, *Trends in Public Administration* (New York: McGraw-Hill, 1933); Yearley, *Money Machines*; William R. Doezema, "Railroad Management and the Interplay of Federal and State Regulation, 1885–1916," *Business History Review* 50 (Summer 1976): 153–178.

Studies of individual states provide valuable glimpses into their administration. See, for example, Gerald D. Nash, *State Government and Economic Development: A History of Administrative Policies in California, 1849–1933* (Berkeley: University of California Press, 1964), esp. 352–357; William A. Link, *The Paradox of Southern*

Progressivism, 1880–1930 (Chapel Hill: University of North Carolina Press, 1992), ch. 1; Robert C. Nesbit, *The History of Wisconsin: Urbanization and Industrialization, 1873–1893* (Madison: State Historical Society of Wisconsin, 1985), ch. 12. On the Massachusetts Railroad Commission, see Thomas K. McCraw, *Prophets of Regulation* (Cambridge, MA: Harvard University Press, 1984), ch. 1. Interstate, interlevel, and gender influences in enacting and enforcing factory regulations are examined in Kathryn Kish Sklar, *Florence Kelly and the Nation's Work* (New Haven, CT: Yale University Press, 1995), ch. 9. The Illinois Supreme Court struck down the state's eight-hour law. Courts played an ongoing role in state and local administration, as discussed later in this chapter.

30. See, for example, Rudy Higgens-Evenson, "From Industrial Police to Workmen's Compensation: Public Policy and Industrial Accidents in New York, 1880–1910," *Labor History* 39 (November 1998): 365–380. He documents the New York Factory Board's woeful record on the prosecution and fining of factory operators for workplace accidents. Also see Donald F. Tingley, *The Structuring of a State: The History of the Illinois, 1899–1928* (Urbana: University of Illinois Press, 1980), ch. 4; Mansel G. Blackford, *The Politics of Business in California, 1890–1920* (Columbus: Ohio State University Press, 1997), ch. 5; William Forbath, *Law and the Shaping of the American Labor Movement* (Cambridge, MA: Harvard University Press, 1991).

31. Brock, *Investigation and Responsibility*, 44–57, 227; Teaford, *Unheralded Triumph*, ch. 6; White, *Trends in Public Administration*, table C1 (291–298).

32. Leonard D. White, *The Republican Era, 1869–1901: A Study in Administrative History* (New York: Macmillan, 1958); Carpenter, *Forging of Bureaucratic Autonomy*, ch. 2; Stephen Skowronek, *Building a New American State: The Expansion of National Administrative Capacities, 1877–1920* (New York: Cambridge University Press, 1982), chs. 2–5.

33. Richard F. Bensel, *Yankee Leviathan: The Origins of Central State Authority in America, 1859–1977* (New York: Cambridge University Press, 1990), table 6.5; Fabricant, *Trend of Governmental Activity*, table B13; White, *Trends in Public Administration*, 243–244; US Bureau of the Census, *Historical Statistics of the United States* (Washington, DC: Government Printing Office, 1975), series Y241, 242, 247. To put the increase in federal employees in perspective, New York City had a payroll of 30,000 in 1900; local and state governments hired three and a half times more staffers than the federal government did that year.

34. Carpenter, *Forging of Bureaucratic Autonomy*, ch. 2; James R. Beniger, *The Control Revolution: Technological and Economic Origins of the Information Society* (Cambridge, MA: Harvard University Press, 1896), 234, 282–283, 325, 430–431; Constance M. Green, *Washington*, vol. 1 (Princeton, NJ: Princeton University Press, 1962–1963), 316, 328–329; Morris, *Rise of Theodore Roosevelt*, 441, 574, 585. Roosevelt took advantage of his boss's vacation to prepare Admiral George Dewey for an attack on the Spanish fleet in the Philippines once war was declared.

35. Nicholas R. Parillo, *Against the Profit-Motive: The Salary Revolution in American Government, 1780–1940* (New Haven, CT: Yale University Press, 2013); Paul P. Van Riper, "American Administrative State: Wilson and the Founders," in *A Centennial History of the Administrative State*, ed. Ralph C. Chandler (New York:

Free Press, 1987), 14–21; White, *Republican Era*, ch. 4; Skowronek, *Building a New American State*, ch. 5. University appointments to chairs of public administration began in the 1920s. See White, *Trends in Public Administration*, 311–326.

36. Oscar Kraines, "The Cockrell Committee, 1887–1889: First Comprehensive Congressional Investigation into Administration," *Western Political Quarterly* 4 (December 1951): 596–599; Margery Davies, *Woman's Place Is at the Typewriter: Office Work and Office Workers, 1870–1930* (Philadelphia: Temple University Press, 1982), ch. 3; Cindy Sondik Aron, *Ladies and Gentlemen of the Civil Service: Workers in Victorian America* (New York: Oxford University Press, 1987), 86–89, 94; Richard E. Welch, *The Presidencies of Grover Cleveland* (Lawrence: University Press of Kansas, 1988), 49; Morton Keller, *Affairs of State: Public Life in Late Nineteenth Century America* (Cambridge, MA: Harvard University Press, 1977), 118, 141, 298; White, *Republican Era*, 101–103, 203; Stanley Lebergott, *The American Economy: Income, Wealth, and Want* (Princeton, NJ: Princeton University Press, 1976), 248–298, on household facilities in the Gilded Age.

37. Beniger, *Control Revolution*, 282–283; Kraines, "Cockrell Committee," 590, 596–598. The committee recommended financial retrenchment and more efficient work habits, not more staff, as the solution for administrative backlogs, but it also suggested the use of duplicating machines and the installation of modern plumbing. The United States published *The Statistical Abstract of the United States* annually between 1878 and 2012; private publishers have continued the series.

38. Herbert Kaufman, "The Growth of the Federal Personnel System," in *The Federal Government Service*, ed. N. Wallace Sayre (Englewood Cliffs, NJ: Prentice-Hall, 1965), 41–43. By 1916, 62 percent of federal employees were part of the civil service. On the creation of administrative units in the USDA, see Carroll H. Wooddy, *The Growth of the Federal Government, 1915–1932* (New York: McGraw-Hill, 1934), ch. 12.

39. See table A.3 in the appendix for a more complete list of state actions. Carpenter, *Forging of Bureaucratic Autonomy*, ch. 6; Wooddy, *Growth of the Federal Government*, ch. 12; Hart, *Actual Government*, 438; Skocpol, *Protecting Soldiers and Mothers*, table 3, ch. 2, esp. 128–129, 134.

40. Mark Sullivan, *Our Times: The United States, 1900–1925*, vol. 3 (New York: Scribner's Sons, 1930), 302; A. Hunter Dupree, *Science in the Federal Government: A History of Policies and Activities* (Baltimore: Johns Hopkins University Press, 1957), 189, 192; Carpenter, *Forging of Bureaucratic Autonomy*, 205, chs. 4, 6; White, *Republican Era*, 244, 246, 256; Ari Hoogenboom, *The Presidency of Rutherford B. Hayes* (Lawrence: University Press of Kansas, 1988), ch. 5, esp. 114–120, 105; Michael J. Lacey, "The World of Bureaus: Government and the Positivist Project in the Late Nineteenth Century," in *The State and Social Investigation in Britain and the United States*, ed. Michael J. Lacey and Mary O. Furner (Washington, DC: Woodrow Wilson Center Press, 1993), 157–163.

Political scientists who point to administrative capacity as a criterion of American statebuilding have emphasized the development of semiautonomous bureaucrats, defined as officials who gained policymaking discretion. See Skowronek, *Building a New American State*; Bensel, *Yankee Leviathan*; Carpenter, *Forging of Bureaucratic*

Autonomy. I use the term "administrative capacity" in a broader sense; functionally oriented administrative units can exercise real power even if bureau heads lack wide "autonomous" policy authority.

41. Josephson, *Politicos*, 344.

42. Richard Hofstadter, William Miller, and Daniel Aaron, *The American Republic*, vol. 2 (Englewood Cliffs, NJ: Prentice-Hall, 1959), 95.

43. Fine, *Laissez Faire*, chs. 3–5; Herbert Hovenkamp, *Enterprise and American Law, 1836–1937* (Cambridge, MA: Harvard University Press, 1991), 5, 96–97, 204, 330, 347; John G. Sproat, *The Best Men: Liberal Reformers in the Gilded Age* (New York: Oxford University Press, 1968), chs. 1, 8; Michael Les Benedict, "Laissez Faire and Liberty: A Re-evaluation of the Meaning and Origins of Laissez-Faire Constitutionalism," *Law and History Review* 3 (Fall 1985): 293–331. Merle Curti, *The Growth of American Thought* (New York: Harper & Brothers, 1943), ch. 25, provides an incisive exposition on these points.

44. The cases are *Wabash, St. Louis, and Pacific Railway Co. v. Illinois* (1886), *Pollock v. Farmers' Loan and Trust Co.* (1895), *U.S. v. E. C. Knight Co.* (1895), *Interstate Commerce Commission v. Cincinnati, New Orleans, and Texas Pacific Railway Co.* (1897), *In Re. Debs* (1895), and *Plessy v. Ferguson* (1896). Summaries of the decisions appear in Melvin I. Urofsky and Paul Finkelman, *A March of Liberty: A Constitutional History of the United States* (New York: Oxford University Press, 2011), chs. 22–24; Michael Kammen, *A Machine that Would Go of Itself: The Constitution in American Culture* (New York: Vintage, 1986), ch. 7.

45. Harold M. Hyman and William M. Wiecek, *Equal Justice under Law: Constitutional Development, 1835–1875* (New York: Harper & Row, 1982), 356–357; Brock, *Investigation and Responsibility*, ch. 3; Howard Gillman, *The Constitution Besieged: The Rise and Demise of Lockner Era Police Powers Jurisdiction* (Durham, NC: Duke University Press, 1993), 87–94; Keller, *Affairs of State*, 336, 362, 401–408; G. Edward White, *Justice Oliver Wendell Holmes: Law and the Inner Self* (New York: Oxford University Press, 1993), ch. 8; Margaret Virginia Nelson, *Judicial Review in Virginia, 1789–1928* (New York: Columbia University Press, 1947), ch. 4; Ernest L. Bogart and John M. Matthews, *The Modern Commonwealth, 1893–1918* (Springfield: Illinois Centennial Commission, 1920), ch. 15; Melvin I. Urofsky, "State Courts and Protective Legislation during the Progressive Era: A Re-evaluation," *Journal of American History* 72 (June 1985): 75, 88.

46. Michael L. Benedict, "Law and Regulation in the Gilded Age and Progressive Era," in *Law as Culture and Culture as Law*, ed. Hendrick Hartog and William E. Nelson (Madison, WI: Madison House, 2000), 227–263; Charles W. McCurdy, "The Knight Sugar Decision of 1895 and the Modernization of American Corporate Law, 1869–1903," *Business History Review* 53 (1979): 304–342; Hovenkamp, *Enterprise and American Law*, 123; Forbath, *Law and the Shaping of the American Labor Movement*, appendix A; Fine, *Laissez Faire*, 127, 132, 154; Alan Jones, "Thomas M. Cooley and 'Laissez Faire Constitutionalism': A Reconsideration," *Journal of American History* 53 (March 1967): 763–766. Also see notes 44 and 45.

47. Bryce, *American Commonwealth* (1888 ed., rev. 1890), 2:422. The table on governmental actions was omitted from the 1893 edition. Robert H. Wiebe, *The*

Segmented Society: An Introduction to the Meaning of America (New York: Oxford University Press, 1975), 149, 165–166, agrees with Bryce that Americans venerated the Constitution as a template of national ideals, a sentiment that conveyed authority to the Supreme Court's resolution of conflicts.

48. Charles Beard and Mary Beard, *The Rise of American Civilization*, vol. 2 (New York: Macmillan, 1927), chs. 23, 27; Samuel Eliot Morison and Henry Steele Commager, *The Growth of the American Republic*, vol. 2 (New York: Oxford University Press, 1930), ch. 10, esp. 214–215; Hofstadter, *American Political Tradition*, 164.

I am not arguing that liberal historians deliberately used history to advance a political agenda; rather, their value systems disposed them to emphasize the negative dimensions of the Gilded Age. State governments' inability to remedy the problems of the Great Depression of the 1930s reinforced progressives' support for national action. On the political orientation of historians, see Richard Hofstadter, *The Progressive Historians: Turner, Beard, Parrington* (New York: Knopf, 1968), 25–41, 182–196, 220, 256, 265, 298–299; John Higham, *History: Professional Scholarship in America* (Baltimore: Johns Hopkins University Press, 1983), pt. I, chs. 1, 2, pt. II, ch. 3; Clyde E. Barrow, "Beyond Progressivism: Charles A. Beard's Social Democratic Theory of American Political Development," *Studies in American Political Development* 8, 2 (1994): 236–253; David Thelen, "The Practice of History," *Journal of American History* 81 (December 1994): 933–960. The 1,047 historians included in Thelen's survey considered Eugene Debs and Jane Addams the most admired people in the Gilded Age (table 3, 952).

For the political orientation of historians and humanists during the middle decades of the twentieth century, see Seymour M. Lipset, *Political Man: The Social Basis of Politics* (New York: Anchor Books, 1963), 337–338, 365; Everett C. Ladd and Seymour M. Lipset, *The Divided Academy: Professors and Politics* (New York: McGraw-Hill, 1975), 20, 27, 29–30, 368–369; Paul F. Lazarsfeld and Wagner W. Thielens Jr., *The Academic Mind: Social Scientists in a Time of Crisis* (Glencoe, IL: Free Press, 1958), 16–17, 150–152. Elements of laissez-faire minimalism concerning the proper scope of government in the United States remained vibrant through the twentieth century and into the twenty-first; see Ballard C. Campbell, *The Growth of American Government: Governance from the Cleveland Era to the Present*, updated ed. (Bloomington: Indiana University Press, 2015), ch. 11.

11. *The Progressive State*

1. Ron Chernow, *The House of Morgan: An American Banking Dynasty and the Rise of Modern Finance* (New York: Simon & Schuster, 1990), ch. 7; J. Lawrence Broz, *The International Origin of the Federal Reserve System* (Ithaca, NY: Cornell University Press, 1997), 175–178; James Livingston, *Origins of the Federal Reserve System: Money, Class and Corporate Capitalism, 1890–1913* (Ithaca, NY: Cornell University Press, 1986), esp. 173; Robert Bruner and Sean D. Carr, *The Panic of 1907: Lessons Learned from the Market's Perfect Storm* (Hoboken, NJ: John Wiley & Sons, 2007), 151; Arthur S. Link, *Woodrow Wilson and the Progressive Era,*

1910–1917 (New York: Harper & Row, 1954), 44–51; Ballard C. Campbell, "Economic Causes of Progressivism," *Journal of the Gilded Age and Progressive Era* 4 (January 2005): 7–22.

2. Richard A. Greenwald, *The Triangle Fire, the Protocols of Peace, and Industrial Democracy in the Progressive Era* (Philadelphia: Temple University Press, 2005), esp. chs. 6, 7; John D. Buenker, *Urban Liberalism and Progressive Reform* (New York: Scribner's, 1973), 48–50.

3. On economic crises as triggers of political change, see Ballard C. Campbell, "Tax Revolts and Political Change," *Journal of Policy History* 10 (1998): 153–178; Ballard C. Campbell, introduction to *American Disasters: 201 Calamities that Shook the Nation* (New York: Checkmark Books, 2008). On windows of opportunity for policymaking, see John W. Kingdon, *Agendas, Alternatives, and Public Policies* (N.p.: HarperCollins, 1984), 99–105, 177–178.

4. "Inaugural Address of Governor Eugene N. Foss," January 5, 1911, *Journal of the Massachusetts House of Representatives* (1911); William Allen White, *The Autobiography of William Allen White* (New York: Macmillan, 1946), 428; Theodore Roosevelt, "Annual Message, Dec. 5, 1905," in James D. Richardson, comp., *Messages and Papers of the Presidents*, vol. 10 (Washington, DC: Bureau of National Literature and Art), 7355 (Roosevelt referred to "problems" three times in his very short inaugural address); Woodrow Wilson, *The New Freedom* (New York: Doubleday, Page, 1913), 281.

Influential interpretations of progressivism include Richard Hofstadter, *The Age of Reform* (New York: Random House, 1955), 16 ("Americans do not abide very quietly the evils of life"); Samuel Hays, *The Response to Industrialism, 1885–1914* (Chicago: University of Chicago Press, 1957); Robert Wiebe, *The Search for Order, 1877–1920* (New York: Hill & Wang, 1967); Buenker, *Urban Liberalism and Progressive Reform*; Richard L. McCormick, *From Realignment to Reform: Political Change in New York State, 1893–1910* (Ithaca, NY: Cornell University Press, 1981); Arthur S. Link and Richard L. McCormick, *Progressivism* (Arlington Heights, IL: Harlan Davidson, 1983); Daniel T. Rodgers, *Atlantic Crossings: Social Politics in a Progressive Age* (Cambridge, MA: Harvard University Press, 1999). Maureen A. Flanagan, *America Reformed: Progressives and Progressivism, 1890s–1920s* (New York: Oxford University Press, 2007), and James J. Connolly, *An Elusive Unity: Urban Democracy and Machine Politics in Industrializing America* (Ithaca, NY: Cornell University Press, 2010), provide extensive citations to pertinent literature.

5. David Montgomery, "The 'New Unionism' and the Transformation of Workers' Consciousness in America, 1909–1922," *Journal of Social History* 7 (Summer 1974): 509–529, esp. table 1 on strikes and unemployment.

6. Clay McShane, *Down the Asphalt Path* (New York: Columbia University Press, 1994), ch. 9; James J. Flink, *America Adopts the Auto, 1895–1910* (Cambridge: Massachusetts Institute of Technology, 1970). See motor vehicle registration in table A.3 in the appendix.

7. John Duffy, *The Sanitarians: A History of American Public Health* (Urbana: University of Illinois Press, 1990), ch. 15; Gerald N. Grob, *The Deadly Truth: The History of Disease in America* (Cambridge, MA: Harvard University Press, 2002),

ch. 8; Martin V. Melosi, *The Sanitary City: Urban Infrastructure in America from Colonial Times to the Present* (Baltimore: Johns Hopkins University Press, 2000), chs. 6–9.

8. Louis Galambos, "Technology, Political Economy, and Professionalization: Central Themes of the Organizational Synthesis," *Business Historical Review* 57 (Winter 1983): 471–493; James R. Beniger, *The Control Revolution: Technology and Economic Origins of the Information Society* (Cambridge, MA: Harvard University Press, 1986); Mary O. Furner and Barry Supple, eds., *The State and Economic Knowledge: The American and British Experience* (Washington, DC: Wilson International Center for Scholars, 1990). W. Brooke Graves, *Uniform State Action: A Possible Substitute for Centralization* (Chapel Hill: University of North Carolina Press, 1934), 293–294, counted forty-three national organizations of civic professionals created between 1878 and 1916; eleven were formed before 1900.

9. For intellectual challenges to conservative political beliefs, see Sidney Fine, *Laissez Faire and the General Welfare State: A Study of Conflict in American Thought, 1865–1901* (Ann Arbor: University of Michigan Press, 1956), chs. 6–8.

10. Wiebe, *Search for Order*, 166. Also see Robert Wiebe, *Self-Rule: A Cultural History of American Democracy* (Chicago: University of Chicago Press, 1995), 141–157; Michael McGerr, *A Fierce Discontent: The Rise and Fall of the Progressive Movement in America, 1870–1920* (New York: Free Press, 2003), ch. 2. Robert D. Johnson, *The Radical Middle Class: Populist Democracy and the Question of Capitalism in Progressive Era Portland* (Princeton, NJ: Princeton University Press, 2003), ch. 1, explores the imprecision in the concept of middle class and suggests that the term "middling" classes best fits some situations.

11. Maureen Flanagan, "Gender and Urban Political Reform: The City Club and the Woman's City Club of Chicago in the Progressive Era," *American Historical Review* 95 (October 1990): 1032–1050; Maureen Flanagan, *Seeing with Their Hearts: Chicago Women and the Vision of the Good City, 1871–1933* (Princeton, NJ: Princeton University Press, 2002); Theda Skocpol, *Protecting Soldiers and Mothers: The Political Origins of Social Policy in the United States* (Cambridge, MA: Harvard University Press, 1992), 52, 457, chs. 6–8; Frank Felsenstein and James J. Connolly, *What Middletown Read: Print Culture in an American Small City* (Amherst: University of Massachusetts Press, 2015), esp. ch. 6; Eleanor Flexner and Ellen Fitzpatrick, *Century of Struggle: The Woman's Rights Movement in the United States* (Cambridge, MA: Harvard University Press, 1996); William A. Link, *The Paradox of Southern Progressivism, 1880–1930* (Chapel Hill: University of North Carolina Press, 1992), 134–140. The adoption of the Nineteenth Amendment (women's suffrage) is discussed in chapter 12.

12. Buenker, *Urban Liberalism and Progressive Reform*. Also see Kenneth Finegold, *Experts and Politicians: Reform Challenges to Machine Politics in New York, Cleveland, and Chicago* (Princeton, NJ: Princeton University Press, 1995); Mansel G. Blackford, "Reform Politics in Seattle during the Progressive Era, 1902–1916," *Pacific Northwest Quarterly* 59 (October 1968): 177–185; Michael P. Rogin and John L. Shover, *Political Change in California: Critical Elections and Social Movements, 1890–1966* (Westport, CT: Greenwood, 1970), chs. 2, 3. Elizabeth Sanders,

Roots of Reform: Farmers, Workers, and the American States, 1877–1917 (Chicago: University of Chicago Press, 1999), argues that southerners spearheaded progressivism in Congress. Also see Robert Harrison, *Congress, Progressive Reform, and the New American State* (New York: Cambridge University Press, 2004), ch. 9.

Key actions of Congress in the Progressive Era:

1906 Hepburn Railroad Regulation Act (Interstate Commerce Commission rate powers); Pure Food and Drug Act
1909 Income tax amendment passed by Congress; Payne Aldrich tariff; corporate excise tax
1910 Mann-Elkins Act (physical evaluation of railroads)
1912 Adoption of Seventeenth Amendment (popular election of US senators); Pujo Commission; immigration literacy test (Taft veto)
1913 Income tax law; Underwood tariff; Federal Reserve Act
1914 Clayton Act; Federal Trade Commission
1916 Child Labor Act (overturned by Supreme Court); Federal Highway Act
1917 Eighteenth Amendment (Prohibition) adopted (ratified 1919)

13. Roger E. Wyman, "Middle-Class Voters and Progressive Reformers: The Conflict of Class and Culture," *American Political Science Review* 68 (June 1974): 488–504; James Wright, *The Progressive Yankees: Republican Reformers in New Hampshire, 1906–1916* (Hanover, NH: University Press of New England, 1987), esp. chs. 4, 5; J. Joseph Huthmacher, *Massachusetts People and Politics, 1919–1933* (New York: Athenaeum, 1959), ch. 1. Also see Paul Kleppner, *Continuity and Change in Electoral Politics, 1893–1928* (New York: Greenwood, 1987), 131–136, 191–197; Michael E. McGerr, *The Decline of Popular Politics: The American North, 1865–1928* (New York: Oxford University Press, 1986), 148–151, 209, ch. 5; Laurence James Holt, *Congressional Insurgents and the Party System, 1909–1916* (Cambridge, MA: Harvard University Press, 1967). Congressional policymaking during the Progressive Era, including voting alignments by policy domains, is an area that needs further analysis.

14. Thomas Bender, *A Nation among Nations: America's Place in World History* (New York: Hill & Wang, 2006), ch. 5; Rodgers, *Atlantic Crossings*, esp. chs. 2, 4, 6; Michael Mann, *The Sources of Social Power*, vol. 2 (Cambridge: Cambridge University Press, 1993), ch. 18. Also see Kenneth O. Morgan, "The Future at Work: Anglo-American Progressivism, 1890–1917," in *Contrast and Connection: Bicentennial Essays in Anglo-American History*, ed. H. C. Allen and Roger Thompson (Columbus: Ohio University Press, 1976), 245–271; Seth Koven and Sonya Michel, "'Women Duties': Materialist Politics and the Origins of the Welfare State in France, Germany, Great Britain, and the United States, 1880–1920," *American Historical Review* 95 (October 1990): 1076–1108.

15. Jacqueline Van Voris, *Carrie Chapman Catt: A Public Life* (New York: Feminist Press at City University of New York, 1987), 10; Richard J. Evans, *The Feminists: Women's Emancipation Movements in Europe, America and Australasia, 1840–1920* (London: Croom Helm, 1977), 246–259; David Morgan, "Woman Suffrage in Brit-

ain and America in the Early Twentieth Century," in Allen and Thompson, *Contrast and Connection,* 279–288; Ida Husted Harper, "The World Movement for Woman Suffrage," *American Review of Reviews* (December 1911): 725–729.

16. David P. Thelen, *The New Citizenship: Origins of Progressivism in Wisconsin, 1885–1900* (Columbia: University of Missouri Press, 1972); Clifton K. Yearley, *The Money Machines: The Breakdown and Reform of Governmental and Party Finance in the North, 1860–1920* (Albany: State University of New York Press, 1970); Bender, *Nation among Nations,* 250–253; John Higham, *Writing American History: Essays on Modern Scholarship* (Bloomington: Indiana University Press, 1970), ch. 4. James L. Huston, "The American Revolutionaries, the Political Economy of Aristocracy and the American Concept of the Distribution of Wealth, 1765–1900," *American Historical Review* 98 (October 1993): 1079–1105, dates the transition from republican-era assumptions about the creation of wealth, which hinged on political control of public policy, to the Progressive Era emphasis on private capitalism to the last years of the nineteenth century.

17. Campbell, "Economic Causes of Progressivism."

18. Samuel Haber, *Efficiency and Uplift: Scientific Management in the Progressive Era, 1890–1920* (Chicago: University of Chicago Press, 1964); Martin J. Schiesl, *The Politics of Efficiency: Municipal Administration and Reform in America, 1800–1920* (Berkeley: University of California Press, 1977), ch. 5; Jonathan Kahn, *Budgeting Democracy: State Building and Citizenship in America, 1890–1928* (Ithaca, NY: Cornell University Press, 1997).

19. Campbell, "Economic Causes of Progressivism"; John D. Buenker, *The Income Tax and the Progressive Era* (New York: Garland, 1985).

20. Link and McCormick, *Progressivism,* 117.

21. Table A.3 in the appendix lists major statutes and ordinances adopted in eight states. Each policy adoption in the United States has its own story, for three primary reasons. First, the structure of governance under American federalism grants policymaking authority to thousands of governing units that contain many thousands of policy actors. Second, policy proposals engage diverse subjects, which differ in content and connection to constituent groups. The literature demonstrates that differences in policy content can produce different policymaking scenarios. Third, the socioeconomic environment varies between places and changes over time, which alters the context of policymaking. These dimensions of lawmaking form an interactive matrix that produces a wide variety of influences on policy actions.

Academic disciplines have approached this subject from different angles. Historians tend to see a variety of causal determinants behind policy innovations, while political scientists and economists seek to identify dominant causal factors. Both approaches have merit. A model of policy diversity in the Gilded Age and Progressive Era appears in Ballard C. Campbell, "Federalism, State Action, and 'Critical Episodes' in the Growth of American Government," *Social Science History* 16, 4 (Winter 1992): 561–577.

22. Campbell, "Federalism, State Action, and 'Critical Episodes,'" table 2; Advisory Commission on Intergovernmental Relations, *Significant Features of Fiscal Federalism, 1976–1977 Edition,* vol. 2, *Revenue and Debt* (Washington, DC: Gov-

ernment Printing Office, 1977), table 66; John C. Burnham, "The Gasoline Tax and the Automobile Revolution," *Mississippi Valley Historical Review* 68 (December 1961): 435–459.

23. David Brian Robertson, *Federalism and the Making of America* (New York: Routledge, 2012), 77, 99, 105; David Brian Robertson, *Capital, Labor, and State: The Battle for American Labor Markets from the Civil War to the New Deal* (Lanham, MD: Rowman & Littlefield, 2000), 17; William Graebner, "Federalism in the Progressive Era: A Structural Interpretation of Reform," *Journal of American History* 64 (September 1977): 311–357.

24. On the South, see Link, *Paradox of Southern Progressivism*; C. Vann Woodward, *The Origins of the New South, 1877–1913* (Baton Rouge: Louisiana State University Press, 1951); Edward L. Ayers, *The Promise of the New South: Life after Reconstruction* (New York: Oxford University Press, 1992), ch. 15. Carl V. Harris, *Political Power in Birmingham, 1871–1921* (Knoxville: University of Tennessee Press, 1977), ch. 11, traces how utility companies pushed for a state regulatory commission in Alabama to avoid political fights with city officials in Birmingham.

Important studies of policy diffusion in the states by political scientists include Jack L. Walker, "The Diffusion of Innovations among the American States," *American Political Science Review* 63 (September 1969): 880–899; Jack L. Walker, "Communication," *American Political Science Review* 63 (September 1969): 900–903 (about the South's anomalous relation to state innovations); Virginia Gray, "Innovation in the States: A Diffusion Study," *American Political Science Review* 67 (December 1973): 1174–1185; Robert L. Savage, "Patterns of Multi-linear Evolution in the American States," *Publius* 3 (Spring 1973): 75–108.

25. Yearley, *Money Machines*; Kahn, *Budgeting Democracy*; Campbell, "Economic Causes of Progressivism." Evidence of budget deficits and debt defaults in cities and states is based on financial studies listed in the appendix, other local sources, and Ballard C. Campbell, "Depressions and Taxes in the United States, 1873–1915," in *Taxation, State, and Civil Society in Germany and the United States from the 18th to the 20th Century*, ed. Alexander Nutzenadel and Christoph Strupp (Baden-Baden, Germany: Nomos, 2007), 67–81. Also see Eric Monkkonen, *The Local State: Public Money and American Cities* (Stanford, CA: Stanford University Press, 1995), 26 (for Illinois); Harris, *Political Power in Birmingham*, tables A1, A2.

26. Alfred D. Chandler, *The Visible Hand: The Managerial Revolution in American Business* (Cambridge, MA: Harvard University Press, 1977), 109–120, 272–281; James H. Potts, "The Evolution of Municipal Accounting in the United States, 1900–1935," *Business History Review* 52 (Winter 1978): 518–536. The American Association of Public Accountants was established in 1886.

27. Kahn, *Budgeting Democracy*, chs. 1–4; Leonard D. White, *Trends in Public Administration* (New York: McGraw-Hill, 1933), 221; Schiesl, *Politics of Efficiency*, 4, 90–94, chs. 5, 6.

28. Charles Phillips Huse, *The Financial History of Boston, 1822–1909* (Cambridge, MA: Harvard University Press, 1916), 231–233; James J. Connolly, *The Triumph of Ethnic Progressivism: Urban Political Culture in Boston, 1900–1925* (Cambridge, MA: Harvard University Press, 1998), 94–109; *Report of the City Audi-*

tor, Boston (Boston: Auditor's Office, 1906–1915); Massachusetts Bureau of Statistics, *Statistics of Municipal Finance* (Boston, 1912).

29. Rudy Higgens-Evenson, *The Price of Progress: Public Services, Taxation and the American Corporate State, 1877–1929* (Baltimore: Johns Hopkins University Press, 2003), 93–101, ch. 7; Thomas R. Pegram, *Partisans and Progressives: Private Interests and Public Policy in Illinois, 1870–1922* (Urbana: University of Illinois Press, 1992), 194–199; *Massachusetts Auditor's Report for 1910* (Boston, 1911), esp. viii–ix; *Massachusetts Auditor's Report for 1912* (Boston, 1913), viii; White, *Trends in Public Administration*, 189; William F. Willoughby, *The Movement for Budgetary Reform in the States* (New York: Appleton, 1918); sources for table A.3 in the appendix. Also see Thomas Schick, *The New York State Constitutional Convention of 1915 and the Modern State Governor* (Lebanon, PA: National Municipal League, 1978), chs. 4, 5. Massachusetts established a Commission on Efficiency and Economy in 1912, New York and Illinois established theirs in 1913, and Virginia established one in 1916.

30. On legislative voting in the states, see Wright, *Progressive Yankees*, 76, 108, 118; John M. Wegner, "Partisanship in the Ohio House of Representatives, 1900–1911," *Ohio History Journal* 106 (Summer–Autumn 1997): 146–170; John D. Buenker, "Progressivism in Connecticut: The Thrust of the Urban, New Stock Democrats," *Connecticut Historical Society Bulletin* 35 (October 1970): 97–109; Buenker, *Income Tax*, 35–37, 108–115, 154–155, 168, 179–180, 273, 276, 285, 289, 316–317; my analysis of sixty-two votes in the Illinois house (1907–1913) and eleven votes in the Massachusetts house (1909–1913). Also see David Sarasohn, *Party of Reform: Democrats in the Progressive Era* (Jackson: University of Mississippi Press, 1989), 112–118; Pegram, *Partisans and Progressives*, 7–15, 191–211; Robert Stanley, *Dimensions of Law in Service of Order: Origins of the Federal Income Tax, 1861–1913* (New York: Oxford University Press, 1993), table 5.8, 233. State legislative behavior in the Progressive Era remains understudied.

31. For example, a wide variety of educational matters, including professional certifications, were put under the supervision of the New York Board of Regents, the state's chief educational administration. Edger Fuller and Jim B. Pearson, eds., *Education in the States*, vol. 1, *Historical Development and Outlook* (Washington, DC: National Education Association, 1969), appendix C, 895–896.

32. Schick, *New York State Constitutional Convention*; Ernest L. Bogart and John M. Mathews, *The Modern Commonwealth, 1893–1918* (Springfield: Illinois Centennial Commission, 1920), chs. 10, 11; W. Brooke Graves, *American State Government*, 3rd ed. (Boston: D. C. Heath, 1946), 406–436, esp. 419.

33. White, *Trends in Public Administration*, 243–245; Solomon Fabricant, *The Trend of Government Activity in the U.S. since 1900* (New York: National Bureau of Economic Research, 1952), 188–197.

34. US Bureau of the Census, *Historical Statistics on Governmental Finances and Employment* (Washington, DC: Government Printing Office, 1979), 10–11, tables 2, 4–6; Campbell, "Federalism, State Action, and 'Critical Episodes'"; Ballard C. Campbell, *The Growth of American Government: Governance from the Cleveland Era to the Present* (Bloomington: University of Indiana Press, 2015), table 2.2; Advi-

sory Commission on Intergovernmental Reform, *Significant Features of Fiscal Federalism, 1976–77*, vol. 2, *Revenue* (Washington, DC, 1977), 99–101; Yearley, *Money Machines*, 195–207; Jon C. Teaford, *The Rise of the States: Evolution of American State Government* (Baltimore: Johns Hopkins University Press, 2002), ch. 3.

35. Elizabeth Brandeis, "Labor Legislation," in *History of Labor in the United States*, vol. 3, ed. John R. Commons et al. (New York: Macmillan, 1935), 636–637, 649–654; Carl Gersuny, *Work Hazards and Industrial Conflict* (Hanover, NH: University Press of New England, 1981), ch. 2; Gerald N. Grob, *The Deadly Truth: A History of Disease in America* (Cambridge, MA: Harvard University Press, 2002), 164–165; Link, *Paradox of Southern Progressivism*, 304–308; Robert J. Gordon, *The Rise and Fall of American Growth: The U.S. Standard of Living since the Civil War* (Princeton, NJ: Princeton University Press, 2016), 287–289.

36. Kimberley S. Johnson, *Governing the American State: Congress and the New Federalism, 1877–1929* (Princeton, NJ: Princeton University Press, 2007), ch. 4, esp. 88–93; Marc T. Law and Gary D. Libecap, "The Determinants of Progressive Era Reform: The Pure Food and Drug Act of 1906," in *Corruption and Reform: Lessons from America's Economic History*, ed. Edwin L. Glaeser and Claudia D. Goldin (Chicago: University of Chicago Press, 2006), ch. 10.

37. Eileen L. McDonagh, "Representative Democracy and State Building in the Progressive Era," *American Political Science Review* 86 (December 1992): 938–950.

38. William Howard Taft's inaugural address, *Congressional Record*, 61st Congress, March 4 and 16, 1909, 3, 49. The complex politics behind the adoption of the income tax amendment is traced in Buenker, *Income Tax*, 37–43, 90–136. Also see James D. Savage, *Balanced Budgets and American Politics* (Ithaca, NY: Cornell University Press, 1988), 141–144; Sarasohn, *Party of Reform*, ch. 3; Sanders, *Roots of Reform*, 224.

39. Stanley Coben, *A. Mitchell Palmer, Politician* (New York: Columbia University Press, 1963), 76, 79; Holt, *Congressional Insurgents*, ch. 6; Sanders, *Roots of Reform*, 228–229.

40. Joseph A. Pechman, *Federal Tax Policy: Revised* (New York: Norton, 1971), 255, table A-1; Stanley, *Dimensions of Law*, 201, 215–225.

41. Oscar Anderson, *The Health of a Nation: Harvey W. Wiley and the Fight for Pure Food* (Chicago: University of Chicago Press, 1958), ch. 10; Johnson, *Governing the American State*, 107–110.

42. Morton Keller, *Regulating a New Economy: Public Policy and Economic Change in America, 1900–1933* (Cambridge, MA: Harvard University Press, 1990), chs. 2, 3, 9; Thomas K. McCraw, *Prophets of Regulation* (Cambridge, MA: Harvard University Press, 1984), chs. 3, 4; Gabrial Kolko, *The Triumph of Conservativism: A Reinterpretation of American History, 1900–1916* (Chicago: Quadrangle, 1967); Hofstadter, *Age of Reform*, ch. 6, esp. 254n8 on enforcement capacity.

43. See table A.5 in the appendix. Herbert Kaufman counted fifty-six new administrative units between 1900 and 1916; cited in Advisory Commission on Intergovernmental Relations, *A Crisis of Confidence and Competence* (Washington, DC, 1980), 115, table A-6.

44. Herbert Kaufman, "The Growth of Federal Personnel System," in *The Federal*

Government Service, ed. N. Wallace Sayre (Englewood Cliffs, NJ: Prentice-Hall, 1965), 41–43; John M. Gaus and Leon O. Wolcott, *Public Administration in the United States Department of Agriculture* (Chicago: Public Administration Service, 1940); Wayne F. Fuller, *RFD: The Changing Face of Rural America* (Bloomington: Indiana University Press, 1964), 34–77; Daniel P. Carpenter, *The Forging of Bureaucratic Autonomy: Networks and Policy Innovation in Executive Agencies, 1862–1928* (Princeton, NJ: Princeton University Press, 2001), chs. 4, 7. On the conflicted history of reconstructing administrative government, see Stephen Skowronek, *Building a New American State: The Expansion of National Administrative Capacity, 1877–1920* (New York: Cambridge University Press, 1982), ch. 6.

45. Per capita federal expenditures shrank from $7.52 in 1903 to $6.92 in 1913 (in 1913 inflation-adjusted dollars), according to calculations of the National Industrial Conference Board, *Cost of Government in the United States, 1929–1930* (New York, 1932), 85.

46. Paul Studenski and Herman E. Krooss, *Financial History of the United States* (New York: McGraw-Hill, 1963), 264, 299; Skocpol, *Protecting Soldiers and Mothers*, 109–110, 113–114; A. Hunter Depree, *Science in the Federal Government: A History of Policies and Activities* (Baltimore: Johns Hopkins University Press, 1957), 169–182.

47. Carpenter, *Forging of Bureaucratic Autonomy*, ch. 6; Gaus and Wolcott, *Public Administration in the United States Department of Agriculture*, 5–6, 2, 278; Anderson, *Health of a Nation*, chs. 7–9.

48. Brian Balogh, *The Associational State: American Governance in the Twentieth Century* (Philadelphia: University of Pennsylvania Press, 2015), ch. 2, 202–204; Bruce E. Seely, *Building the American Highway System: Engineers as Policy Makers* (Philadelphia: Temple University Press, 1987), chs. 1–3; Bruce E. Seely, "Logan W. Page," in *American National Biography*, ed. John A. Garraty (New York: Oxford University Press, 1999); Carpenter, *Forging of Bureaucratic Autonomy*, ch. 4; McCraw, *Prophets of Regulation*, 63; Kahn, *Budgeting Democracy*, ch. 6.

49. Campbell, *Growth of American Government*, 223–229.

50. John Kincaid, "From Cooperation to Coercion in American Federalism: Housing, Fragmentation and Preemption, 1780–1992," *Journal of Law and Politics* 9 (Winter 1993): 356–367; Clifford L. Staten, "Theodore Roosevelt: Dual and Cooperative Federalism," *Presidential Studies Quarterly* 23 (Winter 1993): 129–143; David B. Robertson, "The Bias of American Federalism: Political Structure and the Development of America's Exceptional Welfare State in the Progressive Era," *Journal of Policy History* 1 (1989): 261–291; Johnson, *Governing the American State*, ch. 1; W. Brooke Graves, *American Intergovernmental Relations: Their Origins, Historical Development, and Current Status* (New York: Scribner's Sons, 1964), esp. chs. 14, 15, 798–799 (Elihu Root on changes in federalism); Graves, *Uniform State Action*; Graebner, "Federalism in the Progressive Era." James Q. Dealey, *The Growth of American State Constitutions, 1776–1914* (Boston: Ginn, 1915), 295–296, illustrates the alarm over national centralization.

51. George E. Mowry, *The Era of Theodore Roosevelt and the Birth of Modern America, 1900–1912* (New York: Harper Torchbook, 1962), 220–224; Kathleen M.

Dalton, *Theodore Roosevelt: A Strenuous Life* (New York: Vintage, 2004); Donald A. Ritchie, *Press Gallery: Congress and the Washington Correspondents* (Cambridge, MA: Harvard University Press, 1991), ch. 11. Newspapers published pictures of William Howard Taft and Woodrow Wilson throwing the first pitch to open the professional baseball season, a tradition that began in 1910. This symbolized the dawning of the presidential persona in American civic life.

52. Jonathan Lurie, *William Howard Taft: The Travails of a Progressive Conservative* (New York: Cambridge University Press, 2012); A. Scott Berg, *Wilson* (New York: Putnam, 2012). On presidential references to classic dual federalism, see Campbell, *Growth of American Government*, 15–16; Skowronek, *Building a New American State*, ch. 6; Carpenter, *Forging of Bureaucratic Autonomy*, 13.

12. *The Wartime State*

1. Donald Smythe, *Pershing: General of the Armies* (Bloomington: Indiana University Press, 1986), chs. 23–26; Frank Freidel, *Over There: The Story of America's First Great Overseas Crusade*, rev. ed. (New York: McGraw-Hill, 1990); Michael Adas, "Ambivalent Ally: American Military Intervention and the Legacy of World War I," in *Beyond 1917: The United States and the Global Legacies of the Great War*, ed. Thomas W. Zeiler, D. Ekbladh, and B. Montoya (New York: Oxford University Press, 2017), ch. 5.

2. Thomas G. Patterson, J. Garry Clifford, and Kenneth J. Hagan, *American Foreign Relations: A History*, vol. 2 (Boston: Houghton Mifflin, 2000), chs. 1, 2; Kenneth J. Hagan, *This People's Navy: The Making of American Seapower* (New York: Free Press, 1991), chs. 6–8, 239.

3. See Patterson et al., *American Foreign Relations*, ch. 3, for details about the route to war and a comprehensive bibliography. David M. Kennedy, *Over Here: The First World War and American Society* (New York: Oxford University Press, 1980), 20–25.

4. The unemployment rate was 9 percent in 1915 and 1.24 percent in 1918. Susan B. Carter, *Historical Statistics of the United States: Millennial Edition*, vol. 2 (New York: Cambridge University Press, 2006), table Ba475.

5. Russell F. Weigley, *History of the United States Army* (Bloomington: Indiana University Press, 1984), ch. 15; Walter Millis, *Arms and Men: A Study in American Military History* (1956; reprint, New Brunswick, NJ: Rutgers University Press, 1981), 211–238.

6. Robert Lansing, *War Memoirs of Robert Lansing* (Indianapolis: Bobbs Merrill, 1935), 23, 236.

7. A brief but insightful analysis of Wilson's position on the war and the peace settlement is Richard Hofstader, *The Age of Reform: From Bryan to FDR* (New York: Vintage, 1955), 272–282.

8. Kennedy, *Over Here*, 93, 144, 151, 168–191; Christopher Capozzola, *Uncle Sam Wants You: World War I and the Making of the Modern American Citizen* (New York: Oxford University Press, 2008), esp. chs. 1, 6; Howard Zinn, *LaGuardia in Congress* (New York: Norton, 1969), 17n1; Jeanette Keith, "The Politics of Southern

Draft Resistance, 1917–1918," *Journal of American History* 87, 4 (March 2001): 1335–1361; Allan R. Millett and Peter Maslowski, *For the Common Defense: A Military History of the United States of America* (New York: Free Press, 1994), 349–352.

The Supreme Court upheld the constitutionality of conscription in *Arver v. United States,* 245 U.S. 366 (1918), stating that a draft was an implied component of Congress's power to maintain an army and declare war and that it was a citizen's duty to serve.

9. Freidel, *Over There*, 30–31.

10. Paul A. C. Koistinen, *Mobilizing for Modern War: Political Economy of American Warfare, 1865–1919* (Lawrence: University Press of Kansas, 1997), chs. 8–13; Hugh Rockoff, *America's Economic Way of War* (Cambridge: Cambridge University Press, 2012), esp. ch. 5; Marc Allen Eisner, *From Warfare State to Welfare State: World War I, Compensatory State Building, and the Limits of the Modern Order* (University Park: Pennsylvania State University Press, 2000), chs. 2, 3; Edward M. Coffman, "The Battle against Red Tape: Business Methods in the War Department General Staff, 1917–1918," *Military Affairs* 26 (Spring 1962): 1–10; Kennedy, *Over Here*, ch. 2, 254–255.

11. Paul Studenski and Herman E. Krooss, *Financial History of the United States* (New York: McGraw-Hill, 1963), ch. 23; Rockoff, *America's Economic Way of War*, 111–125; John F. Witte, *The Politics and Development of the Federal Income Tax* (Madison: University of Wisconsin Press, 1985), ch. 4.

12. Advisory Commission on Intergovernmental Relations, *The Condition of Contemporary Federalism: Conflicting Theories and Collapsing Constraints* (Washington, DC, 1981), 224–226. The commission noted dissenting opinions on the hypothesis that a portion of wartime spending became institutionalized in the financial system. Robert Higgs, *Crisis and Leviathan: Critical Episodes in the Growth of American Government* (New York: Oxford University Press, 1987), chs. 2, 4; Ballard C. Campbell, "Federalism, State Action, and 'Critical Episodes' in the Growth of American Government," *Social Science History* 16 (Winter 1992): 561–577.

13. Weigley, *History of the United States Army*, 368; Jonathan Kahn, *Budgeting Democracy: State Building and Citizenship in America, 1890–1928* (Ithaca, NY: Cornell University Press, 1997), 176–181.

14. Theda Skocpol et al., "Patriotic Partnerships: Why Great Wars Nourished American Civil Voluntarism," in *Shaped by War and Trade: International Influences on American Political Development*, ed. Ira Katznelson and Martin Shefter (Princeton, NJ: Princeton University Press, 2002), 154–169.

15. K. Austin Kerr, *Organized for Prohibition: A New History of the Anti-Saloon League* (New Haven, CT: Yale University Press, 1985); Richard F. Hamm, *Shaping the 18th Amendment: Temperance Reform, Legal Culture, and the Polity, 1880–1920* (Chapel Hill: University of North Carolina Press, 1995); William A. Link, *The Paradox of Southern Progressivism, 1880–1930* (Chapel Hill: University of North Carolina Press, 1992), 311–320; Carroll H. Woody, *The Growth of the Federal Government, 1915–1932* (New York: McGraw-Hill, 1934), 81, 93–106.

16. Jacqueline Van Voris, *Carrie Chapman Catt: A Public Life* (New York: City

University of New York, 1987); Eleanor Flexner, *Century of Struggle: Woman's Rights Movement in the United States* (Cambridge, MA: Harvard University Press, 1975), 216–298.

17. Kennedy, *Over Here*, 87–89; Paul L. Murphy, *World War I and the Origin of Civil Liberties in the United States* (New York: Norton, 1979), chs. 3, 4; H. C. Peterson and Gilbert C. Fite, *Opponents of War, 1917–1918* (Madison: University of Wisconsin Press, 1968).

18. Murphy, *World War I and the Origin of Civil Liberties*, 228–229, 266–267; Peterson and Fite, *Opponents of War*, 276–277; William Preston Jr., *Aliens and Dissenters: Federal Suppression of Radicals, 1903–1933* (Cambridge, MA: Harvard University Press, 1963), chs. 3, 4; Kennedy, *Over Here*, 75–83.

The Espionage Act was upheld in *Schenck v. United States* (1919), in which Justice Oliver Wendell Holmes held that the conviction of an individual who had distributed antidraft leaflets was not an unconstitutional violation of First Amendment rights because his action presented a "clear and present danger." In *Abrams v. United States* (1919) the Supreme Court upheld the Sedition Act, under which the author of a pamphlet calling for a general strike had been convicted. The court said that the First Amendment did not protect the right to excite disaffection, riot, or revolution. In this case Justice Holmes dissented, finding that "no clear and present danger" existed.

19. Murphy, *World War I and the Origin of Civil Liberties*, ch. 4. Also see David Williams, "The Bureau of Investigation and Its Critics, 1919–1921: The Origins of Federal Political Surveillance," *Journal of American History* 68 (December 1981): 560–579; Eldridge F. Dowell, *A History of Criminal Syndicalism Legislation in the United States* (Baltimore: Johns Hopkins University Press, 1939), esp. appendix I; John Higham, *Strangers in the Land: Patterns of American Nativism, 1860–1925* (New York: Atheneum, 1963), chs. 8, 9; Donald F. Tingley, *The Structuring of a State: The History of Illinois, 1899–1928* (Urbana: University of Illinois Press, 1980), 199, 210–221.

20. Paul Kleppner, *Continuity and Change in Electoral Politics, 1893–1928* (New York: Greenwood, 1987), 141–154, 186–187, 208–210; Alan Ware, *The Democratic Party Heads North, 1877–1962* (New York: Cambridge University Press, 2006), tables 4.6, 4.7; Koistinen, *Mobilizing for Modern War*, 262–263; George Soule, *Prosperity Decade: From War to Depression, 1917–1919* (New York: Holt, Rinehart & Winston, 1947), chs. 1–4, 9. Henry Cabot Lodge, the dean of Senate Republicans, interpreted 1918 as "a country-wide revolt against dictatorship . . . and constitutional limitations." Kennedy, *Over Here*, 244.

21. A. Scott Berg, *Wilson* (New York: Putnam, 2013), 558, 572, 586, 616, suggests that Wilson's increased resistance to alterations in his League of Nations plan, coupled with his willingness to appease European leaders to gain their consent, may have been the result of minor strokes suffered in the spring of 1919, exacerbated by a case of influenza. His doctor and others had noticed a mental decline by summer.

Philip Bobbit, *The Shield of Achilles: War, Peace and the Course of History* (New York: Anchor, 2002), ch. 14, esp. 391, argues that the League of Nations failed because Europeans did not share Americans' democratic conception of the state, a conflict that forced Wilson to barter away his Fourteen Points to win European acceptance of a league. Wilson's break with his political mentor Colonel Edward House in the latter stages of the treaty negotiations, Bobbit contends, removed the one person who might have persuaded Wilson to adopt a more politically realistic strategy. On the economic effects of the war, see Rockoff, *America's Economic Way of War*, 136–154.

22. Richard Gid Powers, *Secrecy and Power: The Life of J. Edgar Hoover* (New York: Free Press, 1987), chs. 2–4; Williams, "Bureau of Investigation"; Preston, *Aliens and Dissenters*, ch. 8.

23. Kleppner, *Continuity and Change*, 124, 152–154, 186–187, 208; David Burner, *The Politics of Provincialism: The Democratic Party in Transition, 1918–1932* (New York: Norton, 1967), ch. 2, esp. 43–44, 234–241; Ware, *Democratic Party Heads North*, tables 4.6, 4.7; John M. Allswang, *A House for All Peoples: Ethnic Politics in Chicago, 1890–1936* (Lexington: University Press of Kentucky, 1971), 42, 78, 129, 186; Donald R. McCoy, "Election of 1920," in *History of American Presidential Elections, 1789–1968*, ed. Arthur M. Schlesinger Jr. (New York: Chelsea House, 1971), 2349–2385; J. Joseph Huthmacher, *Massachusetts People and Politics, 1919–1933* (New York: Atheneum, 1969), ch. 2.

The stagflation rate (unemployment rate plus inflation rate) totaled 24.5 percent in 1920. In 1980, when Ronald Reagan won the presidential election over Jimmy Carter, stagflation registered 20.6 percent. Franklin Roosevelt won the 1932 election when the unemployment rate hit 23 percent but deflation prevailed. Economic indicators suggest that most voters suffered real income declines between 1919 and 1920. Soule, *Prosperity Decade*, chs. 4, 5, 9. On the link between depressions and elections, see Ballard C. Campbell, "Depression and Politics in American History," *Long Term View* 4 (Spring 1998): 13–21.

24. Capozzola, *Uncle Sam Wants You*, esp. ch. 6; Edward G. Hartmann, *The Movement to Americanize the Immigrant* (New York: Columbia University Press, 1948), chs. 7, 8; Murphy, *World War I and the Origin of Civil Liberties*, 116–126.

25. Powers, *Secrecy and Power*, 68; Wooddy, *Growth of the Federal Government*, 92.

26. Information about collecting data on individuals was obtained from the references concerning administration cited in chapters 6 and 10 and the sources for tables A.2, A.3, and A.6 in the appendix. Also see Michael Haines, "The Population of the United States," in *The Cambridge Economic History of the United States*, vol. 2, ed. Susan Carter (New York: Cambridge University Press, 2008), 147–149; Margo J. Anderson, *The American Census: A Social Survey* (New Haven, CT: Yale University Press, 1988), 6; Dorothy Ross, *The Origins of Social Science* (New York: Cambridge University Press, 1991), chs. 7, 8.

27. John Torpey, "The Great War and the Birth of the Modern Passport System," in *Documenting Individual Identity: The Development of State Practices in the Modern World*, ed. Jane Caplan and John Torpey (Princeton, NJ: Princeton University Press, 2001), 256–270.

28. Anderson, *American Census*, ch. 5.

13. *The End of the Long Nineteenth Century*

1. Robert S. Lynd and Helen Merrell Lynd, *Middletown: A Study in Modern American Culture* (1929; reprint, New York: Harcourt, Brace, 1956), ch. 24.

2. Charles A. Beard, *American Government and Politics* (New York: Macmillan, 1928), 3–5, 476; Walter F. Dodd, *State Government* (New York: Century, 1923), 42–47, 143; Leonard D. White, *Introduction to the Study of Public Administration* (New York: Macmillan, 1926), 78–79, 466; Leonard D. White, *Trends in Public Administration* (New York: McGraw-Hill, 1933); Carroll H. Wooddy, *The Growth of the Federal Government, 1915–1932* (New York: McGraw-Hill, 1934); Dodd, *State Government*, chs. 1, 2; William B. Munro, *Municipal Administration* (New York: Macmillan, 1934), 15, 155–157; E. P. Buford, "Federal Encroachment on State Sovereignty," *American Law Review* 57 (December 1923): 801–827; Walter Thompson, *Federal Centralization: A Study and Criticism of the Expanding Scope of Congressional Legislation* (New York: Harcourt Brace, 1923), 325–326; Arthur N. Holcombe, *State Government in the United States* (New York: Macmillan, 1926), 10; Pendleton Herring, *Group Representation before Congress* (Baltimore: Johns Hopkins University Press, 1929), esp. chs. 2, 3, appendix 2. Many organizations with offices in Washington had "National" as the first word in their names. Although perceptions of Washington as the political nerve center of America rose after World War I, the city still fell short of being a commercial or cultural capital similar to London or Paris, as James Bryce remarked in *The American Commonwealth*, vol. 2 (New York: Macmillan, 1893), ch. 113. Modern scholars have affirmed these contemporary observations. See James T. Patterson, *The New Deal and the States: Federalism in Transition* (Princeton, NJ: Princeton University Press, 1969), ch. 1; John Kincaid, "From Cooperation to Coercion in American Federalism: Housing, Fragmentation and Preemption, 1780–1992," *Journal of Law and Politics* 9 (Winter 1993): 353–368; Randall G. Holcombe, "The Growth of the Federal Government in the 1920s," *Cato Journal* 16 (Fall 1996): 175–199; Kimberley S. Johnson, *Governing the American State: The New Federalism, 1877–1929* (Princeton, NJ: Princeton University Press, 2007).

3. Susan B. Carter, *Historical Statistics of the United States: Millennial Edition* (New York: Cambridge University Press, 2006), vol. 1, pt. A. Fifty-six percent of white males in the United States were younger than thirty years old in 1920; another 15 percent were in their thirties. On generational succession as an agent of political change, see Alan B. Spitzer, "The Historical Problem of Generations," *American Historical Review* 78 (December 1973): 1353–1385; Allan R. Bass, "Generational Analysis: Description, Explanation, and Theory," *Journal of Social Issues* 30, 2 (1974): 55–72; Amanda Cox, "How Birth Years Influence Political Views," *New York Times*, July 7, 2014.

4. Julie A. Golia, "Courting Women, Courting Advertisers: The Woman's Page and the Transformation of the American Newspaper, 1895–1935," *Journal of American History* 103 (December 2016): 606–628; Claudia Goldia, "America's Graduation from High School: The Evolution and Spread of Secondary Education," *Journal of Economic History* 58 (June 1998): 345–374. High school curriculum changed sub-

stantially between 1890 and the early 1920s, with less time spent learning Latin and increased attention to vocational arts, history, and civics. Lynd and Lynd, *Middletown*, 191–199.

5. Richard Hofstadter, *The Age of Reform* (New York: Vintage, 1955), 166–167; Samuel P. Huntington, *American Politics: The Promise of Disharmony* (Cambridge, MA: Belknap Press, 1981), ch. 5, 76–77; Arthur M. Schlesinger Jr., *The Cycles of American Politics* (Boston: Houghton, Mifflin, 1986), 27–30; David R. Mayhew, *Divided We Govern: Party Control, Lawmaking, and Investigations, 1946–1990* (New Haven, CT: Yale University Press, 1991), 162, 179; Arthur M. Schlesinger Jr., *Paths to the Present* (New York: Macmillan, 1949), 77–92; Leonard D. White, *States and the Nation* (Baton Rouge: Louisiana State University Press, 1953), 47.

Mood shifts are sometimes linked to long waves (cycles). See Joshua S. Goldstein, *Long Cycles: Prosperity and War in the Modern Age* (New Haven, CT: Yale University Press, 1988), 5–8, ch. 7; David Hackett Fischer, *The Great Wave: Price Revolutions and the Rhythm of History* (New York: Oxford University Press, 1996), 29, 132, 297–300; Andrew Tylecote, *The Long Wave in the World Economy: The Current Crisis in Historical Perspective* (New York: Routledge, 1993); Robert W. Fogel, *The Fourth Great Awakening and the Future of Egalitarianism* (Chicago: University of Chicago Press, 2000). On the long cycles and crises, see Jack A. Goldstone, *Revolution and Rebellion in the Early Modern World* (Berkeley: University of California Press, 1991).

6. To underscore this point, virtually everyone my age has a vivid recollection of the assassination of President John Kennedy (1963), including where they were and what they did in the immediate aftermath. Younger adults probably have similar experiences concerning the 9/11 terrorist attacks (2001), while the attack on Pearl Harbor (1941) was seared in the memory of adults alive at that time.

7. Marc Allen Eisner, *From Warfare State to Welfare State: World War I, Compensatory State Building, and the Limits of the Modern Order* (University Park: Pennsylvania State University Press, 2000), analyzes the impact of war mobilization on the political economy in the 1920s and 1930s. On the salience of "focusing events" and crises, see John W. Kingdon, *Agendas, Alternatives, and Public Policies* (New York: HarperCollins, 1984), 99–108.

8. Robert H. Wiebe, *The Search for Order, 1877–1920* (New York: Hill & Wang, 1967), xiii–xiv.

9. A notable constancy in the structural framework of national politics is equal state representation in the US Senate. In 1920 New York had 10,385,277 residents, 134 times more than Nevada; both were allotted two Senate seats.

10. Jack L. Walker, "The Diffusion of Innovations among the American States," *American Political Science Review* 63 (September 1969): 880–899; Virginia Gray, *Politics in the American States: A Comparative Analysis* (Washington, DC: Congressional Quarterly Press, 1999). For policy diffusion among the industrializing states, see Michael Mann, *The Sources of Social Power*, vol. 2, *The Rise of Classes and Nation-States, 1760–1914* (New York: Cambridge University Press, 1993), 473.

11. Grover Cleveland served as mayor of Buffalo and governor of New York prior to his election as president. Benjamin Harrison, elected president in 1888, had run

unsuccessfully for governor of Indiana. William Howard Taft, elected president in 1908, had been appointed governor of the Philippines (1900–1904), an American colony.

12. Imperialists and naval enthusiasts such as Theodore Roosevelt, who favored the expansion of American influence internationally, were partial exceptions. The Bellamy nationalists, socialists, and the Communist Party of America proposed major political reformulations that were rejected.

13. This conclusion does not contradict the truism that groups seek to shape policy in their own interest; nor does it deny that public policy can favor some individuals more than others.

14. Lynd and Lynd, *Middletown*, 198, 484–493; Theda Skocpol, "Patriotic Partnerships: Why Great Wars Nourished Civic Voluntarism," in *Shaped by War and Trade: International Influences on American Political Development*, ed. Ira Katznelson and Martin Shefter (Princeton, NJ: Princeton University Press, 2002), ch. 6.

15. National Industrial Conference Board, *Cost of Government 1929–30* (New York, 1932), 17; US Bureau of the Census, *Historical Statistics on Governmental Finances and Employment* (Washington, DC: Government Printing Office, 1979), 30, 43, 51, 55.

16. Jack L. Walker, "Origin and Maintenance of Interest Groups in America," *American Political Science Review* 77 (June 1983): 390–406. Theda Skocpol, *Protecting Soldiers and Mothers: The Political Origins of Social Policy in the United States* (Cambridge, MA: Harvard University Press, 1992), documents the success of women's organizations in enacting early social welfare programs. On legislator and administrator careerism, see Ballard C. Campbell, *The Growth of American Government: Governance from the Cleveland Era to the Present* (Bloomington: Indiana University Press, 2015), ch. 9.

17. See Woody, *Growth of the Federal Government*, for details on federal activities in 1915–1930, esp. 94–95 on federal prisons. Wooddy attributes roughly one-half the increase in federal activity to "increased demand" for programs in place before World War I (549). Also see Lisa McGirr, *The War on Alcohol: Prohibition and the Rise of the American State* (New York: Norton, 2015).

18. On the expansion of state and local activities, see White, *Trends in Public Administration*, 143; Munro, *Municipal Administration*, 15; Lynd and Lynd, *Middletown*, 413; Margaret W. Cahalan, *Historical Corrections Statistics in the United States, 1850–1984* (Washington, DC: US Department of Justice, 1987), tables 3-1, 8-4, 8-6, appendix table 7. For the extent of paved roads in Maine in 1926, see Stephen J. Horsnby and Richard Judd, *Historical Atlas of Maine* (Orono: University of Maine Press, 2015), plate 64. Robert Moses, famed builder of parks and highways, got his start in the 1920s under Al Smith, governor of New York. See Robert A. Caro, *The Power Broker: Robert Moses and the Fall of New York* (New York: Vintage, 1974), chs. 7–17.

19. Alexis de Tocqueville, *Democracy in America*, abridged ed. (New York: New American Library, 1956), 163.

INDEX